Global Linguistic Flows

Located at the intersection of sociolinguistics and Hip Hop Studies, this cutting-edge book moves around the world—spanning Africa, Asia, Australia, the Americas and the European Union—to explore Hip Hop Cultures, youth identities, the politics of language, and the simultaneous processes of globalization and localization. Focusing closely on *language*, these scholars of sociolinguistics, linguistic anthropology, (Hip Hop) cultural studies, and critical pedagogies offer linguistic insights to the growing scholarship on Hip Hop Culture, while reorienting their respective fields by paying closer attention to processes of globalization and localization.

The book engages complex processes such as transnationalism, (im)migration, cultural flow, and diaspora in an effort to expand current theoretical approaches to language choice and agency, speech style and stylization, codeswitching and language mixing, crossing and sociolinguistic variation, and language use and globalization. Moving throughout the Global Hip Hop Nation, through scenes as diverse as Hong Kong's urban center, Germany's Mannheim inner-city district of *Weststadt*, the Brazilian *favelas*, the streets of Lagos and Dar es Salaam, and the *hoods* of the San Francisco Bay Area, this global intellectual *cipha* breaks new ground in the ethnographic study of language and popular culture.

H. Samy Alim is Assistant Professor in the Department of Anthropology, University of California, Los Angeles, USA.

Awad Ibrahim is Associate Professor, Faculty of Education, University of Ottawa, Canada.

Alastair Pennycook is Professor of Language Studies, Faculty of Arts and Social Sciences, University of Technology, Sydney, Australia.

Global Linguistic Flows
Hip Hop Cultures, Youth Identities, and the Politics of Language

Edited by

H. Samy Alim
University of California, Los Angeles, USA

Awad Ibrahim
University of Ottawa, Canada

Alastair Pennycook
University of Technology, Sydney, Australia

Routledge
Taylor & Francis Group

NEW YORK AND LONDON

First published 2009
by Routledge
270 Madison Ave, New York, NY 10016

Simultaneously published in the UK
by Routledge
2 Park Square, Milton Park, Abingdon, Oxon OX14 4RN

Routledge is an imprint of the Taylor & Francis Group, an informa business

Typeset in Minion Pro by EvS Communication Networx, Inc.
Printed and bound in the United States of America on acid-free paper by Edwards Brothers, Inc.

Library of Congress Cataloguing-in-Publication Data
Global linguistic flows: hip hop cultures, youth identities, and the politics of language/edited by H. Samy Alim, Awad Ibrahim, Alastair Pennycook.—1st ed.
p. cm.
Includes bibliographical references and index.
1. Culture and globalization. 2. Hip-hop—Influence. 3. Education in popular culture. 4. Language and culture. 5. Intercultural communication. 6. Group identity. I. Alim, H. Samy. II. Ibrahim, Awad. III. Pennycook, Alastair, 1957-
HM621.G578 2009
306.44089'9607301732—dc22
2008009107

ISBN 10: 0-8058-6283-8 (hbk)
ISBN 10: 0-8058-6285-4 (pbk)
ISBN 10: 0-203-89278-X (ebk)

ISBN 13: 978-0-8058-6283-6 (hbk)
ISBN 13: 978-0-8058-6285-0 (pbk)
ISBN 13: 978-0-203-89278-7 (ebk)

Contents

Check Out Receipt

Cape Coral-Lee County Public Library (CC)
239-533-4500
library.leegov.com
Fri 06/08/2012 9:12:52 AM

12100

Item: 33069035729165
Title: ILL Global linguistic flows : hip hop
cultures, youth identities, and the politics of
language
Material: ILL
Due: 6/22/2012

Total Items: 1

Thank you for using the Cape Coral -
Lee County Public Library
Hours:
Monday-Wednesday 9-8
Thursday 9-6
Friday-Saturday 9-5

Preface

One of Hip Hop's central speech events is *tha cipha*, an organic, highly charged, fluid circular arrangement of rhymers wherein participants exchange verses. This volume itself is constructed as a global intellectual Hip Hop cipha, with each contributor *spittin* ("writing") about particular contexts and *buildin* ("collaborating, challenging, and theorizing") with others to produce a whole that is greater than the sum of its parts. Highlighting the intersections between issues of language, Hip Hop Culture, and globalization, this volume pulls together various scholars of sociolinguistics, linguistic anthropology, (Hip Hop) cultural studies, and critical pedagogies in an effort to contribute to the growing scholarship on "Hip Hop Culture," as well as to reorient those fields by paying closer attention to the processes of globalization and localization. Contributors attempt to do this by combining the rigorous microanalysis of linguistic exchanges with the richness of ethnographic engagement with the production of the popular.

This volume addresses a constellation of concerns: Hip Hop Cultures, youth identities, the politics of language, and the simultaneous processes of globalization and localization. The recent outpouring of literature on the globalization and localization of "Hip Hop Culture(s)"—and the tensions between the two concurrent processes—suggests that scholars are turning to the study of global Hip Hop cultures as a means toward both illuminating our understanding of this abstract, discursive, popular cultural zone ("Hip Hop Culture") and delving deeper into the workings of complex processes such as transnationalism, cultural flow, syncretism, indigenization, hybridity, (im)migration, and diaspora, to name a few of the concepts that permeate this volume.

There is a final significant reason to explore these issues, one that is central to this book but ironically is taken for granted in most of the scholarship on Hip Hop Culture: *Language*, the omnipresent medium through which Hip Hop cultural practices, performances, and productions are both expressed and constituted, is perhaps one of the least analyzed aspects of Hip Hop Culture. Given the dominance of *rappin* in Hip Hop cultural practice, language is perhaps one of the most useful means by which to read Hip Hop Culture. By placing language squarely at the center of their analyses, the studies in this volume aim to shed light on both our understanding of Hip Hop Culture(s) as well as expand our theoretical approaches to language choice and agency, speech style and stylization, codeswitching and language mixing, crossing and sociolinguistic variation, and language use and globalization.

What we hope we have done in this volume is to invigorate scholars of language through our analyses and our engagement with key concepts in sociolinguistics, linguistic anthropology, and critical applied linguistics (and in some cases, creating our own concepts) in an effort to engage the sociolinguistics of globalization. We also hope that we have enlivened Hip Hop Studies by calling attention to language as a key to understanding Hip Hop cultural practices, productions, and performances (and in some cases, in contexts heretofore unexplored). We also hope that our attention to the simultaneous processes of globalization and localization will contribute to broader discussions in the social sciences and humanities.

Shout Outs

Alim

It's been quite a journey, a fantastic voyage, as we've worked extremely hard over the last coupla years to put this joint together. I'd like to give a worldwide shout out to all the folks who helped us out along the way, including the many contributors, editors (particularly Naomi Silverman), and reviewers of this volume who have shared their insights with us and brought us one step closer to understanding how language works in a global, popular cultural landscape that is increasingly dominated by Hip Hop Culture(s). I think I speak for all of us when I say that this was truly one of the most exciting collaborations I've been involved in. The organic, highly-charged conversations, multiple rounds of reviews, debates and, yeah, battles, have shown me the value of global collaboration, whether in person, via email, and even Facebook chats. Real talk. We been rollin *deep* for the last coupla years, straight *grindin*. Because of this, the end result is something that is mos DEF(initely) bigger than the sum of its parts, and we are indebted to all of you for your hard work and brilliant insights. One Love.

I also wanna give a shout out to three working groups at UCLA who have been instrumental in helping me think about these issues: the Discourse Lab, Culture Power & Social Change, and the Working Group in Hip Hop Cultural Studies. Specifically, I'd like to thank Alessandro Duranti, Darnell Hunt, Kris Gutierrez, Candy and Chuck Goodwin, Paul Kroskrity, Reynaldo Macias, Claudia Mitchell-Kernan, Elinor Ochs, and the whole CLIC (Center for Language, Interaction, and Culture) for being extremely supportive; Karen Brodkin, Akhil Gupta, Sondra Hale, Sherry Ortner, Kyeyoung Park, Susan Slyomovics and all of CSPC; Sabela Grimes, Cheryl Keyes, Jooyoung Lee, Lauren Mason, Emilee Woods, Christina Zanfagna and the WGHHCS (I see you). Props to the entire UMUM family, James G. Spady (it *been* global, right?), Samir Meghelli (thanks for that killa cover photo, homie, and for www.thaglobalcipha.com), Stefan Dupres, Charles G. Lee, Leandre Jackson, and David White. Uknowhowweroll. Shout outs also go out to John Baugh, Mary Bucholtz, Jeff Chang, Davey D, Michael Eric Dyson, Penny Eckert, Dawn-Elissa Fischer, Kira Hall, the Society for Linguistic Anthropology, John Jackson, Robin Kelley, Bakari Kitwana, Imani Perry, James Peterson, Ben Rampton, John Rickford, and Geneva Smitherman.

Much love to the Stanford Humanities Center for a wonderful opportunity to really concentrate on and engage these issues of language and globalization as they intersect with Hip Hop Culture (2007–2008). I've benefited greatly from my interactions with Michael Bratman, Jim Clifford, Babacar Fall, Liisa Malkki,

Richard Roberts, Chris Rovee, Carol Shloss, and the whole gang. Let's keep buildin. Much love to Stanford's "Hip Hop Lectures," put on by Michelle Elam and Marcyliena Morgan among others. Thanks for the invitation to share some of these ideas with you and for lettin me kick it all year. Big, family love to the Alim Clan (scattered all over the globe) and Cesar y toda mi familia de Nayarit for holdin me down. *Andale pues!*

Finally, I can't end without givin props to the homies, Alastair and Awad. Double A, I can't begin to express how much I've learned by workin with both of you and I can't thank you enough for your intellectual rigor, creativity, patience, understanding, and most of all, for makin one *helluva* team. Much respect. Like Onyx say, let's K.I.M. [Keep It Movin]! And to the rest a y'all—space is short, but y'all know who y'all is! One love to all the Hip Hop youth all over the world doin da damn thang. This for y'all… P.E.A.C.E.

Awad

Alim, the kids done did it again! Mad love to them, the Hip Hop Nation in da house, BIG TIME. They have taken the academy by storm. And we (Triple A) have engaged this incredibly exciting socio-cultural and linguistic space. And let me tell ya, this was a off da hook project. We got into this iiissshhhhhh so *deep* that Alim once emailed us and said, "I wish this project would never end." Clearly, all good things come to an end, at least from our side as editors. It is your turn, as W. E. Du Bois would say, "my gentle reader," to enjoy and struggle with this text as much as we enjoyed and struggled with it. Part of our struggle was that, we as editors met face-to-face only once. We know each other from our published work. We performed the postmodern in this book. Mad love to all who made it possible for us to do so.

Yo, it starts at home. Shout out to my crew at the University of Ottawa: Tim Stanley, Marie-Josée Berger, Judith Robertson, Nick Ng-A-Fook, Joel Westheimer, Diana Masny, Claire Maltais, Doug Fleming, Francis Bangou, Meredith Terretta (*merci mes chers amis*), Ruth Kane, Boulou Ebanda de B'beri, Lorna McLean, Sharon Cook. My OMEGA crew in Ottawa: K.I.M! Elmo: Our best is here, and our absolute best is yet to come. Selma, loud cheers! Brother Hafiz, much, much love my boy. My people in Sudan, BIG UP: Abir, Mohaid, Hisham, Hatim, Najat, Mohamed, Ahmed, Sawsan, Ishraga; brother Hassan's family; the aunties: Sitana & Batoul; Sinnar, I see y'all; Halaween, your secret will be revealed one day; Ala, Malaz, Mazin, Mohamed, Roa, Inshirah: mad love.

Of course, my journey has taken me to different places, meeting different people. Shout out, BGSU: the Subreenduths, the Booths, the Aguianos, the Currans (I see with both eyes), the Craddocks, John, James Brown and all you students who shower me with love. My people in Casablanca (Morocco): Said, Meriem, Imran, Youssef, the Imads, El Asri, Mubarak, Idriss, and the whole crew: I am diggin y'all. You have shown me that theory is a lived thing that is yet to be fully deciphered. Unconditional hospitality, *jouissance*. My crews in South Africa and Senegal (Salam Boubakar): shout out! Space is short, you know who you are: BIG UP!

Of course this project would not have been possible, as Alim already indicated, without the Double A Team: Alim and Alastair. Some things are meant to be felt, and to talk about them is to spoil them. This team simply *is*, and *is* slips language. Yet, the closest two words that might capture how The Triple A works are: elegance and rigor. Nothing passes without a rigorous and elegant discussion. It was simply a blessing to work with you two, my homies.

There are four people who have the biggest impact in my life: my sisters Osailat (my absolute best friend), Aziza (Can you see me?), and my brother Hassan: Boy, I owe you BIG TIME. Did I ever tell you how deeply I love you? But, every inch and cell of my body is owed to Her Majesty, my mother, Fatima Salih. I bow my head and ask for her forgiveness and blessing. May I kiss your hands one more time? I know you hear me: Wad Boro is doing it big ma, and Keeping It Moving. For you who hope, tell her the journey has begun. For you who love, tell her love is a round the corner. LOVE YA MA!

Alastair

Awad, Alim – Double A – I'm not going to add much to all this. Seems like the world has been acknowledged! Thanks, guys, this has been a great ride through theory, text and imagination. Thanks to all the contributors, who had to put up with us coming back, and coming back again, with ideas and questions and suggestions. And thanks to the Sydney crew—Tony Mitchell, Nick Keys, and Astrid Lorange (for the index too)—for all the good times, and to all those makin some local noise (www.localnoise.net.au).

Intro

Straight Outta Compton, Straight aus München: Global Linguistic Flows, Identities, and the Politics of Language in a Global Hip Hop Nation

H. SAMY ALIM

Addressing a large audience at the University of Pennsylvania's conference on "Islam and the Globalization of Hip Hop," James Peterson (2001) offered critical insight into one of Hip Hop's central speech events, *tha cipha*, an organic, highly charged, fluid circular arrangement of rhymers wherein participants exchange verses: "The use of the term *cipha* in the Hip Hop vernacular is important. Ciphas are marvelous speech events. They are inviting and also very challenging. They have become a litmus test for modern day *griots*. Ciphas are the innovative formats for battles (the ritual of rhyming is informed by the physical arrangement of Hip Hop)." Peterson continued by further noting that the concept of the cipha "is essential to Hip Hop Culture and to its vernacular," not only because it is the height of linguistic creativity and competition in the Hip Hop Nation, but also because it "indicates an epistemology that is non-linear."

As Spady, Alim, and Meghelli (2006) write: "If Hip Hop were a material object, tha cipha would represent Hip Hop at its molecular level" (p. 11). One could argue that, at least in the ethnographic, microanalytic sense, tha cipha might represent the fundamental unit of analysis in the interpretation of the Hip Hop cultural practice of *rappin*. In a move that privileges local epistemologies and views the contemporary global situation as less singly dominated and increasingly interactive (as does Appadurai, 1990), Spady et al. (2006) theorize Hip Hop Culture and its global diffusion as a cipha. "In the same way that local Hip Hop artists build community and construct social organization through the rhyming practices involved in tha cipha, Hip Hop communities worldwide interact with each other (through media and cultural flow, as well as embodied international travel) in ways that organize their participation in a mass-mediated, cultural movement" (p. 11).

Exemplifying this, Jeff Chang (2007, p. 58), writing about a "Hip Hop World" in *Foreign Policy*, takes us inside the annual rap battle known as the "Iron Mic." As he describes it, the youth in this hot, urban nightclub look like "typical hip-hop artists, dressed in baggy pants and baseball caps." But a closer look, and listen, reveals that these Hip Hop heads are rappin in multiple language varieties. "One rapper spits out words in a distinctive Beijing accent, scolding the other for not speaking proper Mandarin," while "his opponent from Hong Kong snaps back to the beat in a trilingual torrent of Cantonese, English, and Mandarin, dissing the Beijing rapper for not representing the people." The crowd—not in Los Angeles, not in New York, *but in Shanghai*—"goes wild!" Centrally for this volume, the *cipha* becomes a space where language ideologies and identities are shaped, fashioned, and vigorously contested, and where languages themselves are flexed, created, and sometimes (often intentionally) bent up beyond all recognition.

As we shall see, this volume itself is constructed as a global intellectual Hip Hop cipha, with each contributor *spittin* ("writing") about particular contexts and *buildin* ("collaborating, challenging, and theorizing") with others to produce a whole that is greater than the sum of its parts. Highlighting the intersections between issues of language, Hip Hop Culture, and globalization, this volume pulls together various scholars of sociolinguistics, linguistic anthropology, (Hip Hop) cultural studies, and critical pedagogies in an effort to contribute to the growing scholarship on "Hip Hop Culture," as well as to reorient those fields by paying closer attention to the processes of globalization and localization. Contributors attempt to do this by combining the rigorous microanalysis of linguistic exchanges with the richness of ethnographic engagement with the production of the popular. At the outset, particularly since we are dealing with a relatively specialized, hotly contested, and often-misunderstood area of inquiry (and perhaps since as linguists, we are hyperattentive to language as a signifier of theoretical perspectives and ideological stances), a definition of several key terms is needed.

Although the terms *rap* and *Hip Hop* are sometimes used interchangeably, *Hip Hop* is used by practitioners to refer to a vast array of cultural practices including MCing (rappin), DJing (spinnin), writing (graffiti art), breakdancing (and other forms of streetdance), and cultural domains such as fashion, language, style, knowledge, and politics, all of which give us "Hip Hop Culture." "Rap" then, or "rappin," is constructed as one practice within "the whole culture of the movement," as U.S. Hip Hop pioneer Afrika Bambaataa would put it (Interviewed by Davey D on http://www.daveyd.com). To the most devoted Hip Hop heads, it is "a way of life," or a "lifestyle," and "worldview."

Until very recently (Alim, 2006b; Alim & Pennycook, 2007a; Pennycook 2007b; Spady et al., 2006), many scholars have referred to "Hip Hop Culture," or just "Hip Hop," in the abstract, without ever delineating its parameters. Perhaps because of its ubiquity (in everything from university curricula to fast food commercials to the background music in *boujie* Whole Foods supermarkets), there is this sense in both the public and academic discourse on "Hip Hop" that "we all know what we're talking about" when we use the term. However, as the contributors to this volume can attest, this normative use of "Hip Hop Culture" becomes problematic when one engages in ethnographic studies of Hip Hop cultural practices across wide-ranging and diverse scenes and contexts. While "Hip Hop Culture" is still valuable in its broad usage (at a particular level of abstraction), engagement with specific sites of Hip Hop cultural practice, production, and performance demands a perspective that favors the plurality of *Hip Hop Cultures* over the singular and monolithic "Hip Hop Culture." For this volume, the term *Hip Hop Cultures* refers not only to the various manifestations of the above-mentioned practices outside the United States, but to the often overlooked diversity of Hip Hop practices in the many regional scenes both inside and outside the United States that provide contexts for studies in this volume. All of these scenes comprise the "imagined community" (Anderson, 1991) known as the "Global Hip Hop Nation (GHHN)," a multilingual, multiethnic "nation" with an international reach, a fluid capacity to cross borders, and a reluctance to adhere to the geopolitical givens of the present.

These terms were not interrogated at the time when then graduate student Tricia Rose began writing one of the earliest and most oft-cited cultural analyses of Hip Hop in the United States in the early 90s (eventually published in 1994). It was not lost on her that she was deconstructing what would potentially become the most profound and the most perplexing cultural, musical, and linguistic movement of the late 20th/early 21st century. Within the first several pages of that book, she imagined the emergence of Hip Hop scholarship about diverse global scenes. "It is my firm belief that this project—which grounds black cultural signs and codes in black culture and examines the polyvocal languages of rap as the 'black noise' of the late twentieth century—will foster the development of more globally focused projects," she wrote (p. xiv). In a startling moment of intellectual foresight, she continued:

> Some of these might center on the pleasure that hip hop style and rap music affords suburban white teenagers in small, relatively homogenous midwestern towns [Kitwana, 2005], or the rich hip hop hybrids nurtured in Mexican [McFarland, 2006] and Puerto Rican [Rivera, 2003] communities in Los Angeles and New York, the Chinese [Lin, this volume] and Japanese [Condry, 2006] break-dancers with whom I spoke in a downtown Hong Kong mall and in Tokyo in 1984. The French North African immigrant hip hop scene [Prevos, 2001; Meghelli, 2004] in Paris or the German [Androutsopoulos, 2003], British [Peterson, 2002], and Brazilian [Roth-Gordon, 2002, this volume; Pardue, 2004a, 2004b] rap scenes could each fill its own book. (pp. xiv–xv)

The area of "global Hip Hop studies" was codified in large part due to the publication of Tony Mitchell's (2001) edited collection *Global Noise* (using the Hip Hop practice of *sampling* in forming the title). The volume featured Hip Hop scholarship from locations as linguistically and culturally diverse as

Europe, Canada, Japan, and Australia and sought to explore the expression of local identities globally through participation in Hip Hop Cultures. Several book-length treatments about global Hip Hop Cultures have appeared, such as Remes's (1998) study of Hip Hop in Dar Es Salaam, Kaya's (2001) study in Berlin, Maxwell's (2003) treatment of Hip Hop in Sydney, Condry's (2006) and Fisher's (2007) analyses of "Hip-Hop Japan," Henderson's (2007) engagement with "the hip hopping Samoan diaspora," and Osumare's (2007) exploration of the "Africanist aesthetic in global Hip Hop," as well as several other edited volumes and journal issues, such as Alim (2002), Alim and Pennycook (2007b), Durand (2002), Basu and Lemelle (2006), and Spady et al. (2006).

Kinshichoo de Freaky daburu no Japanese: Hip Hop Linguistics, Transcultural Flows, and the Sociolinguistics of Globalization

For the editors of this current volume, there are significant reasons for addressing the following constellation of concerns: Hip Hop Cultures, youth identities, the politics of language, and the simultaneous processes of globalization and localization. The recent outpouring of literature on the globalization and localization of "Hip Hop Culture(s)"—and the tensions between the two concurrent processes (partially captured by the term *glocalization* (Robertson, 1995)—suggests that scholars are turning to the study of global Hip Hop cultures as a means toward both illuminating our understanding of this abstract, discursive, popular cultural zone ("Hip Hop Culture") and delving deeper into the workings of complex processes such as transnationalism, cultural flow, syncretism, indigenization, hybridity, (im)migration, and diaspora, to name a few of the concepts that permeate this volume.

Our focus on Hip Hop is as related to the global presence of other musical forms, such as Reggae (Veal, 2007) and Jazz (Hobsbawm, 1998), for example, as it is to the globalization of entities "outside" of music, such as the proliferation of Muslim networks through communications technology (cooke & Lawrence, 2005) or the "globalization of food" through "movable feasts" (Kiple, 2007). However, as Krims (2000, p. 5, cited in Pennycook, 2007a, p. 8) has noted, "There is now scarcely a country in the world that does not feature some form of mutation of rap music, from the venerable and sophisticated hip-hop and rap scenes of France, to the "swa-rap" of Tanzania and Surinamese rap of Holland." Such widespread participation in Hip Hop leads Pennycook (2007a, pp. 6–8) to argue that the "transcultural flows" of Global Hip Hop Culture(s)—that is, "the ways in which cultural forms move, change and are reused to fashion new identities" as well as the processes of "borrowing, blending, remaking and returning, to processes of alternative cultural production"—may in fact be one of the most important sites of the study of globalization in general.

Further, scholars of this increasingly globalizing (and localizing) world are viewing the flow of Hip Hop cultural materials, practices, and ideologies with an eye toward understanding the multiple processes of identification. Specifically, for this group of scholars of language, we ask a related and significant set of questions. Just how is it that "Hip Hop Culture" has become a primary site of identification and self-understanding for youth around the world? And even more specifically, what linguistic resources do youth manipulate, (re)appropriate, and sometimes (re)create, in order to fashion themselves as members of a "GHHN"? And in doing so, what challenges do they face and pose, within distinct, local scenes, which privilege their own often competing, locally relevant categories of identification? How do these "Hip Hop headz," through their use of multiple language varieties and speech styles, negotiate their membership within the GHHN as they index the multiplicities of their identities through the often dangerous and contentious cultural terrains of race, gender, class, ethnicity, sexuality, and other locally relevant sites of identification? Furthermore, given Hip Hop Culture's historical focus on "knowledge," its relentless and consistent critique of educational systems, as well as its espousal of subversive language ideologies (from China, Brazil, and Cuba to the United States, Nigeria, and Canada), how does Hip Hop challenge dominant ideologies of language at the same time that it functions as an important site of language pedagogy? What are the implications for language policies, pedagogies, and the politics of language?

There is a final significant reason to explore these issues, one that is ironically taken for granted in most of the scholarship on Hip Hop Culture: *Language*, the omnipresent medium through which Hip Hop cultural practices, performances, and productions are both expressed and constituted, is perhaps one of the least analyzed aspects of Hip Hop Culture. Given the dominance of *rappin* in Hip Hop cultural practice, language is perhaps one of the most useful means by which to read Hip Hop Culture. By placing language squarely at the center of their analyses, the studies in this volume aim to shed light on both our understanding of Hip Hop Culture(s) as well as expand our theoretical approaches to language choice and agency, speech style and stylization, codeswitching and language mixing, crossing and sociolinguistic variation, and language use and globalization.

The scholars in this volume, in one way or another, are as committed to the study of language and culture, as they are to the potential of social transformation through intellectual inquiry. That is, we are not interested in a linguistics that narrowly presents speech as dislocated from the lives of its speakers. In this important sense, as well as the others mentioned above, this volume represents what I would call the first book-length, global intellectual *cipha* of what I have referred to as "Hip Hop Linguistics (HHLx)" (Alim, 2006, p. 10)—an interdisciplinary field of scholars committed to the study of language and language use in Hip Hop "communities." HHLx is interested in Hip Hop language practices in a global context, with particular attention to the global social and linguistic processes that both gave rise to Hip Hop Nation Language (Alim, 2004) in the United States, and to processes of transformation, reconfiguration, and appropriation, as well as to the agentive creation of HHNL varieties and their performance in diverse locales (such as Cairo, Tokyo, and Soweto, for example).

In a broader sense, we view this volume as an exploration into the developing "sociolinguistics of globalization" (Blommaert, 2003). Often looking beyond linguistic structure and viewing language as culture, the contributors in this volume confirm Blommaert's claim that "what is globalized is not an abstract Language, but specific speech forms, genres, styles, and forms of literacy practice" (p. 608). This is certainly the case with Hip Hop. Hip Hop rhyming practices have altered poetic genres across the globe, with Japan being a particularly intriguing case where Hip Hop artists restructure Japanese in order to rhyme and flow (Tsujimura & Davis, this volume), and along with Chinese (Lin, this volume), Korean (see Pennycook, 2007a, p. 128), and Italian artists (see Androutsopoulos & Scholz, 2003, pp. 474–475), have produced similar poetic structures such as the *back-to-back chain rhymes* and *bridge rhymes* described in Black American Hip Hop. This is all the more interesting because rhyme, as Tsujimura and Davis (this volume) inform us, is not found in traditional Japanese verse. In line with the major thrust of this volume, they complicate this picture by noting that while this may appear to be simply a "reflection of a global form of expression characteristic of Hip Hop world-wide, the way in which rhyme is adapted into Japanese Hip Hop is localized to the context and resources of the Japanese language by having it faithfully conform to the notion of *mora*, a crucial linguistic concept of the language, but not necessarily relevant in many others."

In another incredibly complex case of Hip Hop poetics, Lin (this volume) explores the global and local dimensions of the Cantonese verbal art of Hip Hop rhyming. Encouraged by "Western Hip Hop" to spit that *fo* (Cantonese for "fire") —that is, to "speak in the voice of *siu shih-mahn* (grassroots people)," to disrupt dominant, middle-class norms with their use of *chou-hau* (vulgar mouth), and to compose similarly complex multirhyme matrices (as in Alim, 2003)—artists like the Muslim-aligned MC Yan not only critique American foreign policy in songs like "War Crime" but they also "capitalize on the special tonal and syllabic features of the Cantonese language" to do so. As Lin (this volume) writes, Yan calls this "double-rhyming" or "3-dimensional rhyme," meaning that "several levels of phonetic parallelism can be drawn upon to create a multilevel rhyming aesthetic: e.g., rappers can use words with same vowels (rhyming), same consonants (alliteration), same sounds (homonyms), same number of syllables, and same or similar syllable pitch (tone) patterns for multisyllabic words." (Now that's what you call some serious next level rap *ishhh*!)

The sociolinguistics of globalization requires us not only to take these sociolinguistic details into account in our consideration of cultural processes, but it also pushes us to critique and expand even our very notions of language. For example, in writing about Rip Slime, Pennycook (2003, 2007a) describes a Japanese group that is partially influenced by Black American Hip Hop Nation Language—the group's name itself builds upon the tradition of creative wordplay in that it exploits the sometimes globally marginalized r/l distinction in "Japanese English" to produce "Lips Rhyme" (2003, p. 530)—while priding themselves on speaking a "*Kinshichoo de* freaky *daburu no* Japanese" (Freaky mixed Japanese from Kinshichoo). In addition to the more obvious global influence, the use of language by these artists is indexical of multiple cultural affiliations and identifications. As Pennycook concludes, Rip Slime's uses of multiple forms of Japanese—"Japanese which may locate these rappers as decidedly local (*Kinshichoo*) or which may signal their sense of cultural mixing"—and multiple forms of English—which "at times explicitly echoes African American English while other times seems more Japanese in its usage"—seems to avoid designations of local or global and to "flow itself across the boundaries of identity" (p. 527). As we witness this complex linguistic remixing across the globe, as evidenced in this volume, the multiplicity of indexicalities brought forth by such multilayered uses of language demands a sociolinguistics of globalization that gives a more central role to linguistic agency on the part of youth, as their appropriations and remixes of Hip Hop indicate that these heteroglot language practices are important technologies in the fashioning of their local/global identities.

"It's Still the Same *Corroboree*": Hip Hop Cultures, Contested Origins, and "Wireless Identities" in an *Abo-Digital* Age

As we enter the *abo-digital* age, many Black (and other) American Hip Hop heads and scholars alike are not aware that Hip Hop's "origins" in what Murray Forman (commenting at the Stanford Hip Hop Archive in 2005) referred to as "the essential Bronx moment" are being challenged by Hip Hop practitioners and scholars around the globe. Many of the chapters in this volume, in fact, present alternative origins of "Hip Hop Culture," with Pennycook and Mitchell, Androutsopoulos, Omoniyi, and Sarkar doing so most directly. The "original origin myth" (to use an oxymoron) has been told and retold numerous times in the Hip Hop literature (George, 1999; Toop, 1984/1999; Yasin, 1999, to name a few), but very rarely, if at all, with an explicit metanarrative of the immense cultural labor that Hip Hop heads engage in as they make a "culture" with a "history" and "traditions," and of course, an "origin."

Interestingly enough, this metacultural-analysis first appears in Maxwell's (2003) cogently theorized study of a small group of mostly White boys in Sydney, Australia. In his year and a half of ethnographic engagement, he examines these youths' "intense desire…to *constitute* themselves as a community," and "to *claim* for that community the status of a culture, a claim accompanied and supported by claims to specific knowledges, traditions, and practices, and to *locate* that culture as part of a transnational movement, the Hip Hop Nation" [emphasis mine] (p. 20). I italicize the verbs in the above quotation to emphasize the significance of Maxwell's cultural analysis; that is, his attempt to characterize how White boys in Sydney constructed their identities by *writing* themselves into an "already existing" Hip Hop cultural text (rather than an "already local" one; see below) and *working* together constantly to *claim* Hip Hop as theirs.

Pennycook and Mitchell (this volume) present us with an alternative, and yet complementary, view of the diverse Hip Hop scenes in Australia. By doing this, they provide us with an interesting moment of cross-racial comparison of

Hip Hop ideologies in Australia. Whereas the White boys in Maxwell's study worked to create an ideology of Hip Hop as racially inclusive in order to distance the equally available "culture" from a "Blackness" that they could never embody (despite their expressed desire "to be black," ["When I was getting into it all, I was um, I'd wish that I was black because then I could rap," p. 66]), the Aboriginal and African rappers in Pennycook and Mitchell worked equally hard to construct Hip Hop as an extension of a "Blackness" or "Africanness" that they actually embodied. In some cases, these rappers constructed themselves as the "originators" of Hip Hop, with globalization being described as a "return to Africa."

In the Aboriginal case, we have a prime example of what Pennycook and Mitchell refer to as the "already local" construction of Hip Hop's origins. As the Aboriginal Wire MC explains, we are living in an age of *wireless identities*, or the *abo-digital* age: "I'm abo-digital because I'm a Twenty-first century Aboriginal, I'm down with laptops and mobile phones and home entertainment. But digital also means your hands and your fingers, so I'm still putting my fingers in the dirt; I'm still using my hands to create things. So that's the ambiguity" (cited in Pennycook & Mitchell, this volume, p. 26). By exploiting the ambiguity of the word *digital,* Wire MC further describes Hip Hop as "still the same *corroboree*," a term that the authors explain is used widely throughout "Indigenous communities in Australia to refer to events or meetings (as opposed to ceremonies) which typically include songs, dances, and other social and cultural activities." (p. 26). The *re-re-appropriation* of *corroboree* actually comes close to capturing the view of Hip Hop's origins by Aboriginal and African MC's as "already local." Corroboree, as an indigenous term, was first appropriated into English, then reappropriated by Aboriginal communities, and now further reappropriated by Aboriginal Wire MC to refer to Hip Hop. Similarly from these MCs' perspective, Hip Hop, as an Indigenous practice, was first appropriated by Black Americans, then reappropriated by Aboriginal and African peoples, and then further reappropriated by MCs to shape local Hip Hops within already existing local traditions.

The strength of Pennycook and Mitchell's analysis is that they radically reshape the ways in which we think about global and local cultural and linguistic formations, from "global hip hops" to "global Englishes." As Maxwell (2003) wrote, it is very difficult to deny—though one has to wonder, like Perry (2004), why attempt denial in the first place—that Hip Hop "originated in a culturo-historical specific—the African-American inner-cities of the United States" (with many recognizing the global flows that worked upon this "womb," including Dyson cited in Jones, 2006; and Hebdige, 1987; Kelley, 2006). Denial of Black American influence does not interest Pennycook and Mitchell, however; theirs is a different point. They point to the need to consider "the dynamics of change, struggle, and appropriation" in the process of globalization and to the advantages of viewing the processes of "hip hop indigenization" as a "highly complex process of struggle and two-way flows." Importantly, their work, along with other contributions in this volume, restores a sense of agency to cultural workers who are busy carving out and creating spaces for themselves in the GHHN.

When read together with Maxwell's (2003) work, one is struck by the ability of African, Aboriginal, and other Indigenous cultures—as opposed to non-African and non-Indigenous ones—to lay claim to "Hip Hop Culture" by, as Omoniyi writes (this volume), "self-constructing as the essential core from which the dominant cultural flow [of Hip Hop] derived," even as they are being "discursively other-constructed on the periphery of a global mainstream." Capturing this tension to define oneself through the eyes of "the Other"—this Hip Hop double-consciousness, if you will (see Dyson cited in Jones, 2006)—Nigeria's Afrolution Records writes:

> What has always held African Hip Hop back is a struggle for our own identity, our own sound—something that belongs to us and is not a second rate replication of the Western sound. Sure we all grew up on US Hip Hop, we acknowledge that and we are grateful for the opportunities it has created for us but one cannot deny the true essence of Hip Hop is "keeping it real." (cited in Omoniyi, this volume)

The search for the "real," in this case, is a Hip Hop that "carves out a recognizable creative patch and a legitimate non-subordinate local identity whilst retaining membership" in a GHHN (Omoniyi, this volume). Again, these comments point to the fact that there is a great deal of (often self-conscious) cultural work being done by the agents of global Hip Hops in an effort to express local identities through engagement with the global.

Given the possibility, as raised by Omoniyi, Sarkar, and Pennycook and Mitchell, that much of the world no longer relies exclusively on Hip Hop's Black American "origins," still for most contexts, as Androutsopoulos (2003, this volume) writes about German Hip Hop—and Higgins (Tanzania), Roth-Gordon (Brazil), Cutler (White America; all in this volume), Ibrahim (2003) and several chapters in Basu and Lemelle (2006) demonstrate—diverse global Hip Hop Cultures evolve "in a constant dialogue with its 'mother culture,' by drawing on US hip-hop as a source for new trends and as a frame for the interpretation of local productions" (p. 1). Despite this, it is not the intention of this volume to pit the "American" versus the "global"; global Hip Hop Cultures are comprised of multiple "circuits of flow" (Pennycook, 2007a) and numerous, overlapping, interactive ciphas (Spady et al., 2006). This persistent "back-back, forth-and-forth motion" between the local and the global gives rise to the creative linguistic choices, styles, and varieties that are the central subject of investigation in this volume.

"He No Fit Rap *Foné* Pass American, So I Decide to Do Am Naija Style": Crossing, Codeswitching, and Styling in Diverse Hip Hop Politico-Linguistic Contexts

As stated above, it is primarily the *languages* of global Hip Hop Cultures that interest the contributors to this volume. From the perspective of linguistic anthropology, which views language "as a cultural resource and speaking as cultural practice" (Duranti, 1997, 2004), speakers make use of the linguistic resources available to them to index multiple identities (Ochs, 1990, 1992). An understanding of the dialectical, mutually constitutive relationship between languages and identities is central to an understanding of key sociolinguistic concepts such as crossing, language mixing, codeswitching, styleshifting, and styling, all of which are featured heavily in this volume. This perspective views speakers as both producers and products of language, using language in ways that simultaneously reproduce social structures and individual subjectivities. As Kroskrity (1993) further notes, specific linguistic resources can also be employed across contexts by very different speakers, who through their behavior seek to exploit the potential multiple indexicalities of particular linguistic resources (see also Eckert, 2005).

Our focus on language engages, quite centrally, sociolinguistic concerns about style and styling, or what Bakhtin (1981) referred to as "stylization." This area of inquiry, as noted in Eckert and Rickford (2001) and Rampton (1999a), along with the work on language ideologies (Kroskrity, 2000; Schieffelin, Woolard, & Kroskrity, 1998), has produced perhaps the most fruitful and engaging theoretical developments in sociolinguistics and linguistic anthropology in the last two or three decades. Many of the contributors to this volume ground their analyses in these recent developments, and I would add that it is this theoretical work that keeps them grounded. That is, work in this area, despite our living in an age of "wireless identities," demands that we "keep our ear to the street" (Baugh, 1983), so to speak, and that we engage the local even as scholars of poststructuralism, postmodernism, and "posteverything" (Fred Erickson, personal communication, 2006) insist that we are living in a world of "aerials rather than roots," and that our societies resemble "lifestyle communities" and "neo-tribes without socialization" (Rampton, 1999b, p. 425, citing Bauman, 1992).

This point could not have been more clearly demonstrated through the work of Johnstone (1999) and Hill (1999), who consider "styling locally" and "styling globally," while recognizing the potential strength of posttheories to account for particular moments of language use. As sociolinguists and linguistic anthropologists renew their disciplinary connections (Bucholtz & Hall, in press), there is a growing consensus to view identities as defined *not* by the correlation of particular linguistic resources and whatever social categories scholars deem relevant (region, race, class, gender, sexuality, etc.). Rather, as Bucholtz and Hall (2004, p. 376) argue, identities are perhaps better understood as outcomes of language use, requiring us to shift our focus from identity (which suggests a set of fixed categories) to "identification as an ongoing social and political process." This consensus has developed, in part, because of a growing view that identities are being fashioned in a world of increasingly decentralized authority, a proliferation of nonregionalized virtual place (Meyrowitz, 1985), and the loosening of boundaries of inclusion and exclusion (Rampton, 1999b).

Though speech has never been "innocent" (Rampton, 1999b), many chapters in this volume affirm Rampton's perspective by problematizing "**production within** particular cultural spaces" by looking at "**projection-across**," at speech's "transposition into and out of arenas where social conditions and social relations are substantially different." (p. 423). Of course, as much of the work in this volume also points out, the deployment of specific linguistic resources, and their reception, is contingent upon the local configurations of cultures, languages, and politics (Pennycook, 2007b; see also Omoniyi, 2006; Sarkar & Allen, 2007). As Higgins (this volume) asks about Tanzanian Hip Hop heads, for example, raising important questions about "crossing," "styling the other," and authentication: "Are these youth *crossing* (Rampton, 1995) from Tanzanian varieties of English into AAE [African-American English]," and thus "borrowing the linguistic and semiotic styles of another culture" of and by which they are generally perceived as outsiders? Or, are they "*appropriating* AAE for the local East African context" with their language use "resulting in a simultaneously localized, yet global, form of expression, such as *raplish*" (Pennycook, 2003)?

In a similar vein, Androutsopoulos' chapter focuses on German and Greek Hip Hop heads who "split styles"; that is, shift in and out of language varieties and discourse genres in their lyrics, writings, conversations, and computer-mediated communication. Productively reworking the concept of *crossing*, Androutsopoulos points out that the usual emphasis on "identity work" has led us to overlook the aesthetic and poetic work being accomplished through the related linguistic practices of styling, crossing, and codeswitching. Further, he suggests that, at least in this specific case, the use of an "(African American) English from below as an identity resource" may have as much to do with "*stepping into* an alien ethnic territory ('blackness')" as "*stepping out* of one's own national boundaries" and "into a global hip-hop nation that is not necessarily imagined of primarily in racial or ethnic terms." Of primary concern for him, as well as Higgins, is how these artists negotiate the tensions inherent in any attempt to simultaneously "go global" while "keepin it local."

Regarding these cultural-linguistic tensions, language use in any context is subject to the interpretation of those languages through local ideologies of language (and race, ethnicity, gender, etc.), which in turn, may be transformed through local youths' participation in global cultural formations. The ethnographic work on language ideologies takes us beyond a vision of "language choice" and opens up instead an understanding of the relations between diverse language practices and the (trans)formation of local realities. As already noted, these studies, as well as many of the studies of global Hip Hop Cultures in this volume, not only force us to contend with the "on-the-ground" realities and the specific ethnographic contexts, but they also force us to take into account the sociopolitical arrangement of the relations between language use, identities, power, and pedagogies.

In the case of the subheading above, a Nigerian Hip Hop artist rhymes in what

Omoniyi (this volume) refers to as "Hip Hop Nation Language-Nigeria," which often includes a complicated mix of "multiple indigenous languages including those that are not necessarily their mother tongues…with Nigerian Pidgin as a common denominator," often codeswitching with Yoruba, Igbo, and (African) American English (p. 124). The use of all of these language varieties is certainly counterpositioned, as Omoniyi notes, to the kind of "establishment identity" that we might associate with "English-as-official language" policy. The on-the-ground reality in Nigeria is complex, to say the least. While language use in Nigerian Hip Hop threatens the establishment of a sociolinguistic order that privileges English, it simultaneously draws upon (African) American English, which some local speakers describe as a failed attempt and an "excruciating encounter" with "Yankee drawl." (p. 125). In this context, the language of Hip Hop in Nigeria is a new site for the articulation and contestation of multiple identities, during an age of globalization where neocolonial subjects and nations are "exploring strategies of reinvention in order to break completely either from the colonial yoke or neocolonial elite domination" (Omoniyi, this volume).

The Hip Hop politico-linguistic context is equally complex in Canada (Sarkar, this volume), Tanzania (Higgins, this volume), and China (Lin, this volume), where in each instance, we witness youth deeply engaged in identity construction through diverse linguistic practices and what I (this volume) refer to as "language ideological combat." In her chapter on Tanzania, for example, Higgins describes the practices of Hip Hop youth who use a combination of "African American English," specifically Hip Hop Nation Language in the United States, a glocal street code known as *Kihuni*, and kiSwahili to identify *not* as "marginalized, or as inauthentic wannabes," nor are they simply "trying to relocate themselves in another culture"; rather, they are "redefining their local environments" through participation within a "transcultural, multilingual, and multiracial" GHHN. Drawing on the work of Blommaert (1999, pp. 93–98), Higgins points out (like Omoniyi, this volume) that a complete understanding of this context would need to consider Tanzania's complex history of colonialism, independence from Britain in 1961, the subsequent economic changes (from socialism to capitalism), and linguistic shifts (from an "anti-English" language policy to a policy (not a reality) of "Swahili-English bilingualism").

As a final example of the language ideological combat taking place in diverse Hip Hop politico-linguistic contexts, Sarkar (this volume) explores the transformative power of Hip Hop language mixing in Montreal, Quebec, a city that has witnessed a complete, demographic overhaul in the last two decades. Montreal has become "multiethnic and multilingual," especially since the 1970s, as "non-White" or "non-Christian" immigrants (from Haiti, the Dominican Republic, and various predominantly Muslim countries) arrive to make Canada their home. In the face of such radical demographic shifts, an intense struggle over nationhood, and a staunch effort by the state to maintain a "rigidly normative, prescriptive" French-language dominance, Hip Hop language mixing in Quebec simultaneously threatens the myopic plans of language policy-makers as it operates, at least for the present generation, as a "positive and cohesive social force" (Sarkar, this volume).

Importantly, Sarkar theorizes language and race together to help further our understanding of identity formation in Quebec (as Ibrahim, 2003 has done for Ontario). The arrival of Afrodiasporic youth, their subsequent subjugation due to skin color, and their familiarity with Malcolm X and Black American ideologies of race and nationalism (Sarkar & Allen, 2007), has influenced non-White Montreal MCs to introduce narratives of local racism in order to critique a global system of racialized oppression. Hip Hop artists, wherever they are located (as evidenced in Alim & Pennycook, 2007b; Basu & Lemelle, 2006; Mitchell, 2001), often challenge the sociopolitical arrangement of the relations between languages, identities, and power. Critically, in predominantly non-White, male-dominated Hip Hop contexts, constructions of Blackness and masculinity are transported globally and interact with local constructions to produce, in some cases, a radically new racial consciousness.

Fear of a Black Male Planet: Hip Hop, Intertextuality, and the Racialized, Gendered Process of "Becoming Black"

Constructions of Blackness and masculinity in the United States have interacted most notably with those in Brazil (Roth-Gordon, this volume; Pardue, 2004a), Cuba (Fernandes, 2003; Wunderlich, 2006), France (Helenon, 2006; Meghelli, 2007), South Africa (Magubane, 2006), and other locales such as Columbia, Venezuela, Senegal, Mali, and other African and Afrodiasporic communities (as noted in Basu & Lemelle, 2006; Fernandes, 2003; Osumare, 2007). It is well-documented that Hip Hop Culture in the 1980s and 90s in the United States was driven in large part by an ideological commitment to Black nationalism, various forms of Islam and Afrocentrism (Alim, 2006a), and a race-consciousness that centered Blackness and pushed Whiteness to the periphery (see Spady & Eure, 1991, in particular, as well as Chang, 2005; Decker, 1993; Perry, 2004; Rose, 1994). The group Public Enemy perhaps looms largest in the global Hip Hop imagination as the greatest advocates of a Black-centered ideology of race, with their albums *It Takes a Nation of Millions to Hold Us Back* (1988) and *Fear of a Black Planet* (1990) hailed by Hip Hop heads around the world as two of the most important Hip Hop releases of all time. These albums, along with the works of legions of both male and female "nation conscious rappers" (Spady & Eure, 1991), articulated, in large part through their inspiration from Elijah Muhammad's *Message to the Black Man in America* (1965), a recognition not just of a fear of "Blackness" but also a fear of a particular form of "Black masculinity."

Without denying significant female and non-Black participation in various local Hip Hop communities in the United States, and female and non-Black attempts to challenge the status of Blackness and masculinity, both constructions maintain their dominance (Pough, 2004; Richardson, 2006), in part due to female and non-Black complicity and coconstruction of these identities as dominant

(Morgan, interviewed in Carpenter, 2006). In Cutler's chapter in this volume, she explores the coconstruction of Whiteness in a Hip Hop cultural sphere where Blackness is seen as normative. In her chapter, she builds upon her research (1999) that examines the ways in which a "white upper middle class New York City teenager" employs "African American Vernacular English" to accomplish various tasks, including the production of himself as a member of the Hip Hop Nation as well as the reproduction of White male privilege and racism. In this volume, she takes on the participation of a White MC in a predominantly Black rap battle and how both he and his competitors work together to coconstruct Whiteness through adopting particular *stances* (Goffman, 1981), and the linguistic practices of *marking* (Mitchell-Kernan, 1974) and *styling the other to define the self* (Bell, 1999). While research on styling the other focused almost exclusively on members of dominant linguistic groups styling the linguistically marginalized, Cutler's chapter raises an interesting question about what happens when a member of an otherwise privileged group finds himself styling *himself* as the other within a popular cultural sphere that marks Whiteness as the racial other and White masculinities as inferior. (Contrast with Black American youth's daily struggle speaking what Alim, this volume, refers to as "Black Language in White public space.")

Language, race, and styling the other are also themes in much of Ibrahim's (1999, 2000, 2001) critical ethnographic research which traces how a group of immigrant, francophone African youth, living in an urban metropolitan city in southwestern Ontario, Canada, were in the process of "becoming Black." This process was on the one hand marked by an identification with and a desire for North American Blackness; and it was, on the other, as much about the performance of gender, race, and language in a Canadian context. The research delineated these youths' desire for and identification with Blackness through their learning of "Black English as a Second Language (BESL)," which they accessed in and through their participation with U.S. Hip Hop Culture (see also Sarkar this volume for a related, yet different case in Montreal, Quebec).

In her chapter, Roth-Gordon also explores the linguistic practices by which Hip Hop youth "become Black" through their engagement with American ideologies of race found in U.S. Hip Hop Culture. Importantly, in addition to the examinations of crossing, codeswitching, styling, and language mixing in this volume, Roth-Gordon's chapter delves into what Androutsopoulos (this volume) calls the "third sphere of Hip Hop discourse." In Androutsopoulos' sociolinguistic and discourse analytic schema of Hip Hop discourses, he builds upon Fiske's (1987) concept of *vertical intertextuality* to outline three interrelated spheres: "artist expression (corresponding to Fiske's 'primary texts'), media discourse ('secondary texts'), and discourse among Hip Hop fans and activists ('tertiary texts')" (p. 44). Besides being one of the few studies of the "third sphere of Hip Hop discourse" (see also Woods, 2006, for indexicalization among Black-American and Korean-American Hip Hop youth in Los Angeles, and Lee, 2005 for Black-American discourse in the street ciphas of southcentral Los Angeles), Roth-Gordon's study of "rap as daily discourse" introduces and labels the highly remarked upon but seldom studied practice of "conversational sampling."

In terms of the production of a Black, male planet, Roth-Gordon's studies remind us that along with the flow of languages comes the flow of ideologies, as in Appadurai's "ideoscapes" (1996), in this case, what she terms "race trafficking." Through race trafficking—"the controversial and underground importation of US racial and political ideology" (p. 70)—Brazilian youth "become Black" despite the embodied stigma of Blackness in Brazil and the efforts of the Brazilian nation-state to endorse "race mixture…under the racist assumption that Whiteness would bleach both African and Indigenous racial impurities." The public performance of *negritude* ("Black consciousness") by these artists, along with their revival of terms like *mano* (Black brother) and *playboy* (White, wealthy male youth), points to the complex interaction of the introduction of American racial ideologies with local ideologies and conceptions of race and racism.

Blackness's normative status in American Hip Hop crosses borders to Australia as well, where some White Australians' attempts to colonize Hip Hop Culture are met with exasperation by some Black MCs' (as if colonizing Black territory wasn't enough). As Wire MC describes in Pennycook and Mitchell (this volume, p. 37):

> As for the whole Aussie accent thing, man, I have a struggle going on with that one personally. First, I don't talk ocker [stereotypical white Australian male]. I talk how I'm talkin'…I don't say "g'day mate." I say, "how you going brother." That's what I say…. But on a more personal outlook, it's like wait a minute. Hip hop comes from a black background. I live in a country where it was a penal system before it was a colony, as we were told—or forced— to assimilate us. And this is just a personal thing, but I find now through hip hop, having white boys come up to me and saying "you know, maybe you should rap a bit more Aussie." And I'm like "What?! Are you trying to colonize me again dude?! Stop it. Stop it."

In their attempts to distance Hip Hop from Blackness (mentioned above), some White MCs may be identifying more with a national identity as Australian, while other Black MC's may be aligning themselves with a transnational Black identity. At the same time, when Wire MC identifies himself as "B.L.A.C.K." (Born Long Ago Creation's Keeper), this is a "B.L.A.C.K.ness" that operates within a dual space of appeal to a sense of "transnational Blackness," which is equally concerned with broader racial politics and specific Indigenous histories. Underscoring a central methodological point of this book, this doubling of racial identity can easily be missed by scholars (admittedly, I first read the Aboriginal/Australian "how you going brother?" as the Black American "how you doing brother?"!) who assume solely Black American kinship and fail to engage ethnographically with Hip Hop scenes in Australia.

Regardless of the different ways that "transnational Blackness" is accomplished throughout the world, Hip Hop heads from the diverse locales of the *favelas* of Rio de Janeiro, Brazil, the *banlieues* of Paris, France, the *townships* of South Africa, and the *barrios* of Cuba—all existing on the peripheries of their respective nation-states—have turned to a Global Hip Hop "Nation" for a rearticulation of their race, gender, class, and political positions as well as an empowered view of themselves as transnational subjects.

Listening with Both Ears: Future Directions in the Study of Hip Hop(s), Language(s), and Culture(s)

What we hope we have done in this volume is to invigorate scholars of language through our analyses and our engagement with key concepts in sociolinguistics, linguistic anthropology, and critical applied linguistics (and in some cases, creating our own concepts) in an effort to engage the sociolinguistics of globalization. We also hope that we have enlivened Hip Hop Studies by calling attention to language as a key to understanding Hip Hop cultural practices, productions, and performances (and in some cases, in contexts heretofore unexplored). We also hope that our attention to the simultaneous processes of globalization and localization will contribute to broader discussions in the social sciences and humanities.

There are several research directions that need further development, however, if we are to accomplish these grand goals. They are: (1) Ethnographic studies of Hip Hop and hiphopographies that *en-voice* the often silencing cultural studies approaches (see Spady et al., 2006). (2) Analyses of the languages of Hip Hop Cultures that move us beyond structure to a broader semiotic, multimodal (Goodwin, 2006; Mendoza-Denton, 2007) system of representation and toward a theorizing of style as *glocal distinctiveness* (building upon Irvine, 2001). (3) Studies of language use in what Androutsopoulos (this volume) refers to as the third sphere of Hip Hop discourse, primarily because interaction is a critical site for the development of ideologies and identities (Bucholtz & Hall, 2005). (4) A more direct engagement with critical language pedagogies in the education of linguistically profiled and marginalized Hip Hop youth (and all youth, of course; see Pennycook, 2007b; Alim, Ibrahim, this volume). (5) A need for comparative, multisited, cross-cultural studies that are situated within historical analyses (see Hill, 1999, with particular reference to "styling locally, styling globally") and that attempt to understand the "translocalities" (Appadurai, 1996; Clifford, 1997) of Hip Hop Cultures. (6) Studies of language and the construction of gender in Hip Hops that take us beyond the tired "bitch" and "ho" critiques to an ethnographic understanding of how youth interpret and make use of "misogynistic" and "homophobic" texts (see Newman, this volume, for male practices and Richardson, 2006, for critical Black female literacies).

Newman's chapter, building upon Dimitriadis' (2001, p. 63) stellar demonstration that meaning-making in Hip Hop could not possibly be "prefigured by textual analysis of rap lyrics alone," provides a welcome engagement with the "lifeworlds" of Jamaican-American and Latino Hip Hop youth in New York City. Tackling what others refer to as "Hip Hop's most notorious problems"—sexism, violence, misogyny, and homophobia (widespread problems of global societies in general)—Newman, who self-identifies as gay in his chapter, finds a disjuncture between the youth's use of terms like *faggot* and *homo* in their lyrics and their life experiences and treatment of homosexuals. Newman's analysis, which is based on interviews and extended ethnographic observation, complicates the simplistic reading of the relationship between Hip Hop texts and their consumers by exploring *empirically* "how creators and listeners construe a text."

Extended ethnographic engagement and hiphopographical approaches to the study of Hip Hop cultural practices point out the potential shortcomings of distanced, ungrounded approaches. Maxwell (2003) eloquently critiques what he refers to as the "disturbing cultural studies approaches in which 'the media'... is reified and theorized without regard to cultural agents (other than the cultural theorist doing the writing)" (p. 19). Even Maxwell, though, like many others grappling with the scholarly representation of Hip Hop, struggles with this critique (as do I, Alim, 2006), namely by dominating the text, but also by his lack of significant attention to the translocal dynamics of race. Rose's (1994) insightful analysis provides another instance of this difficulty. For example, despite conducting interviews and a particular level of ethnographic engagement, her chapter on gender relations in U.S. Hip Hop reads not as an attempt to explore the dynamics of gender and race in Hip Hop practitioner's lived experiences, but rather as a belabored attempt to have Black women Hip Hop artists claim Rose's particular vision of "feminism"—compare this with Joan Morgan's (1999) work in developing a "Hip Hop feminism".

Further, despite their significant contributions, Mitchell (2001) and Gilroy (1993) miss the mark on U.S. Hip Hop by failing to problematize the construction of Black American Hip Hop Culture as a monolith (as noted in Dyson in Jones, 2006; Magubane, 2006). For example, Mitchell's (2001) misrepresentation of Black American Hip Hop (see Fernandes, 2003) as becoming "increasingly atrophied, clichéd, and repetitive" as well as his reading of "gangsta rap" as an "espousal of urban ugliness, greed, misogyny, capitalism, crime, homophobia, joyless sex, male physicality, and violence" (p. 2) appear reductive. Evidence gained from critical readings of U.S. Hip Hop texts (Perry, 2004; Quinn, 2005) and ethnographic engagement with the creators and consumers of the said "atrophied" Hip Hop of the same time period (see Spady et al., 1999) present us with a far more complex picture, one that pushes against uncritical popular discourses. The difficulty of ethnographic engagement remains an issue for leading scholars of Hip Hop, including some of the contributors in this cipha; that is, it is something that we must work through as a collective.

Several of the chapters in this volume draw on ethnographic methods or grow out of longer ethnographies of language and Hip Hop cultural practice in particular locales. There is still a need, however, to engage what Alim, Meghelli, and Spady (2006) outline as *hiphopography* (first exemplified in Spady, 1991; Spady, Alim, & Lee, 1999; Spady, Dupres, & Lee, 1995)—a critical methodology that "integrates the varied approaches of ethnography, biography, and social, cultural, and oral history" and obligates scholars "to engage the cultural agents of the Hip Hop Culture-World directly, revealing rappers as critical interpreters of their own culture" (p. 28). Viewing Hip Hop artists as both "cultural critics" and "cultural theorists" (see also Dyson, 2004, p. xiv), hiphopography attempts to uncover what it means "to *be* Hip Hop, to exist in a Hip Hop Culture-World, and to possess a Hip Hop mode of being and way of viewing the world" (p. 29; see also Ibrahim, this volume on "affect").

Hiphopography's insistence on direct engagement with the "culture creators" also demands the inclusion of theories of linguistic practice into the study of Hip Hop Cultures. While this current volume clearly views language as central to our understanding of Hip Hop Cultures, hiphopography presents language as not only central to the notion of a GHHN, and to reading the "nation" theoretically, but as central to its study in the field and the narration of its histories. As I have previously written (Alim, 2006a, pp. 11–12), hiphopography seeks to reinvigorate cultural studies' commitment to the people and put into practice what cultural anthropology espouses, that is, a nonhierarchical, anticolonial approach that humanizes its subject.

This call for humanizing Hip Hop comes at a time when, at least according to critically acclaimed Black American rapper Nas, *Hip-Hop Is Dead* (the title of his top-selling album released on the eve of 2007). It also comes at a time when New York City's (and East Coast's) hegemony on global Hip Hop aesthetics has been considerably weakened, if not *deadened*, by southern (Dirty Souf) "Crunk" Hip Hop from places like Young Jeezy's and T.I.'s Atlanta and Chamillionaire's and Paul Wall's Houston. Further, the West Coast has made its own resurgence with E-40's and Keak da Sneak's Bay Area "Hyphy" Movement. And check it: It's been a long time since Hip Hop came "straight outta Compton," and it ain't only The Game that's bringin it back. Hip Hop youth in Germany have turned that classic Hip Hop phrase (and moment) into one that breathes new life into Hip Hop as it turns Germany's Mannheim inner-city district of *Weststadt* into *Westcoast*. When these youth remake Hip Hop, and provide wonderfully new Hip Hop moments, they are drawing on a "variety of linguistic and multimodal resources to construct their *glocal* identities" (Androustsopoulos, this volume). Like Hip Hop heads around the world, they're simultaneously *representin* their hood and what Osumare (2002) called the "Global Hip Hop Hood" through language...straight *aus München*!

Surely, Nas is listening. Although *Hip-Hop Is Dead* is a prime example of the contradictions inherent in popular culture (sounding like both a moratorium and celebration of Old School New York Hip Hop), to Nas, Hip Hop is dead in part because "intellectuals only half-listen." If we have attempted anything in this volume, it is to listen fully, with both ears, and to pay close attention to the languages, styles, ideologies, and cultures of global Hip Hops. To paraphrase

Robin Kelley (2006, p. xvi), Hip Hop ain't dead simply cuz it ain't finished—it is "a living culture, constantly re-making itself, and it is a reflection of the concerns and struggles, hopes and desires, of at least two generations." This is a Hip Hop that hasn't just recently "gone global" (as most media reports would have it). It is a Hip Hop that's both *been* global and is already local at the same time. As co-editor of this volume Awad Ibrahim has been known to shout, "B-boys and b-girls, make some (Black, Brown, and global) nooooiiiise!"

References

Alim, H. S. (Ed.). (2002, Spring). Black culture's global impact [Special issue]. *The Black Arts Quarterly, 7*(1).

Alim, H. S. (2003). On some serious next millennium rap ishhh: Pharoahe monch, hip hop poetics, and the internal rhymes of internal affairs. *Journal of English Linguistics, 31*, 60–84.

Alim, H. S. (2004). Hip hop nation language. In E. Finegan & J. Rickford (Eds.), *Language in the USA: Perspectives for the 21st century* (pp. 387–409). Cambridge, UK: Cambridge University Press.

Alim, H. S. (2006a). *Roc the mic right: The language of hip hop culture.* London & New York: Routledge.

Alim, H. S. (2006b). "The Natti ain't no punk city": Emic views of hip hop cultures. *Callaloo, 29*(3), 969–990.

Alim, H. S., & Pennycook, A. (2007a). Introduction: Glocal linguistic flows. *Journal of Language, Identity, and Education, 6*(2), 89–100.

Alim, H. S., & Pennycook, A. (2007b). Glocal linguistic flows: Hip hop culture(s), identities, and the politics of language education [Special issue]. *Journal of Language, Identity, and Education, 6*(2).

Anderson, B. (1991). *Imagined communities: Reflections on the spread of nationalism.* London: Verso.

Androutsopoulos, J. (2003*). Hip hop: Globale kultur, lokale praktiken.* Bielefeld: Transcript Verlag.

Androutsopoulos, J., & Scholz, A. (2003). Spaghetti Funk: Appropriations of hip-hop culture and rap music in Europe. *Popular Music and Society, 26*(4), 463–479.

Appadurai, A. (1990). Disjuncture and difference in the global cultural economy. *Public Culture, 2*(2), 1–23.

Appadurai, A. (1996*). Modernity at large: Cultural dimensions of modernity.* London & Minneapolis: University of Minnesota Press.

Bakhtin, M. M. (1981). *The dialogic imagination* (M. Holquist, Ed.; C. Emerson & M. Holquist, Trans.). Austin: University of Texas Press.

Basu, D., & Lemelle, S. (Eds.). (2006). *The vinyl ain't final: Hip hop and the globalization of black popular culture.* London & Ann Arbor, MI: Pluto Press.

Baugh, J. (1983). *Black street speech: Its history, structure, and survival.* Austin: University of Texas Press.

Bauman, Z. (1992). *Intimations of postmodernity.* London: Routledge.

Bell, A. (1999). Styling the other to define the self: A study in New Zealand identity making [Special issue]. *Journal of Sociolinguistics, 3*(4), 523–541.

Blommaert, J. (1999). *State ideology and language in Tanzania.* Köln: Koppe.

Blommaert, J. (2003). Commentary: A sociolinguistics of globalization. *Journal of Sociolinguistics, 7*(4), 607–623.

Bucholtz, M., & Hall, K. (2004). Language and identity. In A. Duranti (Ed.), *A companion to linguistic anthropology* (pp. 369–394). Malden, MA: Blackwell.

Bucholtz, M., & Hall, K. (2005). Identity and interaction: A sociocultural linguistic approach. *Discourse Studies, 7*(4–5), 585–614.

Bucholtz, M., & Hall, K. (Eds.). (in press). Undoing the disciplinary divide in sociolinguistics and linguistic anthropology [Special issue]. *Journal of Sociolinguistics.*

Carpenter, F. C. (2006). An interview with Joan Morgan. *Callaloo, 29*(3), 764–772.

Chang, J. (2005). *Can't stop won't stop: A history of the hip hop generation.* New York: St. Martin's Press.

Chang, J. (2007, November/December). It's a hip hop world. *Foreign Policy, 163*, 58–65.

Clifford, J. (1997). *Routes: Travel and translation in the late twentieth century.* Cambridge, MA: Harvard University Press.

Condry, I. (2006). *Hip-hop Japan: Rap and the paths of cultural globalization.* Durham, NC: Duke University Press.

cooke, m., & Lawrence, B. (Eds.). (2005). *Muslim networks: From Hajj to hip hop.* Chapel Hill & London: University of North Carolina Press.

Cutler, C. (1999, November). Yorkville crossing: White teens, hip hop, and African American English [Special issue]. *Journal of Sociolinguistics, 3*(4), 480–504.

Davey D. (1996). *Afrika Bambaataa's definition of hip hop.* Retrieved April 18, 2008, from http://www.daveyd.com/whatisbam.html.

Decker, J. L. (1993). The state of rap: Time and place in hip hop nationalism. *Social Text, 34,* 53–84.

Dimitriadis, G. (2001). *Performing identity/performing culture: Hip-hop as text, pedagogy, and lived practice.* New York: Peter Lang.

Durand, A. (Ed.). (2002). *Black, blanks, beur: Rap music and hip hop culture in the francophone world.* Lanham, MD & Oxford: Scarecrow Press.

Duranti, A. (1997). *Linguistic anthropology.* New York: Cambridge University Press.

Duranti, A. (Ed.). (2004). *A companion to linguistic anthropology.* Malden, MA: Blackwell.

Dyson, M. E. (2004). Foreword. In M. Forman & M. A. Neal (Eds.), *That's the joint! The hip-hop studies reader* (pp. xi–xiv). London & New York: Routledge.

Eckert, P. (2005, January 7th). *Variation, convention, and social meaning.* Plenary address, Linguistic Society of America, Oakland, CA. Retrieved January 1, 2007, from http://www.stanford.edu/~eckert/EckertLSA2005.pdf

Eckert, P., & Rickford, J. (Eds.). (2001). *Style and sociolinguistic variation.* Cambridge, UK: Cambridge University Press.

Fernandes, S. (2003). Fear of a Black nation: Local rappers, transnational crossings, and state power in contemporary Cuba. *Anthropological Quarterly, 76*(4), 575–608.

Fischer, D. (2007). *'Kobudhi Agero! (Pump Ya Fist!)': Blackness, "Race" and Politics in Japanese Hiphop.* Unpublished dissertation, University of Florida.

Fiske, J. (1987). *Television culture.* London & New York: Routledge.

George, N. (1999). *Hip hop America.* New York: Penguin Books.

Gilroy, P. (1993). *The Black Atlantic: Modernity and double consciousness.* London: Verso.

Goffman, E. (1981). *Forms of talk.* Oxford: Blackwell.

Goodwin, M. (2006). *The hidden life of girls: Games of stance, status, and exclusion.* Malden, MA: Blackwell.

Hebdige, D. (1987). *Cut'n'mix: Culture, identity, and Caribbean music.* New York: Methuen.

Helenon, V. (2006). Africa on their mind: Rap, blackness, and citizenship in France. In D. Basu & S. Lemelle (Eds.), *The vinyl ain't final: Hip hop and the globalization of black popular culture* (pp. 151–166). London: Pluto Press.

Henderson, A. (2007). *Gifted flows: Engaging narratives of hip hop and Samoan diaspora.* Unpublished dissertation, University of California, Santa Cruz.

Hill, J. (1999). Styling locally, styling globally: What does it mean? [Special issue]. *Journal of Sociolinguistics, 3*(4), 542–556.

Hobsbawm, E. (1998). *Uncommon people: Resistance, rebellion, and jazz.* New York: New Press.

Ibrahim, A. (1999). Becoming Black: Rap and hip-hop, race, gender, identity, and the politics of ESL learning. *TESOL Quarterly, 33*(3), 349–369.

Ibrahim, A. (2000). Trans-re-framing identity: Race, language, culture, and the politics of translation. *trans/forms: Insurgent Voices in Education, 5*(2), 120–135.

Ibrahim, A. (2001). Race-in-the-gap: Emigrés, identity, identification, and the politics of ESL learning. *Contact, 27*(2), 67–80.

Ibrahim, A. (2003). "Whassup homeboy?" Joining the African diaspora: Black English as a symbolic site of identification and language learning. In S.Makoni, G. Smitherman, A. Ball, & A. Spears (Eds.), *Black linguistics: Language, society, and politics in Africa and the Americas* (pp. 169–185). London: Routledge.

Irvine, J. (2001). "Style" as distinctiveness: The culture and ideology of linguistic differentiation. In P.Eckert & J. Rickford (Eds.), *Style and sociolinguistic variation* (pp. 21–43). Cambridge, UK: Cambridge University Press.

Johnstone, B. (1999, November). Uses of Southern-sounding speech by contemporary Texan women [Special issue]. *Journal of Sociolinguistics, 3*(4), 505–522.

Jones, M. D. (2006). An interview with Michael Eric Dyson. *Callaloo, 29*(3), 786–802.

Kaya, A. (2001). *"Sicher in Kreuzberg" Constructing diasporas: Turkish hip-hop youth in Berlin.* Bielefeld: Transcript Verlag.

Kelley, R. (2006). Foreword. In D. Basu & S. Lemelle (Eds.), *The vinyl ain't final: Hip hop and the globalization of Black popular culture* (pp. xi–xvii). London: Pluto Press.

Kiple, K. (2007). *A moveable feast: Ten millennia of food globalization.* Cambridge, UK: Cambridge University Press.

Kitwana, B. (2005). *Why White kids love hip hop: Wankstas, wiggers, wannabes, and the new reality of race in America.* New York: Basic Civitas.

Kroskrity, P. (1993). *Language, history, and identity: Ethnolinguistic studies of the Arizona Tewa.* Tucson, AZ: University of Arizona Press.

Kroskrity, P. (Ed.). (2000). *Language ideologies: The cultures of language in theory and practice.* Santa Fe, NM: School of American Research.

Lee, J. (2005). *"You wanna battle?" Negotiating respect and local rules in the emcee cipher.* Paper presented at The Lehman Conference on Hip-Hop: From Local to Global Practice, New York.

Magubane, Z. (2006). Globalization and gangster rap: Hip hop in the post-apartheid city. In D. Basu & S. Lemelle (Eds.), *The vinyl ain't final: Hip hop and the globalization of Black popular culture* (pp. 208–229). London: Pluto Press.

Maxwell, I. (2003). *Phat beats, dope rhymes: Hip hop down under comin' upper.* Middletown, CT: Wesleyan University Press.

McFarland, P. (2006). Black-Brown cultural exchange and the making of a genre. *Callaloo, 29*(3), 939–955.

Meghelli, S. (2004). Returning to The Source, En Diaspora: Historicizing the emergence of the hip hop cultural movement in France. *Proud Flesh*, (3). Retrieved April 18, 2008, from http://www.africaresource.com/proudflesh/issue3/meghelli.htm

Meghelli, S. (2007, Winter). The making of a global hip hop nation, from the Bronx to the *Banlieues*: An oral history with Sidney Duteil. *The Black Arts Quarterly, 12*(1),. 21–26.

Mendoza-Denton, N. (2007). *Homegirls: Symbolic practices in the making of Latina youth styles.* Oxford: Blackwell.

Meyrowitz, J. (1985). *No sense of place: The impact of electronic media on social behaviour.* Oxford: Oxford University Press.

Mitchell, T. (Ed.). (2001). *Global noise: Rap and hip-hop outside the USA.* Middletown, CT: Wesleyan University Press.

Mitchell-Kernan, C. (1974). *Language behavior in a Black urban community* (2nd ed.). Berkeley, CA: University of California Press.

Morgan, J. (1999). *When chickenheads come home to roost: My life as a hip hop feminist.* New York: Simon & Shuster.

Muhammad, E. (1965). *Message to the Black man in America.* Chicago: Muhammad Mosque of Islam.

Ochs, E. (1990). Indexicality and socialization. In J. Stigler, R. Shweder, & G. Herdt (Eds.), *Cultural psychology: Essays on comparative human development* (pp. 287–308). Cambridge, UK: Cambridge University Press.

Ochs, E. (1992). Indexing gender. In A. Duranti & C. Goodwin (Eds.), *Rethinking context: Language as an interactive phenomenon* (pp. 335–358). Cambridge, UK: Cambridge University Press,

Omoniyi, T. (2006). Hip-hop through the world Englishes lens: A response to globalization. *World Englishes, 25*(2), 195–208.

Osumare, H. (2002). Troping Blackness in the hip hop global "Hood" [Special issue]. *The Black Arts Quarterly, 7*(1), 24–26.

Osumare, H. (2007). *The Africanist aesthetic in global hip-hop: Power moves.* New York: Palgrave Macmillan.

Pardue, D. (2004a). Putting *mano* to music: The mediation of race in Brazilian rap. *Ethnomusicology Forum, 13*(2), 253–286.

Pardue, D. (2004b). "Writing in the margins": Brazilian hip-hop as an educational project. *Anthropology and Education Quarterly, 35*(4), 411–432.

Pennycook, A. (2003). Global Englishes, Rip Slime and performativity. *Journal of Sociolinguistics, 7*(4), 513–533.

Pennycook, A. (2007a). *Global Englishes and transcultural flows.* London: Routledge.

Pennycook, A. (2007b). Language, localization, and the real: Hip-hop and the global spread of authenticity. *Journal of Language, Identity, and Education, 6*(2).

Perry, I. (2004). *Prophets of the hood: Politics and poetics in hip hop.* Durham, NC: Duke University Press.

Peterson, J. (2001). *Islam and globalization*. Paper Presented at the University of Pennsylvania's conference on Islam and the Globalization of Hip Hop.

Peterson, J. (2002). Ethnographic revelations of nationalism in London Hip Hop. *The Black Arts Quarterly* , 1–5.

Pough, G. (2004). *Check it while I wreck it: Black womanhood, hip hop culture, and the public sphere.* Boston, MA: Northeastern University Press.

Prevos, A. (2001). Postcolonial popular music in France. In T. Mitchell (Ed.), *Global noise: Rap and hip-hop outside the USA* (pp. 39–56). Middletown, CT: Wesleyan University Press.

Quinn, E. (2005). *Nuthin but a "G" thang: The culture and commerce of gangsta rap.* New York: Columbia University Press.

Rampton, B. (1995). *Crossing: Language and ethnicity among adolescents.* London: Longman.

Rampton, B. (Ed.). (1999a, November). Styling the other [Special issue]. *Journal of Sociolinguistics, 3*(4).

Rampton, B. (1999b). Introduction [Special issue]. *Journal of Sociolinguistics, 3*(4), 421–427.

Remes, P. W. (1998). *Karibu Geto Langu/Welcome in my ghetto: Urban youth, popular culture and language in 1990s Tanzania.* Doctoral dissertation, Northwestern University, Evanston, IL.

Richardson, E. (2006). *Hiphop literacies.* London: Routledge.

Rivera, R. (2003). *New York Ricans from the hip hop zone.* New York: Palgrave Macmillan.

Robertson, R. (1995). Time-space and homogeneity-heterogeneity. In M. Featherstone, S. Lash, & R. Robertson (Eds.), *Global modernities* (pp. 25–44). London: Sage.

Rose, T. (1994). *Black noise: Rap music and Black culture in contemporary America.* Middletown, CT: Wesleyan University Press.

Roth-Gordon, J. (2002). Hip hop Brasileiro: Brazilian youth and alternative Black consciousness movements. *The Black Arts Quarterly, 7*(1), 9–10.

Sarkar, M., & D. Allen. (2007). Hybrid identities in Quebec hip-hop: Language, territory, and ethnicity in the mix [Special issue]. *Journal of Language, Identity, and Education, 6*(2), 117–130.

Schieffelin, B., Woolard, K., & Kroskrity, P. (Eds.). (1998). *Language ideologies: Practice and theory.* New York: Oxford University Press.

Smitherman, G. (1997, September). The chain remain the same: Communicative practices in the Hip Hop Nation. *Journal of Black Studies, 28*(1), 3–25.

Spady, J. G (1991). Grandmaster Caz and hiphopography of the Bronx. In J. G. Spady & J. Eure (Eds.), *Nation conscious rap: The hip hop vision* (pp. xi–xxxi). Philadelphia: Black History Museum Press.

Spady, J. G., Alim, H. S., & Lee, C. G. (1999). *Street conscious rap.* Philadelphia: Black History Museum Press.

Spady, J. G., Alim, H. S., & Meghelli, S. (2006). *Tha global cipha: Hip hop culture and consciousness.* Philadelphia: Black History Museum Press.

Spady, J. G., Dupres, S., & Lee, C. G. (1995). *Twisted tales in the hip hop streets of Philly.* Philadelphia: Black History Museum Press.

Spady, J. G., & Eure, J. (1991). *Nation conscious rap: The hip hop vision.* Philadelphia: Black History Museum Press.

Toop, D. (1999). *Rap attack: From African jive to New York hip hop.* London: Pluto Press. (Original work published 1984)

Veal, M. (2007). *Dub: Soundscapes and shattered songs in Jamaican reggae.* Middletown, CT: Wesleyan University Press.

Woods, E. (2006). *"That MF Doom flow": Identity construction and intertextuality in underground hip hop.* Unpublished master's thesis, Department of Anthropology, University of California, Los Angeles.

Wunderlich, A. (2006). Cuban hip hop: Making space for new voices of dissent. In D. Basu & S. Lemelle (Eds.), *The vinyl ain't final: Hip hop and the globalization of Black popular culture* (pp. 167–179). London: Pluto Press.

Yasin, J. (1999). Rap in the African-American music tradition: Cultural assertion and continuity. In A. Spears (Ed.), *Race and ideology: Language, symbolism, and popular culture* (pp. 197–223). Detroit: Wayne State University Press,.

Styling Locally, Styling Globally

*The Globalization of Language and Culture
in a Global Hip Hop Nation*

Hip Hop as Dusty Foot Philosophy

Engaging Locality

ALASTAIR PENNYCOOK AND TONY MITCHELL

When asked what he means by the *Dusty Foot Philosopher* (the title of his recent CD, which received a 2006 Juno Award for Rap Recording of the Year, and was nominated for the inaugural Polaris Music Prize), Somali-Canadian MC K'Naan explains that this is both how he sees himself and a broader image of global representation. When images of Africa are shown on charity television (the most common means by which people view Africa, he suggests),

> the camera always kind of pans to the feet, and the feet are always dusty from these kids. What they're trying to portray is a certain bias connected to their own historical reasoning, and what I saw though instead, was that that child with the dusty feet himself is not a beggar, and he's not an undignified struggler, but he's the dusty foot philosopher. He articulates more than the cameraman can imagine, at that point in his life. But he has nothing; he has no way to dream, even. He just is who he is. (K'Naan interview, April 25, 2004)[1]

In his track "For Mohamoud (Soviet)" he explains further:

> Dusty foot philosopher means the one that's poor, lives in poverty but lives in a dignified manner and philosophizes about the universe and talks about things that well-read people talk about, but they've never read or traveled on a plane. (K'Naan, 2005)

K'Naan's vision raises several key themes we wish to pursue here. By looking at Hip Hop as dusty foot philosophy, as both grounded in the local and the real, and capable of articulating a broader sense of what life is about, K'Naan is not only talking about localization, about the ways in which Hip Hop becomes a means for the local articulation of identity, but also about a deeper sense of locality. To have one's feet in the dust is an image of localization that goes beyond appropriation of sounds, or references to local contexts. It speaks to a particular groundedness, a relationship to the earth that is about both pleasure and politics. To walk barefoot is to be located in a particular way. In his adopted home, Canada, the impossibility of walking barefoot makes him "feel like a foreigner." By contrast, "walking on the sand with your bare feet is therapeutic, you feel the sun" (Interview). Far from being a trivial point only about the weather or sartorial politics, this is a much more significant issue to do with the ways in which our histories, bodies, desires, and localities are intertwined.

Indigenous Australian Wire MC articulates this relationship in a different way, picking up the importance of the earth, dirt, and dust while simultaneously linking to a new digital era. Asked to explain what he means by his phrase *abo-digital*, Wire MC explains that it

> has an ambiguous meaning because of the word digital. I'm abo-digital because I'm a 21st century Aboriginal, I'm down with laptops and mobile phones and home entertainment. But digital also means your hands and your fingers, so I'm still putting my fingers in the dirt; I'm still using my hands to create things. So that's the ambiguity. (Wire MC interview, March 31, 2006)

This image is important for several reasons: It pulls a sense of indigeneity away from an indelible link only to traditional ways of doing things. This is a 21st century Aboriginal performer at home in a digital, global era. Yet at the same time, like K'Naan's dusty feet, he has dirty hands, fingers that create from the land to which Aboriginal Australians have been so deeply connected for thousands of years. Wire MC links the traditional and modern in another way, through his notion of Hip Hop as "the modern day corroboree."[2] Hip Hop brings people together in new ways, to tell stories, to sing and dance, but "It's still the same corroboree, still singing and dancing and telling the same stories about the immediate environment" (Wire MC).

Both Wire MC and K'Naan articulate the complexity of cultural and political influences here: They are 21st century digital artists who draw on and change traditional cultural forms; they are part of the global Hip Hop movement, identifying with and also rejecting different aspects of its global formation; they benefit from and participate in the rapid flows of music and ideas made possible in the digital age and yet they remain highly critical of Western ways of viewing the world and of the bias in particular forms of historical reasoning. Dusty foot philosophy is an argument to understand the impoverished of this world not as undignified strugglers but as dusty foot philosophers, as capable of articulating more than the outside observer can imagine. This chapter aims to open up an understanding of the ways in which localized Hip Hop can on the one hand still be part of a global, digital world and yet at the same time have its feet and fingers in the dirt; how it can participate in the global spread of Hip Hop and yet at the same time be part of the critique of those forms of global media that participate in the denigration of African and Aboriginal people; how local Hip Hop can be both part of international popular culture while at the same time articulating local philosophies of global significance; both dusty footed and philosophical. In taking up this line of argument, we are trying to get beyond common images whereby localization is merely the appropriation of the preexisting global, in order to explore instead how these artists' articulation of the *coevalness of origins* obliges us to spatialize time and think differently about the already local (cf. Mignolo, 2000).

Localizations: Struggle, Engagement, Transformation

A central concern of this chapter, therefore, is to pursue what it means for Hip Hop to become localized. This has implications not only for an understanding of Hip Hop but also for broader concerns in anthropology and linguistics, particularly with respect to concerns about the global spread of English. If we only have a vision of a global spread of Hip Hop or English, emanating from one source before becoming localized through the adoption of various cultural or linguistic forms, we may be missing the dynamics of change, struggle and appropriation. As Robbins (2001) notes, in trying to understand the relationship between tradition and modernity, the tendency, at least among anthropologists, is to emphasize processes of localization and appropriation so that aspects of modernity become localized: "No matter what modernity is to begin with" this argument goes,

> once cooked in the heat of local fires it will have lost its shape to a significant extent and become something indigenous and distinctive, a homemade product of the kind anthropologists have long studied. In this practice, keeping things culturally local implicitly becomes the only way of keeping them ethnographically real. (p. 901)

While it might be tempting to follow this line of thought in our approach to Hip Hop localization, thus suggesting that keeping it real means keeping things culturally local (Pennycook, 2007), we also want to develop Robbins' concern that the proposition "when local cultures cut modernity to fit their own dimensions, they can make it assume almost any form they like" (pp. 901–902) is problematic.

This does not imply that there is an unchangeable essence to Hip Hop that resists localization; but nor does it assume that once cooked in the heat of local fires, Hip Hop loses its shape to such an extent that it becomes something else. What it does suggest is that when local practices of music, dance, story-telling, and painting encounter diversifying forms of globalized Hip Hop, they enable a recreation both of what it means to be local and of what then counts as the global.

"In these self-consciously multicultural, globalized times" suggests Robbins, "reports of cultural difference do little to disrupt our own settled understandings" (p. 909). In order to come to terms with forms of linguistic and cultural localization, therefore, we need to look very carefully at current conceptualizations of the global spread of Hip Hop. In the same way that accounts of the current state of English as nothing but a global spread from the center to the periphery—whether from a triumphalist or a critical perspective (e.g., Phillipson, 1992)—fail to account for the many local identifications and appropriations, so it is still common to view the global spread of Hip Hop as if this were only the global take-up of a particular cultural form. An international Hip Hop conference in the German city of Chemnitz in August 2006, for example, which dealt mainly with Hip Hop in Germany, as well as France, Cuba, Slovenia, Poland, Australia, and the United States, was opened by the U.S. consul from Leipzig, who referred to the "uniquely American" nature of Hip Hop.

From this perspective, then, the global spread of Hip Hop is the global spread of (African) American culture: "Hip Hop is and always will be a culture of the African-American minority. But it has become an international language, a style that connects and defines the self-image of countless teenagers…" (Bozza, 2003, p. 130). While this perspective captures several important points—Hip Hop is indeed a globally marketed phenomenon, and American Hip Hop is dominant, particularly in English-language media—it fails to engage with the different circuits of flow through which Hip Hop circulates globally (Pennycook, 2007), the diversity of local appropriations of Hip Hop, or the coevalness of origins and the roles of mimicry and enactment (what may appear very similar may not in fact be so). Accusations of cultural imperialism, as with accusations of linguistic imperialism (Phillipson, 1992), while important as critiques of media dominance and cultural commercialization, may ultimately fail to engage with the complexity of cultural flows and appropriations. Thus when Brown (2006, p. 138) in his discussion of German Hip Hop refers to the "'cultural imperialism' that overwhelmed local cultures with a flood of products and ideas, erasing old traditions and replacing them with new ones" in postwar Europe due to "U.S. military and economic dominance," this critique of U.S. media dominance falls into the trap of denying cultural agency to others. There is no doubt that U.S. films such as *Wild Style* (1983) and *Beat Street* (1984) exerted a global influence on fledgling Hip Hop cultures, as Brown acknowledges, but so too did Hip Hop's origins in Jamaican DJs toasting and sound system culture in the 1960s and 1970s, a factor dealt with extensively by Toop (1984) and Hebdige (1987) in two of the first books to deal seriously with Hip Hop. Thus, in the same way that a critique of English linguistic imperialism overlooks the complexity of local engagement, so arguments that simultaneously critique and celebrate African American dominance of global Hip Hop media fail to develop an appreciation of the complexity of localization.

Our point is not to deny the massive influence of American, and particularly

African American Hip Hop on contemporary global Hip Hop, nor to overlook the diversity within Hip Hop in the United States, but rather to explore what is meant by localizations of Hip Hop. In his preface to the book *The Vinyl Ain't Final*, which devotes half its space to African American Hip Hop scenes in the United States and half to Hip Hop scenes in Hawai'i (contentiously incorporated into the U.S. section), the UK, Germany, France, Cuba, the Samoan diaspora, Japan, South Africa, and Tanzania, Robin Kelley draws attention to this problem by suggesting that "In most academic circles nowadays, acknowledging that the ghettoes of North America continue to be the primary cultural referent for Hip Hop around the globe will easily draw charges of 'Americocentrism'" (2006, p. xiv). By "uniquely embrac[ing] writings on the subject inside and outside of North America" Kelley goes on to argue, the book neither denies "the centrality of the U.S. in the culture and distribution of Hip Hop culture" nor overlooks the ways in which "artists incorporate local cultural forms, language and stories that speak specifically to their experiences." The problem, however, is that even when viewed from this perspective, there is a danger that the focus on the perceived similarities between local "clothing styles, dance styles, vocal styles, even down to their stances and poses" and those of African American urban youth may obscure the differences. To assume that "the look and the sound of Hip Hop around the world shares much in common with what emerged out of the States" (2006, p. xiv) may be not only to see similarities rather than differences but also to assume that similarity implies directionality.

An understanding of Creole languages and continua may offer a useful parallel here. To categorize African American vernacular English (AAVE) as a "subvariety" of American English, as do some researchers in world Englishes (Kachru & Nelson, 2006) for example, or to see Aboriginal English as a "subcategory" of Australian English, is, amongst other faults, to fall under the sway of a trickle-down model of language spread, where a language seeps from the center into different communities, changing as it diversifies. It assumes that observed similarity is a result of nondivergence rather than reconvergence. Such a model misses entirely the far more dynamic role of pidgins and creoles, the exclusion of which from world Englishes, as Mufwene has noted, "has to do more with the racial identity of those who speak them than with how these varieties developed and the extent of their structural deviations" (2001, p. 107). The serious analysis of Creole development and decreolization processes (Ewers, 1996; Mufwene, 2001; Rickford, 1997) suggests by contrast that in spite of apparent similarities between AAVE and American English, the former may be better understood as a Creole-based language carrying numerous elements of African languages that has been gradually gaining similarities with American English, rather than as a subvariety of English. Similarly, Aboriginal English in Australia may have far more to do with divergence from Kriol than from Australian English (Malcolm, 2001). Apparent similarity, therefore, should not be the basis for assuming unidirectional spread. Convergence and multiple origins are equally possible.

The echoes around the world of new Hip Hop cultures may be understood not so much as subvarieties of global Hip Hop, but rather as local traditions being pulled toward global cultural forms while those traditions are simultaneously reinvented.

While there is therefore clearly a worthwhile critique to be made of the "bankrupt images of gangsterism and materialism" that "dominate the global airwaves," we need to understand not only the "tragic consequences as well as resistive urges" (Kelley, 2006, p. xvi) of the global spread of Hip Hop, but also the dynamism that underlies processes of localization. At the very least, by analogy with world Englishes, we would do better to talk of global Hip Hops. Yet the processes of localization are more complex than global Hip Hop taking on local flavors: While an analogy with world Englishes may bring us pluralization, the shortcomings of a vision of English with local flavors also has limitations. It is not so much the case that Hip Hop merely takes on local characteristics, but rather that *it has always been local.* As Wire MC says, "Hip Hop is a part of Aboriginal culture, I think it always has been" (Interview). This is not of course to suggest that Hip Hop as a global cultural formation was invented by Indigenous Australians; rather, it is to argue that what now counts as Aboriginal Hip Hop is the product of a dynamic set of identifications—with African American music, style, and struggle—and a dynamic set of reidentifications—with indigenous music, style, and struggle.

Not only have indigenous clothing, dance, vocal styles, stances, and movements combined with Hip Hop styles to form indigenized hybrids where U.S. Hip Hop is no longer the host culture, but Hip Hop is seen as having a direct link back to traditional ways of singing, dancing, and telling stories. The two MCs in Australian Aboriginal Crew Street Warriors, for example, both have a background in traditional Aboriginal dance which invests their stances and movements with an authority that dates back way beyond the 1970s. Similarly, Upper Hutt Posse draw on Maori traditional dances such as the *haka*, a war dance, to invest their Hip Hop with Indigenous culture, just as K'Naan draws on the "hand-me-down poetry" of his Somalian grandfather, and Native American MC Litefoot draws on indigenous American culture. Indeed, in the case of indigenous cultures such as New Zealand Maori, Indigenous Australians, and Somalian Africans, not to mention Native Americans, entrenched oral traditions of storytelling and poetry stretching back thousands of years have incorporated Hip Hop into their cultures rather than the other way around. While it is evident that African American, and African French, and African Brazilian influences on global Hip Hop are central to its development, the question we are confronted by is this: At what point does the local take over the global, or at what point do we need to focus on the local host culture appropriating Hip Hop rather than Hip Hop becoming localized? And if we take Robbins' (2001) concern seriously that we need to understand the stakes over which struggles to appropriate are fought, what meanings do forms of language and culture moving in different directions come to have? Put another way, rather than trying "to sort out the autochthonous from the borrowed, we need to consider the uses musicians make of hip-hop, how they understand its relationship to their own condition, and what new meanings are generated by its use" (Urla, 2001, p. 185).

The Struggle for Localization

As Robbins (2001) suggests, the struggle for localization is one that has to deal with the content of what is being localized. Thus Wire and K'Naan are obliged to revise the dominant narrative of Black American exclusive ownership of Hip Hop and construct themselves as artists who have an equal right to claim Hip Hop.[3] Thus, at the same time that K'Naan takes up Hip Hop as a means of expression, he also engages in a rejection of certain U.S. Hip Hop styles and meanings, simultaneously critiquing the violence in Somalia and the glorification of violence in some U.S. rap. The view of an individual and violent struggle against oppression in the ghettoes of North America he compares with the everyday realities of life in Somalia:

> in my country, everyone is in that condition. So it's not special. So therefore we don't have an element which makes it a thing that is possibly glorifiable. And that's why, for me, what I was talking about was these are the people who don't speak about it, they live it. And when there's a gangster, quite a few of which exist in my life, who I know, they never say that they are. They don't have that mentality; it's not linked to "cool." In fact, it is uncool. And they know it, and that's the misfortune. (Interview, K'Naan)

This theme is a feature of his tracks "Hardcore," and "If Rap Gets Jealous," where he mocks the posturing of Gangsta Rap when set against the violence on the streets of Mogadishu, "the most dangerous city in the universe, where people get shot at birth." "Hardcore's" chorus, "So what's hardcore, really? Are you hardcore? Mmmm," intersperses detail about life on the Somalian streets with a bemused questioning about the reference points and values of so-called "hardcore" Hip Hop. And in his track "Strugglin," he says 'I'm more gangsta than you are, but I ain't about the raw route," which he interprets as

> talking to the privileged mentality that is called "keepin' it gangsta." That's pretty suburban to me. Real gangsters don't want to keep it that way. In my view, a gangsta is the would be revolutionary, who is dying to survive, and awaits the opportunity to change. (2005, p. 2)

Global Hip Hops can thus be highly critical of dominant themes in global Hip Hop, in particular, features of violence, consumerism, and misogyny, especially when confronted by very different local conditions. Senegalese crew Daara J note a similar move away from American themes toward more local elements. According to Faada Freddy, the Hip Hop movement in Senegal was at first just imitating certain forms of U.S. rap, "carry a gun, go down to the streets and try to show that you are someone that you can express yourself with violence." But eventually they realized that

> we should care more about our hunger problems…we live in a country where we have poverty, power, race…you know ethnic wars and stuff like that. So we couldn't afford to go like Americans, talking about "Bling Bling," calling our pretty women "Hoes" or stuff like that. So we couldn't afford that! So that's why we went out at a point where we begin to realise…you know…that rap music was about the reality and therefore we went back to our background and see that…OK…and not only rap music is a music that could help people…you know…solve their problems, but this music is ours. It is a part of our culture! (Daara J interview, March 3, 2005)

At the same time that Daara J identify with aspects of Black American Hip Hop, they also resist and change parts of its message and style that they find inappropriate to their local circumstances. On the one hand there may be an identification with music, style, and antiracist struggles; on the other hand, there may be a resistance to the dominance of particular worldviews. In making this dual move to render Hip Hop "part of our culture" while rejecting what are perceived as common values in U.S. Hip Hop, there is a tendency to deal only with a very particular and stereotypical image of U.S. Hip Hop, while also potentially reifying and romanticizing local cultural practices: Resistance all too often comes at the expense of simplification. Wire MC likewise rejects what he sees as the misogyny in the use of the term *bitch* in U.S. rap, linking this not only to his view of proper Indigenous Australian relations to women but also to an understanding of Aboriginal land as a maternal force:

> we have a deep innate sense of community obligation, we are born with it, and that's why you don't hear Black [Aboriginal] MCs…using words like "bitches," they won't diss women. Because my mum isn't a bitch, my grandma isn't a bitch, and my mother the land ain't a bitch. (Wire MC)

Becoming Already Local

Senegalese Hip Hop group Daara J also draw on many other possible influences, from the Francophone Hip Hop scene (which connects the *banlieues* of Paris and Marseille with the multilingual urban scenes of Dakar, Libreville, and Montreal; see Auzanneau, 2002; Sarkar & Allen, 2007; Sarkar this volume), to other African musics and traditions. When Daara J claim that "this music is ours. It is a part of our culture," they point not only to a level of appropriation but rather to a different form of ownership. As K'Naan argues, African Hip Hop has had to draw on very limited resources, and work with minimal means, and is born out of poverty, hardship, and war:

> Hip Hop in Africa is made out of nothing, and for nothing. Hip Hop in
> the U.S. is made out of dreams and for everything. Hip Hop in Canada is
> made out of dreams and for nothing…. In North America, I am introduc-
> ing a culture, in Africa, I am reviving one. (2005, p. 2)

Not only does K'Naan usefully contrast here the material and economic
bases from which Hip Hop emerges in the three contexts, but he also points to
the issue we shall develop further in this section: While one part of his agenda
is to make North Americans aware of the violence and degradations suffered
by Somalians (and the concomitant shallowness of a glorification of violence),
another part of his agenda is to use Hip Hop to revive oral traditions in Somalia.
From this point of view, then, Hip Hop can be a tool not so much of cultural
imperialism, nor even of cultural affiliation or appropriation, but rather of
cultural revival.

K'Naan, whose name means "the traveler," moved from Wardhiigleey (River
of Blood), his 'hood in Mogadishu, to New York's Harlem and then to Toronto
because "we felt the immigration situation was more friendly in Canada" (2005,
p. 1). He taught himself to rap before he spoke a word of English while he was
still living in Mogadishu, where his father, who was working as a taxi driver in
Harlem, sent him new vinyl releases from New York by artists such as Rakim
and Nas:

> But seriously,
> I remember I was seven
> When rap came mysteriously
> And made me feel eleven
> It understood me
> and made my ghetto heaven
> I understood it as
> the new poor peoples' weapon

He lists among his musical influences African artists such as Sulva, Magool,
Marian Mursal, Youssou N'Dour (with whom he worked on the 2001 musicians
in exile project, *Building Bridges*) as well as Salif Keita and Ali Farka Touré. He
describes his style as "an outcome of my personal experiences, travels and musical tastes. It's also born out of the struggles and beauties that I remember from
our ancient culture" (2005, p. 2). Rather than using a DJ, he prefers to perform
with a band, and plays the traditional African drum the *djembe*. He also draws
on the tradition of oral poetry in Somalia for inspiration, particularly Arays Isse
Karshe, whom he rates (along with his own grandfather and Pablo Neruda) as one
of the great poets of the world. He explains that not only did Arays Isse Karshe
have his own unique rhythm and style, to which K'Naan pays homage in his
track "Until the Lion Learns to Speak," and at the beginning of his video clip to
"Strugglin," but also "everything that he talked about was concerning the struggle

of the country and its power struggle with independence and colonialism." That a 21st century Hip Hop artist can draw on a tradition of Somalian oral poetry draws attention to the possibility that rather than focusing centrally on processes of spread and localization, we also need to account for processes by which local traditions are changed and spread. Hip Hop makes it possible for the local to be put on a global stage, not as the dusty feet caught through the lenses of a camera intent on depicting poverty, but rather as the dusty feet that are grounded in local philosophical and poetic traditions.

As K'Naan goes on to explain, with the West African tradition of griots and the East African traditions of oral poetry, it is easy to see the connections between traditional African practices and Hip Hop.

> I'm certain that any country, any given country in Africa, you will find an ancient form of Hip Hop. It's just natural for someone from Africa to recite something over a drum and to recite it in a talking blues fashion, and then it becomes this thing called Hip Hop.

As he suggests elsewhere (www.thedustyfoot.com, 2006), in the context of the finding of the oldest human fossils 140 miles east of Addis Ababa, Ethiopia, "We are…and always have been, your forefathers." There are several ways we can read this: It sits well with those Afrocentric arguments that draw strong connections between contemporary African American cultures and their African origins. But rather than viewing Hip Hop as an American cultural form with African origins, K'Naan suggests that it is first and foremost an African form that has been Americanized. It might be tempting to dismiss such claims as fanciful when viewed against the standard histories of the development of Hip Hop (e.g., Chang, 2005), or to see this only as a local construction for very particular purposes. We are trying in this chapter, however, to take this more seriously in order to grasp the ways in which both histories are plausible once localization is dealt with in its complexities. Senegalese Hip Hop group Daara J, as we have seen, claim Hip Hop as their own, not merely as an act of appropriation but rather as a claim to origins. According to their track "Boomerang," "Born in Africa, brought up in America, Hip Hop has come full circle." As their MC Faada Freddy explains, the traditional Senegalese form of rhythmic poetry, *tasso* is the original form of rap:

> So that's why we arrive at the statement where the American people brought out all that culture that was slumbering at the bottom of their soul.… And this is…it was the beginning of rap music. This music went around the world because…it applied a certain influence over the world and all over. But now just realise that music is coming back home because it is about time that we join the traditional music, we join yesterday to today. (Daara J, March 5, 2006)

In joining yesterday to today, Daara J present a different possibility from the image of Hip Hop emerging from U.S. urban ghettoes and spreading across the world, since from their point of view all such movements can be traced back to African contexts.[4] From this point of view, the arguments over the multiple influences of the Black Atlantic (Gilroy, 1993) or the Jamaican role in the development of Hip Hop, become subsumed under a wider argument that all are part of the wider influence of the African diaspora. The development of Hip Hop in Africa from this point of view is merely a return to its roots. Thus while Perry (2004) rightly critiques "romantic Afro-Atlanticism" (p.17) for overlooking the point that "Black Americans as a community do not consume imported music from other cultures in large numbers" and thus ultimately the "postcolonial Afro-Atlantic Hip Hop community is...a fantastic aspiration rather than a reality" (p. 19), this in turn may overlook the point that African American Hip Hop is only a part of a much wider circuit of musical and cultural influences.

Yet Daara J's image of the boomerang also undercuts their own claim that everything started in Africa. The boomerang also brings us spinning in a circle back to Indigenous Australia and Wire MC:

> The reason I was attracted to it was the song and dance aspect to it, because the culture I come from, The Dreamtime, we always expressed our stories, our beliefs, our fears, our superstitions through song and dance. So being an Abo-digital in the 21st century, it was a natural evolution for me to move into Hip Hop and continue the corroboree, but with the modern day aspect. (Wire MC interview, March 31, 2006)

The point, then, is that it is not fruitful to pursue the true origins of Hip Hop, as if these could be found either in the villages of Africa or the ghettoes of North America, but rather to appreciate that once Hip Hop is taken up in a local context, the direction of appropriation starts to be reversed: No longer is this a cultural form that has been localized; now it is a local form that connects to several worlds: Australian Aboriginal Hip Hop does connect to African oral traditions but not as much as it connects to Australian Aboriginal practices. It is in this sense that Hip Hop has always been Aboriginal Australian just as it has always been African. Hip Hop from this point of view is a continuation of Indigenous traditions; it draws people into a new relationship with cultural practices that have a history far longer than those of current popular music. Yet in doing so, it also changes those cultures and traditions, rendering them anew. From rappers in Berlin of Turkish background who draw on the traditions of medieval Turkish minstrels (*halk ozani*), acting as "contemporary minstrels, or storytellers,...the spokespersons of the Turkish diaspora" (Kaya, 2001, p. 203), to Fijian Australian MC Trey's invocation of the connections between Hip Hop and Pacific Islander cultures, Hip Hop becomes not merely a cultural formation that has spread and been locally taken up, nor even one that has its origins in Africa and has returned, but rather one that has always been local.

Language Localizations

Here, too, language plays an important role, but in more complex ways than an assumption that English implies globalization and other languages local appropriations. It is a common process for the localization of Hip Hop to involve a move into other languages. Thus, from Italy to Aotearoa/NZ, Greenland to Germany, Japan to Tanzania, Hip Hop has typically been taken up in local languages (Mitchell, 2003; Pennycook, 2007). Such a move, however, is subject to the cultural politics of local language use: It is one thing to use German in Germany, but quite another to use Turkish, or as Kaya's (2001) study of Turkish Hip Hop culture in Berlin suggests, a "mix of Turkish, German and American-English…a verbal celebration of ghetto multiculturalism, twisting German, Turkish and American slang in resistance to the official language" (p. 147). It is something quite different again to use Maori in Aotearoa/NZ, where it remains a minority indigenous language spoken by a relatively small proportion of the population. Rapping in Maori thus becomes a political and cultural statement about the legacy of British colonialism, especially when no English translation is provided, as in some of Te Kupu and Upper Hutt Posse's tracks. As Te Kupu has said of the Upper Hutt Posse's 1998 video clip "Tangata Whenua" (People of the Land):

> It's all in the Maaori language, which is our native language, the native language of Aotearoa…Tangata Whenua is indigenous people, literally "Tangata"/person, and "whenua"/land…. Throughout the video you will notice that there is a meeting house, a wharenui, involved there. There's carvings. What we do is carve depictions of our ancestors and they're spread throughout the video, there's constant reference to them, and that's to say that they are here with us right now. That's a Maaori belief that our ancestors are with us all the time, through wider spirituality. (2000, p. 202)

So the track draws on traditional Maori spirituality and belief, as well as using pre-European Maori musical instruments such as the purerehua (bull roarer), to eliminate the legacy of colonialism and White settlement of Aotearoa, and return the Maori to sovereignty of the land, as well as asserting the importance of the Maori language and its belief systems. And like K'naan in his Somali language track "Soobax" (Come out), which calls on Somalian gods to help him to gain wisdom from his experience, and find freedom through struggle, Upper Hutt Posse invoke the Maori deities to combat pollution.

K'Naan, however, uses mainly English in his music—he grew up in Canada after his family fled Somalia as refugees—but laments the paucity of the language. While it is useful for bringing awareness of Somalia to a wider audience—and thus, as he suggests, his use of English is an advantage to Somalian people rather than to him personally—English cannot compare with Somali, which is entirely poetic, I mean, even if I was to speak to you in Somali just in conversation, you'd hear rhythm, and you'd hear rhyme, and most of the words I would use would have to begin in the same letter. It's just because it is set up in poetry. So, when I compare it to Somali, English is very dry, and also very young sounding. It's blatant. Whereas in Somali, if you had done something wrong, I would have to take three minutes to address the universe, and then say to you, "…this is why you've done something wrong." (K'Naan interview)

The struggle for K'Naan, then, is how to use English-language Hip Hop on the one hand to speak to a wider world about the violence and desperation of life in Mogadishu and, on the other, to use this dry, young, blatant language to convey the richness of Somalian oral poetic tradition.

Wire MC also has to struggle with the role of English. He rejects the new colonialism that insists that he should use a particular Australian accent and verbal repertoire to represent his localization:

as for that whole Aussie accent thing, man, I have a struggle going on with that one personally. Firstly, I don't talk ocker.[5] I talk how I'm talkin'. I don't say "g'day." I don't say "g'day mate." I say, "how you going brother." That's what I say. As for this push for a more ocker MC, I find that a bit too tokenistic in one sense, like some of them seem to force it…. But on a more personal outlook, it's like wait a minute. Hip Hop comes from a Black background. I live in a country where it was a penal system before it was a colony, and we were told—or forced—to assimilate us. And this is just a personal thing, but I find now through Hip Hop, having White boys come up to me and saying "You know, maybe you should rap a bit more Aussie." And I'm like "What?! Are you trying to colonise me again dude?! Stop it. Stop it." (Wire MC)

Here again we see the double identification: "Hip Hop comes from a Black background" where it is simultaneously African American and part of local relations of racial discrimination. One way to think about this, is to take up Perry's (2004) argument that Hip Hop in the United States is "situationally black, that is to say that the role it occupies in our society is black both in terms of its relationship to other segments of the black community and of its relationship to the larger white segment of the country and of the 'global village'" (p. 29). Thus, for many Hip Hop artists around the world, there is an identification not only with aspects of the music, style, and language of U.S. Hip Hop, but also with the racial politics that surround it. Yet, to be "situationally black" is also to be tied to local relations of race: For Wire MC, this is to be confronted not by the history of slavery that continues to define parts of African American identity, but by the colonial history of Australia. While there are many parallels of death, dispossession, and denigration, as well as massive linguistic and cultural disruptions, there are also deep differences in terms of relation to land, language, and culture.

Wire does incorporate some words of his traditional language into his Hip Hop, but since he didn't grow up speaking the language, English is his dominant medium.

> I started a crew up at home, up at Bowraville [in northern New South Wales] and the group was called Barrung Buljurr Girrawa, which in Gumbainggir is Brrung, "Bowra," Buljurr "Rhythm," and Girrawa "Mob," so Bowra Rhythm Mob….we weren't rapping in language, unless you consider English to be language. There are indigenous words that I might use in some of my raps, but I don't speak the language or practice the language, so I don't want to make any tokenistic gestures towards my Gombangi heritage through that. I'll use more modern day slang that we use up home, I'll take that and put that in the raps, and if I do that then up home they go "oh, yeah, we know what he's talking about." But if I say something in language a lot of people up home don't really know language so it's like "what's he saying and why is he saying that?"

If we do "consider English to be language" (referring in this context to English as an Indigenous language), the question of how English can be used to serve his own purposes becomes important: The "M.C." after his name means "My Cousin," affirming the strong family and kinship links in Aboriginal communities, and his track "B.L.A.C.K." stands for "Born Long Ago Creation's Keeper," a reference to 30,000 years of Aboriginal culture in Australia. He does not do Hip Hop for its own sake, to advance Hip Hop, but rather

> to advance myself as a human and as an Aboriginal, advance the awareness of my culture, especially on a contemporary tip…right now, I'm international, I'm in another man's land, the nation of Gadagul, I come from the nation of Gombangi. I also try to bring that awareness through Hip Hop, there are so many different shades of Aboriginal. One of the biggest personal achievements for me has been going to communities and performing. From somewhere like the Block to somewhere like Noombuwa,[6] where it's very different but still the same. Having elder aunts come up to me and saying, "We like what you're doing, we're listening to what you're saying, and what you're doing is a good thing. We weren't too sure if you were gonna be swearing, but we like you." So that's one of my big achievements, to be accepted by communities as a positive force.

For Wire then, the most important form of legitimation is not via a global/ international Hip Hop forum but rather through the local/international contexts where he visits other Aboriginal nations across Australia and is accepted by Aboriginal elders. The same applies to K'Naan, who sees himself as representing the diasporic Somali community around the world, as it does for Te Kupu and the Maori people of Aotearoa/New Zealand.

Taking Self-Fashioning Seriously

Dusty foot philosophy, then, can be taken to mean a number of things. K'Naan found himself accused by leading Canadian M.C. K-os of colonialism and pretentiousness for filming the video for "Soobax" with Kenyan musicians and DJs amongst Somali exiles in Mombassa and Nairobi, in a track called "B-boy Stance":

> They took cameras to Africa for pictures to rhyme
> Over; Oh yes the great pretenders
> Religious entertainers who want to be life savers

K'Naan replied to this slur in a track entitled "Revolutionary Avocado," in the process contrasting not only his own struggles between promoting peace and needing to fight battles, but also the relationship between Plato and Aristotle:

> I'm trying to be a peaceful poet
> But the warrior in me just can't sit back
> You the all-knowing with a beer bottle
> Wishing you was Plato and me Aristotle?...
> Suburban negro turned Hip Hop hero
> Is there a reason he really hates me, though? (McKinnon, 2005, p. 1)

As Darby and Shelby (2005) note, "taking both Hip Hop and philosophy seriously furthers our quest for knowledge" (p. xvii). Indeed, they draw connections between some of the North American artists that K'Naan recalls listening to back in Mogadishu, and philosophy as European metaphysical thought: "Rakim and St. Thomas Aquinas school us in the nature of God.... Nas and Hegel probe the depths of self-consciousness" (p. xvii).

The idea of dusty foot philosophy, however, does not by and large refer to this formal disciplinary domain of philosophy. Shusterman's (2005) view of Hip Hop as "a whole philosophy of life, an ethos that involves clothes, a style of talk and walk, a political attitude, and often a philosophical posture of asking hard questions and critically challenging established views and values" (p.61), brings us closer to the way of thinking we are trying to open up here. For K'Naan, dusty foot philosophy is a political statement about local knowledge and respect for the dignity of the disenfranchised. Dusty foot philosophy is juxtaposed not only with Nike-clad mundanity, but also with ways of thinking that overlook the importance of the locus of enunciation (Mignolo, 2000): It is Hip Hop that deals with the politics of location and inequality, Hip Hop that is located in traditions and philosophies embedded in long histories. We have argued in the chapter for the importance of taking the local seriously. As David Scott (1999) argues, the "real question before us is whether or not we take the vernacular voices of the popular and their modes of self-fashioning seriously, and if we do, how we think through their implications" (p. 215). If indeed we take modes of self-fashioning seriously, and allow competing voices that claim Hip Hop as part of their history into the discussion, we are obliged at the very least to account for the constant struggles between identification, rejection, engagement with local cultural forms, and uses of language that not only localize but also transform what it means to be local.

Ultimately, therefore, whether we are dealing with the global spread of English or the global spread of Hip Hop, we need to move beyond an image only of spread and adaptation, beyond only a pluralization by localization (global Englishes and global Hip Hops) in order to incorporate as well the self-fashioning of the already local. If we take Wire's view seriously that Hip Hop has always been Aboriginal, if we view the dusty feet and the abodigital fingers as linked to the histories and traditions of locality in a different way, we are confronted by the need to articulate a new sense of history and location. The global locatedness of Hip Hop demands that we rethink time and space, and adopt what Mignolo (2000) refers to as a historiography that "spatializes time and avoids narratives of transition, progress, development, and point of arrivals" (p. 205). If we can allow for "multiple, heterogeneous, and uneven temporalities and histories that the dominant historical narrative, often presenting itself as singular and linear, suppresses" (Inoue, 2004, p. 2), it becomes possible conceptually to question the linearity at the heart of modernist narratives about origins. Global Hip Hops do not have one point of origin (whether that be in African griots, New York ghettoes, Parisian suburbs, the Black Atlantic, or Indigenous Australia) but rather multiple, copresent, global origins. Similarly, global Englishes are not what they are because English has spread and been adapted but because language users refashion themselves, their languages, their histories, and their cultures. Just as Hip Hop has always been Aboriginal, so has English. Such an understanding of Hip Hop as dusty foot philosophy, we are suggesting, radically reshapes the ways in which we can understand global and local cultural and linguistic formations.

Notes

1. Interviews and other materials used in this chapter are drawn from two Australia Research Council (ARC)-funded projects, Postoccidental Englishes and Rap (Pennycook) and Local Noise: Indigenizing Hip Hop in Australasia (Mitchell & Pennycook). For other versions of interviews, see also Mitchell (2006).
2. The word *corroboree* is used fairly widely across Indigenous communities in Australia to refer to events or meetings (as opposed to ceremonies) which typically include songs, dances, and other social and cultural activities. Like a number of such terms, it is a word that has been appropriated into English and then reappropriated by Aboriginal communities. There is a further reappropriation of the term in Wire MC's use here.
3. Here and in other parts of this chapter, Alastair Pennycook is indebted to extensive discussion and negotiation with coeditor Samy Alim in helping to clarify such arguments so that the goal in taking the local voices of Hip Hop artists seriously does not start to look like yet another

effacement of the key role of African American creativity in global arts (where jazz is another example). Tony Mitchell does not necessarily share this view.

4. Indeed, they elsewhere invoke the arguments of the Senegalese Afrocentric philosopher Cheikh Anta Diop's that development implies acceptance of new elements: "sans acceptation d'éléments nouveaux, il n' y a pas de développement; nous avons accepté d'éléments nouveaux dans les langues, les instruments, etc., et nous avons guardé notre base." (Without accepting new elements, there is no development; we've accepted new elements in languages, instruments etc., and we have still kept our base). (Interview)

5. Ocker is an Australian slang term for a (stereo)typical, White Australian male.

6. The comparison here is between the poor and predominantly indigenous inner-city area of Redfern in Sydney, known as the Block, and small rural indigenous communities such as Noombuwa.

References

Auzanneau, M. (2002). Rap in Libreville, Gabon: An urban sociolinguistic space. In. A-P Durand (Ed.), *Black, blanc, beur: Rap music and hip-hop culture in the Francophone world* (pp. 106–123). Lanham, MD: Scarecrow Press.

Bozza, A. (2003). *Whatever you say I am: The life and times of Eminem.* London: Bantam.

Brown, T. (2006). "Keepin it real" in a different 'hood: (African-)Americanization and hip hop in Germany. In D. Basu & S. Lemelle (Eds.), *The vinyl ain't final: Hip and the globalization of black popular culture* (pp. 137–150). London: Pluto Press.

Chang, J. (2005) *Can't stop won't stop: A history of the hip-hop generation.* New York: St Martin's Press.

Darby, D., & Shelby, T. (2005). From rhyme to reason: This shit ain't easy. In D. Darby & T. Shelby (Eds.), *Hip hop and philosophy: Rhyme 2 reason* (pp. xv–xviii). Chicago, IL: Open Court.

The Dustyfoot. (2006). http://thedustyfoot.com

Ewers, T. (1996). *The origin of American Black English:* Be-*forms in the hoodoo texts.* Berlin: Mouton de Gruyter.

Gilroy, P. (1993). *The Black Atlantic: Modernity and double consciousness.* London: Verso.

Hapeta, D. (Te Kupu). (2000). Hip hop in Aotearoa/New Zealand. In Tony Mitchell & Peter Doyle (Eds.), *Changing sounds: New directions and configurations in popular music, IASPM 1999 international conference proceedings* (pp. 202–207). Sydney: University of Technology.

Hebdige, D. (1987). *Cut 'N' mix.* London: Routledge.

Inoue, M. (2004). Introduction: Temporality and historicity in and through linguistic ideology. *Journal of Linguistic Anthropology, 14*(1), 1–5.

Kachru, Y., & Nelson, C. (2006). *World Englishes in Asian contexts* Hong Kong: Hong Kong University Press

Kaya, A. (2001). "*Sicher in Kreuzberg*" *Constructing diasporas: Turkish hip hop youth in Berlin.* Bielefeld: Transcript Verlag.

Kelley, R. (2006). Foreword. In D Basu & S Lemelle (Eds.), *The vinyl ain't final: Hip and the globalization of Black popular culture* (pp. xi–xvii). London: Pluto Press.

K'Naan (2005a). *The dusty foot philosopher.* Sony/BMG CD.

K'Naan (2005b). Retrieved February 24, 2005, from http://www.HiphopCanada.com

Malcolm, I. (2001). Aboriginal English: Adopted code of a surviving culture. In D. Blair & P. Collins (Eds.), *English in Australia* (pp. 201–222). Amsterdam: Benjamins.

McKinnon, M. (2005). Kicking up dust: The remarkable hip hop odyssey of Toronto's K'naan. *Artists Network of Refuse and Resist,* retrived June 30, 2005, from http://www.artistsnetwork.org/news16/news763html

Mignolo, W. (2000). *Local histories/global designs: Coloniality, subaltern knowledges and border thinking* Princeton, NJ: Princeton University Press.

Mitchell, T. (2003). Doin' damage in my native language: The use of "resistance vernaculars" in hip hop in France, Italy, and Aotearoa/New Zealand. In H. Berger & M. Carroll (Eds.), *Global pop, local language* (pp. 3–17). Jackson: University Press of Mississippi.

Mitchell, T. (2006). A modern day corroboree—Wire MC. *Music Forum, 12*(4), 26–31.

Mufwene, S. (2001). *The ecology of language evolution.* Cambridge, UK: Cambridge University Press.

Pennycook, A. (2007). *Global Englishes and transcultural flows.* London: Routledge.

Perry, I. (2004). *Prophets of the hood: Politics and poetics in hip hop.* Durham, NC: Duke University Press.

Phillipson, R. (1992). *Linguistic imperialism*. Oxford: Oxford University Press.

Rickford, J. (1997). Prior creolization of AAVE? Sociohistorical and textual evidence from the 17th and 18th centuries. *Journal of Sociolinguistics, 1*. 315–336.

Robbins, J. (2001). God is nothing but talk: Modernity, language, and prayer in a Papua New Guinea Society. *American Anthropologist, 103*(4), 901–912

Sarkar, M., & Allen, D (2007). Hybrid identities in Quebec hip-hop: Language, territory, and ethnicity in the mix. *Journal of Language, Identity and Education, 6*(2), 117–130.

Scott, D. (1999). *Refashioning futures: Criticism after postcoloniality*. Princeton, NJ: Princeton University Press.

Shusterman, R. (2005). Rap aesthetics: Violence and the art of keeping it real. In D Darby & T Shelby (Eds.), *Hip hop and philosophy: Rhyme 2 reason* (pp. 54–64). Chicago, IL: Open Court.

Toop, D. (1984). *Rap attack: African jive to New York hip hop*. London: Pluto Press.

Urla, J. (2001). "We are all Malcolm X!" Negu Gorriak, hip-hop, and the Basque political imaginary. In T. Mitchell (Ed.), *Global noise: Rap and hip-hop outside the USA* (pp. 171–193). Middletown, CT: Wesleyan University Press.

Language and the Three Spheres of Hip Hop

JANNIS ANDROUTSOPOULOS

Introduction

Looking at Hip Hop through the lenses of sociolinguistics and discourse analysis implies approaching Hip Hop as discourse; that is, as a "complex area of practice" (Fairclough, 1995, p. 185), in which social knowledge and social reality are produced, reproduced, and transformed through a variety of speech genres, mediated by a variety of communications technologies. To be sure, Hip Hop's traditional "four elements"—breaking, DJing, rapping, and writing—rely on performance modes that go well beyond language, such as visual representation, sound, movement, and technical manipulation of objects. But more than verbal art, language in Hip Hop is the medium in which artist performances and member identities are contextualized and negotiated.

This chapter aims at complementing the widespread conception of Hip Hop as a "universal language" or "global idiom" (Mitchell, 2001, pp. 12, 21) in a two-fold way: By an account of the interplay of Hip Hop's global spread and local appropriations, on the one hand, and of the diverse social and generic contexts in which Hip Hop discourse is articulated, on the other. The first point is hardly controversial: A growing body of research on Hip Hop outside the United States documents how its various local articulations depart from the "original" in significant ways—in rap music, for example, in terms of language choice, song topics, cultural references, and sampling practices (see papers in Androutsopoulos, 2003a; Kimminich, 2003; Mitchell, 2001). However, even though local Hip Hop acquires features and invites interpretations that no longer rely exclusively on its African American origins, it does not lose its global imprint, but rather evolves in a constant dialogue with its "mother culture," by drawing on U.S. Hip Hop as a source for new trends and as a frame for the interpretation of local productions. This persistent dialogue between the global and the local is manifested in both discourse and in language style, as my discussion of English will highlight later on.

However, less attention has been paid to the second point. As the references I just quoted suggest, most language-centered studies on Hip Hop focus on rap lyrics. Although this focus has yielded many important results so far, it seems to overlook the emic distinction between Hip Hop as a cultural hyperonym and rap as one of its hyponyms, or put differently: Hip Hop as a set of social practices unfolding around its "four elements," one of them rap, itself being conceived as a "genre system" (Krims, 2000). A integrative view on language and Hip Hop would need to encompass a much wider range of discourse practices, such as talk at work among rappers, writers, and breakers; the discourse of Hip Hop magazines and broadcast shows; artist-fan communication during live events; and an array of everyday talk and computer-mediated discourse in what is often termed the *Hip Hop Nation* (Alim, 2002).

This chapter aims at contributing to such a wider approach by using the concept of "vertical intertextuality" (Fiske, 1987) to develop an understanding of Hip Hop as a system of three interrelated "spheres" of discourse: artist expression (corresponding to Fiske's "primary texts"), media discourse ("secondary texts"), and discourse among Hip Hop fans and activists ("tertiary texts"). I shall outline some discursive and sociolinguistic properties of each sphere, focusing on the interplay of Hip Hop's global and local characteristics. Most evidence comes from German and Greek; that is, the languages and Hip Hop discourses I am most familiar with. My discussion emphasizes how the language of rap lyrics is adapted to local contexts by retaining global features; how Hip Hop media use language to index Hip Hop affiliation, by attending to mass media conventions; and how resources from the primary and secondary sphere are used by fans and activists in their face-to-face and computer-mediated discourse. Against that backdrop, I examine nonnative English in Hip Hop discourse, focusing on German as an instance of the "expanding circle" of English (Crystal, 2004). As is well documented (e.g., Mitchell, 2001), rap outside the United States goes through a process of linguistic "emancipation," in which early attempts in English are soon followed by a shift to the rapper's native language(s). This does not forcibly lead to a monolingual local rap landscape, but it does establish the local/national language as default, against which other languages may gain symbolic meaning. Pennycook (2003) argues that Hip Hop provides a prime example for the relation between globalization and English as a lingua franca, challenging the "overly simple view that English is for intercultural communication and local languages for local identities" (Pennycook, 2003, p. 83). I extend this line here by examining uses of English across Hip Hop's three spheres, and by relating them to the notion of *glocalization*, a term coined by Robertson (1996) to refer to the process by which globally circulating cultural resources are recontextualized in local settings. I argue that English (including stylized African American

English) is a main resource for constructing "glocal" Hip Hop identities, which gain their meaning as local performances of a global cultural paradigm (see also Higgins, this volume).

Vertical Intertextuality and Hip Hop Discourse

Intertextuality is a notion with diverse understandings in linguistics. Some disciplines, such as text linguistics, traditionally adopt a "narrow" view of intertextuality as a process in which textual elements are integrated in other texts, such as quotations or allusions (e.g., Klein & Fix, 1997). A "broader" understanding of intertextuality gained currency in sociolinguistics and discourse studies with the reception of Bakhtin (1981) who views any text as being fundamentally related to other texts, its meanings being shaped by that relationship. Intertextuality in such a wide sense includes the relationship between a text and its sources, or the functional cross-linking between different genres within a given cultural domain.

Both types of intertextuality are articulated in a framework by popular culture theorist John Fiske, an amended version of which I use in this chapter. In *Television Culture* (1987) and other writings (e.g., 1989, 1992), Fiske conceives of television texts as a "web of intertextual relations" (1987, p. 85), which he explores by distinguishing between "horizontal" and "vertical" intertextuality. The first is about explicit relations between individual texts, such as a video clip's allusions to a particular film, and thus corresponds to the "narrow" sense of intertextuality mentioned above. Vertical intertextuality refers to relations between texts with different functions in the circuit of popular culture. Fiske distinguishes here between primary, secondary, and tertiary texts. Primary texts, such as soap operas or video clips, are the centerpieces around which popular culture is formed. Operating "around" them are secondary texts such as reviews and commercials, whose main task is to promote "selected meanings" (Fiske, 1987, p. 117) of primary texts. Secondary texts may thus determine which of the multiple meanings implied in a primary text will be activated by viewers. Tertiary texts are located on the level of audiences. They are "the texts that the viewers make themselves out of their responses which circulate orally or in letters to the press, and which work to form a collective rather than an individual response" (Fiske, 1987, p. 124). Two types of tertiary texts are distinguished: Social interaction and fan productivity, which is in turn subdivided in expressive productivity (e.g., fans styling themselves after popular culture models), and textual productivity; that is, fans appropriating and transforming primary texts to produce their own cultural artifacts (cf. Winter, 1995).

Even though Fiske's framework was originally devised for television, it can be applied straightforwardly to Hip Hop. While horizontal intertextuality captures quotations, references and other processes of "textual sampling" that are ubiquitous in rap lyrics and songs (Mikos, 2003; see also Roth-Gordon, this volume), vertical intertextuality models relationships across texts following the main subject positions within popular culture; that is, those of producers, mediators, and audiences. Consider the example of rap music in Germany: A record release constitutes a primary text, to the extent, of course, it is attended to by fans. It is reviewed or promoted in a variety of secondary texts such as Hip Hop magazines or on websites; and it is listened to, commented upon, or sampled by fans in a variety of speech events. The release itself, its treatments in media discourse, and its discursive appropriations by audiences constitute a chain of vertical intertextuality, the elements of which interact with each other. Secondary texts such as record reviews may no doubt have an impact on fans' interpretations of a record release, and, ultimately, on its reputation and sales; however, music fans may also access releases without the aid of professional mediators, as in the case of unadvertised underground productions.

My notion of "sphere" extrapolates from single texts to conceive vertical inter-textuality as a relationship between "text collectives" or conglomerates of primary, secondary, and tertiary texts. In this sense, and still using rap as a case in point, Hip Hop's "primary sphere" encompasses all productions which originate (or are accessible) in a particular country, together with their corresponding video clips and other broadcast performances. All these are potential rather than actual primary texts, depending on the attention they are being given by audiences. The "secondary sphere" includes all media texts that are dedicated to describing, evaluating, and merchandising primary texts. The "tertiary sphere" would then encompass all speech events in which Hip Hop fandom is performed, such as enjoying a concert, discussing music, or making a Hip Hop homepage.

The application of vertical intertextuality to Hip Hop, however, is not without its conceptual problems. Three points seem particularly problematic. First, the far too rigorous separation of the spheres: Fiske conceives of television as a closed, highly professionalized arena of media production and distribution. However, Hip Hop's emphasis on local/street activities and its blurring of boundaries be-tween producers and consumers (cf. Bennett, 1999; Mikos, 2003) challenge a neat separation of spheres. At the same time, the development of communications media in the last decades favors amateur media productions. As a consequence, we need to rethink the relation between the three spheres in terms of mixed and transitional forms. For instance, we might think of some Hip Hop artists as "primary," even in the absence of published productions, to the extent their lo-cal discourse has an impact on local communities.[1] Likewise, we might think of newcomer artists who publish their amateur productions on Internet platforms as located in a transitional space between the tertiary and primary sphere. Rather than being hermetically closed, Hip Hop's first sphere receives constant input and feedback from the third one, and digital media enhance this trend.

A second problem is the rich intermediality of contemporary popular culture. It seems that what characterizes Hip Hop's cultural reality is the merging of aspects of all three spheres within particular media contexts. Consider the case of freestyle radio shows (Berns & Schlobinski, 2003), in which callers improvise live on beats played by a DJ in the studio, while the show host comments on the performance. In Fiske's terms, this is a hybrid of secondary texts (presenter talk) and tertiary texts (fan performance), referencing primary texts (i.e., professional rap). On the Internet, commercial web portals such as Germany's www.rap.de and www.hiphop.de offer primary texts (songs, video clips) for downloading; they feature magazine-like content such as reviews or interviews; and they make available to their visitors message boards for computer-mediated social interaction. Likewise, private Hip Hop homepages are first and foremost tertiary texts (an outcome of fans' textual productivity), but they may also include secondary texts (e.g., reports on the local Hip Hop scene), and even primary texts (e.g., home productions).

A third issue is the relation of vertical intertextuality to the global spread and local appropriation of Hip Hop culture. The preceding discussion tacitly assumed that spheres will be constructed within a particular country; however, from a reception point of view, primary texts are an amalgam of global and local input, since most fans, in Germany and elsewhere, listen to both local and U.S.-American (and perhaps also other international) productions. Some U.S. secondary texts have a global reach, such as "Yo! Mtv Raps" in the 1980s or *The Source* magazine today, but as local Hip Hop infrastructures emerge, local secondary spheres assume more authority and independence over the U.S.-American one. And while tertiary texts are anchored locally by definition, this too is changing with the Internet, since fan productions, such as personal homepages, now have a potentially international reach, and fan conversations can now be carried out on the net across the globe.

In sum, while I suggest that Fiske's notion of vertical intertextuality is a useful starting point for an integrative examination of the language and discourse of Hip Hop, I also argue that it needs to be extended by rethinking interfaces and transitions among the three spheres. In the subsequent discussion, I will therefore pay particular attention to fuzzy boundaries and transition paths between Hip Hop's three spheres, and to closure mechanisms that eventually keep them apart.

In terms of methodology, understanding these blurred boundaries has essentially benefited from my ethnographic engagement with various facets of Hip Hop. What is meant is not a canonical (in-depth, long-term) ethnography of a Hip Hop community, but rather adopting an ethnographic perspective, and using elements of ethnographic method in various sites and research settings since 2000. First, these methods include research on Hip Hop on the German-speaking web, in which I systematically observed online Hip Hop activities and conducted interviews with web authors and editors (Androutsopoulos, 2006, 2007). Second, fieldwork on "splash!" a large Hip Hop festival in Germany, in which expert group discussions and interviews with journalists and event organizers were used to study the festival's marketing discourse (Androutsopoulos & Habscheid, 2007). Third, the organization of "academy" meets community-type events which focused on local rap and Hip Hop in Germany and Greece (Androutsopoulos, 2003a). Taken together, these activities offered valuable insights into the complexity and multiperspectiveness of Hip Hop discourses. Ultimately, however, it is the combination of ethnographic knowledge with sociolinguistically informed discourse analysis that shapes this chapter.

Language in the Primary Sphere: Local Resources for Global Actions

Sorting out what might be specifically local in the contemporary worldwide instantiations of rap music requires a *tertium comparationis*, against which global generic patterns and their local reconfigurations may be established. Such a framework was developed by Androutsopoulos and Scholz (2002, 2003) for a study of French, German, Greek, Italian, and Spanish rap songs. These were compared against a "genre profile" consisting of four main categories: song topics, speech act patterns, rhetorical resources, and linguistic variation. Although this does not provide for some important dimensions of rap, notably rhyme and flow (Krims, 2000), it nonetheless captures a number of features that seem fairly typical of rap genres worldwide. I'd like to illustrate their local instantiation by focusing on the relationship between rhetorical resources, in particular metaphor and cultural referencing, and speech act patterns, in particular self-referential speech (talk about one's own verbal performance) and audience-directed speech (talk about the effects of rap on listeners, and inviting them to react).

We examined metaphorical language in rap lyrics with cognitive metaphor theory in the legacy of Lakoff and Johnson (1981), in which metaphor is defined as the conceptual mapping of two experiential domains. Well-established rap metaphors include RAP IS BATTLE, RAP IS KNOWLEDGE, and RAP IS A DRUG (cf. also Lüdtke, 2007). Consider the last one: It essentially constructs a rapper's verbal performance as a powerful substance that is intoxicating and addictive for the audience. Three of its instantiations are given in 1 to 3 below. While the first two are void of local referencing, the pattern exemplified by the Greek example localizes the metaphor by referring to a detoxification center (*Strofi*, lit. "turning point") known throughout the country.

(1) *I crystallize the rhyme so you can sniff it*
    (Wu-Tang Clan, "It's yourz," in *Forever*, Lou/Sony, 2000)
(2) *mein stoff 100% pure dope ohne verschnitt*
    "my stuff 100% pure dope uncut"
    (Spax, "Ich komm," in *Privat*, Moto Music, 1998; Germany)
(3) *μια τζούρα από το ραπ μου είναι υπεραρκετή να σε στείλει στη Στροφή γι αποτοξίνωση*
    "a hit of my rap is more than enough to send you to Strofi for detox"
    (Ζωντανοί Νεκροί, "Το ραπ μου είναι πρόκληση," in *Ο πρώτος τόμος*, FM Records, 1998; Greece)

Cultural referencing is attested since the earliest rap productions and presumably goes back to the sounds and dozens of African American youth, from which rapping originally evolved (cf. Toop, 2000). In the ritual insults elicited by Labov (1972, pp. 277–353), names of popular artists, celebrities, cartoon figures, institutions, consumer products, and so on are embedded in comparative or copulative constructions to qualify the speaker's opponents or their relatives (e.g., *you look like Jimmy Durante's grandfather; your mother James Bond*). In contemporary rap discourses, rappers draw on cultural referencing for self-reference, boasting or dissing. Cutler's analysis (in this volume) offers excellent examples of referencing to mark race in U.S. battling. In European rap lyrics, the sources of referencing are of essentially the same kind in terms of their cultural domains, but hybrid in terms of national provenience (see also Scholz, 2001). Some examples:

(4) *du bist weich wie ein Kissen, ich bin hart wie Thyssen Stahl*
    "You are soft like a cushion/I'm coming hard like Thyssen steel"
    (Rödelheim Hartreim Projekt, "Reime," in *Direkt aus Rödelheim*, MCA, 1994; Germany)

(5) *tortellini sti loops che c'ho fini più di Fini*
    "these loops like tortellini that I have finer than Fini"
    (Neffa, "Gran Finesse," in *Chico Pisco*, Black Out/Universal, 1997; Italy)

(6) *όταν κάνω ραπ στέλνω κάθε άταχτο MC sto KAT σαν τον Ζαν Κλοντ Βαν Νταμ*
    "When I'm rapping, I send any undisciplined MC to KAT/like Jean-Claude Van Damme"
    (ZEN, "Ασταμάτητες ρίμες", in *Πάλι κουνάς το κεφάλι*, FM Records, 2003, Greece)

(7) *con più storie a raccontare dei fratelli Grimm/questo è il mio dream team/"The Boss" più di Springsteen* "with more stories to tell than the Grimm brothers/ this is my dream team/'The Boss' more than Springsteen"
    (Chief & Soci, "Soci," in *Il mondo che non c'è*. Best Sound/BGM, 1997, Italy)

Consider the mention of *Thyssen*, a German steel industry, in (4); *Fini*, an Italian vinegar brand, in (5); and *KAT*, an Athens hospital, in (6). Being locally anchored and therefore presumably as opaque to U.S. audiences as are Cutler's examples to European ones, cultural references of this sort construct a fragmented panorama of local knowledge that includes history and traditions, high art and mass culture, places and institutions. But as examples 6 and 7 illustrate, referencing in fact indexes a hybrid cultural horizon, in which global media culture, European cultural heritage, and specifically local traditions merge. In this respect, referencing works much like audio sampling (Mikos, 2003), though on a different semiotic plane (see Roth-Gordon, this volume).

Thus I suggest that the relationship between genre-typical verbal actions and rhetorical resources is a "hot spot" of discursive localization in the primary sphere. Other "hot spots" no doubt exist, some of them located closer to more traditional sociolinguistic interests. In the framework by Scholz and myself, these are captured by the notion of *linguistic variation*, which entails asking to what extent rap's vernacular orientation is maintained in various local contexts, examining language variation in rap lyrics by region, gender, and market placement (cf. Morgan, 2001; Scholz, 2003), and reconstructing the linguistic repertoire of rap artists in each particular local context. As rap enters new speech communities, the original predominance of African American English is replaced by new, and often more complex, sociolinguistic conditions. Depending on speech community, rap lyrics are variably positioned in the space between standard and nonstandard varieties, national monolingualism and societal multilingualism. Wider language ideologies as well as individual market placement are crucial for the extent to, and the manner in which, societal heteroglossia surfaces in rap discourse, and for the chances of new "resistance vernaculars" (Potter, 1995) to emerge, be it regional dialects, minority languages, or mixed talk (cf. Auzanneau 2001; Sarkar, this volume).

Talking about "Greek rap" or "German rap" might be a useful shortcut for comparative purposes, but turns out to be a crude simplification as we focus on a particular local scene. German rappers and fans, for instance, make clear distinctions between rap styles from Berlin and Hamburg, just as their U.S. counterparts do between the West and East Coasts (cf. Berns & Schlobinski, 2003). Regardless of where it is carried out, Hip Hop is a process of symbolic competition within a community of peers, in which the construction of individual style is a powerful resource of locally achieved distinction. All players are referencing the same cultural models and discursive rules, but aim at outcomes as individual as possible. What this suggests is that "the local" may be expected to contain an almost infinite range of variation on the same theme, which still waits to be explored.

Language in the Secondary Sphere: "Stylistic Splits" in Media Discourse

I delimit the secondary sphere to what Thornton (1996) terms "niche media" (e.g., dedicated Hip Hop magazines, broadcast shows, commercial websites) and "micromedia" (e.g., nonprofit fanzines, Internet newsletters, flyers). In contrast to mainstream mass media, "niche" and "micro" media speak, at least to some extent, "from within." They are recognized by participants as constitutive of Hip Hop's public sphere, and are often part of local activism.[2] But even so, the secondary sphere imposes its own institutional conditions as an arena of public discourse, which involve the negotiation of the relationship of Hip Hop traditions to local "journalese" standards. While it seems safe to assume that the discourse of dedicated Hip Hop media will take a degree of background cultural knowledge and intimacy with in-group jargon for granted, it will also need to attend to expectations of correctness and professionalism. Hip Hop media must negotiate the conflicting relationship between "street culture" and the exigencies of the media and advertising industries. A central aspect of language use in secondary texts is therefore the way in which language styles that are characteristic of professional journalism are articulated with those that index familiarity with, and membership to, the (local chapter of the) Hip Hop Nation.

In this process, Hip Hop's primary and tertiary sphere offer resources that media actors may draw on in varying degrees. For instance, broadcast hosts may converge to stylistic imperatives of rap discourse, such as the celebration of "resistance vernaculars" (Potter, 1995), the creative combination of language styles, and the aesthetic attention to linguistic form. They may also implement speech styles that are (perceived to be) common in the everyday speech of the Hip Hop Nation. Hip Hop media are no doubt subject to the wider process of conversationalization of public discourse (Fairclough, 1995), though they do so by targeting the specific conversational style of the Hip Hop scene. Adopting these resources will lead to an increase in hybridity and interdiscursivity, as the boundaries between editorial style, performance arts, and conversational style are blurred or even consciously subverted. But the extent to which this actually occurs will vary by particular media institutions, particular genres, and individual authors or presenters.

I use two German examples to illustrate the range of differences that might be expected in the discourse of the secondary sphere, and in particular its differential appropriation of indexes from the primary and the tertiary sphere. The first (example 8) is a promotional text from the program booklet of a large Hip Hop festival. The second (example 9) is an initial host sequence from "Wordcup," a now defunct weekly Hip Hop show on German music television channel Viva. For reasons of space, both examples are given in English translation only; *italics* indicate English lexical items in the German original, the wording of which is quoted in the discussion where needed (full original texts are provided in Androutsopoulos, 2003b, 2005).

(8) Excerpt from program booklet of "Hip Hop Open 2001"; English translation
    1. Berlin *MC* Kool Savas who attracted attention mainly
    2. through his cooperation with…, thinks
    3. the label "scandal *rapper*" is an appropriate
    4. description. "A pint of bananas for you monkeys" or "*Fame and Cash*"
    5. stand for his rather direct manner of bringing things down
    6. to the point…. Currently, Kool Savas works
    7. absolutely motivated and painstakingly on his new album "*Battle*
    8. *Kings*." More straight words can be expected. And
    9. one thing is for certain in Savas' live performances:
    10. *Fake MC* heads will roll. Rough shit! Word on that!!

(9) Host opening sequence of "Wordcup," February 7, 1999; English translation

1. hey y'all what's up
2. welcome to Wordcup
3. great you tuned in again.
4. like you probably know, Wordcup is produced here in Cologne,
5. and we thought
6. so that you at home and most of all we here get to see some of the culture
7. that we come here to the Cathedral.
8. world-famous, Cologne Cathedral,
9. we hang out here at the Cathedral terrace with all the *skaters*,
10. let's go see if Method Man is up there somewhere,
11. uhm, what else do we have for you in this show.
12. we prepared an interview with Outcast,
13. you get to see that,
14. and we were in Paris at the Rang Division, right,
15. and we brought back something from our time in Paris
16. where we show you what's going on graphics-wise in *hiphop* Paris.
17. anyway, stay tuned to Wordcup,
18. let's watch Method Man now, Judgment Day.
19. at Wordcup. *word.*

I read the first example as an instantiation of a secondary sphere model peppered up by lexical elements from the primary and tertiary sphere. As indicated by its complex syntax with relative clauses and passive constructions (cf. lines 1, 2, 8) and by collocations such as *höchst akribisch* (original wording of "painstakingly," line 7), this is a professional writing style, which at the same time indexes its target group by using appropriate terminology (*MC, Rapper*) and slang items such as *fake* and *derb* ("rough"; line 10). The most interesting part as far as the tension between Hip Hop's global and local dimension is concerned, are the two concluding phrases in line 10: In the first, *Derber Schiet!* ("rough shit!"), the context makes clear that the noun *Schiet* is used as a calque of Eng. *shit* in its Hip Hop usage (i.e. "stuff"). What is remarkable here is the choice of *Schiet*, a northern German regional form, instead of colloquial standard German *Scheiss*. As this selection is apparently not motivated by topic, it can be read as a means of increasing similarity (phonologic and orthographic) between the calque and its English model. The second phrase is a colloquial German assertion, *Wort drauf!* ("Word on that!"), which is strongly reminiscent of *word up*, the globally spread African American Hip Hop formula. Both phrases are emblematic of the discursive cultural localization of Hip Hop: As these texts address German-speaking audiences, they are with good reason linguistically "local" (and quite markedly so in the first case), yet they evoke bits and pieces of the global Hip Hop idiom.

The second example suggests that Hip Hop media talk can go further than that. This passage, lasting about 30 seconds, is more or less standard procedure in terms of generic activity: there is an introductory welcome (lines 1–3), a description of the local setting (4–10) which playfully references the U.S. artist of the first clip (line 10), a preview of this show's content (11–16), and the announcement of the first clip (17–19). The host, Afro-German ex-rapper Tyron Ricketts, holds a microphone, and gesticulates a lot. The opener, *hey leute was geht ab* (original wording of line 1) is fairly common in German Hip Hop talk. Ricketts consistently uses an inclusive "we," speaking on behalf of his production team. His vocabulary includes colloquialisms (*rumlümmeln* "hang out"; *was grafikmäßig abgeht* "what's going on graphics-wise"), and he switches to English for the closing formula, which is once again *word*. Compared to other music shows on the same channel, Ricketts' style is remarkably unplanned, as indicated by hesitation markers and meta-communicative expressions (lines 11, 13, 14), though it is impossible to tell whether the host is genuinely spontaneous here.

This is an example of extensive drawing on primary and tertiary sphere resources in constructing the show's cultural identity. "Wordcup" constructs its niche status in terms of content, multimodal style in the opening credits (featuring scratching sounds, a graffiti-style logo, and "Black" sounding English background voices), the host's use of a microphone, and, crucially, his speech style. Being an ex-rapper, the host himself blurs the boundary between the primary and secondary sphere. By approximating a mode of everyday talk in his delivery, he blurs the boundary to the tertiary sphere as well.

The examples suggest that authors and presenters, the main actors of the secondary sphere, perform "stylistic splits" between Hip Hop speech styles and commercial media conventions. By converging toward the speech style of the scene, they convert "street language" into symbolic capital in the realm of Hip Hop's niche media. At the same time, they draw on other resources, such as a fluent delivery or discourse-organizing devices, for their professional performance. We might have expected that mainstream conventions be subverted altogether in Hip Hop's secondary sphere, but so far as Germany's niche Hip Hop media are concerned, this is very limited the case indeed. While they cannot afford to ignore the need of a stylistic fit to their target audience, they cannot ignore journalistic conventions either.

The boundary between the secondary and the tertiary sphere is reinforced both in the outcome, that is, the actually published text or show, and by selection processes that precede it. For instance, interviews with the managers of leading German Hip Hop portals such as www.hiphop.de and www.rap.de suggest that they expect from their freelance authors a strong command of written German, and a "smooth and punchy tone," as one manager put it (cf. Androutsopoulos, 2003c, 2006). Active competence of Hip Hop slang is necessary, but not the only prerequisite for participation in the secondary sphere. In this respect, commercial Hip Hop websites differ from tertiary texts, such as the personal homepages discussed in the next section.

Language in the Tertiary Sphere: Crafting Member Identities

Research on Hip Hop's tertiary sphere is sparse (see also the Intro to this volume), and most of it is concerned with relations between tertiary sphere practices and primary sphere models. One way of looking at this is in terms of language variation, asking whether the vernacular speech so typical of rap lyrics reflects, or rather overshoots, variation in rappers' nonlyrical speech (cf. Alim, 2002). Another approach examines how primary texts are appropriated in the everyday discourse of their audiences, and inspire their textual productivity (cf. Dimitriadis, 2004). In research situated outside the United States, the blend of U.S. primary sphere resources with local linguistic practices takes center stage. In an early instance of such research from Germany, Schneider (1997) offers an ethnography of an amateur crew of second-generation migrants. This crew consumes both U.S.American and German rap productions and clearly distinguishes between the two markets. Although they are fully aware of the differences between Hip Hop's original context and their own situation, they nonetheless use the former to make sense of their migrant experience. They dissociate themselves from gangsta rap and orient to Public Enemy, whose work they read as a political message against racism and social injustice. Global and local resources merge in this crew's home productions, which explicitly represent their ethnic "roots" and at the same time make use of English chunks. Another example is an ethnography of a breakdance crew of ethnic Italians in the Southern German city of Mannheim (Bierbach & Birken-Silverman, 2002). Based on interactional sociolinguistics, this work affords detailed insights into the impact of Hip Hop discourse on the group's verbal interaction. Its members develop an "in-between space," in which mediated Hip Hop knowledge is articulated with elements of their ethnic origin. This process is epitomized in their renaming practices, such as turning the Mannheim inner-city district of *Weststadt* into *Westcoast*. Hip Hop discourse permeates the group's speech style, including breakdance terminology, references to U.S. as well as German artists, as well as boasting and dissing rituals, in which the group's multilingual repertoire of German, Italian, and Sicilian dialect, is employed.

A less explored area of the tertiary sphere is computer-mediated communication (CMC), which is used extensively across the globe as an additional "means of representing, critiquing and contradicting the images and issues of Hip Hop culture" (Richardson & Lewis, 2000, p. 251; see also Richardson, 2006). In Fiske's terms, Hip Hop engagement with CMC extends both types of tertiary texts: Participating in message boards and other platforms of online talk extends Hip Hop focused interaction, and making a homepage or weblog extends practices of fan productivity. In my research on German Hip Hop on the web (Androutsopoulos, 2003b, 2003c, 2006), I found that maintaining a personal homepage and engaging in online talk are clearly distinct participation formats. Homepages presume a clear notion of authorship: Their authors may not always reveal their real names, but they stage themselves as active members; for example, by narrating their local engagement and sharing home productions; they "represent" their town or region by drawing attention to its Hip Hop activities; and they invite exchange with their visitors by customarily offering a guest book. By contrast, Hip Hop message boards are characterized by anonymity and a reduced responsibility of authorship. Getting in touch on a board may well consolidate regional contacts and lead to new co-operations, but many board entries are limited to ritual communication, such as dissing artists or greeting fellow crews and friends (cf. example 13 below).

In view of this variety of media formats and communicative activities, Hip Hop language style on the web is obviously vastly heterogeneous. To be sure, there is a common stock of multimodal "style insignia" that cuts across all forms of Hip Hop engagement on the web. For instance, casting homepage logos in graffiti type, signifying Hip Hop's four elements by means of visual metonyms, drawing on specific word-formation patterns to craft crew names (such as *Beat Skill Crew* in example 11 below), and using a large set of English lexis and formulaic speech all unmistakeably contextualize Hip Hop affiliation. But beneath this web of surface markers, a striking range of variability with respect to generic models and language style remains. The framework developed in this chapter allows us to understand this variability in terms of which sphere the relevant models for tertiary communication on the web are derived from.

I illustrate this with the case of www.webbeatz.de, a website that offers web space to amateur artists to present their work on a personal homepage (Androutsopoulos, 2007). An analysis of spelling variation across three genres on this website, that is, record reviews, personal homepages, and discussion boards, suggests that the latter feature written representations of colloquial speech to a significantly greater extent than homepages, with reviews being closest to normative German orthography. In terms of the vertical intertextuality framework, this means a differential orientation of literacy practices: While review authors attend to orthographic conventions expected from public discourse, board conversationalists rather orient themselves to the informal speech of offline tertiary talk. Significantly, however, the language style of the homepage sample is much more internally diverse than in the other two genres. This is illustrated by the two examples below, in which italics again indicate English lexical items in the original and bold print (in example 11) highlights representations of colloquial and regional pronunciation.

(10) Homepage text from webbeatz.de
      Einer der erfolgversprechendsten Gruppen der Flensburger HipHop-Szene ist die BeatSkill Crew. Durch Zusammenarbeit mir Künstlern von Flensburg bis Salzburg, diverse von ihnen geplante Events und vor allem durch ihre Auftritte haben sich M und D bereits einen Namen gemacht. Während M durch ihren einzigartigen, teils mit Gesangspassagen gemischten Reimstil Eindruck macht, sorgt D für die passenden, teils asiatisch und teils funk-inspirierten Beats.

One of the most promising bands from the Flensburg *hiphop* scene is *BeatSkill Crew*. M and D have made a name through cooperations with artists from Flensburg to Salzburg, through the planning of various *events*, and especially through their gigs. While M impresses through her unique rhyming style, which is partly interspersed with singing parts, D is in charge of the appropriate, partly Asian and partly *funk*-inspired *beats*.

(11)   Homepage text from webbeatz.de
       Straight Up Hip Hop—Straight aus München

> A: Wir **wolln** halt, dass **ma** München **ned** ausschließlich mit Sound wie Blumen-topf oder David P verbindet. Wo **is** der dreckige, abgefuckte Scheiß hier? Ich kann mir **nimmer** diesen,"Was geht ab digga" Sound anhören, so **isses ned**. Das Leben **is ned** nur aus Party und feiern und cool rappen, **oider**!

Straight up hip hop – straight from Munich

> A: What we **want** is that people won't associate Munich only with the *sound* of Blumentopf or David P. **Where's** that dirty, fucked-up shit here? I can't hear this "What's up *digga*" sound **no more, that's not** how it is. Life **is not** just *party* and having fun and *cool rapping*, **mate**!

Even without detailed linguistic analysis, it is obvious that example (10) is modeled on genres from the secondary sphere, in particular promotional discourse, as indicated by its elaborated syntax, its use of standard orthography, and a content focus on the band's success potential and their current production activities. By contrast, the authors of (11) use direct speech, rather than third-person mode, to foreground issues of style in their local Hip Hop community, and they heavily mark that speech as vernacular by means of spelling and wording (this includes the use of *Scheiss* as a calque of "shit" in its Hip Hop usage, and *digg*a, a German Hip Hop term of address). In terms of the quantitative analysis of spelling variation outlined above, example 10 is closer to reviews, 11 closer to discussion boards.

One might object that being authored by newcomer artists, these examples are not typical for the tertiary sphere. However, they in fact reflect one important aspect of Hip Hop's cultural circulation, namely, the fuzzy boundary between production and reception: Fans are seldom "just fans," but experiment with the boundaries to other arenas of Hip Hop engagement. In doing so, they may variably orient themselves to discourse conventions from Hip Hop's other spheres, and CMC offers them a space of vernacular literacy, in which they may draw on a variety of linguistic and multimodal resources to construct their *glocal* Hip Hop identities—a process that is nicely epitomized by the headline of example 11, *Straight Up Hip Hop—Straight aus München*.

English "From Below": A Cross-Sphere "Glocal" Identity Resource

As that headline illustrates, English is a hallmark of the interplay of the global and the local in Hip Hop discourses. In German Hip Hop—and, I would dare to extrapolate, in the "expanding circle" generally—English is a set of linguistic resources, which are embedded in the respective national language by means of borrowing, code-switching, or code-mixing (cf. Androutsopoulos, 2004, 2007). Moreover, that headline also illustrates how English goes beyond lexical borrowings to encompass formulae, slogans, and other chunks, which are best viewed as instances of (emblematic, formulaic) code-switching. In written discourse, it also includes a set of spelling variants such as the determiner forms *tha*, *da* and the <z> plural marker, as in *beatz*. And not least, English is often the language of choice for naming, as illustrated by names for events, media features, rap crews, and websites across examples 8 through 14.

It is useful to think of English in Hip Hop discourses as *English from below*, a term coined by Preisler for "the informal—active or passive—use of English as an expression of subcultural identity and style" (Preisler, 1999, p. 241). In contrast to "English from above," which is promoted "by the hegemonic culture for purposes of international communication," English from below is motivated by "the desire to symbolize subcultural identity or affiliation, and peer group solidarity" (Preisler, 1999, pp. 241, 246). It is acquired via noninstitutional channels and is much more variable than officially promoted, institutionally transmitted English as a Foreign Language (Preisler, 1999, p. 260; Androutsopoulos, 2004). My own research suggests that from the participants' point of view, English is an essential part of their "Hip Hop slang" (Androutsopoulos, 2006, 2007). It gains its significance by originating from exclusive Hip Hop sources and is intertextually saturated, perhaps all the more so as we move from the lexicon to chunks.

While Hip Hop English "from below" is strongly present across spheres in my German data, its precise use depends on the different contextual constraints and exigencies of each sphere. Consider how some English resources are instantiated in rap lyrics (example 12) and guest book entries (example 13); again, italics in the glosses indicate English items in the original.

(12)   Excerpt from Azad, "Faust des Nordwestens," in *Faust des Nordwestens*, 3p/Intergroove, 2004; Germany
Ich steh auf zum Weedrauchen/lass laut Musik laufen/werd taub wie Pete Townshend/lass Crowds zum Beat bouncen/wenn ich meine Stile kick/völlig natürlich, wie wenn ich auf der Wiese lieg/steh ich ständig unter Strom und geh MCs zerficken mit miesem Shit/ihr weaken Bitchez werdet gepoppt vom Chief im Biz/AAAU/how you like me now?
"I get up to smoke *weed*/let music play loud/get deaf like Pete Townshend/ let *crowds bounce* to the *beat*/when I *kick* my styles/fully naturally, as if I'd lay on a meadow/I'm always full of adrenaline and fucking MCs with ugly *shit*/you *weak bitches* are being screwed by the *chief* in the *biz*/au/*how you like me now*?'

(13)   Guest book entry
Hej hej…sehr fette Page…cool…keep this shit online :-) und checkt mal www.timeless-x.de

Hey hey…that's a phat *page…cool…keep this shit online* :-) and *check* out
www.timeless-x.de

The lyrics by Frankfurt-based hardcore rapper Azad illustrate how English in
German rap lyrics goes beyond referential demands to serve the organization of
performative discourse and the refinement of poetic form (cf. Androutsopoulos
& Scholz, 2002; Auzanneau, 2001; Pennycook, 2003; Higgins, this volume; Sarkar,
this volume). Most English lexis in excerpt (12) belongs to Hip Hop's core international terminology and slang (*beat, crowds, bounce, kick styles, MCs, weak,
bitch*) and is integrated in such a way as to facilitate rhyme: Note how German
rauchen and *laufen* rhyme with English *Townshend* and *bouncen*, and German
lieg with English *kick* and *shit*. Azad's code-switching in the last verse (*how you
like me now?*) is also drawing on English for rhyme-making as well as, on the
propositional level, to claim authority over his fictitious opponent. Short switches
of this kind are fairly common in German rap, as are English discourse markers
to signal turn taking, and African American voices sampled into a song's intro
or chorus. As a result, German rap songs featuring both extrasentential switching and heavy lexical borrowing are quite common. Yet the dominant language
of these songs is clearly German, and they seldom, if ever, reach international
audiences.

By contrast, the secondary sphere relies more heavily on the referential dimension of English lexis, as witnessed in examples 8 and 9 above, though not without
drawing on chunks and formulae (cf. *word* in example 9). On the Internet, the
patterns of English that are circulating in rap lyrics and media discourse are
tailored to new generic demands. Thus producers of personal homepages lift bits
and pieces from their favorite U.S. rap artists to design navigation bars, browser
page titles and headings, their body text being mainly in colloquial German.[3] On
discussion boards and guest books, the prevalence of expressive interpersonal
discourse boosts short English switches of the kind illustrated by example 13.
A comparison across German Hip Hop media in fact reveals that chunks and
formulae amount to almost one-fourth of English instances in web guest books,
but less than 5% in magazines (Androutsopoulos, 2004).

Elsewhere (Androutsopoulos, 2004), I suggest that such short, formulaic
switches into English—*word* in 9, *Straight up Hip Hop* in 11, *how you like me
now* in 12, *keep this shit online* in 13—may be viewed as instances of *language
crossing*, a term coined by Rampton (1995) for the purposeful use of (elements
of) a language that does not "belong" to the speaker, but to another ethnic or
social group. As the metaphor implies, crossing is a process by which speakers
transgress a social boundary by language use, thereby engaging with aspects of
the identity of the legitimate users of that language. Now, the English switches
in question here are clearly doing some sort of identity work in terms of their
propositional content and the speech acts they convey: They are used to affirm
cultural engagement, to address and praise ("give props") other members, and to

appeal to common values—in short to carry out ritual activities in and through which participants perform being a Hip Hopper. Moreover, their contexts of use fit the notion of liminality in the language crossing framework; that is, situations in which the normal assumptions of social order are softened or suspended, as is the case with lyrical performance, media performance, or pseudonymous computer-mediated discourse.

To be sure, such crossing practices are not uncontested; appropriating superficial features of African American English to construct Hip Hop identities may be rejected as "fronting," in the U.S. context and elsewhere (cf. Richardson & Lewis, 2000). However, the crucial point seems to be their identity target: Does the use of Hip Hop English by German Hip Hoppers lay a claim to African American identities? My suggestion, at least in the German case, is that the point is less *stepping into* an alien ethnic territory ("Blackness") than *stepping out* of one's own national boundaries (in this case: "Germanness") and into a global Hip Hop terrain that is not necessarily imagined in primarily racial or ethnic terms. And this is consonant with the initial observation of this chapter: Although "original Hip Hop" is a permanent point of reference, its local appropriations no longer rely exclusively on its African American origins.

Conclusion

This chapter attempts to interrelate the different arenas of discourse in which Hip Hop culture is continuously constructed and transformed, and to examine how the tension between globalness and localness is negotiated within each of these arenas. In concluding, we saw that language use across the three spheres of Hip Hop is by necessity heterogeneous, because it attends to the purposes and constraints that are particular to each sphere. Rather than being hermetically delimited, the three spheres of Hip Hop have fuzzy boundaries with respect to their conditions of access and language style. As a result, Hip Hop discourses are characterized by interfaces, in which elements that are typical for one sphere are indexically incorporated in others. Thus rap lyrics converge towards "street language," though without being identical to it; media talk may draw on the performative style of rap lyrics as well as the style of casual conversation, though without fully adopting either; verbal rituals from the primary sphere, such as practices of boasting and dissing, are articulated with local experience in the everyday life of the Hip Hop nation; and on the Internet, patterns of rap and media talk are adapted to new purposes. These interfaces need to be understood as significant resources of Hip Hop discourse, and should be paid more attention to in future research. Equally needed is more comparative research across local contexts. With respect to computer-mediated communication, for example, preliminary observations suggest that Hip Hop boards across Europe (notably from Italy, Norway, and Greece) share a common stock of (African American) English. Frequency differences still need to be examined, but qualitatively, what is characteristic for the German case seems, more generally, an instance of global Hip Hop English "from below." From a transnational perspective, then, Hip Hop English emerges as a "universal" strategy of Hip Hop identity marking. It establishes a symbolic connection between verbal art, media, and fan discourse, on the one hand, as well as between various localized Hip Hop discourses on the other.

Acknowledgments

This chapter is a considerably revised and updated version of a German paper (Androutsopoulos, 2003b) and its English translation (Androutsopoulos, 2005). I am indebted to Alastair, Alim, and Awad for their excellent editorial work, and to Arno Scholz, my partner in the "European rap research" project, in which many ideas and findings presented here were developed. The usual disclaimers apply, of course.

Notes

1. I am indebted to Samy Alim for emphasizing this point.
2. Hip Hop's secondary sphere will mostly consist of print media and websites; that is, the media types that may flourish at the fringe of the media and culture industry, whereas its extension to broadcast will be restricted to countries in which Hip Hop is commercially successful; in other words, the type of media involved in the secondary sphere index the degree of Hip Hop's popularity and commodification in a particular country.
3. One of my informants, 15-year-old "Aspa," decorated her website with headings such as *Welcome 2 tha World of AspA*; *MIX UP THA $#!T*; *Ein paar freshe Linkz von AspA* ("Some fresh links by Aspa"). In the interview we conducted, she credited her spelling practice to U.S. band Wu-Tang Clan, which she claimed to listen to "since I was eleven" (Androutsopoulos, 2003b, p. 129).

References

Alim, H. S. (2002). Street-conscious copula variation in the hip hop nation. *American Speech, 77*(3), 288–304.
Androutsopoulos, J. (Ed.). (2003a). *HipHop: Globale Kultur—lokale Praktiken.* Bielefeld: Transcript.
Androutsopoulos, J. (2003b). HipHop und Sprache: Vertikale Intertextualität und die drei Sphären der Popkultur. In J. Androutsopoulos (Ed.), *HipHop: Globale Kultur—lokale Praktiken* (pp. 111–136). Bielefeld: Transcript.
Androutsopoulos, J. (2003c). Musikszenen im Netz: Felder, Nutzer, Codes. In H. Merkens & J. Zinnecker (Eds.), *Jahrbuch Jugendforschung* (Vol. 3, pp. 57–82). Opladen: Leske & Budrich.
Androutsopoulos, J. (2004). Non-native English and sub-cultural identities in media discourse. In H. Sandøy (Ed.), *Den fleirspråklege utfordringa* (pp. 83–98). Oslo: Novus.
Androutsopoulos, J. (2005). Hip hop and language: Vertical intertextuality and the three spheres of pop culture. In P. Dyndahl & L. A. Kulbrandstad (Eds.), *High fidelity eller rein jalla? Purisme som problem i kultur, sprak og estetikk* (pp. 161–188). Vallset: Oplandske Bokforlag. (English version of Androutsopoulos, 2003b, Catrin Gersdorf, Trans.)
Androutsopoulos, J. (2006). Online hip hop culture. In S. Steinberg, P. Parmar, & B. Richard (Eds.), *Contemporary youth culture: An international encyclopedia* (Vol. 1, pp. 217–233). Westport, CT: Greenwood Press.
Androutsopoulos, J. (2007). Style online: Doing hip hop on the German-speaking web. In P. Auer (Ed.), *Style and social identities: Alternative approaches to linguistic heterogeneity* (pp. 279–317). Berlin: de Gruyter.

Androutsopoulos, J., & Habscheid, S. (2007). "Von der Szene—für die Szene"? Stil und Stilisierung in der Vermarktung des HipHop-Festivals "splash!" In K. Bock, S. Meier, & G. Süß (Eds.), *HipHop meets academia* (pp. 289–310). Bielefeld: Transcript.

Androutsopoulos, J., & Scholz, A. (2002). On the recontextualization of hip hop in European speech communities: A contrastive analysis of rap lyrics. *PhiN–Philologie im Netz, 19*, 1–42. Retrieved from http://www.phin.de/pi2002.htm.

Androutsopoulos, J., & Scholz, A. (2003). Spaghetti funk: Appropriations of hip hop culture and rap music in Europe. *Popular Music and Society, 26*(4), 489–505.

Auzanneau, M. (2001). Identités africaines: le rap comme lieu d'expression. *Cahiers d'Études africaines, 41*(3–4), 163–164.

Bakhtin, M. (1981). *The dialogic Imagination: Four essays* (M. Holquist, Ed., C. Emerson & M. Holquist, Trans.). Austin: University of Texas Press.

Bennett, A. (1999). Hip hop am Main: The localisation of rap music and hip hop culture. *Media, Culture and Society, 21*, 77–91.

Berns, J. & Schlobinski, P. (2003). Constructions of identity in German hiphop culture. In J. Androutsopoulos & A. Georgakopoulou (Eds.), *Discourse constructions of youth identities* (pp. 197–219). Amsterdam: Benjamins.

Bierbach, C., & Birken-Silverman, G. (2002). Kommunikationsstil und sprachliche Symbolisierung in einer Gruppe italienischer Migrantenjugendlicher aus der HipHop-Szene in Mannheim. In I. Keim & W. Schütte (Eds.), *Soziale Welten und kommunikative Stile* (pp. 187–216). Tübingen: Narr.

Crystal, D. (2004). *English as a global language* (2nd ed.). Cambridge, UK: Cambridge University Press.

Dimitriadis, G. (2004). *Performing identity/performing culture: HipHop as text, pedagogy and lived practice*. New York: Peter Lang.

Fairclough, N. (1995). *Media discourse*. London: Edward Arnold.

Fiske, J. (1992). The cultural economy of fandom. In L. Lewis (Ed.), *The adoring audience: Fan culture and popular media* (pp. 30–49). London: Routledge.

Fiske, J. (1987). *Television culture*. London, New York: Routledge.

Fiske, J. (1989). *Understanding popular culture*. London, New York: Routledge.

Hebdige, D. (1979). *Subculture: The meaning of style*. London: Methuen.

Kimminich, E. (Ed.). (2003). *Rap: More than words*. Frankfurt am Main: Lang.

Klein, J., & Fix, U. (1997). (Eds.). *Textbeziehungen*. Tübingen: Stauffenburg.

Krims, A. (2000). *Rap music and the poetics of identity*. New York: Cambridge University Press.

Labov, W. (1972). *Language in the inner city: Studies in the Black English vernacular*. Philadelphia: University of Pennsylvania Press.

Lakoff, G., & Johnson, M. (1980). *Metaphors we live by*. Chicago: University of Chicago Press.

Lüdtke, S. (2007). *Globalisierung und Lokalisierung von Rapmusik am Beispiel amerikanischer und deutscher Raptexte*. Münster: LIT.

Mikos, L. (2003). Interpolation and sampling: Kulturelles Gedächtnis und Intertextualität im HipHop. In J. Androutsopoulos (Ed.), *HipHop: Globale Kultur—lokale Praktiken* (pp. 64–84). Bielefeld: Transcript.

Mitchell, T. (Ed.). (2001). *Global noise: Rap and hip hop outside the USA*. Middletown, CT: Wesleyan University Press.

Morgan, M. (2001). "Nuthin' but a G thang": Grammar and language ideology in hip hop identity. In: S. Lanehart (Ed.), *Sociocultural and historical contexts of African American English* (pp. 187–210). Amsterdam/Philadelphia: Benjamins.

Pennycook, A. (2003). Global Englishes, Rip Slyme, and performativity. *Journal of Sociolinguistics, 7*(4), 513–533.

Potter, R. A. (1995). *Spectacular vernaculars*. New York: SUNY.

Preisler, B. (1999). Functions and forms of English in a European EFL country. In T. Bex & R. J. Watts (Eds.), *Standard English: The widening debate* (pp. 239–267). London: Routledge.

Rampton, B. (1995). *Crossing: Language and ethnicity among adolescents*. London: Longman.

Richardson, E. (2006). *Hiphop literacies*. New York: Routledge.

Richardson, E. & Lewis, S. (2000). "Flippin' the Script/Blowin' up the Spot": Puttin' hip hop online in (African) America and South Africa. In G. E. Hawisher & C. L. Selfe (Eds.), *Global literacies and the world wide web* (pp. 51–76). London: Routledge.

Robertson, R. (1996). *Globalization: Social theory and global culture*. London: Sage.

Schneider, S. (1997). Gewaltrhetorik in der Selbstpräsentation jugendlicher HipHopper. In M. Charlton & S. Schneider (Eds.), *Rezeptionsforschung* (pp. 268–286). Opladen: Westdeutscher Verlag.

Scholz, A. (2001). Intertestualità e riferimento culturale in testi rap italiani. *Horizonte, 6*, 139–162.

Scholz, A. (2003). Rap in der Romania. "Glocal approach" am Beispiel von Musikmarkt, Identität, Sprache. In J. Androutsopoulos (Ed.), *HipHop: Globale Kultur—lokale* Praktiken (pp. 147–167). Bielefeld: Transcript.

Thornton, S. (1995). *Club cultures: Music, media and subcultural capital.* Cambridge, UK: Polity Press.

Toop, D. (2000). *Rap Attack 3: African rap to global hip hop.* London: Serpent's Tail.

Winter, R. (1995). *Der produktive Zuschauer.* München: Quintessenz.

Conversational Sampling, Race Trafficking, and the Invocation of the *Gueto* in Brazilian Hip Hop

JENNIFER ROTH-GORDON

Introduction

When I arrived in Rio de Janeiro in 1997 to conduct ethnographic research on the slang of poor Black youth, politically conscious rap was getting a lot of play in Brazil's *favelas* (shantytowns) and impoverished suburbs, even experiencing a brief period of crossover success. The São Paulo based group Racionais MC's (The Rationals) was on the verge of going platinum with their album *Sobrevivendo no Inferno* (Surviving in Hell) and would take home awards for "Best Rap Group" and "Audience's Choice" at the 1998 MTV Brazilian Music Video Awards. Signs of Hip Hop culture were all over the *favela*: large murals and graffiti depicted album covers and song lyrics; U.S. sports teams and references to New York adorned the most coveted clothing items; and fans took on nicknames of popular rappers. Youth I met swapped, borrowed, and sometimes bought rap CDs to listen to on individual headphones and on boom boxes at nightly impromptu gatherings in the streets of their neighborhood. As I explore in this chapter, Hip Hop culture even influenced daily linguistic practice, as fans integrated particularly catchy refrains into conversations, singing rap songs together and quoting well-known lyrics.

Though most Brazilian rappers and rap fans have limited access to English, this infusion of Hip Hop culture relied heavily on ideas and images of the United States. Taking inspiration from groups such as Public Enemy and KRS-One, politically conscious Brazilian rap focuses on the daily realities of Brazil's social and geographic periphery, highlighting the transnational similarities between situations of social inequality, crime, drug use, police brutality, and racism. They perform the aggressive and confrontational style of conscious rap and attract attention in particular for embracing U.S. ideas of structural violence (including institutional racism) and a Black–White racial dichotomy, as these themes directly contradict Brazilian ideals of racial democracy (Fry, 2000; Sansone, 2003). In what follows, I draw on Osumare's (2007) idea of "connective marginalities" to illustrate the ways in which youth actively create connections between Brazil and the United States. As they "traffic" in nationally opposed racial ideologies, Brazilian rappers construct ideas of racial similarity between themselves and the United States. In particular, I explore how global Hip Hop relies on—and helps construct—the racialized urban ghetto as a site of power and prestige.

In order to foreground local understandings of global Hip Hop culture, or the "glocal" (Alim, this volume; Robertson, 1995), I move into what Androutso-poulos (this volume) calls the "third sphere of Hip Hop discourse," recording the daily conversations of politically conscious rap fans. I turn to linguistic studies of intertextuality and indexicality to analyze a practice I call "conversational sampling," which includes the seamless integration of rap lyrics into everyday speech. Though Brazilian youth quote lyrics almost exclusively in Portuguese,[1] linguistically marking their affiliation with domestic rap when they "sample," I argue that these linguistic practices invoke the racialized urban ghetto in order to forge connections to the United States and First World modernity. Conversational sampling thus provides a ready example of intertextuality, where speakers recycle song lyrics, using these linguistic recontextualizations to make new statements about their participation in both local communities and the world at large.

Have Hip Hop, Will Travel: Constructing Brazilian Marginality

As this volume and others attest (Condry, 2006; Mitchell, 2001), the assertion that Hip Hop has "gone global" now has at least 25 years under its belt. Seeking to explain the appeal of global Hip Hop, Osumare (2007) points to Hip Hop's "connective marginalities," which attract youth worldwide living in situations of global social inequality. She argues that Hip Hop resonates across four main fields: culture, class, historical oppression, and youth rebellion. Through these connective marginalities embedded in Hip Hop, youth latch on to "perceived linkages across nation-states and language groups" (2007, p. 15). In this chapter, I take up this notion in order to interrogate how *and why* Brazilian rappers and rap fans emphasize, and even invent, similarities between themselves and the U.S. conscious rap scene. While it may be far more common to investigate the construction of difference, I argue that likeness must be actively constructed, in global Hip Hop as anywhere else.

Hip Hop arrived in Brazil in the 1980s, and Brazil's largest city, São Paulo, quickly established itself as its epicenter.[2] The success of Racionais MC's in the late 1990s helped to launch like-minded groups such as Gog (from Brasilia) and M.V. Bill (from Rio de Janeiro). These groups follow in the style of politically conscious rap in the United States—what Pardue (2005) calls "marginal" rap in

São Paulo—taking seriously Chuck D's charge to be "the CNN of black America." The globalization of Hip Hop culture has made urban space particularly salient, and the ghetto (or "the 'hood") is arguably one of U.S. Hip Hop's most visible exports, iconically linking Blackness to urban space (Forman, 2002; Krims, 2002; Rose, 1994). Politically conscious rappers and rap fans in Brazil are deeply influenced by these spatial and racial metaphors, through which they associate the ghetto with African Americans and both with the global dominance of the United States. For them, the ghetto cannot be separated from the power and prestige of the United States.

My own relationship with rappers and rap fans offers evidence of their slippage between "Black America" and the United States. As a White middle-class American, I was a far cry from the Hip Hop ambassador these youth craved: I was from New York (and a Yankees' fan), and yet I had never met Chuck D; I spoke English but had only limited knowledge of African American English and thus had limited ability to translate U.S. rap lyrics; and my musical background was spotty at best, leading one local rapper to finally exclaim, "*Você não anda no ghetto, né?*" ("You don't hang around in the ghetto, do you?"). And yet, despite these disturbing contradictions, I provided Brazilian youth with tangible connections to Black America, transporting U.S. rap CDs (both by request and as gifts), discussing U.S. racial politics at length, and allowing them to "speak" to African Americans as I collected their personal tales of racism to include in my "American book."

As physical distance, scarce financial resources, and linguistic differences all limit the abilities of Brazilian youth to connect directly with the U.S. Hip Hop scene, small references to the racialized ghetto carry significant meaning. To indicate their affiliation with the legendary birthplace of U.S. Hip Hop, the fans I knew constantly evoked images of New York: They renamed buildings in their *favela* after the boroughs of Brooklyn and the Bronx; they displayed New York logos whenever possible; and they explicitly spoke of imagined similarities in lifestyles. In one conversation on racism, a poor Black *favela* youth explained: "*Aqui é mais ou menos igual ao pessoal do Harlem.... Discriminação geral, polícia enchendo o saco o tempo todo.*" ("Here it is more or less like the people from Harlem.... General discrimination, police bothering us the whole time.") These connections were mostly symbolic and often imagined: While this youth had actually lived in Connecticut for a short time, and could have possibly visited New York, the majority (if not all) of the residents of the "Bronx" and "Brooklyn" buildings knew these names only from U.S. popular culture.

Brazilian youth also forge connections to the United States by importing the Civil Rights-inspired rhetoric of North American politically conscious rap (Alim, 2006). As in the United States, young Black males are an increasingly endangered population in Brazil, the most likely targets of police brutality and the most frequent victims of the violence that surrounds drug trafficking (Huggins, 2000; Mitchell & Wood, 1999; Scheper-Hughes & Hoffman, 1994). They

Example 3.1 *Periferia é Periferia* (Periphery is Periphery) by Racionais MC's.

1 *Pedir dinheiro é mais fácil que roubar mano*	Begging is easier than stealing brother
2 *Roubar é mais fácil de trampar mano*	Stealing is easier than working brother
3 *É complicado, o vicio tem dois lado*	It's complicated, vice has two sides
4 *Depende disso ou daquilo então tá tudo errado*	It depends on this or that or then it's all wrong
5 *Eu não vou ficar do lado de ninguém porquê?*	I'm not going to stand on anyone's side why?
6 *Quem vende droga pra quem? Há*	Who sells drugs to whom? Ha!
7 *Vem pra cá de avião ou pelo porto ou cais*	They arrive by planes or by the ports or piers
8 *Não conheço o próprio dono de aeroporto e mais*	I don't know the real owner of the airport and what's more
9 *Fico triste por saber e ver*	It makes me sad to know and see
10 *Porque quem morre no dia-a-dia*	Because who dies on a daily basis
11 *É igual a eu e a você*	Is equal to you and me
[*refrão:*]	[refrain:]
12 *Periferia é periferia*	Periphery is periphery

are commonly referred to as *marginais* (marginals), a term that signifies poverty, social inferiority, and disenfranchisement, in addition to presumed criminality (Goldstein, 2004; González de la Rocha et al., 2004). Politically conscious rappers identify the youth of the Brazilian periphery as their primary audience, and continuously affirm, "*Nós somos marginalizados, mas não somos marginais*" ("We are marginalized, but we are not marginals"). As they highlight the institutional causes of violence and suffering in their communities, they seek to empower themselves through the confrontational stance they associate with U.S. racialized urban spaces.

In the rap song *Periferia é Periferia* ("Periphery is Periphery"), excerpted in Example 3.1 above, Racionais MC's take up the example of drug trafficking to explain the marginalization of poor Black youth. This song reveals what rappers see as direct parallels between their situation and that of the U.S. ghetto (including drugs, structural violence, and social inequality).

It also draws on these connections, importing the power and prestige associated with the U.S. ghetto, attempting to unite the youth of Brazil's socially and geographically marginalized communities through a refrain of solidarity: *Periferia é periferia* ("Periphery is periphery"). In so doing, rappers link marginalized Brazilian spaces to Black America and its location in the First World.

Conversational Sampling: Intertextuality in Daily Discourse

The ubiquitous practice of sampling in Hip Hop (Smitherman, 2000; Woods, 2007) provides a valuable opportunity to explore how rappers and rap fans actively construct transnational connections by reworking well-known and familiar references. While sampling can be found in all branches of Hip Hop (DJing, MCing, graffiti, and breakdancing), I focus here on how rap lyrics can be recontextualized into the daily conversation of poor Black male fans.[3] In the linguistic practice that I call "conversational sampling," speakers quote or sing rap lyrics as part of their conversation—often following up on key words or phrases from their interlocutor's speech. Recycling and recontextualizing lyrics in conversation is not unique to the daily discourse of rap fans (Rampton, 2006). Yet as I will argue, through these memorable phrases, youth do more than merely recall popular songs or rehash familiar themes. They creatively draw on global youth culture to align themselves with the power and prestige they associate with U.S. First World modernity.

In order to demonstrate the process through which politically conscious rap is embraced to forge transnational connections for poor Black Brazilian youth, I turn to the daily conversations that I recorded between 1997 and 1998 among youth in a Rio *favela* that I call Praia do Cristo (Christ's Beach) or Cristo. Because of its status as a government-built project, Cristo is more accurately described as a *conjunto habitacional* (housing project), though it is commonly called a *favela* by residents and outsiders alike. In contrast to the squatter status and self-constructed properties of Rio's many *favelas*, Cristo affords residents legal home ownership with water, plumbing, and electricity. And yet Cristo also shares many of the trappings that mark the social and physical distinction of a *favela*: lack of adequate garbage collection, constant police surveillance, and the open disdain of middle-class neighbors. The White and wealthier live in condominium buildings right next door, with doormen, security gates, and access to the modern conveniences (such as washing machines and cable TV) that connect them, both symbolically and literally, to the First World. Cristo's location—on a few blocks of Rio's most valuable real estate—means residents are surrounded, quite literally, by the reality of Brazilian inequality.

Initially, I began conducting research in a local public high school (which served working-class and *favela* youth in the wealthy South Zone of Rio), where I met CW, who invited me back to Cristo and became my main research assistant. Because *favela* residents are often suspicious of the White middle-class people who rarely enter their communities (except to purchase drugs), CW served as my guide to Cristo. He facilitated access to daily conversations among his friends, mostly in their late teens and early 20s, helped translate rap songs into my more standard Portuguese, and taught me how to speak in rap lyrics. Conversational sampling was an important conversational norm within CW's peer group. Common phrases such as "*É complicado…*" ("It's complicated…") and "*Pronto para…*" ("Ready to…") necessarily inspired the catchy refrains from popular rap songs. Other times, youth followed up on key themes of politically conscious rap, as in Example 3.2 below. The lines in bold are recontextualized song lyrics, examples of conversational sampling.

Example 3.2 Rap as Daily Discourse

1	Karate:	*Ih se levar isso*	Karate:	Ooh if she takes this [the tape]	
2		*pra 14° vai dar*		to the 14th [squad] it's going to	
3		*um pirimbo::lo. Pô::, não faz*		cause cha::os. Da::mn, don't do	
4		*isso não heim?[Risos]*		that OK? [Laughter]	
5	Beavis:	*Vai vendo o estrago!*	Beavis:	Wait and see what will happen!	
6		*[Risos]*		[Laughter]	
7	Jennifer:	*Não, eu também tá com medo da*	Jennifer:	No, I'm also afraid of the	
8		*polícia aqui. Eu não vou pra*		police here. I'm not going to the	
9		*14° não. … De jeito nenhum.*		14th. … No way.	
10	Karate:	*Cê tá com medo dos cara chato?*	Karate:	You're afraid of the cops? [lit. 'the annoying guys']	
11	Jennifer:	*Da polícia que anda aqui*	Jennifer:	Of the police who walk around	
12		*já com … já pronto assim,*		here ready with … all ready like,	
13		*já pronto pra-*		ready to-[4]	
14	Karate:	**"Pronto pra atirar,**	Karate:	**"Ready to shoot,**	
15		**pronto pra matar."**		**ready to kill."**	
		[….]		*[….]*	
16	Wilson:	**"Os cara chato. Os cara chato."**	Wilson:	**"The police. The police."**	
17		**"Não é não é quinze pra onze**		**"It's not it's not 10:45**	
18		**ainda não!"**		**yet!"**	
19	Karate:	**"Não é quinze para onze não.**	Karate:	**"It's not 10:45 yet.**	
20		**Não. Falta pouco ainda pra**		**No. There's still a little time**	
21		**quinze para onze."** *[…]*		**until 10:45."** […]	
22		**"Não vou muito longe.**		**"I'm not going very far.**	
23		**Os cara já-"** *[Risos]*		**The cops already-"** [Laughter]	
24		**Vou andar só uns 5 ou 6**		I'm only going to walk 5 or 6	
25		**passos."** *[…]*		steps." […]	
26	Beavis:	*Tá ligado.*	Beavis:	You know what I'm sayin'. [lit. 'are you connected']	
		[….]		*[….]*	
27	Wilson:	*Já falou já com T?*	Wilson:	Have you already talked to T?	
28		*Já falou com T?*		Have you talked to T?	
29	Karate:	*Ele é- ele tem um papo muito*	Karate:	He is- he has a very complicated	
30		*complicado. [Risos]*		story. [Laughter]	
31	Beavis:	*Sofrido.*	Beavis:	He's been through a lot.	
32	Karate:	**"É complicado. O vício tem dois**	Karate:	**"It's complicated. Vice has two**	
33		**lado. Depende disso ou daquilo,**		**sides. It depends on this or that,**	
34		**ou não tá tudo errado."** *[Risos]*		**or it's all wrong."** [Laughter]	

In this conversation, Cristo youth use conversational sampling to joke about what would happen if the conversations I recorded in their community were brought to the corner police station. Conversational sampling offers a ready example of intertextuality as song lyrics are easily detachable (Bauman & Briggs, 1990) and highly transportable from one context to another. Over the course of their conversation, Cristo youth creatively integrate lyrics from three different rap songs. They turn Rio rapper M.V. Bill's refrain, "*Pronto para atirar, pronto para matar*" ("Ready to shoot, ready to kill"), used in the song to discuss a *favela* youth's decline into a life of crime, into a reference to Brazil's notoriously violent and trigger-happy military police.[5] Following up on the theme of police harassment, they reference another Racionais MC's song (provided in Example 3.3), riffing on the all-too-familiar experience of racial profiling and how quick police are to stop poor Black *favela* males. Finally, they use the Racionais line from Example 3.1, "*É complicado*" ("It's complicated") to complicate a prejudicial reading of their friend's lifestyle. In lines 12 and 13, I stumble while trying out my new conversational sampling skills, and Karate beats me to the punch. While my focus in this chapter is on the sociopolitical context of conversational sampling, an important part of the meaning of this practice undoubtedly lies in the linguistic creativity, skill, and pleasure Brazilian youth display when they swap familiar lyrics amongst friends (see also Kelley, 1997; Ibrahim, this volume).

Along similar lines, the collaborative nature of conversational sampling illustrates the role of intertextuality in local peer groups, as youth use these "common linguistic reference points" (Spitulnik, 1997, p. 163) to (re)define themselves and highlight shared aspects of their sociopolitical context. Multiple linguistic studies explore the critical relationship between intertextuality and community formation, as certain "texts" (Hanks, 1989) become key markers of one's communicative competence and group membership (Hill, 2005; Ibrahim, 2003, this volume; Ochs, 1990; Silverstein, 2003; Spitulnik, 1997; Woods, 2007). This suggests that conversational sampling becomes part of a glocal communicative competence, where transnational linguistic practices inform local identity construction and style. It is also important to note how through the act of speaking, fans create new, shared meanings for rap lyrics; for example, by modifying M.V. Bill's song about a youth who has turned to crime into a reference for the (criminal) military police. Sampling, with its juxtaposition of new and old contexts, affords multiple opportunities to construct similarity on both local and global levels.

The excerpt above is one of many I have collected in which *favela* youth use Hip Hop references to address their pressing concerns with police violence. For these youth, encounters with the military police constitute the most common and visceral experience of their exclusion from the Brazilian state. In one of the first studies of Hip Hop, Tricia Rose recounts a time she overheard an African American male quote a KRS-One rap lyric, "Who protects us from you?" to directly challenge a U.S. police officer who was harassing his friends (1994, p. 109). Through conversational sampling, Brazilian youth linguistically perform the confrontational stance of politically conscious rap, invoking the more empowered subject positions they associate with African Americans. As in the excerpt above, however, Brazilian youth most often engage in conversational sampling amongst friends, embracing politically conscious rap to rework their image within the safe space of their peer group.

Race Trafficking: Forging Transnational Connections

While rappers and rap fans can make obvious parallels between U.S. and Brazilian situations of social inequality, police harassment, and violence within their communities, other examples of shared marginality must be shaped and even invented. This is most obvious in politically conscious Hip Hop's embrace of U.S. ideas of institutional racism and a Black–White racial dichotomy. I call this practice "race trafficking" (Roth-Gordon, 2007), drawing on, and paying homage to M.V. Bill's 1999 album title *Traficando Informação* ("Trafficking Information"). Like M.V. Bill, I use the term *trafficking* to highlight the controversial and underground importation of racial and political ideology that often accompanies global Hip Hop. While the press and public have lauded rappers' attention to socioeconomic inequality and conditions of daily life in Brazil's social and geographic periphery, there has been overwhelming disdain for their direct discussion of Brazilian racism.

It is important to recognize the national significance of race trafficking: Brazil's international reputation as a racial democracy has been founded on a comparison with the more polarized context of U.S. race relations (Fry, 2000; Sheriff, 2001; Silva, 1998; Vargas, 2004). Through this implicit and often overt comparison, Brazilians have enjoyed a sense of moral racial superiority. While Brazil may be "Third World" in comparison to the United States and may struggle to improve its status in a global hierarchy, racial democracy brought Brazil international acclaim and pride in having avoided a problem that so obviously plagued the United States. Brazil's racial "cordiality," however, requires that assimilated racial minorities downplay their differences and exclusions from the nation-state (Fry, 2000; Guimarães, 1995; Hanchard 1994; Segato, 1998). In embracing the very race relations that serve as a point of contrast for Brazil (Silva, 1998), rappers must invent points of similarity, erasing historical trajectories that are most commonly read in opposition to each other.

Politically conscious rappers, such as Racionais, take up elements of U.S. Civil Rights Era identity politics that directly contradict Brazil's image as a racial democracy, rejecting this cornerstone of Brazilian nationalism. Within the context of racial democracy, overt racial conflict, legal separatism, and identity politics are readily viewed as "un-Brazilian" (Guimarães, 1995), and socioeconomic class remains the most common (and acceptable) way to interpret inequality. Indeed, though Brazil is ranked among the world's worst in the distribution of income and resources, national discourses promoting racial democracy, miscegenation, and whitening, as well as a lack of "race talk" (Sheriff, 2001) all suggest that race does not explain the shocking levels of disparity. Thus, U.S. rappers frequent mention of Blackness and their public condemnation of racism do not readily map onto past or present race relations in Brazil. This is an example of how Osumare's "connective marginalities" must be forged, rather than assumed.

Politically conscious Brazilian Hip Hop defies national norms promoting a "cultural silence" around race and racism (Sheriff, 2000). In their songs, many rappers openly identify as Black, embracing a Black–White racial dichotomy that aligns them with U.S. racial identity politics and draws on Hip Hop's connections to Black struggle (Condry, 2006). This kind of public statement brazenly subverts the prescriptive push of *embranquecimento* (whitening), a nation-building strategy that included both the subsidized importation of Europeans to "lighten" Brazil and individualized strategies to "improve one's race," often by marrying lighter (Skidmore, 1993). Everyday racial decisions, including terms of racial identification and the use of racial address terms, continue to support the goals of lightening, unless one intends to racially insult and offend (Sheriff,

Example 3.3 *Qual Mentira Eu Vou Acreditar* (Which Lie Should I Believe) by Racionais MC's.

1	*São apenas dez e meia. Tem a noite inteira*	It's only 10:30. The whole night lies ahead
2	*Dormir é embaçado numa sexta-feira*	It would be weird to sleep on a Friday night
	[....]	[....]
3	*Quem é preto como eu, já tá ligado qual é*	Blacks like me already know what's up
4	*Nota fiscal, RG, policia no pé*	Car registration, ID, police on your heels
5	*O primo do cunhado do meu genro é mestiço*	The cousin of my brother-in-law of my son-in-law is half black
6	*Racismo não existe comigo não tem disso*	Racism doesn't exist with me there's none of that
7	*É pra sua segurança*	It's for your own protection
8	*Falô, falô deixa pra lá*	Right, right let it go
	[refrão:]	[refrain:]
9	*Vou escolher em qual mentira vou acreditar*	I'm going to choose which lie I will believe
10	*Tem que saber mentir, tem que saber lidar*	You have to know how to lie, you have to know how to get by
11	*Em qual mentira eu vou acreditar?*	Which lie should I believe?
12	*A noite é assim mesmo então deixa rolar*	The night is like that anyway so let it go
13	*Vou escolher em qual mentira vou acreditar*	I'm going to choose which lie I'm going to believe
14	*Os cara chato ó. Quinze pras onze*	The police hey. [lit. 'the annoying guys'] 10:45
15	*Eu nem fui muito longe os homem embaçou*	I didn't even go very far and the cops nailed me

2001; but see Sansone, 2003 for new trends among youth). Politically conscious Hip Hop identifies race mixture, once thought to be Brazil's salvation and still embraced in national lore, as one of the strongest obstacles to racial consciousness building.

The imported themes of institutionalized racism and Black pride or *negritude* (Pardue, 2004), and their implicit critique of race mixing, are illustrated in the song *Qual Mentira Eu Vou Acreditar* ("Which Lie Should I Believe"). In the excerpt provided in Example 3.3, Racionais MC's narrate the story of a Black male youth who heads out in his car on a Friday night to meet up with friends. It takes only 15 minutes until he is stopped by Brazil's military police, who assume the car must be stolen and proceed with an illegal search.[6]

While the protagonist explains that it is his race that invites this violation of his civil rights (in line 3), he also reveals how racism works in a "racially cordial" Brazil: In lines 5 to 7, the officer quickly dismisses any hint of racism by pointing to race mixing, mentioning a half-Black distant relative as evidence of his lack of racial bias. The song's protagonist, Mano Brown, identifies himself (and his audience) as Black (in line 3) and readily identifies this incident as an example of racial profiling. Example 3.3 thus illustrates the ways in which Brazilian rappers take up U.S. racial ideology to construct racial similarity across national borders, disregarding Brazil's long history of situating itself as the other side of the American racial coin.

Brazilian rappers and rap fans literally attempt to embody U.S. themes of racialized exclusion and a Black–White binary through the male figure of the *mano* (Black brother) and his imagined counterpart, the *playboy* (wealthy White male youth) (Roth-Gordon, 2007; see also Pardue, 2004). The *mano–playboy* divide is signified through a range of U.S.-inspired semiotic practices, from dress, to language, to musical preference: *Manos* wear close-cut Afros or braided hair, ski caps or baseball hats (both clear U.S. references in temperate, soccer-loving Rio de Janeiro), and basketball jerseys or oversized baggy clothes. The *mano* thus draws on the global power and prestige of African Americans and the U.S. racialized ghetto to embody masculine toughness, Black pride, and *favela* loyalty. In contrast, the *playboy* is an outgroup label, used to describe overprivileged Brazilian youth who are self-serving, racist, and slaves to fashion.[7] Name-brand clothes (including American labels), popular Top-40 music, and expensive cell phones and watches are the daily fare of the *playboy*. It is critical to note that both figures rely on symbolic references to the United States, suggesting that Brazilian youth engage in a struggle over valuable First World connections.

The excerpt in Example 3.4 below, which was recorded by my research assistant CW in my absence, illustrates how poor Black *favela* youth articulate their identity through the *mano-playboy* divide. The conflict between these two figures is racialized, as Cristo youth make reference to the wavy forelock of hair (worn most famously by Elvis Presley) that iconically marks White hair and thus Whiteness. They also foreground the significance of urban space and the

Example 3.4 *Manos* (black brothers) vs. *Playboys* (white wealthy kids)

1	CW:	*Deixa eu ver. Deixa*	CW:	Let me see [the walkman]. Let
2		*eu mariar, deixa eu mariar.*		me check it out, let me check it
3		*Não, deixa eu mariar. [...]*		out. No, let me check it out. [...]
4		*Só pra mim criticar.*		Just so I can make fun.
5	Bad Dog:	*(?) Não, tem nada pra*	Bad Dog:	(?) No, there's nothing good
6		*tocar aí.*		playing.
7	Smoke:	*Cho ver, cho ver,*	Smoke:	Lemme see, lemme see,
8		*cho ver.*		lemme see.
9	CW:	*Porra, tá com uma marra*	CW:	Shit, you have the attitude of a
10		*de playboy fudida heim.*		fucking playboy, huh.
		[....]		*[....]*
11	Bad Dog:	*Tá me confundindo com quê?*	Bad Dog:	You are confusing me with what?
12	Smoke:	*Playboy.*	Smoke:	Playboy.
13	CW:	*Daqui a pouco tu tá usando*	CW:	Soon you'll be wearing your hair
14		*topetinho aí.*		with a little forelock.
15	Smoke:	*É.*	Smoke:	Yeah.
16	Bad Dog:	*Sou é* **"periferia é**	Bad Dog:	What I am is **"periphery is**
17		**periferia,"** *rapa.*		**periphery,"** man.
		[....]		*[....]*
18		**"Periferia é periferia,**		**"Periphery is periphery,**
19		**Racionais no ar, filha da**		**Racionais on the air, son of a**
20		**puta, plá plá plá."**		**bitch, uh uh uh."**

Brazilian periphery as direct markers of identity. Lines in bold are taken from the song, *Periferia é Periferia* ('Periphery is Periphery') by Racionais MC's, excerpted in Example 3.1.

Through this conversation, Cristo youth use politically conscious rap to invert global notions of racial hierarchy, stigmatizing Whiteness and elevating the Brazilian periphery. The use of conversational sampling includes implicit references to the U.S. First, as the *mano–playboy* divide offers a glocal interpretation of the U.S. Black–White binary. And second, as Bad Dog's equation of himself with the Brazilian periphery is strengthened through the U.S. export of the racialized ghetto. When Bad Dog claims, in lines 16 to 17, "*Sou é 'periferia é periferia,' rapa*" ("What I am is 'periphery is periphery,' man") to refute CW's racialized insult (accusing him of "selling out" by listening to *playboy* music), his response is grounded in Hip Hop's ready association of Black pride and urban (North American) spaces (see also Alim's, 2003 discussion of "We are the streets"). Through conversational sampling, Bad Dog intentionally erases possible connections between himself and White middle-class Brazilians, seeking instead to forge transnational bonds of Black solidarity.

Conclusion: Indexicality and Invoking the "Gueto"

Reflecting on Hip Hop's ability to transcend national borders, Osumare comments, "Hip-hop creates an encrypted, nuanced youth culture whose members recognize each other even across language barriers" (2007, p. 18). As I have discussed here, Brazilian youth do not draw on preexisting connections between the U.S. racialized ghetto and the Brazilian periphery, as much as they invent and create these connections through acts of strategic essentialism that highlight as much as they erase. This "recognition" must be produced, and it is worth asking what youth have to gain through their direct and indirect affiliation with U.S. Hip Hop.

In her work on mock Spanish, Jane Hill (2005) suggests that intertextuality, or the recycling of certain "texts," also serves as an important source for indexicality, as speakers draw on the shared history of certain words or phrases to align themselves with particular identities and worldviews. As I have discussed, sampling is by definition a form of intertextuality, and as such, it does more than merely send the listener back to an original to "give props" or pay dues. The juxtaposition of old and new, of well worn and just created, invests the current context with new meaning and new intent. Sampling—within music, breakdancing, graffiti, or speech—is especially heteroglossic: multilayered and infused with multiple voices. As I have discussed in this chapter, the rap fans that quote lyrics in their daily conversation do more than just reference rap songs to mark their participation in Hip Hop culture; they simultaneously use lyrics to "point to" (index) ideas and contexts beyond the current situation (Ochs, 1990). This use of indexicality is related to Bourdieu's (1994) notion of linguistic capital, where language lends prestige through what it directly and indirectly references (see also Silverstein, 2003).

It is here that symbolic connections to the United States, including the practice of conversational sampling, allow youth to identify themselves with what they view as the more empowered racial and political subject positions embodied by African Americans (Fry, 2000; Sansone, 2003). It is not that poor Black *favela* youth "see" themselves in African Americans or naturally connect with conditions of shared oppression. Indeed, Brazilian rappers and rap fans work to create points of similarity, often—as in the case of race trafficking—against great odds. It is partly because the U.S. racialized ghetto is wrapped in the power and prestige of First World modernity that Brazilian youth struggle to make familiar notions of the periphery seem more like "the hood."

I have suggested as well that this similarity is constructed, in part, to compete with their White middle-class neighbors who inspire the figure of the *playboy*. Here race and class privilege are signified and bolstered by more direct connections to the United States, including (but not limited to): Disney World vacations and U.S. shopping sprees, costly English classes, and in-home cable connections that offer around-the-clock access to U.S. popular culture. Hip Hop's connections to the racialized U.S. ghetto enable more marginalized youth to transcend national, economic, and linguistic boundaries and to tap into U.S. power and prestige. Conversational sampling and race trafficking thus offer Brazilian youth tangible ways to enhance their symbolic capital, accumulating First World prestige in the face of their increasing marginalization in Brazil.

Appendix

Transcription Conventions

(?)	Transcription not possible
(word)	Uncertain transcription
[laughter]	Transcriber's note (includes background noise as well as clarifications for the reader)
...	Noticeable pause (untimed)
[....]	Excerpt cut
underline	Emphatic stress or increased amplitude
::	Vowel elongation
-	Self-interruption; break in the word, sound abruptly cut off
//	Simultaneous speech (noted before speech of both participants)
.	Sentence-final falling intonation
,	Phrase-final intonation
?	Question rising intonation
bold	Indicates lexical items or example to be illustrated

Acknowledgments

I am grateful to H. Samy Alim, Antonio José da Silva, Awad Ibrahim, Alastair Pennycook, Susan Shaw, Terry Woronov, Leisy Wyman, and two anonymous reviewers for their insightful feedback on this chapter. This research benefited from the generous assistance of the National Science Foundation, the Mellon Foundation, and the Departments of Anthropology, International Studies, and Latin American Studies at Stanford University. I would like to thank the Brazilian youth, especially CW, who made this research possible.

Notes

1. This is in contrast to research on Somali immigrant youth in the United States and Continental Africans in Canada, who turn to African-American English (or Black Stylized English) to affiliate themselves with North American Blackness (Forman, 2002; Ibrahim, 2003).
2. In contrast, Rio de Janeiro is often associated with the national success of crossover pop/rap singers such as Gabriel o Pensador (in the early 90s) and Marcelo D2 (in the early 2000s), who would not be considered part of the politically conscious rap scene.
3. White middle-class youth and *favela* girls I met did listen to rap, particularly during periods of crossover success. While I conducted some comparative research with these groups, I did not observe them participating in the practice of conversational sampling.
4. I was taught to fear the police by both favela youth and members of the Brazilian middle class. In this conversation, I tried (somewhat unsuccessfully) to provide evidence of my familiarity

with insider norms of conversational sampling. Unlike Alim (2004), as a second-language speaker, I was limited in my ability to style shift beyond token slang words and discourse conventions.

5. Though Brazil returned to a political democracy in the 1980s, its law enforcement system was never demilitarized, and studies show that the police have continued the practices of brutality, torture, and homicide exercised during the military dictatorship (Chevigny, 1995; Penglase, 1994).

6. The parallels between this song and L.L. Cool J.'s "Illegal Search" are striking (see Rose, 1994).

7. This definition of the *playboy*, offered by rappers and rap fans, is often disputed by members of the White middle class (see Roth-Gordon, 2007).

Discography

M.V. Bill. (1999). *Traficando Informação*. BMG.
Racionais MC. (1998). *Sobrevivendo no Inferno*. Zambia.

References

Alim, H. S. (2003). "We are the streets": African American language and the strategic construction of a street conscious identity. In S. Makoni, G. Smitherman, A. F. Ball, & A. K. Spears (Eds.), *Black linguistics: Language, society, and politics in Africa and the Americas* (pp. 40–59). New York: Routledge.

Alim, H. S. (2004). *You know my steez: An ethnographic and sociolinguistic study of styleshifting in a Black American speech community*. Durham, NC: Duke University Press.

Alim, H. S. (2006). *Roc the mic right: The language of hip hop culture*. New York: Routledge.

Bauman, R., & Briggs, C. L. (1990). Poetics and performance as critical perspectives on language and social life. *Annual Review of Anthropology, 19*, 59–88.

Bourdieu, P. (1994). *Language and symbolic power* (J. B. Thompson, Ed. & Trans.). Cambridge, MA: Harvard University Press.

Chevigny, P. (1995). *Edge of the knife: Police violence in the Americas*. New York: New Press.

Condry, I. (2006). *Hip-hop Japan: Rap and the paths of cultural globalization*. Durham, NC: Duke University Press.

Forman, M. (2002). "Keeping it real"? African youth identities and hip hop. In R. Young (Ed.), *Music, popular culture, identities* (pp. 101–131). Amsterdam: Rodopi.

Fry, P. (2000). Politics, nationality, and the meanings of "race" in Brazil. *Daedulus, 129*(2), 83–118.

Goldstein, D. M. (2004). *The spectacular city: Violence and performance in urban Bolivia*. Durham, NC: Duke University Press.

González de la Rocha, M., Jelin, E., Perlman, J., Roberts, B. R., Safa, H., & Ward, P. M. (2004). From the marginality of the 1960s to the "new poverty" of today. *Latin American Research Review, 39*(1), 183–203.

Guimarães, A. S. A. (1995). Racism and anti-racism in Brazil: A post modern perspective. In B. P. Bowser (Ed.), *Racism and anti-racism in world perspective* (pp. 208–226). Newbury Park, CA: Sage.

Hanchard, M. (1994). Black cinderella? Race and the public sphere in Brazil. *Public Culture, 7*(1), 165–185.

Hanks, W. F. (1989). Text and textuality. *Annual Review of Anthropology, 18*, 95–127.

Hill, J. H. (2005). Intertextuality as source and evidence for indirect indexical meanings. *Journal of Linguistic Anthropology, 15*(1), 113–124.

Huggins, M. K. (2000). Urban violence and police privatization in Brazil: Blended invisibility. *Social Justice, 27*(2), 113–134.

Ibrahim, A. (2003). "Whassup, homeboy?" Joining the African diaspora: Black English as a symbolic site of identification and language learning. In S. Makoni, G. Smitherman, A. F. Ball, & A. K. Spears (Eds.), *Black linguistics: Language, society, and politics in Africa and the Americas* (pp. 169–185). New York: Routledge.

Kelley, R. (1997). *Yo' mama's disfunktional! Fighting the culture wars in urban America*. Boston: Beacon Press.

Krims, A. (2002). Rap, race, the "local," and urban geography in Amsterdam. In R. Young (Ed.), *Music, popular culture, identities* (pp. 181–196). Amsterdam: Rodopi.

Mitchell, M. J., & Wood, C. H. (1999). Ironies of citizenship: Skin color, police brutality, and the challenge to democracy in Brazil. *Social Forces, 77*(3), 1001–1020.

Mitchell, T. (Ed.). (2001). *Global noise: Rap and hip-hop outside the USA*. Middletown, CT: Wesleyan University Press.

Ochs, E. (1990). Indexicality and socialization. In J. W. Stigler, R. A. Shweder, & G. Herdt (Eds.), *Cultural psychology* (pp. 287–308). Cambridge, UK: Cambridge University Press.

Osumare, H. (2007). *The Africanist aesthetic in global Hip-Hop: Power moves*. New York: Palgrave Macmillan.

Pardue, D. (2004). Putting *mano* to music: The mediation of race in Brazilian rap. *Ethnomusicology Forum, 13*(2), 253–286.

Pardue, D. (2005). Brazilian hip-hop material and ideology: A case of cultural design. *Image & Narrative, 10*, 113–121.

Penglase, B. (1994). *Final justice: Police and death squad homicides of adolescents in Brazil*. New York: Human Rights Watch/Americas.

Rampton, B. (2006). *Language in late modernity: Interaction in an urban school*. New York: Cambridge University Press.

Robertson, R. (1995). Glocalization: Time-space and homogeneity-heterogeneity. In M. Featherstone, S. Lash, & R. Robertson (Eds.), *Global modernities* (pp. 25–44). London: Sage.

Rose, T. (1994). *Black noise: Rap music and black culture in contemporary America*. Hanover, CT: Wesleyan University Press.

Roth-Gordon, J. (2007). Racing and erasing the *playboy*: Slang, transnational youth subculture, and racial discourse in Brazil. *Journal of Linguistic Anthropology, 17*(2), 246–265.

Sansone, L. (2003). *Blackness without ethnicity: Constructing race in Brazil*. New York: Palgrave Macmillan.

Scheper-Hughes, N., & Hoffman, D. (1994). Kids out of place. *NACLA: Report on the Americas, 27*(6), 16–23.

Segato, R. L. (1998). The color-blind subject of myth: Or, where to find Africa in the nation. *Annual Review of Anthropology, 27*, 129–151.

Sheriff, R. E. (2000). Exposing silence as cultural censorship: A Brazilian case. *American Anthropologist, 102*(1), 114–132.

Sheriff, R. E. (2001). *Dreaming equality: Color, race, and racism in urban Brazil*. New Brunswick, NJ: Rutgers University Press.

Silva, D. F. da (1998). Facts of blackness: Brazil is not (quite) the United States…and racial politics in Brazil? *Social Identities, 4*(2), 201–234.

Silverstein, M. (2003). Indexical order and the dialectics of sociolinguistic life. *Language & Communication, 23*, 193–229.

Skidmore, T. (1993). *Black into white: Race and nationality in Brazilian thought*. New York: Oxford University Press.

Smitherman, G. (2000). *Talkin that talk: Language, culture, and education in African America*. New York: Routledge.

Spitulnik, D. (1997). The social circulation of media discourse and the mediation of communities. *Journal of Linguistic Anthropology, 6*(2), 161–187.

Vargas, J. H. C. (2004). Hyperconsciousness of race and its negation: The dialectic of white supremacy in Brazil. *Identities: Global Studies in Culture and Power, 11*, 443–470.

Woods, E. (2007). *"The MF doom flow": Identity construction and intertextuality in underground Hip Hop*. Unpublished master's thesis, University of California, Los Angeles.

"You Shouldn't Be Rappin', You Should Be Skateboardin' the X-Games"

The Coconstruction of Whiteness in an MC Battle

CECELIA CUTLER

Introduction

George Lipsitz writes that Whiteness, "as the unmarked category against which difference is constructed...never has to speak its name [or] acknowledge its role as an organizing principle in social and cultural relations" (1995, p. 369). On the flip side of this equation are people of color who are compelled to measure themselves up to a set of standards based on White American cultural norms. Referring to the mindset of African Americans, W.E.B. Du Bois called this "double consciousness," which he described as the compulsion to see oneself through the eyes of Whites. Spears (1998) describes it as "the dual personality caused by the cohabitation of two consciousnesses or cultural systems within one mind, the White and the African-American" (p. 248).

In pondering this idea, it struck me that double consciousness conceivably plays a role in Hip Hop culture, but in the opposite direction. It would be overly reductionist to analyze Hip Hop culture as an exclusively Black enterprise. Scholars have acknowledged the participation of Latinos and Whites in the formative years of Hip Hop (Morgan 1998; Rivera, 2003,), and now, two decades in, Hip Hop is produced and consumed by young people all over the world (e.g., Pennycook & Mitchell, Androutsopoulos, Higgins, Omoniyi, Roth-Gordon, this volume). Yet in this country it seems that rap music, as Rose writes, "still largely prioritizes Black voices" and "articulates the pleasures and problems of Black urban life in contemporary America" (1994, p. 2; cf. Perry, 2004). The reigning position of African Americans as the chief artistic creators and trendsetters is difficult to dispute. Les Back (1996) has described the Hip Hop Nation as having a "Black culture" but a "multiracial" citizenry (p. 215).[1] In fact the centrality of the Black experience within American Hip Hop culture has led to an interesting role reversal such that Blackness occupies the role of the dominant, unmarked social category. According to Boyd (2002), "Hip Hop and basketball are spaces where Blackness has been normalized, and whiteness treated as the Other" (p. 23). In Hip Hop it is Whites who are forced to see themselves through the eyes of Black people and try to measure up to the standards of authenticity, achievement, and knowledge established by the collective of individuals who make up the Hip Hop Nation.

The normativity of Blackness in Hip Hop stems from a discourse that privileges the Black body and the Black urban street experience (Rebensdorf, 1996). Despite the visibility and popularity of White American rappers such as Eminem, Whiteness is still marked against the backdrop of normative Blackness. This is particularly salient in public Hip Hop performances such as the MC battle analyzed here where every aspect of a performer's identity, including race is subject to scrutiny. This chapter will show how ethnic boundaries get negotiated between a White contestant (Eyedea) and his African American opponents (R.K., E-Dub, and Shells) in an MC Battle. The battle, sponsored by the now defunct *Blaze* Magazine, took place in New York in November 2000.[2]

The analysis will show how Eyedea cooperates with his African American opponents in *marking* his own Whiteness (c.f. Mitchell-Kernan, 1974). *Marking* is normally thought of as a way to parody another person's or group's speech. Marking *White* is a sort of verbal performance that draws on commonly recognized White American linguistic features. In most analyses, marking White is done by African Americans in order to parody or mock White stereotyped ways of talking as well as White American attitudes and behaviors (Alim, 2005). In the present study, White American MCs are drawing on stereotyped linguistic features such as hyper-rhotic /r/ to mark themselves as White. This might seem like a redundant gesture given the fact that the MC in question was, from all outwardly signs, unambiguously White. Yet Whiteness seemed to occupy a unique position in the context of this MC battle that was reflective of its status in the broader Hip Hop culture: it was highly marked and its position vis-à-vis Blackness was being challenged. Discursive and linguistic marking was a way for White and Black competitors to challenge hegemonic Whiteness. I argue that in this context marking plays a functional role in ratifying an alternative social reality in which Blackness is normative and Whiteness is rendered the "other." This is not to suggest that a balancing out of Whiteness and Blackness has occurred, but rather to point out the complicated ways in which they get played out in different domains.

Stance

A useful tool in the attempt to provide a more subtle analysis of how speakers construct, resist, transform, and reject cultural differences is the interpretive framework of *stance*. Jaffe (2004) writes that contemporary work on stance in linguistics, sociolinguistics, pragmatics and linguistic anthropology is related to a number of interpretive traditions, including Goffman's notion of "footing," (1979) and Gumperz' "contextualization cues" (1989, 1992) that focus on how speakers necessarily and simultaneously position themselves with respect to both the form and the content of their utterances and with respect to the social, cultural (including political) identities, values and relationships associated with that form and content.[3]

According to Irvine (2004), stance can take one of three forms: (a) *stance* as "footing," a position within a set of participant roles in an act of speaking; (b) *stance* as point of view, opinion, or ideological position; and (c) *stance* as social position in a larger sense, invoking broad categories of participation in social life such as class or ethnicity. Importantly, stance can index one or more social identities, liberating speakers from static interpretations of their utterances, their identities, and those of others. This makes stance a particularly productive way to look at how speakers manage multiple roles, points of view, and identities in intercultural interactions. In the performance data analyzed in this chapter, speakers adopt stances that invoke their respective positions within a Hip Hop community of practice (Eckert & McConnell-Ginet, 1992) as well as social roles like race and class. This chapter will also show how stance reveals an alternative social order in which normative Whiteness is challenged and ultimately subverted.

Out-Group Language Use within Hip Hop

One interesting question that arises in the study of White American participation in Hip Hop is the link between language and ethnicity. Kira Hall (1995) writes that "the ideological link between language and ethnicity is so potent that the use of linguistic practices associated with a given ethnic group may be sufficient for an individual to pass as a group member" (cited in Bucholtz, 1995, p. 355). Most White American MCs like Eminem, the Beastie Boys, and one of the MCs we'll examine later in the chapter, "Eyedea," employ a speech style that draws features of Hip Hop Nation Language (Alim, 2004) and African American English. Lest they fall victim to the charge that they are wannabes because of the way they speak, White American rappers must adopt a stance that references their Whiteness. They can achieve this by "outing" themselves discursively as the Beastie Boys do in their lyrics when they sing, "I'm a funky-ass Jew and I'm on my way" in the song "Right Here Right Now" or stylistically by playing up socially salient variables that index White American speech such as hyper-rhotic realizations of postvocalic /r/. Taking a racial stance is part of a complex process of "keepin' it real"—an expression that Rickford and Rickford (2000) have described as a Hip Hop mantra, exhorting individuals to be true to their roots, and not to "front" or pretend to be something they are not (cf. Pennycook & Mitchell this volume). It is difficult not to underestimate the centrality of "realness" in Hip Hop and many controversies in Hip Hop surround accusations of "biting" or stealing someone's lyrics or selling out by making one's music palatable to mainstream audiences.

Analysis

Since the late 1990s, there has been a rise in the popularity and visibility of one aspect of Hip Hop culture: MC-ing and MC battles. Within Hip Hop, MC battles are one of the most visible and potentially humiliating ways for an MC to demonstrate his or her rhyming and freestyling skills. Two MCs face one another and each is given a fixed amount of time (usually 30 seconds to a minute) to generate a spontaneous ("freestyle"), rhyming litany of insults at his or her opponent. In most cases, MCs draw on a mix of spontaneous and prewritten rhymes, using hooks like "on the mic" and fillers like "yo" and "check it" to keep their rhymes flowing. A battle may also end in humiliation and defeat if the MC can't make his or her rhymes flow or if the rhymes are obviously written ahead of time rather than generated spontaneously. Ultimately the audience chooses the winner by applauding louder for one opponent than the other at the end of the battle. Crucially, each competitor tries not to take all of this criticism personally lest he or she lose face and the backing of audience.

The first battle is between R.K., (a.k.a. Richard Kimble), a Black MC from Miramar, Florida, and Eyedea (a.k.a. Mike Averill), a White MC from Minneapolis-St. Paul, Minnesota (shown in 1 and 2 below). R.K. is the first to perform and gets a minute to "spit" his rhymes. In the transcript, we can observe some overt references to Eyedea's Whiteness. After a few rather light-hearted jabs at his appearance, R.K. refers to Eyedea as "Telly" in line 15, the polemical White rebel from the 1995 Larry Clark film *Kids*, implying that Eyedea like the lead character Telly is a wannabe—a White kid who wants to be Black.[4] Then in line 23 in a diss against MTV *and* Eyedea, R.K. alludes to a widespread sentiment among Hip Hoppers that MTV has no cachet for authentic hip hoppers when he says that Eyedea is "wacker than MTV's lyricist lounge." Finally, R.K. insinuates that Eyedea is so devoid of talent as an MC that a record deal with the major label Bad Boy still wouldn't help him get any "shine."[5]

(1) R.K., Miramar, Florida vs. Eyedea, Minneapolis, Round 2, Blaze Battle.
     (R.K. and Eyedea are standing on the stage; R.K. has the microphone)[6]
     1. Son, you wanna spit? Nigga, I'mo split your wig.
     2. Motherfucker, lookin' like Telly from "Kids."
     3. R.K. nigga, come in the game.
     4. Understand everything that I'mo spit is flame.
     5. I ((hide)) niggas. I'm glad that you try.
     6. Your career's over like ((inaudible)) when Tupac died.
     7. Yo son, I ((pillage)) niggas that spit.

8. Motherfuckers like me, yo, I'm a *real* lyricist.
9. I got more shit. I ain't feelin' you clown.
10. This nigga is wacker than MTV's lyricist lounge.
11. Yo, R.K. nigga don't (( )).
12. This nigga here, don't got nothin' to do.
13. So I can spit shit. Understand nigga, I rhyme.
14. If you signed to Bad Boy, you still wouldn't see no shine.

Significantly, Eyedea participates in the construction of himself as White. Whereas his competitors rely largely on discursive methods to do this, Eyedea collaborates in his ethnic self-marking phonologically. He possesses a high level of linguistic competence, employing many of the quintessential morphosyntactic patterns found in the rap lyrics of young urban African Americans from New York City such as verbal –s absence, copula absence, negative concord, and multiple negation as well as a range of discourse genres like dissin' and freestyling. He also controls a range of phonological features found in Hip Hop on the East Coast such as monophthongal /ay/, glottalized medial stops, and labialized intervocalic /r/ (Cutler, 2002; Morgan, 2002). But he is careful to temper his displays of competence by deploying linguistic resources that mark him as White. One way he does this is via hyper-rhotic realizations of postvocalic /r/—one of the features that typifies American English in Minnesota where Eyedea comes from. Crucially it also indexes White American speech.

Clark (2002) has described "hyper-rhotic" /r/ as a strategy used by African American teenagers to mark White American speech in the classroom (cf. Rahman, 2007). This contrast relies on the interlocutors' access to linguistic stereotypes that contrast White rhoticity with Black /r/-lessness.[7] Clark (2002) identifies three realizations of /r/ in the speech of his informants: vocalized /r/ (Ø); mildly pronounced (/r/), and strongly pronounced (/rr/). An example of vocalized /r/ is the realization of the word *car* as "cah." Mildly pronounced /r/ is what one typically hears in the speech of American newscasters such as Anderson Cooper. Strongly pronounced or "hyper-rhotic" /r/ involves the tight constriction of the tongue in the center of the mouth, resulting in an exaggerated /r/ sound. Using this three-way distinction, we can see how Eyedea uses hyper-rhotic /r/ to perform and mark his own Whiteness. When it comes to intervocalic /r/, Eyedea employs a labialized variant (/w/) that occurs frequently in New York City Hip Hop (Cutler, 2002). This variant is part of Eyedea's extensive repertoire of features that he uses to mark himself as part of the Hip Hop culture.

Eyedea's performance is shown in 2 below. Examples of hyper-rhotic postvocalic /r/ are found in line 1, *murder* and line 2, *heard* and even more emphatically in the rhyming of *enhancer* and *dancer* in lines 25 and 26. There are also several instances where Eyedea omits postvocalic /r/; in "motherfuckers" [mʌðə'fʌkəz] in line 10 and again in lines 11, 17, and 25. The fact that he retains postvocalic /r/ at a high rate in his performance, and that he chooses the hyper-rhotic variant to do this, points to the role of /r/ as a marker of Whiteness, signaling a racial stance. His puerile rhymes about dog manure and menstrual blood seem to further position him as a nerdy, White teenager. But in the final rhymes of the battle, Eyedea seizes upon an opportunity to position himself as the stronger freestyler. R.K.'s attempt to mock Eyedea by dancing lethargically during his performance allows Eyedea to take the upper hand when he quips that R.K. wants to be "his fuckin' back up dancer" in line 26. The emasculating image of a backup dancer is played out in the final line when Eyedea tells R.K. that he should "sign a deal with little Janet Jackson." The audience immediately roars with laughter and Eyedea wins the round hands down.

(2)   Eyedea vs. R.K., Round 2, Blaze Battle (Eyedea has the microphone)
   1. Hey yo, it's time to mu[**rr**]der you.
   2. From the crowd yo, all I hea[**rr**]d was boos.
   3. Yo, it's all good. On the mic I just straight pound.
   4. And I'll neve[**rr**] get beat by a cat that looks like Homey the Clown.
   5. So try to bring that back.
   6. My mate[**w**]ial's ill.
   7. You[**r**] pants used to be White until your pe[**w**]iod spilled.
   8. What's it make you feel?
   9. Yo, it's difficult. I'm battlin' Mystikal mixed with Bizzy Bone.
  10. Moth[ə]fucke[ə]s can't play me when I freestyle.
  11. Yo, why you got y[ə] hand wrapped in that weak towel.
  12. Comin' up dressed like a clown, yo, you talk a lot.
  13. Yo, you just stepped in dog shit, fo[**rr**]got to wash it off. //R.K. lifts up his foot to check//
  14. It's just like that. I'll grab the mic and straight ((tease me)).
  15. Even if I come off wack, I'll win 'cause it's just easy. //R.K. sits on the floor holding his knees and
  16. bobbing his head to the rhythm//.
  17. Yo, sit down. Oh, that's right because y[ə] nothin'.
  18. And that's the same type like you like to dick suck man.
  19. Yo, man, there [dðɛw] it goes on the mic.
  20. I'm oh so te[**w**]ible.
  21. Look at him tryin' to mock me, knowin' that he jocks me.
  22. You couldn't kick those lyrics with karate.
  23. Come on, bring up the microphone and try to rock me.
  24. //R.K. stand up and starts dancing lethargically in a mock Hip Hop style//.
  25. Yo, I'll grab the mic and try be y[ə] rap enhance[**rr**].
  26. This cat wants to be my fuckin' back-up dance[**rr**].
  27. //audience roars in laughter//
  28. Why Ø you doin' that shit? This man ain't rappin'.
  29. He should go sign a fuckin' deal with little **Janet Jackson**. //thunderous applause//

Eyedea's spit also contains several references to appearance and style as opposed to race. He references two outdated Black rappers in line 9 when he says R.K. looks like a mixture Mystikal and Bizzy Bone, who, like R.K., sported a big afro. In line 26, Eyedea refers to R.K. as "this cat" which could be interpreted as a racialized term, albeit an indirect one. However, looking at all of the performances in which Eyedea participates, it is clear that Whiteness is foregrounded in many more instances and in more overt ways than Blackness. The paucity of references to Blackness points to its unmarked status. For obvious reasons, Black MCs do not resort to race-referenced insults when they battle each other although they may invoke hierarchies of color and use the n-word.[8] Nor do plausible references to Blackness challenge a competitor's legitimacy in the way references to Whiteness often seem to do.

In the next round of the battle, Eyedea faces "E-Dub," a Black MC from Detroit. In Round 3 and Round 4 (the Final Round), there are two spits so each MC must perform twice. E-Dub is older and quite a bit bigger than Eyedea. He has a fair complexion and has his hair braided against his head in cornrows. In the excerpt shown below, Eyedea draws on cultural references from the Simpsons and Hip Hop to create a ridiculous image of his opponent as a mixture between the underachieving son from the long-running cartoon serial "The Simpsons" and the Black MC Mystikal.[9] Eyedea also compares E-Dub with Fred Durst, a White American MC who was popular in the late 1990s. Linking E-Dub to popular White American figures like Bart Simpson and Fred Durst seem to cast doubt on his authenticity as a Black man. It also reinforces the connection between Whiteness and inauthenticity.

(3) Round 3 (Eyedea vs. E-Dub, a.k.a. Edward Dixon, Detroit, Michigan); Spit 1 of 2
   1. Why Ø you walkin' around pretendin' you ain't feelin' me?
   2. That's just so funny when I sta[**rr**]t rippin' a diss on you.
   3. You look like a mixtu[**rr**]e between Ba[**rr**]t Simpson and Mystikal.
   4. ((thinkin' it)) just like when you[**r**] mom made po[**rr**]nos.
   5. You look like fuckin' Fred Du[**r**]st with co[**rr**]n rows.

Competitors can also adopt stances that index an understanding of Hip Hop style. In the next excerpt from Round 3, Eyedea ridicules E-Dub's fashion sense when he suggests that his sweat suit came from the downscale K-Mart.

(4) Round 3 (Eyedea vs. E-Dub); Spit 1 of 2
   1. It's just that. You know I just straight talk.
   2. I've won more battles than you[r] bitch ass has watched.
   3. So why Ø you walkin' around lookin' like that I wrecked you.
   4. This **cat** straight got a K-Ma[r]t sweat suit.
   5. He think he Ø rockin' like that.

6. Yo, the late is night.
7. I'm about to show this moth[ə]fucke[ə] how to break the mic.

Whiteness is invoked again in E-Dub's rebuttal shown in 5 when E-Dub tells Eyedea that he shouldn't be "rappin'—he should be skateboardin' the X-games" in line 2 —a sort of extra-Olympic event featuring a disproportionate number of postadolescent suburban White males who perform daring stunts on boards and bikes. The rhyme frames Eyedea as a White, middle-class suburban skater kid who shouldn't be rapping because he lacks the street credentials. There are additional instances where Whiteness is highlighted in 5. In line 3, E-Dub calls Eyedea a "fake Eminem" with a "long nose." The rhetorical question about Eyedea's origins in line 7 conveys a sense of disbelief that any half-decent MC could come from a place like Minnesota. E-Dub once again casts doubt on his opponent's legitimacy by saying that he belongs on MTV in line 10 and that he couldn't sell a cassette on a Detroit street corner if it came with a bag of marijuana. This final line points to a longstanding practice among MCs in urban Black neighborhoods who would attempt to generate a local following by selling homemade rap cassettes on the street.

(5) Round 3, Spit 2: E-Dub vs. Eyedea (E-Dub on the mic)
1. Believe me. I'm the next to spit the flames.
2. You shouldn't be rappin'. You should be **skateboardin' the X-Games**.
3. You Ø a **fake Eminem** with a fucked up haircut. Long nose.
4. You remind me of my ex-ho. A bitch that don't really work that hard.
5. A faggot rapper that can't rap that hard.
6. And on top of that I'mo have to float ya.
7. Where the fuck are you from? Minnesota?
8. Yo, the home of the Vikings and the ho-ass Timberwolves.
9. I bring shit to kill you.
10. Believe me, you belong on **MTV**.
11. You couldn't sell a cassette on 25th ((and McCane)) if it came with a bag of (( )) weed.

Eyedea in his rebuttal (shown in 6), says, "Yo, I'm doper than you on the mic even if I am a **skater**" in line 5—tacitly acknowledging something about who he really is and where he comes from. Remaining cool-headed in the face of these repeated references to race and embracing a White, middle-class American stance are part of how Eyedea "keeps it real." We can also observe the ubiquitous hyper-rhotic /r/ in lines 2 to 5 (hat*er*, lat*er*, fad*er*, skat*er*).

(6) Round 3, Spit 2: E-Dub vs. Eyedea (Eyedea on the mic)
1. This cat's talkin' 'bout my clothes, he's rockin' an Eyedea shirt.

2. Na, I'm just playin'. Up on the mic, you ain't a hate[**rr**].
3. Here's my backstage pass. Have your momma meet me back there late[**rr**].
4. And if she really wanna a ((fad[**rr**])),
5. Yo, I'm doper than you even if I am a skate[**rr**].
6. So it's all good. Up on the mic you ((slobber)) the nut.
7. Come on, y'all. Who's gonna beat me. Want ((it to be)) **Jabba the Hutt?**

In the last three lines of his spit, Eyedea brutally disparages E-Dub's looks, comparing him to the bloated overlord Jabba the Hutt from the film *Star Wars*, and again when he compares E-Dub to a gopher who couldn't get a girl to look at him if he were a D'Angelo poster.[10]

23. This cat needs to mothe[ə]fuckin' call the dogs off.
24. Yo, you say you poor hoes. You look like a gophe[**rr**].
25. Couldn't ((get a girl)) to stop and look at you if you was a D'Angelo poste[**rr**]

In his second and final spit E-Dub counters by marking Eyedea's Whiteness with a quotative. In line 8, he ventriloquizes Eyedea asking, "What's happinin' *Black*?" The use of the vocative "Black" as a licensed out-group alternative to the in-group term *nigga* is discussed in greater detail in the next section. Here, it offers up a sociolinguistically appropriate lexical alternative to "nigga" for a White speaker. Comparisons between Eyedea and White American rappers like Eminem and Vanilla Ice were also common ways to mark Eyedea as White. E-Dub's allegation that Eyedea is a "light skinned Eminem" (line 13) points up Eminem's status within the Hip Hop community. Eminem is actually quite pale and blond so this latter comparison appears to confer on him an honorary Black status within Hip Hop. It also serves to distinguish some White MCs from others, the implication being that Eyedea is not among the White MCs who are accepted by the Black Hip Hop community.

(7) Round 3, Spit 2: E-Dub vs. Eyedea (E-Dub on the mic)
   1. You Ø in trouble if you try to win.
   2. You heard Aliyah? Try again.
   3. Bill Gates couldn't buy your win.
   4. You Ø hyDRO.
   5. I'm hydroGEN
   6. Who's official. Studio gangstas talk about packin' gat.
   7. E-Dub come through, you ain't clappin' gat. //Eyedea looks quizzically at audience//
   8. You Ø on the ground like, "What's happenin' *Black*?"
   9. I don't sell drugs. I ain't no thug. I'm just rappin' that.

10. Kind of like flashin' gat.
11. Last cat that flashed his gat, left with a bad flashback with my gun in his ass crack
12. (( )) for publishin' your ASCAP, or get your ass capped
13. You ain't fuckin' with me, light skinned **Eminem**.
14. You're not from Detroit. Stop tryna be **Eminem**. //Eyedea mouths the lyrics as if he's heard them before//.

All of Eyedea's opponents make frequent and overt references to his Whiteness; often this is done in ways that appear to challenge his legitimacy as an MC and as a member of the Hip Hop community. A list of all references to Eyedea's Whiteness made by Eyedea's opponents throughout the contest appears in Table 4.1.

The final two excerpts in Table 4.1 show how another White American MC named "See For" gets discursively *marked* as White in similar ways to Eyedea. In this encounter, See For's opponent K.T., a Black MC from Boston, Massachusetts, makes an association between Whiteness and bizarre acts like "blowing up post offices" and "playing records backwards." In the 1970s there were rumors that White rock and heavy metal bands like Queen, Led Zeppelin, and Judas Priest, recorded satanic messages on their records that could be understood subconsciously when a song is played normally to influence the listeners' behavior, or incite them to acts of violence. These kinds of stereotypes parallel a discourse in the Black community about how all of the bizarre, inexplicable crimes and serial murders in the United States seem to have White perpetrators.[11]

K.T. also marks Whiteness when he says that his opponent must be related to Ron Howard, the pale, redheaded star of the TV series "Happy Days." As we can

Table 4.1 References to Eyedea's whiteness in Rounds 2-4 of the *Blaze* Battle

Eyedea vs. R.K. (Round 2)	Motherfucker lookin' like **Telly** from *Kids*.
	This nigga is wacker than **MTV's** lyricist lounge.
Eyedea vs. E-Dub (Round 3)	You shouldn't be rappin', you should be **skateboardin'** the **X-games**.
	You belong on **MTV**.
	You Ø a **fake Eminem** with a fucked up haircut.
	You ain't fuckin' with me, light skinned **Eminem**.
	You're not from Detroit. Stop tryin' to be **Eminem**.
Eyedea vs. Shells (Round 4)	They got Shells battlin' **Lil' Chuck Norris**.
	I'll be damned to lose against **Vanilla Ice**.
	You look like **Buffy the mother fuckin' rhyme slayer**.
See For vs. K.T. (Round 2)	You'd be safer **blowing up post offices** and **playing records backwards**.
	I know you was a coward. I know somehow you was related to **Ron Howard**.

see from these examples, White American culture offers a goldmine of content for rhymes that simultaneously encode the addressee's Whiteness and critique hegemonic White American culture more broadly.

Avoidance as a Strategy for Marking Whiteness

An additional way that White American competitors like Eyedea keep it real and acknowledge racial boundaries here is by avoiding certain themes and terms of address. Black competitors commonly refer to each other as "nigga" throughout the battle. As an in-group form of address, the term indexes a stance of cool solidarity for young Black men (Smitherman, 1994). But its use has expanded so that it is now used as a general, (usually) male gendered address term for young people of diverse ethnic backgrounds in homogenous groupings. Indeed it seems that "nigga" is developing into a discourse marker that more generally encodes the speaker's stance to his or her current addressee(s)—a stance that is cool, urban, usually male, and streetwise.

Although it's quite common for White American male youth to use this term to refer to or address their White friends (Cutler 2002), the public use of this term by White people is still highly controversial in the United States (Kennedy, 2002; Smitherman, 1992). Even the enormously popular White American rapper Eminem who grew up on the border of an economically deprived, Black part of Detroit and who is widely accepted among Black Hip Hoppers has stated publicly that he would never use the term. In the *Blaze* Battle analyzed here, Eyedea *never* employs this term with any of his competitors, whereas R.K. uses the term 11 times when he battles Eyedea (in 1 above). But in Round 2 of the battle, Eyedea's opponent E-Dub who is Black does not use the term to address him even once. It seems to imply that he doesn't take Eyedea seriously and re-fuses to confer on him the insider status that "nigga" might imply. The one other White competitor in this battle, *See For,* similarly avoids the term completely when up against his African American opponent K.T. although K.T. uses it with him on three occasions.

As we might predict based on these general observations, the use of "nigga" as a positive in-group solidarity marker is complicated in biracial interactions; its use is unidirectional in the sense that Black competitors can use it with one another and with Whites, but Whites cannot reciprocate. This allows Black MCs the option of whether or not to ratify their competitor's legitimacy and to express solidarity in a way that is not reciprocal.

Eyedea prevails in Round 3 against "E-Dub" and passes on to Round 4, the final round, where he battles Shells, an MC from New York City (shown in 8 below). As in the previous round, *marking* emerges in oblique ways when Eyedea employs the vocative "Black" to address Shells in line 7. It's the only such token in all of Eyedea's performances and it serves not only to racialize his opponent, but perhaps also index his own Whiteness in that he is not licensed to use "nigga."

In line 1, Shells has begun to mouth Eyedea's lines as if to say that they are prewritten rather than spontaneous or freestyle. Eyedea jumps on this and turns it around, implying that Shells is "biting" or copying his lines—a grave allegation within Hip Hop—and furthermore implies that this is the only way Shells will "ever sell a record." Eyedea places himself in the position of an authority figure vis-à-vis Shells in lines 7 to 8 when he tells him that he and his crew need to "go back to school"—Eyedea being the "teacher" who will set him straight. He finishes off his spit with five rhyming hyper-rhotic realizations of /r/ in which he frames himself as the "grim reaper" who has just finished off his opponent.

(8) Round 4 (final round): Eyedea vs. Shells, New York City, (Eyedea on the mic)
  1. Always spittin' ['spɪʔɪn] my lines, thinkin' that he's freshe[rr], //Shells mouths Eyedea's lines as if
  2. he's heard them before//.
  3. Spittin' ['spɪʔɪɪn] Eyedea lines Ø the only way you'll eve[ə] sell a reco[rr]d.
  4. So why'd you do that?
  5. You don't wanna be (( )).
  6. You know what, you need to take your whole fuckin' crew back to school.
  7. **Black,** that's how it goes. Pull up a stool, I'm the teache[rr].
  8. I'm about to wea[r] your bitch ass ((sounds like you)) sneake[rr]s.
  9. You MCs to me is just geeke[rr]s.
  10. This cat stays close to my dick like a beepe[rr].
  11. He ain't even comin' with the cheape[rr].
  12. You just lost your life by Eyedea the grim reape[rr].

In his rebuttal spit (shown in 9), Shells makes references to Whiteness in line 3 when he calls Eyedea a "lil' Chuck Norris," the White American martial arts actor.

(9) Round 4 (Final Round): Shells vs. Eyedea (Shells on the mic)
  1. Listen man, yo. Hey, yo, listen. Hey yo, hey yo.
  2. I'mo spit hot bars even if this dude is borin'.
  3. They got Shells battlin' lil **Chuck Norris**.
  4. We get it goin' man; you don't really want that.

Shells marks Eyedea's Whiteness later in the spit in line 18 when he says he'll be "damned to lose against Vanilla Ice," the universally reviled White American rapper from the early 1990s. Note Eyedea's physical response to this when he throws up his hands and looks to the audience for a bit of sympathy. It's at least the third time one of his competitors has called him Eminem or Vanilla Ice, and he seems to be saying, "Yes, I'm White. Can't you think of a better rhyme?" Finally, it's noteworthy that Shells—like Eyedea's previous opponent E-Dub—never uses "nigga" to address or refer to him even once. Indirectly, he refers to Eyedea as "this dude" at the outset of his spit. The cumulative effect of these acts seems to suggest that Shells does not accept Eyedea as a full-fledged competitor. As a native of New York City, performing for a home crowd, Shells may have assumed that a White skater from Minneapolis wouldn't have the skills or credibility to pull off a win.

15. You don't know—I'mo let this go.
16. And you talk about my teeth, talk about my flow.
17. I'm a hot ((skimity)) cat. Me Ø mad nice.
18. I'll be damned to lose against **Vanilla Ice**.

Conclusion

There is one more spit in the final round between Eyedea and Shells in which Shells loses face when he starts stumbling on his rhymes, allowing Eyedea to prevail as the overall champion in the tournament. Part of why Eyedea is so successful throughout the battle is because he is careful to maintain racial boundaries and doesn't try to "front." His clean-cut style, absence of head coverings or gang symbols of any kind, show that he is not trying to claim street credibility or indeed be anything more than a White suburban skater kid. His hyper-rhotic /r/ is a way for him to mark himself both ethnically and in terms of class. A crucial part of his success is his ability to let the incessant references to his Whiteness roll off his back, tacitly accepting that his identity is marked in this context, and his impressive skills as a freestyler.

These data show that in MC battles in the U.S. context, Whiteness is a highly marked category that triggers overt and oblique references. Black and White contestants cooperate to construct difference in ways that reflect a shared orientation about the markedness of Whiteness within Hip Hop. The foregrounding of Whiteness serves an important functional role in the MC battle as a way to ratify an alternative social order—an order that must be acknowledged and embraced by White competitors if they are to be accepted by their opponents and the audience as "real."

There are a number of interesting implications that come out of the reversal of hegemonic racial hierarchies within Hip Hop culture: young people who participate in Hip Hop can become aware of what it feels like to experience the other side of the Black/White racial boundary; White American youth can experience a bit of what it feels like to see themselves through the eyes of Black Americans, and Black American youth can experience the sense of entitlement and self-confidence that belonging to the dominant culture entails (although there is a recognition that this dominance is generally limited to the realms of

sports and entertainment). These experiences have the potential to effect societal change by engaging young people in critical conversations about language
and race (Low, 2007) and opening up a dialog about alternative conceptions of
authenticity (Pennycook, 2007). More significantly, the role of hip hop in promoting a kind of subjectivity of Blackness has become a global phenomenon.
As Michael Eric Dyson powerfully affirms in an interview, "America, and indeed
the globe, sees itself through the prism of Blackness" which has become a kind
of home for people around the world seeking "self-definition in the midst of a
global culture of flux" (Jones, 2006, p. 792). Hip Hop's global reach extends this
metaphorical home to a surging wave of culturally, ethnically, and linguistically
distinct young people who are tapping into its power to help them understand
themselve and their place in the world.

Acknowledgments

I would like to express my thanks to Renée Blake for generously providing me
with a videotape of the *Blaze* Battle and for insights into the language of rap
lyrics. I am also indebted to Samy Alim and Awad Ibrahim for their important
suggestions and comments on earlier drafts of this chapter as well as for the
important and inspiring work each has produced.

Notes

1. Back (1996) claims that although Hip Hop's following is multiracial and multicultural, the
dominant culture is Black.
2. The Blaze Battle Face-Off 2000 World Championship was broadcast on HBO on November
25th at 11:30 p.m. EST. The competing MCs were previous winners and runners up from the
Face-Off 2000 Tour. It is important to point out that as a highly commercialized event, the
Blaze Battle is qualitatively different from the spontaneous, informal battles that take place on
street corners and local Hip Hop clubs. It is impossible to know to what extent the final edit
was controlled and shaped by the producers.
3. Gumperz maintains that a given aspect of linguistic behavior (lexical, prosodic, phonological)
can function as a cue for interpreting what is said by a speaker. Contextualization cues hint
at relevant aspects of the social context (via particular codes, styles, and dialects), enabling
participants in a discourse to reason about their respective communicative intentions and
purposes (Gumperz, 1982, 1990). Goffman's related notion of footing (1981) refers to a speaker's
and hearer's shifting alignments in relation to the events at hand.
4. Most reviews of the film *Kids* focus on Telly's amoral sexual behavior—having unprotected sex
with virgins. A less explored aspect of Telly's skater persona is his adoption of Hip Hop style
both in his speech and his dress.
5. Smitherman (1994) defines "shine" as a derogatory reference to a Black male; the website http://
www.urbandictionary.com defines it as a "blow job" (oral sex),"jewelry," or "bling" in addition
to a number of other meanings.
6. Transcription Conventions: (( )) inaudible or questionable utterance; //laughs// = stage directions; Ø = copula absence; [rr] = hyper-rhotic postvocalic /r/; ALL CAPS = increased volume;
Bold text = feature or word pertinent to the analysis.
7. This is not meant to imply postvocalic /r/-lessness is a universal feature of Hip Hop speech style.
It is, however, commonly found in the speech of African American rappers in the Northeast
as well as among many young Whites who want to signal their affiliation with Hip Hop. In the
interview data I collected in New York City for my dissertation, I found rates of postvocalic
/r/-lessness that ranged from 0% to 82% among White Hip Hoppers (Cutler, 2002). Eyedea's

rate based on all the performance data in this battle was 8% (N = 64), suggesting that he can control this feature stylistically. His choice to adopt a hyper-rhotic realization of /r/ appears to be a way for him to emphasize his local (Minnesota) White identity.

8. Alim (personal communication) notes that Black MCs actually do make references to skin color, using terms such as *light-skinned*, *dark-skinned*, or *you Blacker than a*.... Crucially, when Black American rappers call each other "nigga" in an MC battle, it is not an insult.

9. Presumably this comparison refers to Mystikal's braided hairstyle.

10. D'Angelo (Michael D'Angelo Archer) is a successful R&B singer whose career peaked in the mid-1990s.

11. Alim's (2004) Black teenage informants offer further ethnographic evidence for the existence of this mentality in their stereotyping of Whites as "sick, insane, criminals."

References

Alim, S. (2005). *The Whitey voice: Linguistic variation, agency, and the discursive construction of Whiteness in a Black American barbershop*. Paper presented at New Ways of Analyzing Variation 34 Conference, New York University, New York.

Alim, S (2004). *You know my steez: An ethnographic and sociolinguistic study of styleshifting in a Black American speech community*. Durham, NC: Duke University Press.

Back, L. (1996). *New ethnicities and urban culture: Racisms and multiculture in young lives*. London: Routledge.

Beastie Boys, (2004). "*Right here right now.*" On to the 5 boroughs [LP]. New York: Capitol.

Boyd, T. (2002). *The new H.N.I.C. (Head Nigga in Charge): The death of civil rights and the reign of hip hop*. New York: New York University Press.

Bucholtz, M. (1995). From mulatta to mestiza. In K. Hall & M. Bucholtz (Eds.), *Gender articulated: Language and the socially constructed self* (pp. 351–374). New York: Routledge.

Clark, J. C. (2002). Maintaining class and ethnic borders in a North American high school. *Proceedings of II Simposio Internacional Bilingüismo*, 1525–1536. Retrieved May 1, 2006, from http://www.webs.uvigo.es/ssl/actas2002/08/01.%20John%20T.%20Clark.pdf

Cutler, C. (2002). *Crossing over: White youth, hip hop, and African American English*. Doctoral dissertation, New York University.

Du Bois, W. E. B. (1953). *The souls of Black folk*. New York: Blue Heron.

Eckert, P., & McConnell-Ginet, S.. (1992). Think practically and look locally: Language and gender as community-based practice. *Annual Review of Anthropology, 21*, 461–490.

Goffman, E. (1981). *Forms of talk*. Philadelphia: University of Pennsylvania Press.

Gumperz, J. (1982). *Discourse strategies*. Cambridge, UK: Cambridge University Press.

Gumperz, J. (1990). *Language and social reality*. Cambridge, UK: Cambridge University Press.

Hall, K. (1995). Lip service on the fantasy lines. In K. Hall & M. Bucholtz (Eds.), *Gender articulated: Language and the socially constructed self* (pp. 183–216). London: Routledge.

Home Box Office (Producer). (November 2, 2000). *Blaze-battle world championship*. [Television broadcast]. New York: HBO.

Irvine, J. (2004). *Losing one's footing: Stance in a colonial encounter*. Paper presented at the Sociolinguistics Symposium 15. Newcastle upon Tyne, U.K.

Jaffe, A. (2004). Stance in social and cultural context. Workshop abstract for the Sociolinguistics Symposium 15. Newcastle upon Tyne, U.K. Abstract retrieved from http://www.ncl.ac.uk/ss15/panels/panel_details.php?id=64

Jones, M. D.. (2006) An interview with Michael Eric Dyson. *Callaloo, 29*(3), 786–202.

Kennedy, R. (2002). *Nigger: The strange career of a troublesome word*. New York: Pantheon.

Lipsitz, G. (1995, September). The possessive investment in Whiteness: Racialized social democracy and the "White" problem in American studies. *American Quarterly, 47*(3), 369–387.

Low, B. (2007). Hip hop, language, and difference: The N-word as a pedagogical limit-case. *Journal of Language, Identity & Education, 6*(2), 147–160.

Lucas, G. (Producer), Lucas, G. (Director). (1977). *Star wars*. [Motion Picture]. U.S.A. Twentieth Century Fox.

Mitchell-Kernan, C. (1974). *Language behavior in a Black urban community* (Vol. 2). Berkeley, CA: University of California Press.

Morgan, M. (1993). Hip hop hooray! *The linguistic production of identity*. Paper presented at Annual Meeting of the American Anthropological Association, Washington, D.C.

Morgan, M. (1998). More than a mood or an attitude: Discourse and verbal genres in African American English. In S. Mufwene, J. R. Rickford, G. Bailey, & J. Baugh (Eds.), *African American English* (pp. 251–281). New York: Routledge.

Morgan, M. (2002). *Reading between the lines: Language, discourse and power in African American culture*. New York: Cambridge University Press.

Panzarella, P. (Producer), & Clark, L. (Director) (1995). *Kids*. [Motion Picture] U.S.A. Shining Excalibur Films.

Pennycook, A. (2007). Language, localization, and the real: Hip hop and the global spread of authenticity. *Journal of Language, Identity, and Education, 6*(2), 101.

Perry, I. (2004). *Prophets of the hood: politics and poetics in Hip Hop*. Chapel Hill, NC: Duke University Press.

Rahman, J. (2007). An ay for an ah: Language of survival in African American. *American Speech, 82*, 65–96.

Rebensdorf, A. (1996). Representing the real: Exploring appropriations of hip hop culture in the Internet and Nairobi. (Senior undergraduate thesis, Lewis and Clark University, 1996). Retrieved May 1, 2006, from http://www.lclark.edu/~soan/alicia/rebensdorf.101.html

Rickford, J. R., & Rickford, R. J. (2000). *Spoken soul: The story of Black English*. Hoboken, NJ: Wiley.

Rivera, R. (2003). *New York Ricans from the hip hop zone*. New York: MacMillan.

Smitherman, G. (1994). *Black talk: Words and phrases from the hood to the amen corner*. Boston: Houghton Mifflin.

Spears, A. (1998). Language use and so-called obscenity. In S. Mufwene et al. (Eds.), *African-American English* (226–250). New York: Routledge.

Urban Dictionary. (n.d.). Retrieved May 1, 2006, from: http://www.urbandictionary.com

From Da Bomb to *Bomba*
Global Hip Hop Nation Language in Tanzania

CHRISTINA HIGGINS

Introduction

At first glance, the English found in Tanzanian Hip Hop culture shares much in common with the variety of English conventionally known as African American English (AAE). Many linguistic elements associated with AAE occur in casual conversations and electronic communications, and they also appear frequently in Tanzanian Hip Hop music, teen magazines, and certain advertisements that target young consumers. AAE forms typically occur as language mixing and codeswitching with Swahili, but examples comprised entirely of English can also be found. Symbols of urban Hip Hop culture such as clothing (see Figure 5.1), musical styles, and references to African American Hip Hop icons in rap lyrics also point to a strong affiliation with African American Hip Hop culture. Therefore, interesting questions regarding authenticity and identity are raised about their linguistic practices when Tanzanians use varieties of English that seemingly draw on AAE. Are these youth *crossing* (Rampton, 1995) from Tanzanian varieties of English into AAE, borrowing the linguistic and semiotic styles of another culture? Or, are they *appropriating* what may be better described as Global Hip Hop Nation Language to fit their local East African context, their language use resulting in a simultaneously localized, yet global, form of expression, such as a *raplish* (Pennycook, 2003)?

Drawing on examples from youth columns, shout-outs, online bulletin board postings, and Hip Hop lyrics, this chapter investigates the types of English commonly used in expressions of Hip Hop culture among Tanzanians. Like many contributions in this volume, the examples analyzed here treat the study of Hip Hop as "dusty foot philosophy" (Pennycook & Mitchell, this volume) by exploring

Figure 5.1 Rappers Inspekta Haroun and Luteni Kalama of Magangwe Mobb in Kariakoo, Dar es Salaam in 2001. Reproduced with permission of Dr. Alex Perullo.

how global aspects of Hip Hop intermingle with instantiations of localness in specific contexts. While Pennycook and Mitchell's chapter calls attention to the cultural aspects of indigenous Hip Hop, the analysis here focuses on how Tanzanians manage global and local aspects of Hip Hop linguistically.

Specifically, I analyze how youth use language to perform *glocal* identities that are the result of the "tempering effects of local conditions on global pressures," characterized by the "simultaneity of both universalizing and particularizing tendencies" of African American culture and distinctly Tanzanian qualities (Robertson, 1997, n.p.). Taking up Pennycook and Mitchell's perspective, I move beyond a unidirectional analysis of global Hip Hop's influence on the local contexts of Tanzania, and I illustrate aspects of Tanzanian indigeneity that have produced localized Hip Hop language and culture. Within this two-way cultural flow, I show how Tanzanian youths perform a range of identities, as some draw on more local linguistic resources while others orient to more global frameworks in styling themselves as members of the Hip Hop nation.

Crossing or Appropriation?

Much of the research on the use of AAE among non-Black speakers in North America has shown that this usage is substantially different from the "real" AAE spoken by African Americans (Bucholtz, 1999, 2004; Cutler, 1999; Newman, 2005; Reyes, 2005; Wolfram, 1973). Questions about authenticity have led to comparisons between what Bucholtz (1999) calls Cross-Racial African American Vernacular English (CRAAVE) and the AAE of African Americans, as documented in Baugh (1983), Green (2002), Labov (1972), and Rickford (1999). These studies show that although CRAAVE speakers may express a desire to affiliate with African American culture, their lack of linguistic mastery in using AAE marks them as inauthentic. In spite of their implied desire to "sound Black," CRAAVE speakers typically display inconsistency in classic AAE features such as *r*-lessness, pitch, copula deletion, habitual *be*, and lexical items such as *aks* (ask). While a few case studies of non-Black but authentic AAE speakers have shown that is possible for such individuals to be legitimated as members of African American communities (e.g., Hatala, 1976; Sweetland, 2002), most CRAAVE speakers are not insiders in such communities, and many have little or no social contact with African Americans (e.g., Cutler, 1999). Consequently, most CRAAVE speakers' behavior is best described as *crossing* (Rampton, 1995); that is, "code alternation by people who are not accepted members of the group associated with the second language they employ. [Crossing] is concerned with switching into languages that are not generally thought to belong to you...[and] in which there is a distinct sense of movement across social or ethnic boundaries" (p. 280).

Of course, whether crossing leads to inauthenticity or not depends on the interpretation of the linguistic performance by members of situated linguistic communities. Among African Americans, Tanzanians who use terms like *nigga* as a way to refer to their friends may well come off as inauthentic poseurs. However, Tanzanian youths who are greeting one another in shout-outs, or who are attending a rap concert in Dar es Salaam, use this same word to establish a claim to a particular Tanzanian identity. Therefore, speakers can be seen as fashioning selves through language by styling themselves as the other (Rampton, 1999) in order to achieve a particular local identity. Tanzanian youth who import AAE to fashion themselves are therefore creating cosmopolitan, yet very Tanzanian, identities by associating themselves with outside elements. In this view, the use of historically AAE forms among Tanzanians may better be understood as a form of *appropriation* (Ashcroft, Griffiths, & Tiffin, 1989) in which local and global forces intermingle, producing hybrid forms of a new local (and global) order.

Local Identities and the (Imagined) Hip Hop Nation

In his study of urban youth in England, Rampton (1995) found that non-Black youth in England who employ Afro-Caribbean Creole in their daily speech are sometimes treated as speakers of a multiracial youth code.[1] Similarly, in taking up linguistic forms and cultural references associated with street conscious urban African American culture, crossing into AAE can be seen as a means of claiming membership in a multiracial, multinational Global Hip Hop Nation (GHHN) (Alim, 2003, 2004, 2006, this volume), a transcultural, multilingual, and multiracial community. In many ways, the GHHN is an *imagined community* (Anderson, 1991) because of its sheer size: "The members of even the smallest nation will never know most of their fellow-members, meet them, or even hear of them, yet in the minds of each lives the image of their communion" (p. 6). For those with access, the Internet and other forms of globalized media such as MTV have also greatly increased the realness of this nation for youth as well. In Dar es Salaam, Hip Hop fans follow the details of American rapper 50 Cent's career to the same degree as young people in New York, Lagos, and London. Whether or not this community is "real" or "imagined" does not seem so salient in the end; instead, these youths' identities reflect a poststructuralist understanding of *authenticity* as a discursive accomplishment, rather than as a preexisting quality inherent in any individual speaker (Coupland, 2003). As Anderson writes, "Communities are to be distinguished, not by their falsity/genuineness, but by the style in which they are imagined" (1991, p. 6).

Hip Hop Nation Language

In his discussion of Hip Hop Nation Language (HHNL) among African American artists, Alim (2003) identifies HHNL as the linguistic expression of a street conscious identity that offers speakers a way to "connect with the streets as a space of culture, creativity, cognition and consciousness" (p. 54). Alim explains that HHNL includes all of the features of AAE, but HHNL employs these features with much greater frequency. To illustrate these ideas, Alim presents data from his interview with Juvenile, a well-known African American Hip Hop artist. Alim found copula absence to occur at a rate of 56.60% in the interview, while it rose to 75% in an analysis of lyrics from one of Juvenile's full-length CDs. Similarly, in an analysis of African American Hip Hop artist Eve's copula usage, Alim found absences of the linking verb at the rate of 5.95% in her interview, but in her lyrics, the rate climbed to 56.70%. Alim explains that the increase in copula absence and other classic features of AAE are "the strategic construction of a street conscious identity" through which the artists "claim authenticity as members of the HHN through performing their own street credibility" (2003, p. 51). Similar findings have been reported by Edwards and Ash (2004) in their analysis of Tupac Shakur's rhymes.

As the chapters of this volume illustrate, HHNL has expanded far beyond the dominion of African American Hip Hop artists in the United States. Alim (2004) notes that HHNL "is widely spoken across the country, and used/borrowed and adapted/transformed by various ethnic groups inside and outside the US" (p. 394). Speakers of what may better be termed *global* HNNL (GHNNL) include

Anglo and Asian youth in North America and Britain who style themselves using AAE (Bucholtz, 1999, 2004; Cutler, 1999; Rampton, 1995; Reyes, 2005), as well as African immigrants and Puerto Rican newcomers who learn (B)ESL, rather than the English typically associated with the Anglo middle class (Goldstein, 1987; Ibrahim, 2003; Wolfram, 1973). Beyond North America and Britain, musical artists in Turkey (Solomon, 2005), Japan (Pennycook, 2003) and South Korea (Lee, 2004) use their own versions of GHHNL in their musical performances, some of which differ from the HHNL used in the United States. Mitchell (2001) provides an international array of varieties in hybrid codes introduce new forms of locally situated content to the genre, as illustrated by Islamic rap in the U.K. and France, and rap used for political dissent in Mainland China.

Localized versions of GHHNL have also been reported in African nations such as Tanzania and Malawi (Perullo & Fenn, 2003), Nigeria (Omoniyi, 2006), and South Africa (Steingo, 2005). These studies reveal a high degree of linguistic, cultural, and musical hybridity involving local languages alongside global tropes of AAE such as *yo* and rap aliases involving acronyms similar to Chuck D and MC Lyte. Importantly, these studies reveal a strong claim to membership in a GHHN alongside established Hip Hop artists from the the United States. Coming from sub-Saharan African artists, this claim is particularly interesting for questions of authenticity because of the historically racialized nature of Hip Hop and the use of terms such as *wangster, wigger,* and *wannabe* (Kitwana, 2005). It might be the case that race and language become reunited when Black Africans use it; on the other hand, African artists may also be treated as wannabes by their African American counterparts, in spite of their skin color.

Language in Tanzania

The interpretation of GHHNL in Tanzania is complex because of the historically ideological relationship with standard varieties of (British) English. Previously ruled by the Germans, Tanzania (then Tanganyika) was handed over to the British in 1919 as a mandate territory under the League of Nations. Since independence from Britain in 1961, Tanzania has shifted from socialism, economic autonomy, and a language policy designed to bolster Swahili to capitalism, economic liberalization, and institutionalized Swahili-English bilingualism (Blommaert, 1999, pp. 93–98). Swahili officially became a national language in 1967 under the rule of Julius Nyerere, the first president after independence. Nyerere championed the use of Swahili in education, arguing that it was a transmitter for Tanzanian and Pan-Africanist values. Since the 1980s, however, the political economy of English has been steadily growing stronger and currently, English is seen as one of the primary means for achieving success in a globalizing world. This view is especially strong among many Tanzanians who have witnessed structural adjustment programs and the liberalization of the economy (Blommaert, 1999; Higgins, 2004; Neke, 2003; Vavrus, 2002). Increasing reliance on aid from Western donors has required the Tanzanian government to privatize its many previously government run industries, and these economic transformations have increased the perceived importance of English as a tool for success.

English is seen as a link to global opportunity, and standard (British) English remains the idealized medium of instruction in schools; however, it is more often the case that English is used in hybridized and localized ways in Dar es Salaam, rather than in globally comprehensible forms. The variety of language labeled *Kihuni* (tough talk) by Blommaert (1999, 2005) provides a clear example of such localization in Tanzania, as it is a street variety of English-interfered Swahili that involves a great deal of relexification, borrowings, and language play. Kihuni is the sociolect of Swahili spoken by self-ascribed *wahuni* (hooligans, gangsters), living in Dar es Salaam who are largely frustrated with their marginalized positions in the world and who generally lack economic opportunities in their lives. Blommaert (2005) explains that the linguistic development of Kihuni began in the context of Swahili Hip Hop culture, but was to some degree "superimposed by transnational (but essentially African American) 'Gangsta' culture notably focused on international stars such as Tupac" (2005, p. 406). He proposes that Kihuni allows the wahuni to imagine themselves in another space: "it is a repertoire that allows them to 'get out' of Dar es Salaam culturally, to culturally relocate their local environments in a global semiotics of class, status, blackness, marginalization" (p. 408). Blommaert's discussion of this cultural relocation is tinged with tones of disempowerment, for he describes Kihuni and other varieties of Tanzanian English as having limited relevance since they are linguistic codes that "do not count as 'English' as soon as translocal norms are imposed on them" (p. 410). Illustrations of Kihuni appear in Table 5.1.

Kihuni is comparable to *lugha ya mitaani* (street language) a term used by Tanzanians to refer to nonstandard Swahili. In their comprehensive sociolinguistic description and 1100-word dictionary of *lugha ya mitaani* (LyM), Reuster-Jahn and Kießling (2006) make it clear that LyM should not be understood as a variety of English or as a mixed language based on English, even though it is characterized by many appropriations of English idiomatic expressions. They explain that LyM is a sociolect used among youth and is "part of a threefold paradigmatic relationship" in relation to Standard Swahili and English (2006, p. 68). LyM is characterized by unmarked switches between English and Swahili, violations of the grammatical norms of Swahili and English, and semantic shifts which make it difficult for English or standard Swahili speakers to follow. Given

Table 5.1 Examples of Kihuni (from Blommaert, 2005, pp. 406-407)

a. *kukipa*	to leave, to take off (< Standard Swahili 'ku' (infinitive), 'to keep')
b. *macho balbu*	eyes wide open in amazement or fear (Standard Swahili macho 'eyes' and balbu< '[light] bulb')
c. *unga*	cocaine (< Standard Swahili *unga*, 'maize flour')
d. *kupiga bao*	to have sex (< Standard Swahili *kupiga bao*, 'to overtake a vehicle')
e. *mwela:*	police (<Maasai)

its similarities with Kihuni, I will use the umbrella term *street Swahili* to refer to both LyM and Kihuni.

In the next section, I extend Blommaert's discussion of the value of localized languages by examining the glocal elements of GHHNL as it has emerged in Tanzania. Even though Reuster-Jahn and Kießling (2006) are careful to distinguish street Swahili from varieties of English, the data below reveal that in domains strongly oriented to Hip Hop, street Swahili appears alongside English, unmarked mixed and codeswitched forms, and Tanzanian appropriations of AAE. In other words, the data demonstrate (at least) a four-way paradigmatic relationship for language users. In my discussion, I first illustrate how Tanzanian youth reveal imagined connections to the GHHN in locally published shout-outs, nearly all of which are produced in 'errorful' AAE. Next, I examine advertisements which exploit popular music and Internet billboards which discuss popular music to show how GHHNL becomes localized and (re)entextualized through the juxtaposition of AAE, street Swahili, and African American cultural references. Finally, I examine Hip Hop lyrics recorded by Tanzanians that show a high degree of global identification.

Imagining the Hip Hop Nation in Tanzania

Shout-Outs

Shout-outs are a popular form of public communication among young people in Tanzania that appear in daily newspapers. In a typical shout-out, the contributor provides a passport-sized photo, an initial greeting, several sentences about herself or himself, a listing of favorite musical artists, and a message that she or he would like to share with the readers. In the past several years, shout-outs have increasingly been sent to newspapers as text messages via cell phones. The vast majority of contributors are male. Illustrative examples in (1) are taken from newspapers I collected between 2001 and 2005. Street Swahili is in bold italics, standard Swahili appears in italics, and all original spellings and punctuation conventions are preserved.

(1) Shout-outs in Tanzanian newspapers
  (a) ***Kisa Kisangweli*** (**'hey/wassup'**)! all da niggaz in da globe. Ma'
    name
    Is E_____ M_____ a.k.a. 'Eddy'. Born 22 yrz ago. Ma'
    Hobbies are studying an' cultivating small gardens an'
    Listening 2 music. Ma' favourite artistes are Toni
    Braxton, Celine Dion, Mariah Carey an P'Diddy.
    DEDICATIONS: I'd like to dedicate da' song "Ma
    Heart Will Go On" by Celine Dion to ma' lovely daddy
    of Iringa, [6 more names listed].
    MESSAGE: Don do anything b'coz ya friend has done.

(b) How life is it all ladies an' gents around da world.
Ma' name is J_____ K_____ alias 'Figo'. Born one
Decade an' eight yrs went off. Ma' hobbies are playing
Basketball, football an' listenin' 2 music. Ma' best
Artistes are Joe, R. Kelly, Lady JD, EPMD an' Outkast.
DEDICATIONS: I'd like to dedicate da' song "I Believe
In U" by Joe Thomas to [5 names listed]. Also da song "Rise"
by Gabrielle to ma' friend [name listed].
MESSAGE: Education first. Beware of AIDS, it will kill ya men!

(c) HEY! Niggaz an' ladies! Ma' name is V____ M_____
a.k.a. 'Black Vam'. Ma' hobbies are working hard, exchangin'
ideas, reading novels an' listening 2 music. Ma' best entertainers
are Joe Thomas, Celine Dion, Boyz II Men an' R Kelly.
DEDICATIONS: I'd like to dedicate da' song *"Jiwe
Walilolikataa Waashi"* by Kibasa G to [3 names listed]. An' also da
Song "Stutter" by Joe Thomas 2 [4 names listed].
MESSAGE: Golden chance never come twice.

The first shout-out targets "all da niggaz in da globe," the second aims at "all ladies an' gents around da world," and the third greets "niggaz an' ladies!" These greetings are very representative of the many dedications published in Tanzanian newspapers. Here, the contributors are invoking an imagined global community of readers in a weekly magazine whose circulation is limited to East Africa. The use of *"Kisa Kisangweli"* in (a) identifies the readers as street Swahili speakers; however, because this Swahili-medium greeting is written as part of a GHHNL discursive practice (shout-outs) and is juxtaposed with GHHNL features, the greeting becomes *(re)entextualized* (Bauman & Briggs, 1990; Blommaert, 2005; Silverstein & Urban, 1996) here as a hybrid form of global street consciousness. In the process of (re)entextualization, the contributors "take some fragment of discourse and quote it anew, making it seem to carry a meaning independent of its situation within two now distinct co(n)texts" (Silverstein & Urban 1996, p. 2). Conversely, the AAE features are (re)entextualized as local by virtue of the street Swahili, and through their juxtaposition with references to local practices such as cultivating small gardens and listening to Tanzanian artists such as Lady JD and Kibasa G.

Linguistically, membership in the GHHN is claimed through frequent use of AAE forms, including the positive use of the word *niggaz* (friends) and the orthographic representation of consonant cluster deletion in "listenin'," "an'," and "don'," as well as the use of "da" (for Standard English "the") and "ma" (for Standard English "my"). While these features do occur in AAE, a survey of 24 shout-outs reveals highly formulaic language; moreover, the shout-outs are lacking in several important features of AAE including copula absence, habitual *be*, resultative *done*, and multiple negation. Because the shout-outs are submitted on a preprinted form, it is likely that the formulaic quality is due to the fact that the contributors copy existing models while filling out the forms.

If we move along the spectrum toward higher degrees of localization, other shout-outs that are received in the form of text messages and then published by newspapers exhibit more street Swahili. The result is an indexing of street conscious Swahili with street conscious AAE. Example (d), published in 2005, illustrates the resultant new form of HHNL; the words in bold print are street Swahili vocabulary.

(d) *Whatzzup **Mchizi** Mox?*   Wassup **Mchizi** Mox?
    ***Shalotina tina** mzee.*   Everything's **alright**, friend.
    Mambo yako ya Tucheze   Your activities of [the bands] Tucheze
    na Klynn yametulia   and K Lynn have slowed down
    ***kinoma** babu kamua basi*   **a lot** friend, squeeze out already
    *albam **masela**. Tunaisubiri*   the album, **homies**. We are awaiting
    kwa hamu   with eagerness

It is important to recognize the very local street conscious qualities of the bolded words in the original text. The message is a shout-out to Mchizi Mox, a Hip Hop artist whose name contains the street Swahili "*mchizi*" ('fool'). Though it started out as a vocabulary item used among streetwise, typically poor youth, *mchizi* is now well known to Tanzanians of various backgrounds as "silly" or "foolish." Both "*kinoma*" (literally 'in a bad way,' i.e., 'a lot') and "*masela*" (< sailor), meaning 'homies'[2] are somewhat more established as street Swahili, and are often understood by nonstreet Swahili speakers, though not typically used by them. The phrase "*shalotina tina*" ('alright') is relatively new usage in Dar es Salaam, and is apparently not derived from English. In interviews I carried out with five college educated Tanzanians over the age of 40 in 2006, no one knew the meaning of this term.

As the examples above indicate, a strong affiliation between the linguistic forms used and a Black racial identity are rare. The only examples are the GHHN term *niggaz*, used in (1a) and (1c), and the nickname provided by "Black Nam" in (1c). Here, Blackness appears heightened for a young man whose race is typically treated as irrelevant in his local context. This particular example shows how one particular youth makes use of a transcultural resource (the notion of Black as minority) to fashion a local identity. As Bucholtz (1999) suggests, gender may also play a role here since Hip Hop is often ideologically connected to masculinity and Blackness.[3]

Advertisements

The indexicality of street Swahili and Hip Hop culture emanating from the United States is apparent in advertisements aimed at urban youth as well. In a 2005 advertisement for ring tones that can be downloaded to cell phones, standard

Swahili, street Swahili, and the name of a popular rapper from the United States, 50 Cent, become fused into a single context.

(2) Ring tone advertisement that indexes street Swahili with Hip Hop

Pata mlio	Get a ring(tone)
bomba	**awesome/da bomb**
wa simu wa	of the phone of
50 Cent	50 Cent
*na mingine **kibao** kutoka Buzz!*	and **many** other (ringtones) from Buzz!

Here, the street Swahili forms "*bomba*" ('awesome') and "*kibao*" ('many') are relatively well-known forms of street Swahili, though interviews with well-educated adults often revealed that their usage was limited to more streetwise speakers. The word *bomba* was originally a borrowing from Portuguese *bomba* ('pump'), but it is quite possible that the AAE turn of phrase, *da bomb* ('the best') is having an impact on the semantics of this word for GHHNL speakers. The usage of this word offers an example of what Pennycook and Mitchell (this volume) describe as the multiple and copresent origins of Hip Hop language. Rather than appropriating an English word for the Tanzanian context, it may be the case that a Swahili word (albeit of borrowed origin) is being appropriated for the local Hip Hop context.

Newspaper Columns

Varieties of street conscious Swahili which contain a mix of African American HHNL and localized HHNL appear in special columns of daily and weekly newspapers and magazines as well. The otherwise-mainstream daily paper *Mwananchi* publishes a weekly column titled *Kijiwe Shega*, ('the cool street corner'), a title comprised entirely of street Swahili. On one occasion, the column's headline was "*Sugu angalia masoja wanakumaindi?*" The title alone would mystify many non-street Swahili speakers since "*Sugu*" is one of several aliases for Tanzanian rapper Joseph Mbilinyi (a.k.a. Mr. II, 2 Proud), and only Hip Hop aficionados would have the requisite Hip Hop literacy to decipher the headline. Here, "*masoja*" (<soldier, with Swahili plural marker *ma-*) refers to other (Tanzanian) artists; for those with ties to the GHHN, it recalls the use of the word *soldier* in many American Hip Hop lyrics, including those in Master P's (1998) compilation *No limit soldiers* and more recently in 50 Cent's 2006 single "Soldier."

The final word of the title, "*wanaku<u>maindi</u>*," employs the historically British English "mind" inside of Swahili morphology ('Are they minding you?'), but now with a semantic shift to "are they liking/respecting you?" in street Swahili usage. In short, the column, published in 2001, was about whether or not Sugu's fellow rappers were giving him the respect he deserved. Respect is an aspect of AAE that has been studied as a discursive phenomenon with unique importance among African Americans (e.g., Abrahams, 1975), and it is a common theme in American Hip Hop music as well, as exemplified in many song titles such as "Respect" by Notorious B.I.G (1994), "Respect" by Fabolous (2003), and most recently in the titles of Missy Elliot's 2006 album and Hip Hop-inspired clothing line, both called *Respect ME*. The body of the column contains many similar forms (in bold type) that demand a high street Swahili literacy level for comprehension. While I recognize that the choice to translate street Swahili into AAE misrepresents the very hybrid and situated language practices that I am analyzing here, my translations are motivated by suggestions made by consultation with East African sociolinguists and by the indexicalities that are achieved between street Swahili, GHHNL, and Hip Hop cultural references.[4]

(3) Youth column: **Kijiwe Shega** ('cool streetcorner')
    "*Sugu* angalia *ma-soja*   wa-na-ku-*maindi?*"
    Mr. II look.at **pl-soldier** they-pres-you-**mind**
    'Mr. II, are the other **rappers** giving you **respect?**'

    Ai nou ma-chizi wangu hapo *ki-stoni*   lazima   m-ta-kuwa
    m-me-bayi
    I **know pl-cheesy** my   here   **dim-ston**e   necessary you-will-have
    you-have-buy
    '**I know my dawgs** here in the **hood** that you will have bought'

    pepa la Mwananchi ili   *m-ki-cheki ki-jiwe*   chenu. No plobl-
    emu.
    paper of Mwananchi in.order you-if-**check dim-stone** your   no prob-
    lem
    'Mwananchi in order to **check out** your **hood**. No problem.'

Like other youth columns, *Kijiwe Shega* makes use of specialized street Swahili orthography through spelling conventions that make English words appear Swahili, as in "*Ai nou*" (I know) and "*No ploblemu*" (No problem). Furthermore, well-known street Swahili words such as *kijiwe* (literally "small stone," meant to refer to the street corners where jobless youth congregate) are "translated" into more hybrid street Swahili forms such as "*kistoni*," utilizing the English "stone," and thereby increasing their opacity for the uninitiated.

Internet Billboards

Not surprisingly, the Internet also provides a rich array of appropriated forms, especially on sites related to popular music such as http://www.Darhotwire.com, a website maintained in Dar es Salaam. On the site is *Darhotboards*, a service that allows people to post a topic and respond to others using threaded messages which often incorporate a great deal of HHNL. While some can be viewed as a straightforward mimicry of AAE, other examples employ standard Swahili and street Swahili in more localized manners. On one hotboard posted in April of 2006, the initial posting looks a lot like AAE (all spellings, capitalizations, and emoticons are preserved):

(4) Darhotboard Postings
    (a) Yes! Yes! ama abt To Get ya Heads Spininin wit some Swahili Rap Trackz up in this Thread…. Trackz that u never heard b4… the good
        thing is: U can even request the track 🎧 Praise if u down wit this…

Here, in addition to the abbreviated and specialized language used for Internet and text messaging, we also see pronunciations representing AAE such as "ama" (I'm). This is a representation of AAE that is used in a very localized way, however, since "ama" in the AAE context would be the equivalent to "I'm gonna," and hence would not be followed by "abt" (about). Other approximations of AAE here are the deletion of auxiliary verb *have* in "Trackz that u never heard b4," the use of 'z' to mark plurals, and the representation of AAE consonant substitution as in 't' for 'th' in "wit." Follow-up postings reveal even more localization.

    (b) Yo!!!!! A_____ can I get this songs:
        "Mauza Uza" GANGWE MOBB
        "Hukumu Ya Ndotoni" USO WA MBUZI
        "Ana Miaka ya Chini 18" 2 PROUD a.k.a. Mr 2 a.k.a. SUGU
        "Shadow of Dark Destiny's" HASHIM DOGO
        "The Sickers" CHENTO
        mimi hizi ni classic za **bongo**
        amma try to remember some otha cuts, **bongo** Hip Hop has been played out nowadays no
        f**kin' grimy a** joints like back in the days nah' mean ☹?

        Yo!!!!! A_____ can I get this songs:
        "Illusions" GANGWE MOBB
        "Wisdom of a dream" USO WA MBUZI ('face of a goat')
        "She's younger than 18" 2 PROUD a.k.a. Mr 2 a.k.a. SUGU
        "Shadow of Dark Destiny's" HASHIM DOGO
        "The Sickers" CHENTO
        To me these are classic **bongo** ('Dar es Salaam') songs
        amma try to remember some otha cuts, **bongo** Hip Hop has been played out nowadays no
        f**kin' grimy a** joints like back in the days nah' mean ☹?

In (b), though AAE predominates, as in "yo, amma, otha, played out, grimy," and "nah' mean," English-interfered Swahili (e.g., "*mimi hizi ni* classic *za **bongo***) is also used to express opinions about which Tanzanian songs are worthwhile.

Another follow-up posting (c) contains switches from Standard Swahili to abbreviated Internet Swahili (e.g., "*E bwa*" < *eh bwana* 'hey friend'),[5] to approximations of AAE, as in "let me start lil' som' like dis." Also included is some lesser known street Swahili, "*mukide kino*" ("all good," or "all gravy").

> (c) *sawa sawa Mkubwa! E bwa mi list yangu kubwa kwa hiyo nitakupa kila ninapo kumbuka;*
> let me start lil' som' like dis;
> *Wagumu Weusi Asilia* --> *kama unayo tha whole album itakuwa **mukide kino . . . !***
>
> ———————————————————————————
>
> okay okay big-one! Hey bwana (friend), my list is long, so I will give you
> each that I remember;
> let me start lil' som' like dis'
> Wagumu Weusi Asilia (album name) --> if you have tha whole album it will be
> **really all good**

The final posting continues the practice of blending AAE with street Swahili and references to youth culture to produce a claim to GHHN membership. In (d), we see the traditionally AAE use of "props" in combination with Standard Swahili (in regular italics), street Swahili (in bold italics), and a reference to a unified youth culture, signified here through "*moja!!*" (one), appearing as "*pamoja!*" (together) at other times, as reflected in (e). This use of *moja* or *pamoja* to sign off has the same function as the AAE use of 'one' in shout-outs produced in the United States. In Tanzania, this sign-off has another possible (and copresent) origin as an echo from the socialist period of independent Tanzania, in the slogan "*Twende Pamoja!*" ("Let's do it together"), often used to encourage cooperative social welfare projects.

> (d) *halafu props sana kwa kuanika ile link ya kwanza, , , naona yamenikuta iko nusu lakini dah!! **Fresh** tu!! Tupe vitu mwenetu!! **masela** wako **vagalanti**!!!moja!!*
>
> ———————————————————————————
>
> so a lot of props for posting that first link, , , I think
> I had already seen half of them but, dah!! It's **fresh**!! Give us more our friends!!
> your **vigilante gangstas**!!! One!!

(e) *Kuna Jamaa hawaachi Kunipigia simu Hapa wanataka Ni-stop hii kitu...*
Pamoja!

There are people who wont' stop calling me here, they want me to stop this thing (uploading music).... **Together!**

Hip Hop Lyrics

Finally, I provide a few examples of Hip Hop lyrics produced by Tanzanian artists to illustrate how artists localize Swahili rap while claiming membership in the GHHN. First is a stanza from King Crazy GK, featuring East Coast Team, a group whose name is strongly associated with the rap aliases common in the GHHN. The use of "Crazy" as part of the name relates to the AAE usage "silly, fun, wack"; it is no coincidence that an African American rap artist named Krazy exists. The featured group, East Coast Team, creates a globalized indexical tie to the much-publicized tension between the East Coast and West Coast Hip Hop scenes in the United States. As Tanzania is on the East Coast of Africa, this reference is another example of the double identification of Hip Hop pointed out by Pennycook and Mitchell (this volume), and it compares well with Wire MC's double identification of Hip Hop as both African American and as part of Australia's local relations of racial discrimination. Other aspects of the lyrics establish strongly singular identifications with Hip Hop as an American phenomenon, however. In the examples below, underlining is used to mark linguistic and cultural references that are only indexical in the United States (e.g., dialing 9-1-1 will not connect to the police in Tanzania).

(5) Tanzanian Hip Hop lyrics
   (a) <u>King Crazy GK feat.</u> *East Coast Team* "Ama Zao ama Zangu" ('Theirs or mine')

Amiri Jeshi Mkuu sasa naitangaza vita	As an Army commander now, I order a war,
sio ile kuu ya tatu	not the third world war
bali hii ni ya <u>kivietnam</u> yaani mtaa	rather, this is like <u>Vietnam</u>, meaning, street
kwa mtaa	by street
mmoja mmoja nawakamateni afu	one by one, I capture (fans) and then
nazaa nanyi	breed more
utaponiona ita <u>polisi 911</u>	when you see me, call the <u>police at 9-1-1,</u>
la sivyo	otherwise
jua umekwisha	realize that it's over

watoto wa mama siku hizi	children of today,
mnachonga sana	you all think too much of yourselves
yaani nyimbo moja	in other words, if you get one song
hewani	on the air,
mkisifiwa mnajiona wakina <u>P-Diddy</u>	you are praised as if you were <u>P-Diddy</u>

King Crazy GK's cultural references are oriented to African American Hip Hop while his language is mostly standard Swahili, and hence arguably local. Other Hip Hop artists such as Ngwair use AAE references in ways that are also arguably local due to their Tanzanianized forms. In "She Gotta Gwan," the song title alone evokes the AAE expression "She got it goin on," referring to a young woman's physical attractiveness. Ngwair's song title is "inaccurate" as AAE because of its spelling and implied pronunciation, but it carries a great amount of cultural capital in the Tanzanian context. In fact, as of April 2006, it had been one of the top 10 singles for longer than a year. Also of note is Ngwair's use of "*masista*" ("sister" with Swahili plural marker *ma-*). Similarly to the example of "*bomba*" and "da bomb" discussed above, *sista* has experienced several semantic shifts in Tanzania. While *sista* originally came into Swahili as an English borrowing to refer to a nun, it has since shifted among the general population to refer to a young woman. More recently, its meaning has narrowed even further in the form of *sista du*[6] among young males who use it to mark their street credibility and GHHN membership.

(b) *Ngwair, "She Gotta Gwan"* ('She got it goin on')

Tukianzia uzuri tu she gotta gwan	If we start with the best, she got it goin on
Tabia, heshima ndio duh she gotta gwan	Personality, respect, yes, she got it goin on
*Mpaka kwa **masista du** yeeh*	Of all the sisters yeah
nabaki tu kusema	I still say
uuh she gotta gwan	uhh she got it goin on

Conclusion

Within the domain of Hip Hop in Tanzania, the mixing of street Swahili with AAE and other language varieties creates opportunities for the performance of indigeneity alongside transglobal identification. Language in this domain appears to create a largely empowering relationship between the local and the global due to the indexical ties with an (imagined) GHHN. Rather than identifying themselves as marginalized, or as inauthentic wannabes, youths who style themselves by making use of these codes are not (only) trying to escape their marginalized positions, as described by Blommaert (2005). Rather, it seems that they are redefining their local environments in transcultural terms associated with the cultural capital of global Hip Hop, and at least some of the time, they are using mostly local linguistic resources to fashion themselves for this imagined yet locally salient context. In this regard, then, they are no different from other such youth around the world who do the same, including privileged, White teenagers, such as Mike in Cutler's (1999) study, and Asif and Kazim, South Asian teens in Rampton's (1995) study who use Afro-Caribbean Creole in the South of England. Of course, pervasive socioeconomic divisions in Tanzania between the small middle class and the large number of the poor raise a number of issues to address in future examinations of HHNL in Tanzania (and elsewhere), including how access to the Internet, cell phones, and other media regulate the flow of global Hip Hop among consumers and performers and how the economic opportunities associated with Hip Hop in Tanzania affect the linguistic and cultural forms of HHNL.

It is not surprising that young people in many contexts around the world are turning to transcultural resources in the 21st century to style themselves, especially in view of the increased consolidation of global media and the effects of economic liberalization all over the world. Transcultural elements are increasingly present in Tanzania year after year: MTV is now available on Tanzanian cable networks, and in 2006, American Hip Hop artists Ja Rule and Jay-Z gave concerts in Dar es Salaam. The flow has started to trickle in the opposite direction as well. Tanzanian rappers such as Xplastaz, a group that incorporates Masaai lyrics and dancing into their music, have traveled to Europe frequently to record music and perform with other Hip Hop artists from around the world, and events such as B-Connected, an annual concert involving Tanzania and four other countries, offers global connections among Hip Hop artists and audiences. If the trends in Tanzania are any indication of what is to come, what started off as an imagined community loosely bound by a common interest in music and a common language will likely evolve into a much more tightly interconnected global Hip Hop culture.

Notes

1. Sebba and Tate (2002) discuss a parallel phenomenon involving Afro-Caribbean Creole, which has global capital partly due to the worldwide popularity of reggae.
2. My translation of "*masela*" as "homies" is partly motivated by the dictionary of Swahili slang on http://www.darhotwire.com, a popular website based in Dar es Salaam that hosts Tanzanian music videos, song lyrics, gossip, chatrooms, and more.
3. Based on the photos and names published in the shout-outs, all participants were male. Very few female Hip Hop artists have produced albums in Tanzania, so I focus on lyrics composed by male artists only.
4. I am grateful for suggestions made by Mungai Mutonya and Mokaya Bosire at the Annual Conference on African Linguistics in Eugene, Oregon in 2006.
5. An anonymous reviewer suggested that *bwa* could also translate as "dawg" given its alternative reading as a shortened version of *mbwa* (dog).

6. *Sista* is a term widely considered to show respect for women. The addition of the Swahili particle *du* alters the meaning of *sista* to something more like street Swahili *demu* (<dame), a term widely recognized as lacking respect for young women (similar to "'chick" or "broad").

References

Abrahams, R. D. (1975). Negotiating respect: Patterns of presentation among Black women. *Journal of Folklore, 88,* 58–80.

Alim, H. S. (2003). "We are the streets": African-American language and the strategic construction of a street conscious identity. In S. Makoni, G. Smitherman, A. F. Ball, & A. K. Spears (Eds.) *Black linguistics: Language, society and politics in African and the Americas* (pp. 40–59). London: Routledge.

Alim, H. S. (2004). Hip hop nation language. In E. Finegan & J. R. Rickford, (Eds.), *Language in the USA: Themes for the twenty-first century* (pp. 387–409). Cambridge, UK: Cambridge University Press.

Alim, H. S. (2006). *Roc the mic right: The language of hip hop culture.* New York: Routledge.

Anderson, B. (1991). *Imagined communities: Reflections on the origin and spread of nationalism* (rev. ed.). London: Verso.

Ashcroft, B., Griffiths, G., & Tiffin, H. (1989). *The empire writes back: Theory and practice in post-colonial literature.* New York: Routledge.

Baugh, J. (1983). *Black street speech: Its history, structure, and survival.* Austin: University of Texas Press.

Bauman, R., & Briggs, C. (1990). Poetics and performance as critical perspectives on language and social life. *Annual Review of Anthropology, 19,* 59–88.

Blommaert, J. (1999). *State ideology and language in Tanzania.* Koln: Koppe.

Blommaert, J. (2005). Situating language rights: English and Swahili in Tanzania revisited. *Journal of Sociolinguistics, 9,* 390–417.

Bucholtz, M. (1999). You da man: Narrating the racial other in the production of white masculinity. *Journal of Sociolinguistics, 3/4,* 443–460.

Bucholtz, M. (2004). Styles and stereotypes: The linguistic negotiation of identity among Laotian American youth. *Pragmatics, 14,* 127–147.

Coupland, N. (2003). Sociolinguistic authenticities. *Journal of Sociolinguistics, 7,* 417–431.

Cutler, C. (1999). Yorkville crossing: White teens, hip hop and African American English. *Journal of Sociolinguistics, 3,* 428–442.

Edwards, W. F., & Ash, L. (2004). AAVE features in the lyrics of Tupac Shakur: The notion of "realness." *Word, 55,* 165–178.

Goldstein, L. (1987). Standard English: The only target for nonnative speakers of English? *TESOL Quarterly, 21,* 417–436.

Green, L. (2002). *African American English: A linguistic introduction.* Cambridge, UK: Cambridge University Press.

Hatala, E. (1976). Environmental effects on white students in black schools. Unpublished master's essay, University of Pennsylvania.

Higgins, C. (2004). Swahili-English bilingual conversation: A vehicle for the study of language ideology. Unpublished doctoral dissertation, University of Wisconsin-Madison.

Ibrahim, A. (2003). "Whassup, homeboy?" Joining the African diaspora: Black English as a symbolic site of identification and language learning. In S. Makoni, G. Smitherman, A. Ball, & A. Spears (Eds.) *Black linguistics: Language, society and politics in Africa and the Americas* (pp. 169–185). London: Routledge.

Kitwana, B. (2005). *Why White kids love hip hop: Wangsters, wiggers, wannabes, and the new reality of race in America.* New York: Basic Civitas.

Labov, W. (1972). *Language and the inner city: Studies in the Black English vernacular.* Philadelphia: University of Pennsylvania Press.

Lee, J. S. (2004). Linguistic hybridization in K-Pop: Discourse of self-assertion and resistance. *World Englishes, 23,* 429–450.

Mitchell, T. (Ed.). (2001). *Global noise: Rap and hip-hop outside the USA.* Middletown, CT: Wesleyan University Press.

Neke, S. M. (2003). *English in Tanzania: An anatomy of hegemony.* Unpublished doctoral dissertation, University of Ghent, Belgium.

Newman, M. (2005, July). Speakin "bein real": Ideology and dialect among Latino hip hoppers. Paper presented at the 14th World Congress of Applied Linguistics, Madison, Wisconsin.

Omoniyi T. (2006). Hip-hop through the world Englishes lens: A response to globalization. *World Englishes, 25,* 195–208.

Pennycook, A. (2001). *Critical applied linguistics: A critical introduction.* Mahwah, NJ: Erlbaum.

Pennycook, A. (2003). Global Englishes, Rip Slyme, and performativity. *Journal of Sociolinguistics, 7,* 513–533.

Perullo, A., & Fenn, J. (2003). Language ideologies, choices and practices in Eastern African Hip Hop. In H. Berger & M. Carroll (Eds.), *Global pop, local language* (pp. 19–51). Oxford, MS: University of Mississippi Press.

Rampton, B. (1995). *Crossing: Language and ethnicity among adolescents.* London: Longman.

Rampton, B. (1999). Styling the other: Introduction. *Journal of Sociolinguistics, 3/4,* 421–427.

Reuster-Jahn, U., & Kießling, R. (2006). *Lugha ya Mitaani* in Tanzania: The poetics and sociology of a young urban style of speaking (with a dictionary comprising 1100 words and phrases). *Swahili Forum, 13,* 1–196.

Reyes, A. (2005). Appropriation of African American slang by Asian American youth. *Journal of Sociolinguistics, 9,* 509–532.

Rickford, J. (1999). *African American vernacular English.* Malden, MA: Blackwell.

Robertson, R. (1997). Comments on the "global triad" and "glocalization." Globalization and Indigenous Culture Institute for Japanese Culture and Classics, Kokugakuin University. Retrieved April 20, 2006, from http://www2.kokugakuin.ac.jp/ijcc/wp/global/index.html

Sebba, M., & Tate, S. (2002). "Global" and "local" identities in the discourses of British-born Caribbeans. *The International Journal of Bilingualism, 6,* 75–89.

Silverstein, M., & Urban, G. (1996). The natural history of discourse. In M. Silverstein & G. Urban (Eds.), *Natural histories of discourse* (pp. 1–17). Chicago: University of Chicago Press.

Solomon, T. (2005). "Living underground is tough": Authenticity and locality in the hip-hop community in Istanbul, Turkey. *Popular Music, 24,* 1–20.

Steingo, G. (2005). South African music after apartheid: Kwaito, the "party politic," and the appropriation of gold as a sign of success. *Popular Music & Society, 28,* 333–357.

Sweetland, J. (2002). Unexpected but authentic use of an ethnically-marked dialect. *Journal of Sociolinguistics, 6,* 514–536.

Vavrus, F. (2002). Postcoloniality and English: Exploring language policy and the politics of development in Tanzania. *TESOL Quarterly, 36,* 373–397.

Wolfram, W. (1973). *Sociolinguistic aspects of assimilation: Puerto Rican English in East Harlem.* Washington, D.C.: Center for Applied Linguistics.

"So I Choose to Do Am Naija Style"
Hip Hop, Language, and Postcolonial Identities[1]

TOPE OMONIYI

Introduction

Let us begin with a brief initial explanation of the frame imposed on this discussion by the chosen title. Taken from the lyrics of the title song of Nigerian Hip Hop artist 2-Shotz's 2005 album *Nna-Men*, the lines "You no fit yarn *foné* pass American/so I choose to do am Naija style" represent a number of identity-related claims. First, it asserts both complementarity and optionality of "*foné*" and "Naija style" rapping in one and the same vein. But there is a sense in which the choice of Naija style results from a subtle admission or suggestion of American ownership of foné and a conscious decision to diverge and then settle for a Naija alternative. In the lexicon of Nigerian Pidgin, foné is the label for a prestigious Standard English variety often used to describe the highly educated or native-speaker-approximating performance of a nonnative speaker. In other words, native speakers are not described in this term. This is an interesting yet contradictory other-ascribed value considering that the language of much U.S. rap is described as a non-Standard variety of American English that lacks capital in Bourdieu's (1991) terms within the context of U.S. politics. On a hierarchy of languages (Blommaert, 1999, p. 431) and such hierarchies are more often than not managed by the ideological North, Nigerian Pidgin, a South language variety, would occupy a slightly lower stratum than AAVE based on the latter's sheer privilege of location in the North. One significant addition to make to this is the glaring postcolonial dimension entailed by varieties of English and the politics of that relationship and how that frames a discussion of Hip Hop and identity.

In line with the stated aim in Alim's introduction to this volume—to map "the intersections between issues of language, Hip Hop Culture, and globalization"—in this chapter I shall examine how African and Nigerian Hip Hop artists discursively carve out a recognizable creative patch and a legitimate nonsubordinate local identity whilst retaining membership in the global community. I shall examine the discursive strategies deployed by artists in an attempt to articulate Nigerian yet global identities. This will entail tracking evidence of the flow between the two cultural axes; local and global. My exploration will be based on data extracts from transcripts of a BBC 1 Extra audio interview of Daara J conducted by JJC,[2] Ice-T's (a.k.a Tracy Marrow) opening of the 2006 VH1 Hip Hop Honors Award ceremony in New York, commentaries by artists in media reports on Hip Hop websites (*Hip Hop World Magazine*), and song lyrics from the work of a selection of Nigerian artists including Lágbájá, Weird MC, P-Square, Ruggedman, D'banj, and 2-Shotz.

Hip Hop as a Site of Contested Identities

Intellectual exploration of Hip Hop as a site of contested identities with reference to Africa and more specifically to Nigeria is both new and complex. The latter is reflected in the claim by Afrolution Records (2006)[3] to the effect that:

> What has always held African Hip Hop back is a struggle for our own identity, our own sound—something that belongs to us and is not a second rate replication of the Western sound. Sure we all grew up on US Hip Hop, we acknowledge that and we are grateful for the opportunities it has created for us but one cannot deny that the true essence of Hip Hop is "keeping it real". Once we started to learn to do this we planted the fertile seeds that are now seeing our industry grow. If you're a label, an artist or an African Hip Hop disciple please get in touch and register so we can keep you in our loop. (http://www.afrolution.com/, accessed November 15, 2006)

The statement at once sets up "African Hip Hop" that is "our own" in contrast to a "second rate replication of the Western sound." In a sense, this represents a pitch for the local essence, even as it acknowledges that members of the African Hip Hop community "all grew up on US Hip Hop." Growing up on, I would argue, ascribes parental status through nurture if not nature to U.S. Hip Hop and therefore amounts to a subtle acquiescence to the mainstream narrative that assigns the birth of Hip Hop to the Bronx in New York City. In this chapter, I explore two contrasting theoretical constructs of Hip Hop and identity. One construct advocates multiple narratives of origin underlying the contemporary mutation of local and global in the formation of a new identity; a relationship of asymmetry and mutuality. The second, in contrast, constructs a single narrative of origin and one dominant source of dispersal of Hip Hop facilitated by globalization.

Alternative Narrative(s) of Origin and Identity

The claim of a single origin for Hip Hop that is located in the Bronx has fed claims that the versions found outside of the United States are mere imitation art. Toop (1984) credits the Sugarhill Gang's chart hit *Rapper's Delight* in Harlem and the Bronx with the coming "to prominence in 1979" of Hip Hop. Afrolution Record's claim shows that African Hip Hop artists were struggling with the central Hip Hop mantra of "keepin it real" and are then challenged to create a Hip Hop that is more "African" than "American," something that they could claim as their own. This claim also is an indication that Hip Hop communities outside the United States construct themselves as "real" in their particular environments in order to narrate for themselves a history of participation in Hip Hop that privileges the local. The claim of a U.S. origin is pushed internally within the United States as well as without. The following extract from Ice-T's opening speech at the 2006 VH1 Hip Hop Honors Award ceremony is an instance of internal push:

It's so cold, what's up pimpin'? Welcome to the 2006 VH1 Hip Hop Honors. Now you saw tha I'wa'n gon let somebody take my job tonight. Bloomberg may be the mayor of New York but I'm the original gangsta of hip-hop, you dig? This is our third time around and like Hip Hop itself we just get bigger and better every year. We're back to the home of hip-hop, New York City. Respec'. (my emphasis)

Best and Kellner (1992) in a similar vein to the above remarked that:

Hip hop erupted from New York dance and party culture of the 1970s. Encompassing dance and performance, visual art, multimedia, fashion and attitude, hip hop is the music and style for the new millennium. A highly protean and assimilative cultural ethos, it is here to stay, as it absorbs new influences, is appropriated throughout myriad cultural forms and forces across the globe, and has become a major mode of the global popular. (Enculturation, 1999, p. 2)

Outsider Angus Batey made more or less the same claim in a London *Times* article titled "Home Grown—Profile—British Hip-Hop—Music" (2003) noting that:

"UK rap" is a broad sonic church, encompassing anything made in Britain by musicians informed or inspired by hip-hop's possibilities, *whose music is a response to the same stimuli that gave birth to rap in New York* in the mid-Seventies. (my emphasis)

This view, until recently, was not regarded as contentious and has not been the subject of a critical challenge in the literature. However, in an attempt to unravel globalization and the processes of social change that are now associated with it, new worlds and interconnections hitherto either concealed or unobserved and therefore undocumented have been unveiled and with that an accompanying need to revisit existing narratives, theories, and methods that help us to get a clearer understanding of the ways in which the local relates to the global in the contemporary world. It is in this context that the claims above must now be placed side by side with emergent narratives, theories, and methods and reassessed.

The social practices which together make Hip Hop "a way of life" include mc-ing, rapping, freestyling, break/street dancing, graffiti, and overstanding (Toop, 1984). An important question to pose here is that if we take the position that Hip Hop's home is New York, can we regard its emergence in other "homes" around the world as creating a Hip Hop diaspora? It is almost impossible that the Hip Hop diaspora would be mirror replicas of U.S. Hip Hop if they interact with diverse sociocultural realities, a fact not taken on board by an *Imitation or Replica Hypothesis*. Replication invokes a relationship of asymmetry between the original and the replica. This is the framework in which Hip Hop of other parts of the world are represented as imitative (for example, Broder, 2006, p. 40 on Japanese rap). Bradley Winterton writing in the *Taipei Times* in an article titled "Japanese Hip-Hop, Imitation or Art?" (2006) queried:

> Does the spread of hip-hop to Japan mean that everything American, from Wal-Mart to McDonald's, is destined to cover the globe with a uniform and stultifying sameness, or does the exchange of cultural influence quickly mutate into local variations that blend the imported with the inherited and create valuable new cross-bred "species" in innumerable locations? (Japanese Hip-Hop, p. 18)

More recent studies have not only veered away from that position (Condry, 2006), they have also explored the nature of cultural exchange and mutation that globalization supports. An imitation model is simplistic in its assumption that Hip Hop anywhere else is a replica of a U.S. form without appreciating the cultural influences and genetic modification it undergoes in the new environment. Diversity is a firmly established feature of the Global Hip Hop Nation, so the more worthwhile undertaking is an exploration of diversity by looking at less known Hip Hop varieties such as Nigerian Hip Hop with a view to unraveling how such local phenomena respond to and fit into the global, especially against the background of postcolonial reality and "(un)fair trade" ideologies and practices. Alternative narratives of origin interrogate that relationship.

Boomerang Hypothesis

Some of the component features of Hip Hop are now being identified as composite elements of the essential culture and identity of some West African societies. One such claim suggests that the genre is indeed part of a long-standing African oral tradition that was only transplanted to North America through the Middle Passage. I shall call this the *Boomerang Hypothesis* after the Senegalese Hip Hop group Daara J's 2005 album of that title (see also Pennycook and Mitchell, this volume) and the claim by group member Faada Freddie in an interview with artist/broadcaster JJC which was broadcast as a four-part series on BBC 1 Extra between November 2 and 23, 2006:

> The ancestors of Hip Hop itself used to be incarnated by the griots. It was to report the history and the reality that the people were living in the Songhai Realm. The Songhai Realm was Senegal, Mali, Guinea, after came slavery. The culture, the African culture has been deported to America and had to grow in the plantations. Then after came the descendants of the slaves who brought out their modern oral tradition called hip-hop. Now rap music is back home, and that's the reason why we called the latest of the Daara J's album "Boomerang" saying that rap was born in Africa, grew in America but now rap is back home.

Earlier in 2003, Jayne Ifekwunigwe, anthropologist and cultural theorist had been quoted in a University of East London press report as noting that:

> Hip Hop is the single most powerful contemporary influence on music and youth culture world wide. It is an expressive and empowering form of musical resistance, and has been transformed and reborn in its journey through the African diasporas of the United States, Europe and Brazil. Moving full circle, rap and hip hop are now finding new forms of expression in Africa itself. (http://www.uel.ac.uk/news/press_releases/releases/hiphop.htm)

Paul Gilroy's (1993) critique of the quadrilateral transatlantic transactions that constituted the Black Atlantic provides anchorage for that line of argument. If we see the construction of alternative narratives as a strategy of postcolonial deconstruction, then it could be argued that what is described as freestyling in Hip Hop is a version of discursive practices such as *ewi*, a disciplined and tight Yoruba oral poetic form, and *orin ebu* or *orin owe*, the abuse songs and proverbial songs employed in "song-lashing" episodes (Omoniyi, 1995) among the Yoruba of southwestern Nigeria. Similarly, it may be argued that verbal dueling rhymes among Turkish adolescents (Dundes, Leach, & Özkök, 1972, p. 130) with, of course, the expansion of membership of its community of practice to include postteenage youths, is the alternative source of Turkish Hip Hop. Pangie Anno, who manages the oldest music studio in Ghana, claimed in an interview with BBC World Service's Masterpiece program that "The source of Hip Hop is an African tradition, an ancient African tradition of freestyling, which is spontaneous poetry to a rhythmic pattern." Similarly, the Nigerian artist Lágbájá (alter ego Bisade Ologunde) in the lyrics of his 2005 song "Afrocalypso" traces Black diaspora music forms to slave narratives and therefore to Africa:

Africalypso, Africalypso
Some four hundred years ago
They took away my forefathers
From Africa to America
My forefathers took along their music
And some became jazz
Some became soul
Some became rhythm and blues
Swing, big band, bop, hip hop, funk, jazz, rap, reggae, ragga,
And some became calypso

But as with most myths of origin, it is to be expected that there would be variations and sometimes contradictions. For instance, in the BBC program cited above, Reggie Rockstone, described as a Ghanaian Hip Life star (blend of Hip Hop and High Life music), remarked that: "Everything that happened in the South Bronx with hip-hop is what's happening here, except we don't have any guns" thus conceding to the North American root of the genre narrative. Toop (1984) claims in the blurb that his book "takes Hip Hop culture as its central focus for the investigation of Afro-American rapping in all its forms. It begins with the music's African roots and ends in the electro-funk revolution." The reclamation of the origin of Hip Hop by some African artists has implications not only for the identity of the genre but also for the identities of those who (re)produce it.

These counternarratives prompted Omoniyi (2005, 2006a) to suggest that we may in fact be dealing with a case of reappropriation rather than an example of North American cultural imperialism spreading on the wings of globalization's structures. The current claim of reappropriation challenges the idea of an African appropriation of a U.S. form and suggests instead that the form which had been previously appropriated in the US is being reclaimed. The argument echoes Kadiatu Kanneh's (1998) in her exploration of Black American feminisms and women's narratives in which she argued that representations and imaginings of Africa in Black America cannot be anchored solely in histories of exile. In African American appropriations of Africa, she suggests, "memories of Africa and migration surge into the imaginary of Black America, creating representations of American nationality as a multi-layered and contested concept, challenged and redefined by urgent historical remembering" (p. 109). These different narratives of origin are artifacts enabling us to glean source information about the different elements from which contemporary global remixes are being constructed. Our focus ought to be on the determination of the nature of variation between the different forms of Hip Hop in its multiple homes and the identity implications of these variants. This is justification for the characterization I attempt later on in this chapter by identifying the features of Nigerian Hip Hop. I wish to turn next to the agenda of Hip Hop inasmuch as it facilitates a clearer vision of the ideologies that inform it and how these serve identity constructions and negotiations. This agenda is conveyed in discourses of race, nation, class, and ethnicity.

Hip Hop, Race, Nation, Class, and Ethnicity

A discussion of Hip Hop in relation to identity must address its association with race, nation, class, gender, and ethnicity as established variables in the sociolinguistics of identity (cf. Omoniyi & White, 2006). In Hip Hop's multiple locations around the world, these variables may or may not be equally relevant to a discussion of identity. The fact that Hip Hop became a formidable cultural phenomenon in the 1970s in the United States may be an indication of its purposeful evolution as a social and quasi-political movement and a replacement forum for postcivil rights articulation of Black resistance to persisting racial injustices in American society. Best and Kellner (1999) remark that

> Rap artists like Grandmaster Flash, Run DMC, Public Enemy, Ice-T, N.W.A., Ice Cube, Salt 'n' Pepa, Queen Latifah, Wu Tang Clan, Snoop Doggy Dogg, Tupac Shakur, the Fugees, and countless others produced a new musical genre that uniquely articulated the rage of the urban underclass and its sense of intense oppression and defiant rebellion. (p. 2)

This remark and others like it may therefore be seen to assert in part the ideological and political agenda that Hip Hop pursues in the North American context. The literature clearly shows that Hip Hop was extensively racialized in the United States, and justifiably so in the early days, in being predominantly associated with or identified as African American. One is not suggesting that this is no longer the case, but that there is additionally now a social class, nonracial dimension to it with the emergence of non-Black Hip Hop artists like the Beastie Boys (2006 VH1 Hip Hop Award Honorees) and Eminem (Marshall Mathers, III), allegedly the largest selling rap artist at the turn of the 20th century. The former and Vanilla Ice preceded Eminem as relatively successful White Hip Hop artists. The participation of the latter represents both ethnicity and class as legitimate identity variables. In a sense this claim is validated by the issues that underlie the narrative of the Hollywood blockbuster *8 Mile* (2002) which explores a rapper's (Eminem) struggle in coming to terms with his social circumstance and status in Detroit (cf. Kanye West's Fort Minor comment 2007).[4] In spite of belonging to different racial cohorts, all these artists still shared membership of an underclass in the political economy of the United States.

Considering that Hip Hop as a genre is now a global social practice and product, as the studies in this volume demonstrate, the issue arises as to whether or not race and class politics are on the agenda worldwide. Does Hip Hop convey the voice of a racial underclass around the world? If so, what is the nature and history of that underclass and how may it be identified? And if not, whose voice does it convey, and what purpose does it serve in a place like Nigeria? There cannot be one straight and simple answer to these questions considering on one hand the differences between the various contexts as we have already noted above. For instance, for MC Subliminal (Israeli Jew) and DAM (Palestinian Arab-Israeli) Hip Hop presents a forum for engaging with the politics of nation, ethnicity, and religion within the state of Israel. However, in the wider context of Western versus Middle East politics, religion more than race and ethnicity could be applied to the Hip Hop produced by these two groups. On the other hand, the growing entwinement of global destinies so that all humanity is at once involved and implicated irrespective of location, as the debates on global warming and terrorism illustrate, introduce a completely different perspective to these questions.

Similarly, Hip Hop's contention with race in North America does not extend to Hip Hop communities in Africa, except perhaps in South Africa. It certainly is not the case in Nigeria where ethnicity rather than race is the relevant variable in the body-politik. The 30-month civil war of 1967 to 1970 had been ethnicity fueled. The complexity of the identity issue can be seen in the description of East African rapper Big Pin (Chrispin Mwangale) as the "King of Luo rap music," who was quoted as saying that "At the end of the day what matters is that I did my country proud" (http://www.AllHipHop.com, accessed April 16, 2006). The description of Chrispin Mwangale as the proclaimed "King of Luo rap music" invokes ethnicity as an identity variable for describing his art (Luo rap) while the artist himself drew attention to his national affiliation.

This is not to say that one excludes the other. They are copresent though not with the same degree of salience. They belong on different rungs on a *hierarchy of identities* (see Omoniyi, 2006b for an elaboration of this).

In contrast to the Mwangale example, Nigerian rapper, 2-Shotz, introduces an additional level of identification, a regional one, describing himself and Ruggedman, his collaborator, as "Ruggedman and I, Abia State's finest" in the lyrics of his song "Nna Men." Abia is one of the 36 states of the Nigerian federation; it is located in the southeast of the country. Ironically, in the same song 2-Shotz declares that he is "made in Alaba," a commercial suburb of sprawling Lagos City in the southwest, renowned mainly for trade in imported goods, hence its name, the Alaba International Market. Alaba is populated mainly by the Igbo settlers who are originally from the southeast. They are the third largest ethnic group in Nigeria, after the Hausa and Yoruba, with a population of about 18 million (*Ethnologue*, 2005 web edition). The declarative "made in Alaba," resonates with Ice-Cube's self-tagging remark that "My music is a product of who I am and where I came from. I'm made in America. I'm not from Mars or nowhere else" (cited Best & Kellner, 1999, p. 1). It is difficult to rule out the existence of a dialogue between the local and the global that enables 2-Shotz to appropriate and deploy intertextuality as a resource, considering the marking of Alaba as a commercial hub which itself signals certain ways of relating to the global *financescape* (à la Appadurai, 1996). There is also a complex social underclass in Nigeria that comprises youth from both middle- and working class-backgrounds. The economic downturn of the 1980s and extended periods of military dictatorship, World Bank and IMF-imposed structural adjustment programs destroyed the Nigerian middle class, part of the membership of which brain-drained and became global citizens. Still there were large numbers that couldn't leave. Large-scale unemployment (and some were unemployable) bred discontent and anger among young persons, some of whom channeled their frustration into creative enterprises including Hip Hop.

Postcolonial relations also need to be considered here. According to rapper AY (African Yoruba) "there is one painful truth: any form of hip-hop and R'n'B that isn't in English and is from outside of America is regarded as second class" (cited in http://www.bbc.co.uk/africabeyond/africaonyourstreet/hosts/jjc/18567.shtml; accessed April 18, 2008. A Hip Hop/postcolonial identity cross-analysis is as interesting as it is tricky considering that Hip Hop in colonizer nations like Britain and France has a subordinate status to U.S. Hip Hop through a narrative of origin and scale, implicit in which is a reflection of the relative statuses of two subgroups of the Black diaspora vis-à-vis the structure of the global political economy. The asymmetrical relationship between former colonizers (Britain and France) and their former colonies does not extend to Hip Hop Nation Language (HHNL) with the U.S. role-modeling globally. For instance, almost exclusively, rap artists and groups invited to participate in Hip Hop festivals in Africa, and Nigeria in particular, have been drawn from the United States. The official launch of MTV-Base Africa in April 2005 at which U.S. rappers Ludacris, and Will Smith together with DJ Jazzy Jeff performed alongside local artists in Abuja and Johannesburg respectively are an affirmation of this axis of influence. Factoring in the postcolonial experience introduces a further dimension to how we must look at HHNL in Africa and try to understand the intra- and interlanguage, intergenerational and intracultural variations that are discernible. Under a regime of oppositions, African Hip Hop artists can simultaneously be discursively other-constructed on the periphery of a global mainstream while they are self-constructing themselves as the essential core from which the dominant culture flow derived in their own versions of the narrative of origin. This ideological battling is carried on by deploying linguistic resources in constructing a series of propositions as we saw with claim-making in the narratives of origin discussion above. The processes entailed will become manifest in our discussion of language choice and identity in Nigerian Hip Hop.

Nigerian Hip Hop

There are convergences to and divergences from HHN-Global. The local is facilitated through divergences while the global norms are upheld through convergence by the various Hip Hop Nation Language constituencies. By HHNL I am referring to the totality of the codifying and signifying practices of the Hip Hop Nation that are indexical of the nation's identities. Consequently, HHN-Global is a multilingual, multiple, and multifarious codes community (cf. Alim, 2006; this volume). The naming practice is traditional HHNL in most cases following the pattern MC This or MC That, or as we have in the data, Weird MC, 2-Shotz, P-Square. But while the adoption of aliases or street names constitutes a shared social practice of the HHNL-Global community, individual names may index local street realities at an interpretive level. There are postmodern tattoo parlors such as the Galleria on Victoria Island in Lagos, which are different in content from those associated with indigenous aesthetics. Another of the representations of Hip Hop culture is its association with affluence. The local dimension is in the size of the bling which is directly proportional to the size of the host economy. In other words, there are different economies of scale such that affluence in Naira may not necessarily translate into affluence in dollars.[5] Now let us look at the divergences in practice that set Hip Hop Nation-Nigeria apart from other varieties in Hip Hop Nation-Global.

Local Tenor

Hip Hop "a way of life" and "rap" one of its expressive modes seem to be synonymous with the focus on "Hip Hop language" in tracking the local tenor of the global. While it is undesirable to completely discountenance the importance of origin, whether myth or reality, in any consideration of Hip Hop identity, the more interesting task is to explore the ways in which members of various global Hip Hop communities furnish themselves with a Hip Hop history and ideology that demarginalizes them and situates them squarely in the center. This pursuit of a local Hip Hop identity agenda is evident in this response to my e-mail enquiry by Vectortheviper (aka Lanre Ogunmefun) a Nigerian MC, winner of MNet's Channel O's "Storm the Mic" competition in 2006 and one half of the Badder Boyz:

Extract 1

sorry bro,

been really busy with school. yes there are battles in Nigeria, and vector has been undisputed in his battle ecapade [sic] for ever (ask channel O). Grafiti in Nigeria is crazy. check the walls of igbosere street close to city hall, lagos island. and in unilag there are tons of Mc's who do nothing but battle every friday. they range from your mama jokes to you yourself. Brutally, people kill each other here. we got game here in Nigeria nd i hope u'r proud of where ur from now. holla laters.

A number of interesting issues are raised here, including the writing convention adopted which is different from that learned in the formal school system but similar to established global forms in e-mailing and texting conventions. The manner in which these conventions index forms of identity is beginning to attract researchers' attention (see Blommaert & Omoniyi, 2006). We deduce from Vectortheviper's claim that in Nigeria Hip Hop entails more than simply rapping and includes other characteristic elements including graffiti and MC battles (freestyling). Interestingly, when I asked Vectortheviper why there was no graffiti on the University campus where there is evidence of other Hip Hop identity markers, he explains that "it is against the law." This conformity with the law and conventional norm seems to depart from the known stereotype of North American practice.

Couture

Even if one accedes to a theory of the spread of Hip Hop from the United States, still in sharp contrast to the U.S. context, the identities we discern in the HHNL community in Africa are not about "representing the streets" in the U.S. sense because Africa's streets for now have a different subcultural topography and belong to urchins also called *Area Boys* in Lagos. Rather, the HHNL community comprises politically conscious youths liberated by education and critical of the establishment. They display a different kind of angst; a disdain for maladministration, plundering of state resources, and a resultant harsh economic climate that have left them roughshod and battered. This informs MC Vectortheviper's deconstruction of some of Hip Hop's cultural symbols such as baggy jeans and baggy shirts in an interview. According to him, these items are derogated and perceived as either one-size-fits-all prison clothing (not cut to size) or "papa-dash-me" (hand-downs from father or older siblings). This critical view of fashion enables us to explore the moral and ideological concerns subsumed in its interpretation. Besides, the growth in indigenous popular youth fashion that incorporates local textile and design also instantiates divergence. Thus, in clothing styles, HHN-Nigeria contrasts with Robin D.G. Kelley's suggestion cited by Pennycook and Mitchell (this volume) that Hip Hop artists outside of the United States "mirror African American urban youth styles." The mirror is a euphemism for imitation. This difference in values and views on fashion further isolates rap as the shared practice at the core of Hip Hop identity.

Attitudes to Exogenous Standards

Attitude is a significant factor in our treatment and analysis of Hip Hop. Commenting on the nonpopularity of Hip Hop in Malawi, producer Mike Munthali (Dynamike/DJ Lick) remarked in an online article that "Hip Hop is a rejected art in the country mainly because the original proponents of the genre are associated with violence, drugs and crime. It is this stereotyped view that has mainly affected the growth of this music" (cited in http://www.bbc.co.uk/africabeyond/africaonyourstreet/hosts/jjc/18567.shtml; accessed April 18, 2008); youth are more critical of these; the myth of the native speaker and the redefinition of constituency—those we seem to have ratified by having changed between the generations.[6] 2-Shotz articulates his preference for Nigerian Pidgin in "Nna-Men" (featuring Ruggedman) when he says "He no fit yarn fòné pass American, so I decide to do am naija style." Fòné is a colloquial metaphor for prestigious standard native English varieties, especially American and British. Thus his claim may suggest that within the HHN Nigerian community, the latter are recognized as marking an external identity.

Positive attitude toward the local is also reflected in the choice of samples. Samples are the classics that MCs and DJs lay their poetry on. While the macrostructure is a global practice, localization is effected through the samples. In Nigeria, for instance the popular samples include Fela Anikulapo-Kuti, Orlando Owoh, I.K. Dairo, Ebenezer Obey, Haruna Ishola, Olisadebey, from music genres as diverse as Afrobeat, High Life, Fuji, and Apala. Afrobeat is now being sampled beyond the shores of Nigeria in London dance clubs.[7]

Language Choice

I return here to my earlier reference to linguistic resources. While multilingualism is widespread and growing as a result of global cultural flows, it seems that in some environments Hip Hop artists deploy linguistic convergence in performing in the dominant official language of the cosmopolis. This choice ensures optimum efficiency of delivery in terms of outreach and access to an educated community. However, divergence serves a more liberal purpose as demonstrated in Ngugi wa Thiong'o's switch from English to his native Gikuyu in order to reach the grassroots or indigenous peasantry and extensively undermine the political class as an act of subversion (Fox, 2003). Nigerian Afro-beat legend and social critic Fela Anikulapo-Kuti achieved this through Pidgin. Thus language choice can be a conscious act of political subversion and resistance (cf. Mitchell, 2000). Nigerian Hip Hop artists as social critics and activists explore language choice as a multilingual skill and in the process establish for themselves a creative patch and a legitimate nonsubordinate local identity within the global Hip Hop constituency. The multilingual Nigerian HHNL community facilitates this negotiation and construction of identity through language choice. The artists explore what Bucholtz (2003) referred to as strategic essentialism (see also Hall, 1996; Spivak, 1990), in other words, the manner of their use of ethnic languages departs from the traditional pattern of marking ethnolinguistic identity, and yet serves as a difference marking tool in relation to other constituencies around the world.

These artists flag up their membership of a new generation of Nigerians by rapping in multiple indigenous languages including those that are not necessarily their mother tongues, so that language crossing (Rampton, 1995; also Lee, 2006) facilitates the construction of a national/regional rather than an ethnolinguistic identity. In doing this they set up what may be construed as a pan-Nigerian identity that is an ideological departure from the kind of establishment identity we may associate with Nigeria's "English-as-official language" policy. All of the artists in the data perform multilingual rap with Nigerian Pidgin as the common denominator. The pervasive use of Nigerian Pidgin which is accessible to elite and nonelite alike and across ethnic groups undermines the description of

English as the language of unity in early sociolinguistic research in Nigeria. The latter is often cited in justifying the official language policy.

Both Weird MC and D'Banj sing in English, Pidgin English, and Yoruba extensively. 2-Shotz, for instance, raps in Nigerian Pidgin and Igbo but predominantly in the former as we find in the lyrics of his song "Nna-Men"—ft. Ruggedman where he criticizes his peers who adopt an American accent of English. He remarks that: "He no fit rap *fòné* pass American, so I decide to do am naija style." The same criticism is echoed in a blog posting by AbaBoy on the http://www.naijajams.com site dated September 22, 2005, which subsequently attracted 52 responses:

> Listening to some of our hip-hop stars rapping in English (worst still— fake American twang) can sometimes turn into a very excruciating encounter. I am not trying to cut a critical remark just for its sake; the same will also apply to an American artist that decides to dive into the highlife scene. The artist will have to be very good to make it not sound like crap. To cut a long story short, Nigerian hip-hop stars should mc in either Pidgin English or their local language—cut the fake Yankee drawl. By doing this, some of them may perhaps achieve restricted crossover appeal, but more importantly they will essentially reduce the ability to make others cringe. Unfamiliar artists picking fights with world-renowned superstars on planes in Nigeria wouldnt really do the trick. And the Videos....[8]

In Africa where literacy rates are abysmally low according to World Bank statistics, Hip Hop has been deployed to articulate resistance to a dominant elite mainstream. But it is also difficult to describe it as the property of a social underclass when we consider that some of its contemporary exponents come from privileged, educated, and upwardly mobile socioeconomic backgrounds. The artists whose lyrics inform my discussion have a minimum of post-16 education. In other words, they have at least secondary school qualification and in some cases they have had tertiary education, that is, attended a polytechnic or university even though in some cases they may not necessarily have stayed on to graduate, having dropped out by choice in full realization that they wanted to pursue a career in entertainment.

Nigerian Hip Hop, as is the case with other African varieties, deploys a multilingual repertoire with the following discernible patterns:

1. Narrative in Language X and chorus in Language Y;
2. Call in Language X and Response in Language Y;
3. Narrative X and rap in Y;
4. Sample in X and remix in Y
5. Narrative in both Languages X and Y and chorus in X or Y or XY.

Such repertoires are both a property of urban multilingual performers as well as an indicator of groups that comprise individuals drawn from more than one ethnolinguistic community. In the song "If Life" by the multiethnic group Plantashun Boiz (2001), the song is rendered in English, the chorus is in Yoruba while the rap is in Pidgin (see extract below):

Extract 2

A: song extract
(i)
That is what I've got for you
Cos I need you in my life
All the way all the sky ???
I can see it in your eyes

(ii)
We'll be loving one on one
Till we see the morning sun
Girl it's you that I want

B: Chorus [in Yoruba]
Baby iwo ni mo nferan/Baby, it's you I like
Iwo gangan ni mo feran/It's you specifically I like
Iwo ni mo nfe o, girl,/It's you I desire
Iwo gangan ni mo feran 2x/It's you specifically I like

C: Rap extract [Pidgin]
After I check am na you be my desire/
I no dey tell you dis because I wan dey talk am/This is no empty talk
I dey tell you dis based on say na so I dey mean am/I say it because I mean it
And I mean am
So mek you try to understand my point of view/Make an effort
Day and night in fact *I just dey think of you/*
Na you I want and na you I get to have/It's you I want and you I've got to have
Na you dey make cry/You make me cry
Na you sef dey make me laugh ha ha/You also make me laugh
Remaining people na just to see/Others a mere vision
Just **maka** the simple fact say na you I need ["because" in Igbo]

Self-styled "revolutionary rapper" Ruggedman's (2006) "Ruggedy Baba" samples the rhythm of a traditional Edo folksong for his Yoruba chorus, while laying his rap in Pidgin and colloquial American English. Indeed he interrogates the presumed conflict between keepin' it real, language choice, and identity. Ruggedman asserts that:

Extract 3

> From Nigeria the world only know Juju, Fuji and Afro beat
> But we all know hip hop is running the streets
> Wetin go make them know where your music come from [wetin =
> what will]
> In the long run
> Na the fussion of grammar, your slang and your mother tongue
> [na = is]

In the third verse he touches more directly on the subject of identity through an implicit binary opposition of Oyibo (European or White) and "your own people,"

Extract 4

> Now let me address this issue of keeping it real
> The one subject wey I go say dey make me vex still [that I'll say still
> vexes me]
> Cos of how some emcees feel
> About these three words whenever they open their mouths
> Look my guy
> I no fit shout [I can't shout]
> I go only ask what's keeping it real? [I shall only ask]
> Is it singing or rapping like Oyibo or doing what you and your own
> people can feel?
> Some say I sell out because I do dance track they call me Baraje
> master
> Forgetting it got me fame and money faster
> Forget the latter I'll move to the next chapter faster
> I'm just speaking my mind playing my controversial character
> The way I've been known to do when I spit it straight out to you
> You better recognize a real brother that's reaching out to you
> Speaking pidjin and dance tracks no mean say I no keep am real
> That's just me so how else I wan be to be real?
> My rules are spit in whatever language but make sense
> I did that and I've been hot ever since
> (http://www.lyricsmode.com/lyrics/r/rugged_man/ruggedy_baba.
> html)

The same pattern is evident in Jazzman Olofin's "Angelina Remix" which is done in Pidgin, English, and Yoruba. Closely linked with the employment of multiple languages is the phenomenon of codeswitching which I shall discuss next.

Codeswitching

Codeswitching is an identity marker for the Nigerian brand within the global Hip Hop community. Following Alvarez-Cáccamo (2002), I have made the case elsewhere (Omoniyi, 2005) for a reconceptualization of codeswitching so that it accommodates an expanded category that includes not just language in the narrow sense of our understanding of communicative competence in sociolinguistics or discourse competence in sociopragmatics, but also modes of dressing, walking, and other patterns of social behavior. With particular reference to fusion music or remix, it is a relatively straightforward case to make since the basic consideration still is language of the lyrics rendition. However, since Hip Hop is an entire "way of life" with definite and recognizable cultural paraphernalia, we need to examine the totality of its ways of encoding identity, including the talk, the walk, its entire fashion accoutrements including bling; that is, flashy jewelry of all kinds: neck chains, dental grills that adorn Hip Hop artists.

Trilingual codeswitching is a major feature of Nigeria's dialect of HHNL. All three artists have a sample of three languages in their songs. Weird MC has Yoruba, English, and Pidgin with Igbo borrowings. D'Banj has English, Pidgin, and Yoruba, and 2-Shotz has Pidgin and Igbo. The following excerpts taken from the lyrics of "Ijoya" and "Mr. Olopa" by Weird MC and D'Banj respectively illustrate this point:

Extract 5
From Weird MC's "Ijoya" [Yoruba: time to dance]

> Yes, it's time to dance—   [American English accent]
> We own the dance
> Awa la ni ijo
> *Ah trust us, we OWN dis dance*
> Awa la ni ijo
> Na we getam   [Pidgin: We own it]
> Awa la ni *gini*   [Yoruba/*Igbo*: We own *what?*]
> Awa la ni ijo
> *Osigini*   [Igbo: What did he say?]
> Awa la ni ijo

Extract 6
From D'Banj's "Mr Olopa"   [Yoruba: Mr. Policeman]

> When we reached there stori don change [When we got there the story changed]
> Dey even say I dey smoke high grade [They alleged that I smoked cannabis]
> Said it's some cigarette
> No na cigiweed [No it's cannabis in cigarette wrap]

Can I make a phonecall?
If I slap you, you go fall [If I slap you, you'll fall]
They charge me for robbery
Dey even charge Don Jazzy for accessory [They charged Don Jazzy as
an accessory]
Before I know wetin dey happen [Before I realized what was
happening]
All of dem wey dey there join hands again [They all joined in beating
me up]

In the microanalysis of codeswitching, focus is on the structural pattern of the blend with a view to producing a descriptive grammar. However, with regard to codeswitching and identity in a macroanalytical framework, account is taken of the bi/multilingual repertoire and language choice patterns. In relation to Nigerian Hip Hop, codeswitching is both an identity construction tool, and a "language form." The social and political factors that determine the nature of collaboration between languages in codeswitching usage are significant. In other words, colonial history, current language planning, and policy issues and how these impact language practices and attitudes across contexts come into play. In the two extracts above collaboration is between Nigerian major languages: English, Yoruba, Pidgin, and Igbo. This language use practice is already extensively explored in Afrobeat music which Fela Anikulapo-Kuti deployed in over two decades of social commentary and political activism in Nigeria. Thus codeswitching in this mode is conceptually an ideological discursive tool rather than a mere combination of the resources of two languages. It serves Hip Hop's signifying and representing functions.

Working within a modified Three Circles paradigm (Kachru, 1990), one view is that oppositional and asymmetrical (native versus nonnative) relationships abound while an alternative view fueled by an ideology of resistance rejects the existence of unequal partnerships. HHNL is ideologically liberal hence the ease with which it is globalized. Competing myths of origin in the Bronx or precolonial Africa or contemporary urban inner-city all feed the oppositional viewpoint. However, this is only a productive line of inquiry to the extent that it can help our understanding of the complex processes of signifying offered by global rap and Hip Hop. The alternative framework I offer in relation to postcolonial contexts of signification is to conceive of Hip Hop identities as belonging to a global complex within which performers may move freely for whatever reasons they considered salient in the moments of identification in which they find and attempt to define themselves. For the sub-Sahara African HHNL community several frames of reference exist and these frames are interconnected in complex and interesting ways. Some of the more obvious ones include: Anglophone versus francophone, nationality, religion, ethnicity, home versus diasporic, global versus local connections, performing outside, collaborating with "global" or U.S. rappers, etc.

The function of codeswitching is to produce *appropriate* alignments and stances or positionings. These positionings and alignments would be in relation to any of the identity values listed above. Let us consider the following excerpt from Weird MC's interview with Naijajams.com (NJ):

Extract 7

NJ: You've been in the music business for some time now—how has the Nigerian music scene changed since you began performing?

WMC: It's evolved into something really exciting it's unbelievable all *eyes are on Nigeria* right now *we have to let the world know* what's up it's time to *put us on the map.* There's more quality than quantity, *artistes are* putting out great material.

The interviewer's question suggests identity options which the interviewee may or may not take up in her response. On this occasion she claims the offered positioning through an exploration of the pronominal system. "It," referring to "the Nigerian music scene" transposed from object to subject position reveals interviewee's acceptance. The moments within the stretch of utterance at which the italicized information were uttered constitute moments of identification in which Weird MC first isolates the Nigerian Hip Hop community as the object of global gaze, then by choosing the collective "we" and "us" she declares her membership of the community and assumes the role of spokesperson for the group. Weird MC's modest Ego as an objective commentator attributes "great material" to a plural third person, so that her inclusion in the category is only guaranteed if we return to the interviewer's initial ascription to her of a performer's identity. Let us attempt a similar analysis using an excerpt from Weird MC's "Ijoya" from the album *After da Storm*:

Extract 8

[Call and Response]

Yes, it's time to dance—[American accent]	
We own the dance	
Awa la ni ijo	[Yoruba — "we own the dance"]
Ah trust us, we OWN dis dance	
Awa la ni ijo	
Na we getam	[Pidgin: We own it]
Awa la ni *gini*	[Igbo word meaning *what*]
Awa la ni ijo	
Osigini	[Igbo: He said what?]
Awa la ni ijo	
Awa la ni jo o	
Awa la ni ijo	
Yo, take me home.	[Yo: global trope]

The above refrain with which "Ijoya" ends flags up a coconstructed "We–Us" identity between Weird MC and her backup singers. It consists of claim assertions by Weird MC in the lead that are echoed and reinforced by the backup singers. From the line "Awa la ni gini?" to the end, traditional African "call and response" is utilized so that both the lead and backup singers ratify each other and by so doing imply their group solidarity. What is interesting here is that a claim is made to a specific dance—"this dance"—which within the wider system of genre form and brand marking may be regarded as an implicit reference to the local HHNL community. This claim is especially reinforced by the artist's use of Yoruba, English, Pidgin, and Igbo all within a space of 13 lines of refrain.

Another closely related and significant point to make is that the growing practice of using the indigenous languages including Pidgin in the HHNL Nigerian community raises the profile and status of languages that are otherwise subordinated through institutional language in education policies to ex-colonial languages; even more so considering that this is happening among a crucial and vibrant segment of the Nigerian populace, educated youths. 2-Shotz, whom I presented in my introduction, raps almost exclusively in Nigerian Pidgin (Naija style) and claims that he does so by choice for the functional purpose of ensuring that his fans understand him. It challenges the idea of a homogeneous HHNL community and reiterates the diversity within the community.

Further Evidence of Transcultural Flow

Omoniyi (2006a) identified cross-referencing as one of the discursive strategies employed in authenticating their reappropriations. This practice may also be seen as orchestrating a local–global dialogue, exchange, and interpenetration. These are facilitated by participation in transnational events such as the MOBO (Music of Black Origin) Awards, MTV Europe Awards which bring together artists from several countries sharing the same performance and discursive space (see also Pennycook, 2007). In addition to physical collaboration such as these, a borderless global media facilitates interpenetration so that referencing draws on not just the physical/material experience but also a virtual reality within which it is possible to conceptualize membership of a community, the Global Hip Hop Nation. The consequence is an expanded reality that includes local and global references. Nigerian rapper Mode 9 says in Elbow Room, "I'm hungry like snoop in the deep cover of death row" in clear reference to U.S. rapper, Snoop Dogg and Death Row Records. Perhaps the most obvious evidence of transnational culture flow lies in the impact that Nigerian popular culture, including Hip Hop has been having on language use around Africa instantiated especially by Nigerian English forms in Uganda.

Bridging

Bridging is a consequence of cross-referencing and it is achieved in a number of ways. The most obvious of these would be the practice of claiming or tracing links between established artists in one Hip Hop community and those in another community who may themselves not have declared the same publicly. This is often a periphery practice. In other words, within an existing global hierarchical structure that privileges the North, the South lays claims to North artists. The flip side of this coin is when North artists perform on a southern platform and declare that they had a very emotional experience and a sense of home-coming and connecting with Africa. The Africahit Music TV website ran a story on October 11, 2007 titled "The rapper Chamillionaire is Nigerian!" which traced the rapper Chamillonaire's (real name, Hakeem Seriki) roots to Oyo State, Nigeria.[9] Similarly, http://www.Nairaland.com an online forum, carried a discussion on the topic "Is Nas Truly Nigerian?" for a whole year December 4, 2005 to December 20, 2006 in which 51 commentators participated.[10]

Another way that bridging is achieved is simply by allusions, analogies, and comparisons that incorporate values and referents from both local and global constituencies. For example, Hip Hop group P-Square (ft. Alaye) in the lyrics of their song "Temptation," say in Pidgin:

Extract 9

> All my friends dey call me number ten, [dey = habitual "be"]
> cos I dey play like Okocha,
> Dey score like Ronaldinho

Finally, bridging is institutionally achieved through the expansion of award categories to recognize, include, and validate forms of Hip Hop from the "periphery" in previously Western confined industry competitions. Such expansions and validations in turn also consolidate and change regional into global events thus raising their profile. The MOBO (Music of Black Origin) Awards and the MTV Europe Music Awards, both of which now have a Best African Act category, exemplify this. Nigerian Hip Hop artist, Tu Face/2 Face (Innocent Idibia) became the first African to win both these awards in 2005 and 2007 respectively. D'Banj was named the UN Youth Ambassador for Peace in 2007 and Best African Act at MTV EMA 2007. Such international forum appearances complement local events such as the Star Mega Jam organized by multinationals like Nigerian Breweries Plc. The This Day Independence Day Music Festival, also an annual event, takes international stars to Nigeria. Rapper Ruggedman notes in his bio:

Extract 10

> Now I run my own label in Nigeria "RUGGED RECORDS" Have per-
> formed alongside KC n Jojo, Guru, Sean Paul, Wyclef Jean, Akon, Wayne
> Wonder, Ja Rule, Kevin Little, Maxie Priest, Ruggedman's been performing
> all over Nigeria right now and is Nigeria's most wanted rap act. (http://
> www.ruggedmanonline.com/main.html)

The list includes some of the many U.S.-based artists that have performed on these bills and brought the global to the local.

Conclusion

That African Hip Hop or Nigerian Hip Hop is thriving or that U.S. Hip Hop has a transnational pedigree which sets it on a pedestal may not be contentious judging by the pervasiveness of Americanisms in varieties of Hip Hop outside the United States. What is becoming contentious is the relationship between the varieties because this has direct implications for how we construct the global flow of Hip Hop culture and identity. In the foregoing sections I have taken a critical look at two contrasting accounts; one of a sole source of dispersal for Hip Hop and the other of the possibility of multiple origins both equally valid and varying by teller. I cited the evident diversity in form, content, and purpose to question claims that there are two Hip Hops: U.S. Hip Hop on one hand and its imita-tions on the other. I have suggested that there is a universal template to account for similarities while local cultural topographies create differences between the varieties. I presented discursive strategies and tools with which Nigerian Hip Hop artists construct their local identities while situating themselves within HHNL-Global. These include language choice, multilingual rap repertoires, codeswitching, fashion, social criticism, and ideology.

Notes

1. I thank the editors for their comments on an earlier draft. Full transcript of interview conducted in September 2005 is available at: http://www.naijajams.com/weird-mc-interview
2. Abdulrazaq Bello aka JJC is a producer, broadcaster (BBC's "Africa on Your Street" program), and rapper with the award-winning Afropean/Nigerian Hip Hop group JJC & 419 Squad.
3. Afrolution Records is a London-based record producing and marketing company set up in 2006 to specifically to bring African Hip Hop to the world.
4. http://www.inthenews.co.uk/music/types-music/rap/kanye-attacks-white-adoption-HipHop-$15051097.htm
5. "The Infinity Jeep may not only have cruise control, a navigation system, keyless entry, trip/ mileage computer and worth Millions of Naira, it must have a bug disperse censor as it simul-taneously caught Sunny Neji, Faze and even Blackface (assumed unfortunate of the outmoded Plantashun Boiz). They bought one of this 4 wheel drive each last week." Muma Gee's "N15 Million' Infinity Jeep – another point of reference." (http://www.hiphopworldmagazine.com/ newsx.aspx?newsid=126)
6. http://hiphoparchive.org/thecircle/?p=495

7. http://www.npr.org/templates/story/story.php?storyId=1115091
8. AbaBoy is described on his website as "born in Manchester, brought up in Aba, living in London and still loving Nigeria' [http://www.naijajams.com/thoughts-on-the-nigerian-Hip Hop-scene-part-1]. By "unfamiliar artistes picking fights ...' AbaBoy is referring to Eedris Abdulkareem the Nigerian rapper who caused a fracas at the Lagos airport in December 2004 when he attempted to engage 50 Cent in a fight following which the latter broke off his engagement with Nigerian Breweries, organizers of Star Mega Jam and returned to the USA.
9. http://www.africahit.com/news/index.php?mod=article&cat=Nigeria&article=3288&page_order=1&act
10. http://www.nairaland.com/nigeria/topic-3541.0.html

Discography

2-Shotz (2005). "Nna-Men" from the album *2-Shotz: Original Copy*, Umunnamu Music.
Daara J (2005). Boomerang. BMG, WRR, Wrasse, Pony Canyon.
D'Banj (n.d.). "Loke" from the *Run Down Funk U Up* album. Written and produced by D'Banj and Don Jazzy for Mo' Hits Records.
D'Banj (n.d.) "Mr Olopa" from the album *No Long Thing*. Mo' Hits Records.
Jazzman Olofin (2006). "Angelina remix" in *Mr. Funky*. Storm Records.
Lágbájá a.k.a. Bisade Ologunde (2005). "Afrocalypso" in *Africano...mother of groove*. Motherlan' Music.
Mode 9/Modenine (2005). "Elbow Room" Question Mark Entertainment.
Plantashun Boiz (2001). "If Life" in *The biginning BODY & SOUL*. Dove Entertainment.
P-Square (ft. Alaye) (2005). "Temptation" in *Get Squared*. Square Records.
Ruggedman (2006). "Ruggedy Baba," title track. Rugged Style Records.
Weird MC (2005). Ijoya from the album *After Da Storm*. 0907 Entertainment/Ahbu Ventures.

References

Alim, S. A. (2006). *Roc the mic right: The language of hip hop culture*. London: Routledge.
Alvarez-Cáccamo, C. (2002, October 22–26). *Introduction: Class and ideology in code-switching research*. Paper presented at the International Symposium on Bilingualism, Vigo.
Appadurai, A. (1996). *Modernity at large: Cultural dimensions of globalization*. Minneapolis: University of Minnesota Press.
Batey, A. (2003, July 26). Home grown—profile—British hip-hop—music. *The Times*,. Retrieved April 18, 2008, from http://entertainment.timesonline.co.uk/tol/arts_and_entertainment/music/article845985.ece
Best, S., & Kellner, D. (1999). Rap, Black rage and racial difference. *Enculturation, 2*(2), 1–23. Retrieved April 18, 2008, from http://enculturation.gmu.edu/2_2/best-kellner.html
Blommaert, J. (1999). *Language ideological debates*. Berlin: Mouton de Gruyter.
Blommaert, J., & Omoniyi, T. (2006). Email fraud: Language, technology and the indexicals of globalization. *Social Semiotics,16*(4), 573–605.
Bourdieu, P. (1991). *Language and symbolic power*. Cambridge, UK: Polity Press
Broder, C. J. (2006). Hip hop and identity politics in Japanese popular culture. *Asia Pacific Perspectives: An Electronic Journal, 6*(2), 39–43.
Bucholtz, M. (2003). Sociolinguistic nostalgia and the authentication of identity. *Journal of Sociolinguistics, 7* (3), 398–416.
Condry, I. (2006). *Hip hop Japan*. Chapel Hill, NC: Duke University Press.
Dundes, A., Leach, J. W., & Özkök, B. (1972). The strategy of Turkish boys' verbal dueling rhymes. In J. J. Gumperz & D. Hymes (Eds.), *Directions in sociolinguistics: The ethnography of communication* (pp. 130–160). Oxford: Blackwell.
Fox, R. E. (2003). Engaging Ngugi. *Research in African Literatures, 34* (4), 115–128.
Gilroy, P. (1993). *The Black Atlantic*. Cambridge, MA: Harvard University Press.
Gordon, R. G., Jr. (Ed.). (2005). *Ethnologue: Languages of the world*, 5th ed.. Dallas, Tex.: SIL International. Online version: http://www.ethnologue.com/.
Hall, S. (1996). Cultural identity and diaspora. In J. Rutherford (Ed.), *Identity, community, Culture, difference* (pp. 222–237). London: Lawrence & Wishart.

Japanese Hip-Hop: Imitation or Art?, (2006, December 24). Features, 8. Retrieved April 18, 2008, from http://www.taipeitimes.com/News/feat/archives/2006/12/24/2003341835

Kachru, B. (1990). *The alchemy of English: The spread, functions, and models of non-native Englishes.* Urbana: University of Illinois Press.

Kanneh, K. (1998). *African identities: Race, nation and culture in ethnography, Pan-Africanism and Black literatures.* London: Routledge.

Lee, J. S. (2006). Crossing and crossers in East Asian pop music: Korea and Japan. *World Englishes, 25*(2), 235–250.

Mitchell, T. (2000, Fall). Doin' damage in my native language: The use of resistance vernaculars in hip hop in France, Italy and Aotearoa/New Zealand. *Popular Music and Society, 24*(3), 41–54.

Omoniyi, T. (1995). Song-lashing as a communicative strategy in Yoruba interpersonal conflicts. *Text, 15*(2), 299–315.

Omoniyi, T. (2005). Towards a retheorization of codeswitching. *TESOL Quarterly,* 729–734.

Omoniyi, T. (2006a). Hip hop through the world Englishes lens: A response to globalization. In J. S. Lee & Y. Kachru (Eds.), *World Englishes: Symposium on world Englishes in popular culture, 25*(2), 195–208.

Omoniyi, T. (2006b). Hierarchy of identities: A theoretical approach. In T. Omoniyi & G. White (Eds.), *The sociolinguistics of identity* (pp. 11–33). London: Continuum Press.

Omoniyi, T., & White, G. (Eds.). (2006). *The sociolinguistics of identity.* London: Continuum Books.

Pennycook, A. (2007). *Global Englishes and transcultural flows.* London: Routledge

Rampton, B. (1995). *Crossing: Language and ethnicity among adolescents.* London: Longman

Spivak, G. (1990). *The post-colonial critic: Interviews, strategies, dialogues.* New York: Routledge

Toop, D. (1984). *The rap attack: African jive to New York hip hop.* London: Pluto Press.

Winterton, B. (2006, December 2). Japanese hip hop, imitation or art. *Taipei Times,* p. 18. Retrieved April 18, 2008, from http://www.taipeitimes.com/News/feat/archives/2006/12/24/2003341835

The Power of the Word

Hip Hop Poetics, Pedagogies, and the Politics of Language in Global Contexts

"Still Reppin' Por Mi Gente"

The Transformative Power of Language Mixing in Quebec Hip Hop

MELA SARKAR

Introduction

In the Canadian province of Quebec, the urban scene has witnessed a complete makeover in one generation. This traditionally tightly knit, inward-looking enclave of French-speakers within North America has had to open up to outside influences of several kinds over the past half-century. Global Hip Hop is one of them. It has had largely unresearched effects, but the ongoing "glocalization" of Hip Hop in the Quebec context may be one of the more important for the long-range transformation of Quebec society.

Over the short space of a couple of decades, the population of young French-speakers in Montreal (where more than 90% of immigrants to Quebec settle) has become multiethnic and multilingual, for the first time in history. Roughly half of Quebec's total population of about 7 million lives in or near Montreal. The remaining 3.5 million or so people living in "the regions" far from Montreal tend to be much more monolingually French-speaking and "monoethnically" French-Canadian. The Montreal population is now about one-third of ethnic French-Canadian heritage, with non-White and ethnically/linguistically mixed Montrealers on the rise. Since the proportion of newly arriving immigrants from non-White, non-Christian countries has been steadily on the rise in Montreal, hence changing its demographics, the "Montreal/regions" cultural divide seems to be getting more pronounced.

And like a late arrival at the party who ends up moving in, with devastating long-term consequences that the mid-1970s pro-French language planners in Quebec could hardly have foreseen,[1] Hip Hop has landed on the scene as *the* fastest-growing new voice of youth culture and popular artistic expression for a whole generation. While insular Canadian language debates rage and local cultures shift, Quebec Hip Hop has become a cultural force that crosses ethnolinguistic lines, as well as urban/rural lines, to bring together youth across the province and position them as part of a Global Hip Hop Nation (Alim, this volume). In Montreal, descendants of the early 17th-century colonists from France are rubbing shoulders—and rhyming—with other urban youth whose roots go back to very different corners and colors of the globe. Youth in the regions are listening and branching out from their own local roots. In the following pages I will explore some implications of what this may mean for the future of Quebec identity and culture, largely through an examination of the ways language is used in Montreal rap.

Hip Hop Studies and Studying Quebec Hip Hop

Since the early 1990s, Hip Hop studies as a field of inquiry in its own right has gradually been gaining scholarly recognition. This move, from the Hip Hop academic enterprise being marginalized to becoming a valued and legitimized object of scholarship, has followed and then paralleled the ways in which the art forms that find expression through the Hip Hop movement have themselves moved from a marginalized to a central position in popular culture.

Hip Hop Studies in the United States: Black American Beginnings

By far the greater number of book-length studies of Hip Hop have been written from an American perspective. The movement and implications for cultural studies have now been examined in dozens of full-length academic treatments. Kitwana (2005) argues that Hip Hop everywhere is rooted in an identification with Black American culture. While acknowledging the importance of its American roots, I would argue, with Pennycook and Mitchell (this volume), that the global significance of Hip Hop-originated art and cultural forms has gone beyond a simple identification with one originating culture. An up-and-coming Montreal DJ, self-identified as Québécois with Italian roots, put it this way when asked about the Quebec Hip Hop scene:

> Ça l'a un peu ouvert l'esprit aux gens qu'il y avait pas juste les noirs qui pouvaient faire du rap. Pis c'était pas juste important d'venir du ghetto, ou d'être pauvre, pour faire du rap. Parce que maintenant y a des gens qui viennent pas du ghetto aussi qui font du rap. Moi j'pense que ça l'a un peu transformé l'mouvement Hip Hop; c'est devenu plus quelque chose pour les jeunes et non simplement quelque chose pour la communauté noire ou la communauté haïtienne.
>
> [It opened people's minds up to the fact that there weren't just Black people who could do rap. And it wasn't just important to come from the

ghetto, or to be poor, to do rap. Because now there are people who don't come from the ghetto who also do rap. I think that this has changed the Hip Hop movement a bit; it's become more something for young people and not simply something for the Black community or the Haitian community.] (Manzo, interview, March 18, 2005)

Pennycook and Mitchell (this volume) point out that in African and Aboriginal Australian contexts, the interaction of Hip Hop with older local cultural forms makes it possible for MCs to claim Hip Hop as culturally their own and local, in a way that reaches back far beyond the Bronx. In his book on *Global Englishes and Transcultural Flows*, Pennycook questions whether the use of English in rap around the globe is really an indication of massive American triumphal cultural and linguistic spread, or whether there are "other ways of thinking about this" (2007, p. 2). Compared to Africa, Aboriginal Australia, or Maori New Zealand/ Aotearoa, urban Quebec is a more ethnically mixed, brasher, quintessentially North American location for Hip Hop cultural production. But a resistance to domination by English has always been central to the Quebec ethos. Combined with this is a need for urban youth to move away from the navel-gazing traditionalism of monolingual French Quebec culture (C. Bouchard, 2002) in order to create a viable new hybrid culture that can accommodate the diversity of the current youth population. Quebec Hip Hop is the globally derived and locally engaged (Pennycook & Mitchell, this volume) form that this new hybrid culture will be growing into for the next long while, and its origins are multiple despite the shared border with New York State. In particular, to understand Quebec Hip Hop we have to consider the importance of the influence of European French Hip Hop culture as well as of American Hip Hop.

International Hip Hop Studies and Quebec as a Cultural Crossroads

Quebec's geographical position directly north of the American heartland of Hip Hop meant that young people growing up in Quebec in the 1970s and 1980s were exposed to American Hip Hop early on. But because of Quebec's linguistic distinctiveness the exposure of Quebec teenagers to Hip Hop differed from that of their Anglo-Canadian and American contemporaries. Since most school-age children were in French schools, access to cultural influences from France became possible and in fact inevitable, not just for the ethnic French-Canadian population which has always to some extent identified with their historical roots in francophone Europe, but also for a new generation of multiethnic urban Montrealers. When African-origin French rapper MC Solaar started to record in the early 1990s, young French-speakers in Quebec, whatever their ethnolinguistic origin, were able to listen to and understand his politically/poetically complex message. *"L'école du micro d'argent"* (School of the silver microphone), the landmark 1997 recording from the Marseilles Hip Hop group IAM, found an enthusiastic reception in Quebec. Several of the rappers we interviewed mentioned the impact of this CD in particular, one of them remarking: "Tout le monde sonnait comme Akhénaton" (Everybody sounded like [lead MC for IAM] Akhénaton) (Impossible of Muzion, interview, June 4, 2004). Laabidi (2006) refers to this as "le déclic IAM" (p. 172).

To someone situated at the cultural crossroads that, as Laabidi (2006) argues, we inhabit in Quebec, each body of Hip Hop scholarship, both the American and the French, seems hermetically sealed. This is especially true of early American work on Hip Hop, which has, by and large, completely ignored the importance of the Hip Hop phenomenon outside the United States border, except upon occasion to remark on how strong American influence abroad has been (e.g., Rose, 1994, p. 19).[2] The reverse seems to be less true; French scholars, while reserving most of their analytic energies for the European Hip Hop scene, still read and comment on a number of American sources (Bazin, 1995; Durand, 2002; Lapassade & Rousselot, 1998).

A much more recent development in Hip Hop studies has been the slow growth of work outside both the American and the French centers of cultural production. Alim (this volume) points out that the area of global Hip Hop studies was codified mostly through Mitchell's landmark volume, *Global Noise: Rap and Hip Hop Outside the USA* (2001), the first book-length compilation. While there have to date been a few treatments of "Canadian" Hip Hop (Chamberland, 2001, 2006; Krims, 2000), our research team[3] is the first to focus on Quebec Hip Hop specifically as a local (or glocal) instantiation of a global cultural youth movement. We emphasize the local uniqueness of the Quebec Hip Hop scene because of the implications we wish to draw for this particular context, where political forces, language planning decisions, immigration patterns, and global cultural influences have combined to point the way to unexpected new directions for the development of local/national identities.[4] However, we also intend the work described here to be juxtaposed with studies of other urban youth contexts in a "global cipha" of Hip Hop scholarship (Alim, this volume).

This chapter, then, is situated in the context of global Hip Hop studies; specifically, studies that both recognize and resist the centrality of American, and to a lesser extent European French, influences on global Hip Hop as a collection of sites of cultural and intellectual production. As Alim (this volume) recognizes, bodies of work such as those of Mitchell (2001, 2004) and Pennycook (2003; Pennycook & Mitchell, this volume) situate international Hip Hop studies in a postcolonial discourse perspective in which power relations between nation-states, regions, peoples, and individuals are a central object of analysis. Hip Hop themes are some of the many threads being used, in this discourse, to weave together voices—particularly young, nonmainstream, self-aware voices—that are now beginning to discover their own collective power of analysis both within and across borders. These are the voices of this generation's intellectuals; as Pennycook and Mitchell (this volume) point out, signifying on the title of Somali-Canadian rapper K'Naan's best-selling CD, they are "dusty foot philosophers."

Quebec Hip Hop and This Study

Quebec youth moved from being consumers of Hip Hop—first the American, then the European French product—to being producers in their own right in the late 1980s and early 1990s. Many groups were performing to small local audiences and producing mixtapes for local circulation. At first they rapped in English, on the American model, but after the rise to fame of MC Solaar, IAM, Fonky Family, and other European French Hip Hoppers, local Quebec MCs began also to rap in French. The bilingual nature of the youth population, at least in Montreal, and the ease with which many rappers were able to shift between languages, was already in evidence. One group, Dubmatique, rose to local success with sales of over 100,000 between the period 1995 and 2000. Dubmatique rapped only in French, on the European model; several of their members, of African origin, had been schooled in France.

During the second half of the 1990s, very few recordings, with fairly small circulations, were released by Quebec groups other than Dubmatique. In 1999 two CDs were released which achieved local sales in the tens of thousands relatively quickly, considering the restricted Canadian industry market for recordings in French; that is, almost no market outside Quebec (Chamberland, 2001). The 1999 CD *Mentalité Moune Morne*, with a title in Haitian Creole,[5] was the first from Montréal-Nord based group Muzion. This crew of three young Haitian-origin Montrealers, Impossible, Dramatik, and female rapper J.Kyll, all of them fluent speakers of French, Haitian Creole, and English, were notable for the way they mixed their three languages in their lyrics. At the same time, rapper Sans Pression[6] (without pressure, or no pressure) and his then-partner, Haitian-origin Ti-Kid, released *514-50 dans mon réseau* (514-50 in my network).[7] The lyrics on this CD were also remarkable for the way they mixed French, English, and Haitian Creole. Sans Pression, from a family with origins in Congo, had spent time in upstate New York and in small-town Quebec before moving to Montreal; he therefore laid claim to a complex heritage drawing on Black African, African American, and Québécois/Canadian roots.

With these two breakthrough recordings, Quebec Hip Hop exuded a new confidence and linguistic distinctiveness grounded in local sociolinguistic realities. Our project began with an analysis of those two CDs and moved to subsequent work by Muzion and Sans Pression both through their lyrics in other recordings and through interviews with them, as well as with other local artists, notably Dominican-origin rappers SolValdez and 2-Sai, formerly of BlackSunz.[8] We have since extended our lyric analysis and have started an ongoing series of conversations with young Hip Hop fans and aspiring rap, DJ, and graffiti artists. Recordings have proliferated since 1999; dozens are released every year, and new groups are constantly appearing on the scene. The success of most of these groups has not extended beyond one or occasionally two wide-distribution CDs, but many MCs win local small-scale recognition through shows, free Internet distribution and Internet forums, and mixtapes. To explore ways in which the unique mixed language of Quebec rap lyrics is used to challenge existing power relations and denounce local social problems, I will theorize from examples from an analysis of 1999 lyrics and from our formal interviews and informal conversations with local rappers and other Hip Hop insiders between 2002 and 2006.

The Hip Hop Generation in Quebec: Transformative Power

Hip Hop in Quebec has become a diffuse, widely based popular youth movement since the mid- to late 1990s, with adherents everywhere in the province—rural regions as well as Montreal and other urban centers—functioning mostly in French. This diffusion and democratization has gone hand in hand with the diffusion of new ways of mixing non-French loanwords in with both the "standard" and nonstandard varieties of French spoken and written in Quebec.

The Power of Language Mixing

The French that is the base language of Quebec rap, and of talk about rap and Hip Hop, is in some respects a distinct and rapidly evolving French. It is a new language that subtly undermines the original intentions of the Quebec language planners responsible for the legislation that created this multiethnic French-speaking youth population (through obligatory schooling in French) in the first place. By no means all Quebec rap lyrics are linguistically mixed. There are MCs who rap only in English, Spanish, or other nonofficial languages.[9] There are even more who rap only in French.[10] But in lyrics and in the street it is taken for granted that mixing is acceptable on a wide scale. As Pennycook (2004), following Harris (1981, 2002), has pointed out, the reification and subsequent attaching of labels to the supposed entities we call "languages," such as "English," or "French," is bound to be largely arbitrary. The mixing that goes on in the language of much Quebec Hip Hop may call into question, not just Quebec language planning norms, but deep-rooted received notions of what can and cannot be called a language (if indeed anything—any "thing"?—can). The four MCs whose lyrics I focus on here have created texts which both assume and help to construct an audience which is both socially conscious and linguistically open. Multilingualism is positioned "as a natural and desirable condition, whether or not everything is then comprehensible to everyone" (Sarkar & Winer, 2006, p. 189).

In Hip Hop, there is a tension between underground and commercial, between MCs who promote a "conscious" message and those who pursue more materialistic goals (Kitwana 2005; Newman, 2005, 2007). Making it big with Hip Hop carries with it a possible dilution of earlier, less easily accessible, more socially idealistic messages. This tension is present in Quebec Hip Hop, but the restricted nature of the market may make things easier for MCs to a certain extent. When MCs use the mixed language typical of multiethnic youth in Montreal—a mixed language which has both arisen from Hip Hop influences (through the popularity of lyrics by groups such as Muzion and SP), and which, in its local 'hood form, was also at the origin of those Hip Hop influences, according to the MCs—they know that they will not be understood outside a certain youth population in Quebec. The virtual *impossibility* of making it big may permit some MCs to focus on rapping the messages they care about. In our interviews with Muzion and SP, all four MCs emphasized their determination to continue to express a strong social justice message despite the significant level of local success they had attained. Whether they can continue to do so of course remains an open question.

Quebec French has for generations been a source of anxiety and insecurity for its speakers (C. Bouchard, 2002). In this part of the French-speaking world (*la Francophonie*), geographic isolation from the colonizing "mother country" and a few centuries of separate development inevitably resulted in a locally distinctive variety with its own unique vocabulary, pronunciation patterns, and subtle syntactic differences. If it had not undergone the stabilizing influence of a central written standard—particularly powerful for French-speakers because of the weight carried by the pronouncements of the Paris-based *Académie française*—Quebec French might have become a distinct language by now. The adoption of hundreds if not thousands of loanwords from English is a large part of that distinctiveness (Corbett, 1990; Poirier, 1998). But that is not the real problem; the insecurity stems, rather, from the connotations given to "local" varieties in *la Francophonie*. The history of French colonialism has meant that compared to speakers of English around the world, French-speakers in *la Francophonie* have offered much less resistance to the pressures to conform imposed by a European-based metropolitan standard. They have consequently not had the same pride in local linguistic innovation and creative language mixing (Nadeau & Barlow, 2006). With the rise of Hip Hop in French in a number of postcolonial locations outside France—West Africa, for example (Pennycook, 2007)—and including Quebec, that may be about to change (Sarkar, 2006).

Codeswitching in Quebec Hip Hop: The Coding Challenge

When MCs Impossible, J.Kyll, Dramatik, and SP first came out with raps in which several languages were freely mixed over a Quebec French base, the language of the lyrics—according to the MCs themselves—reflected the language of the multiethnic Montreal neighborhoods in which the lyrics were grounded:

> J'**check** Rob : '*What up dog?*'
> — '*What up yo!* **Shit**, les rues sont <u>fucked up</u>!'
> <u>Enough talk</u>. **Check** le reste du <u>squad</u>.
> On *set* un *get* ce soir. *Peace*. <u>Hang up the phone</u>.
> J'<u>step</u> dehors. Dès que j'sors, des nègs <u>blast</u> des *teck*, percent mon corps.
> J'saigne, <u>fuck up</u>, à l'hôpital, presque mort.
> <u>Help me</u> *y'all*!
> (Impossible of Muzion, "666 thème," *Mentalité moune morne*, 1999)

This "dialogue-style" lyric, representing a stylized telephone conversation between Imposs and his interlocutor Rob, is a good example of the language this generation of young Montrealers has evolved to meet their everyday requirements. When we started analyzing the lyrics of this CD and of SP's *514-50 dans mon réseau*, certain coding decisions imposed themselves on the lyric data. In order to indicate the origin of lexical items, we wound up using a coding scheme with nine categories under four superordinate-level headings, as follows:[11]

French
1.   Standard Quebec French (unmarked)
2.   **Nonstandard Quebec French (bold)**
3.   **European French** (bold, and underlined)

English
1.   Standard North American English (underlined)
2.   *African American Vernacular English (AAVE)* (italicized)
3.   *Hip Hop Keywords* (italic and underlined)[12]

Caribbean Creoles
1.   *Haitian Creole* (bold and italic)
2.   *Jamaican Creole* (bold, italic, and underlined)

Other Languages
1.   Spanish (outlined)

Of these nine categories, five are relevant for the "J'check Rob" lyric, which lasts 16 seconds in real time. Quebec youth who listen to local rap and participate in the Hip Hop community in other ways (live shows, Internet forums) would have no difficulty in understanding all of it; it is typical of the way they themselves talk. Imposs introduces the brief simulated phone conversation with a phrase that uses the nonstandard Quebec French verb **checker**, from English "to check," used by Quebec Francophones for decades to mean "to watch, to observe." Here it means "I call up Rob"—we hear the phone ringing—then Imposs continues to Rob with the standard AAVE greeting "*What up dog?*" Rob's voice on the line answers with the equally conventional AAVE "*What up yo!*" then continues with **Shit** [nonstandard Quebec French], les rues sont fucked up! [standard English]. The entire exchange is taking place in a Quebec French context; our decision to code "shit" as French and "fucked up" as English was subjective, based on our understanding that older monolingual French speakers normally have the first epithet, but not the second, integrated into their French lexicon. Younger speakers such as the ones depicted here may not make this fine distinction. The expression "c'est (it's) fucked up" has gained wide currency among members of Quebec's Hip Hop generation, who use it to indicate extremes, both negative (as here) and positive.

The next two lines portray Imposs first answering Rob on the phone, then talking to himself or his Hip Hop audience as narrator of the piece: "Enough talk [English]. **Check** le reste du (the rest of the) _squad_ (Hip Hop word, coded as such because Imposs is speaking in the context of his crew meeting later on). On (we) _set_ (AAVE, "set up") un _get_ (AAVE, "get-together") ce soir (this evening). _Peace_ (coded here as a Hip Hop keyword because it is Imposs's conventional farewell to Rob) Hang up the phone (straight English).

Imposs then "step dehors (outside). Dès que je sors (as soon as I go out), des nègs ("niggas"; the French version has the same negative force as the English in normal language [see Low, 2007, on "the N-word"] and has been reclaimed in a similar way for French by young Black members of the Hip-Hip community) blast des _teck_ ("Tech-1" semiautomatic weapons)." We hear the sound of gunshots: "percent mon corps (put holes in my body). J'saigne (I bleed), fuck up, à l'hôpital, presque mort (at the hospital, almost dead)." We hear an ambulance siren. And the verse ends "Help me y'all!" The rapid-fire code-switching we observe here can be further analyzed in terms of the functions it serves in the composition of raps, which are highly scripted, prewritten forms of language that differ in important ways from normal conversational speech; we have discussed the distinction, and undertaken related analyses, elsewhere (Sarkar & Winer, 2006).

Lyrics, Street Language, and What Speakers Have to Say

It is likely that language like this can only be understood by young Quebec French speakers who are also very familiar with English, both standard North American and AAVE, particularly as it is used and transmuted by Black American rap artists into what Alim (2004) has termed "Hip Hop Nation Language." Furthermore, speakers of this generation, whatever their ethnic background, have also integrated a number of words from both Haitian (French-based) and Jamaican (English-based) Creole into their everyday language and their raps. Some examples of these are **popo** (police), **patnai** (good friend, from English "partner"), **kob** (cash), **ti-moun** (little kid, kid, from French "petit monde"), **kget** (a swearword), all Haitian Creole; _ganja_ (marijuana, one of a long series of words with this meaning), **spliff** (marijuana cigarette, also represented by a long series of words), **_skettel_** (girl, loose woman), **_rude bwoy_** (aggressive youth), all Jamaican Creole.[13]

Several of our interview participants referred to the increasingly widespread use of loanwords from Haitian Creole. One is a recorded rap artist—"Même les Québécois, maintenant, ils commencent à utiliser des slangs créoles" (Even Québécois now are starting to use [Haitian] Creole slang terms) (J.Kyll of Muzion, interview, June 4, 2004); one a rapper at a Montreal high school with an ethnically diverse population:

C'est pas juste les _rappers_ qui font ça. Tu marches dans la rue, pis tu vas parler à un _dude_, pis un p'tit _dude_ québécois va faire "**kgeeettt, pathnai yo!**"

[It's not just *rappers* who do that [language mixing]. You walk down the street, and you're gonna talk to some *dude*, and some little Québécois *dude's* gonna go "**kgeeettt, pathnai** *yo!*"] (Kobir of Red Pill, interview, March 12, 2005).

Our interview with the four young members of Montreal's Hip Hop community who make up the "Red Pill" crew—Anthony, Dace, Maxime, and Kobir— produced many instances of this kind of mixing:

"Hé *yo*, on va **chiller** pis fumer un *spliff*."…"On va aller clubbin"
["Hey *yo*, we're gonna **chill** and smoke a *spliff*."…"We're gonna go clubbin"]
(Maxime and Dace of Red Pill, interview, March 12, 2005)

All these young men were schooled in French; three of them have antecedents outside Quebec. The one member of the crew who declared himself to be "Québecois à 120%" is Maxime, who spoke about his interaction with English through his Hip Hop friends and activities:

J'leur demande tout le temps qu'y me traduisent leur texte [de l'anglais], là, à chaque fois genre, "*A'ight*, explique-moi c'que t'as fait." Pis là, y'est comme: a'ight, là je dis…pis la plupart du temps les rhymes qu'y ont faits en anglais, y riment quand même en français."

[I ask them [other crew members] all the time to translate their texts [from English], every time, like, "A'ight, explain to me what you did." So he's like, a'ight, so I'm telling you…And most of the time the rhymes they did in English, they rhyme in French too.] (Maxime of Red Pill, interview, March 12, 2005)

In another interview with two Dominican-origin Montreal-area MCs, SolValdez and 2Sai, Sol mentioned how natural three-way Spanish-French-English switching is for them: "We don't even notice that we switched languages, we just 'yo, and bla bla bla,' in Spanish and then switch in French" (SolValdez of BlackSunz, interview, April 7, 2004)

In the language of Quebec French-based Hip Hop, this kind of switching extends beyond the original immigrant communities, as all our sources confirm.[14] When we challenged Sol on how his use of Spanish might make his raps incomprehensible for some local listeners, he countered with,

Well, it's kind of a way to slowly teach people, you know. If somebody doesn't know [Spanish], I'm pretty sure that somebody knows somebody that's Spanish and…they'll ask…. [S]ome people might see it as a limitation. But if you look at it on the other side, it's more of an expansion. (SolValdez of BlackSunz, interview, April 7, 2004).

This comment, and Maxime's discussion of the way he has actually learned a lot of English through his work composing raps with crew members who are fluent speakers, leads us to believe that a lot of second language learning may be going on through the medium of Quebec rap lyrics. One development has been a very open-minded attitude to diverse linguistic influences in art and in conversation. The language mixing is becoming something to be proud of rather than something to be ashamed of. A graffiti writer in his mid-20s found it quite natural to say,

> Ça amène beaucoup de diversité, les différences de langage dans le Hip Hop, ça permet au gens d's'exprimer plus facilement pis d'toucher encore plus de monde.
>
> [The language differences in Hip Hop bring in a lot of diversity, that lets people express themselves more easily and reach out to more people.] (Sewk, interview, March 18, 2004)

A comment by J.Kyll from her discussion of the importance of "keepin it real" accords both in content and in style with my interpretation of the power of language mixing in Quebec Hip Hop:

> Les gens y feelent **man,** like if you really like what you're doing, pis si t'es sincère. Tu peux pas rester indifférent à quelqu'un qui te parle, s'y t'parle avec son cœur. *Straight up.*
>
> [People feel, **man,** like if you really like what you're doing, and if you're sincere. You can't stay indifferent to someone who's talking to you, if he's talking to you with his heart. *Straight up.*] (J.Kyll of Muzion, interview, June 4 2004)

In their work, Montreal Hip Hop artists do not just reflect the linguistic and cultural diversity around them—they contribute actively to its creation. In their conscious efforts to teach the urban youth population to use more and different languages and to blend them together in new ways, they articulate a discourse rooted in an alternative vision of community that transcends Quebec's historically intransigent language-against-language divide. As we shall see, this emergent community also has a keen awareness of the social problems that urgently need to be addressed for and by the rising urban generation.

The Power of Representin

Conscious (Social Justice) Focus in Lyrics

To continue with more words from Haitian-origin rapper J.Kyll:

> Show me respect, j'suis la true *ill* **nana**
> Pourquoi t'es venu, si tu *front* **sou kote**?

Fais pas ton **mean**, j'vois ton *bounda* sauter
Si tu sais pas danser, qu'est-ce que t'as à te moquer?
Dis-le, t'aimes mes **moves**, pas vrai, t'es choqué?
Hey! Mais qu'est-ce ta main fait là? <u>Go away</u>!
Neg pa lave, pafume…. <u>No way</u>!
You tha man, toutes les femmes te veulent.. oh! ouais!
You wanna get down, you go down! O.K.[15]

In J.Kyll's work (unlike that of her brother Impossible), straight glossing works reasonably well:

[Show me respect, I'm a **woman** to reckon with
Why did you come, if you're going to sneak *around*?
Don't be **nasty**, I saw your *ass* jumpin'
If you can't dance, quit making fun of me
C'mon, you like my **moves**, admit you're pissed off
Hey! What's your hand doing there? Go away!
Black who'd rather wear perfume than wash…No way!
You tha man, all the girls are after you…yeah, right!
You wanna get down, you go down! O.K.]
(J.Kyll of Muzion, 1999, "Lounge with us", *Mentalité moune morne*)

J.Kyll is one of a handful of female rappers in a landscape where most MCs are men. Here, in the guise of a woman speaking from the dance floor, J.Kyll criticizes a common male attitude, one that combines showing off, acting big, with contempt for the object of his under*hand*ed (what's his hand doing there?) seduction tactics. He thinks he's attractive, but he's not (a personal hygiene problem); he thinks he has something to boast about—yeah, right! There are other and better ways to pleasure a woman (you wanna *get* down, you *go* down). In her work, J.Kyll implicitly and explicitly singles out for special criticism the macho posing that frequently characterizes Hip Hop culture. She frequently points out how important it is for Hip Hop to try to eradicate sexism within the movement if it is to achieve its full transformative potential for young people.

The social commentary proposed in Quebec rap is often informed by analyses of ubiquitous problems such as systemic racism and the poverty endemic to overcrowded urban neighborhoods. SP rings a local change on a common Hip Hop theme in this meditative rap reflecting on what it's like to grow up Black in Montreal:

… le racisme fait partie de ma vie quotidienne
pis je suis pas le seul, <u>goddamn</u>, je le sais, tu le sais,
si t'as une gueule comme la mienne *yo*! *yo*! t'es né suspect
pour les *popos* du réseau, *yo*! j'ai rien à vous cacher:
j'ai le goût de tout casser quand je vous écoute parler,

la même **bullshit** : 'je suis pas raciste moi, les Noirs je les aime
pis dès que je tourne mon dos: 'je les haïs les **crisses** de Nèg's',
'retourne dans ton pays'. On est tous des immigrés…

[…racism is part of my everyday life,
and I'm not the only one, <u>goddamn</u>, you know it, I know it,
if you have a face like mine, *yo! yo!* you're born a suspect
for the *cops* in the system, *yo!* I have nothing to hide from you:
I feel like busting everything up when I hear you,
the same **bullshit**: 'I'm not racist, I love Blacks'
then as soon as my back is turned, 'I hate the **fuckin' niggers'**,
'go back to where you came from'. We're all immigrants….]
(Sans Pression, "Pouki Sa,"[16] *514-50 dans mon réseau*, 1999)]

We hear voices that are "politically correct" in public, but privately racist; we
know they are local francophone Québécois rednecks (no-one else would use
an expression like "les **crisses** de Nègs"). Like many other lyrics by Montreal
MCs, SP's lyric vividly brings out the contradictions inherent in Quebec's public
discourse on immigration, integration, and language,[17] to which SP contrasts
the lived experiences of non-White immigrants. In the 1999 work of SP and of
Muzion, as well as in more recent lyrics by these and a host of other Montreal
rappers, not reported on here, the blended language medium is itself a powerful
part of the convention-challenging message that "speaks truth to power" (Said,
1994). By drawing on words from African American and other Englishes as
well as from languages such as Haitian Creole that arrived in Quebec as part of
postcolonial migrations, Montreal MCs situate Quebec Hip Hop globally as part
of a culture and a movement that lets them bring wide-ranging analytical tools
to bear on supposedly local Quebec social problems.

Representin Cultural and Linguistic Diversity

The availability of rap as an artistic medium for those among the new multiethnic
generation of young Québécois who want to put out a message of some kind is
likely to reshape the local cultural landscape in important ways. As Pennycook
and Mitchell put it (this volume), this is the point where the local takes over
the global, where "we need to focus on the local host culture appropriating Hip
Hop rather than Hip Hop becoming localized." Quebec Hip Hop community
members we talked to felt strongly that Hip Hop as a cultural movement has a
unique ability to enable Quebec youth of many origins to come together and
find a new voice:

C'est grâce au Hip Hop que tous les jeunes sont ensemble maintenant…
Tous les jeunes presque en ce moment l'aiment, soit chinois, arabe, latino,
c'est ça qui relie tout le monde.

[It's thanks to Hip Hop that young people are together now. Almost all young people right now like it, whether they're Chinese, Arab, Latino, it's what's bringing everybody together.]
(Dramatik of Muzion, interview, June 4, 2004)

MCs such as Dramatik, Impossible, and J.Kyll of Muzion therefore see themselves as having a special mission to represent diversity:

Y a beaucoup de monde aussi qui veulent pas parler, mais qui attendent que quelqu'un parle pour eux; ben le Hip Hop ça fait ça pour eux un p'tit peu. Pis dans d'autres styles musicales, ce mélange culturel-là, tu le vois pas vraiment.

[There are also a lot of people who don't want to speak up, but who wait for someone to speak for them; well, Hip Hop does that for them a bit. And in other musical styles, you don't really see that cultural mix.] (Imposs of Muzion, interview, 4 June 2004)

In Quebec, as in so many other places, although Hip Hop means different things to different people, it functions as a powerful unifying force for youth. The particular youth community that is finding its voice through Hip Hop has unique local linguistic and ethnocultural characteristics. The fact that the English used by Montreal MCs is so often drawn from African American and Creole vernaculars aligns the artists as part of a global "resistance to dominant white culture becoming a dominant global cultural form" (Pennycook, 2007, p. 3). The MCs this community speaks through epitomize intellectuals as Edward Said has written about them—"individuals with a vocation for the art of representing" (1994, p. 13), who I take to overlap at many points with Toronto-based Somali-Canadian rapper K'Naan's "dusty foot philosophers" (Pennycook & Mitchell, this volume). Constantly aware and self-marginalizing by choice, in the ways they use language as in other ways, they are quintessential examples of Said's *exilic intellectuals*. These culturally and politically conscious MCs gleefully embrace a condition of marginality which, precisely because it "might seem irresponsible or flippant" (like SP's and Muzion's lyrics), "frees you from always having to proceed with caution" (Said, 1994, p. 63).

In Conclusion: Hybridity, Identity, and the Quebec Hip Hop Generation

The nature of Quebec identity has been the object of theorizing for decades, if not centuries (C. Bouchard, 2002). Political philosophers (Maclure, 2003), sociologists (Labelle & Rocher, 2004), journalists (Gagnon, 2003), and politicians such as Louise Beaudoin, Quebec Minister for the Charter of the French Language (Beaudoin, 1999), have all had their say about whether or not Quebec, whatever the background of its inhabitants,[18] may be said to constitute a "nation" in some sense. In November 2006 the question[19] even came to the Canadian parliament and was passed by a huge majority of 266 to 16. As I write this in 2007, the much-publicized, publicly funded *Commission Taylor-Bouchard*, headed by two prominent academic theorists of identity (G. Bouchard, Jacques, & Taylor, 1999; Taylor, 1989) is touring the province to gather opinions on what "Quebec identity" means to people across the Quebec *nation*. This is a hotly contested forum for public debate. Quebec language legislation from the 1960s through to the present has been grounded in this debate; from the outset, Quebec language planners had as their goal the development of a distinctive national identity based on French as the common public language of an ethnolinguistically diverse population (Termot, 1999). Furthermore, the French they had in mind was the rigidly normative, prescriptive French that typifies attitudes toward language and correctness in *la Francophonie* (Nadeau & Barlow, 2006; Sarkar, 2006).

"Race" has largely been excluded from this debate in Quebec. In other parts of Canada, the importance of skin color for the lives and identities of immigrants and nonimmigrants alike is acknowledged and intensively theorized (Ibrahim, 2003; Walcott, 2000; Yon, 2000, all writing about urban Ontario). In Quebec, the French-English language divide has tended to hijack academic discourse about identity. Language, rather than French-Canadian ethnic identity, or Catholic religious identity, as formerly, is now seen as *the* "élément identitaire" (identity element). Quebec rap lyrics bring skin color and "other" ethnicities back into the agenda. The existence of systemic racism, a common theme in Hip Hop lyrics by non-White Montreal MCs, is downplayed or denied in official discourse and in academic settings (where non-White academics—I am one—are made to feel very uncomfortable if they insist on introducing "the R-word"). This is true in anglophone Quebec, where most of my own professional experience has been; it is even more true in francophone Quebec, as a cursory reading of the Quebec academic discourse on identity will show (Ancelovi & Dupuis-Déri, 1997; Corbett, 1990; Juteau, 1999; Labelle, 2005; Salée, 1995).

Our exploration of the language(s) and message(s) of Quebec Hip Hop has led us to a new way to understand the dynamics of identity creation in Quebec, one in which race and language, the seen and the heard, are theorized together (Sarkar, Low, & Winer, 2007). The rap artists whose work I have explored here are in fact introducing a whole new set of multiple, hybrid, and fluid identities into the debate, thus making possible new ways of unpacking the traditional, tacit, and (I would argue) toxic view of Quebec identity, with its unspoken grounding in "Whiteness" and "Frenchness." Members of Quebec's Hip Hop community, while like all Hip Hoppers acknowledging the importance of being grounded in one's own ethnic origins, still strongly resist being pinned down to societally imposed identities. Quebec Hip Hop brings in the poetic voices and the agency—the power to act—of a new multilingual, multiracial urban generation seemingly left out of the language planners' calculations (Allen, 2006). One of the ways members of this generation are acting decisively is through the creation of new ways of blending the language repertoires available to them.

With new forms of language will come new forms of literature—the poetry of rap is only one example—and new forms of social life which have just begun to be imagined into being. As they reach out to the Global Hip Hop Nation (Alim, this volume), these Hip Hop forms of language and social life extend beyond Quebec's borders, giving youth in this part of the world a way to break out of the purist, French-obsessed ethnocentricity that Quebec has traditionally been known for. Hip Hop in Quebec is indeed, as one of the editors of this volume encapsulated it, a good example of "a moment of translating the global locally" (A. Ibrahim, personal communication). If it goes on as it has begun, Quebec Hip Hop has the potential to be a positive, cohesive, outward-looking social force for this generation—a generation that is experimenting actively with much-needed alternative ways of doing "being Québécois."

Acknowledgments

I am indebted first to the MCs whose lyrics we drew upon and who shared their expertise with us in interviews, as well as to the other Hip Hop insiders who agreed to speak with us. My thanks also go to William Fradette, local Hip Hop head and invaluable resource on the Montreal scene; to Bronwen Low of the McGill-based research team and to Shelagh Plunkett, for their assistance with the first draft of this manuscript; and to Lise Winer and Dawn Allen (also of the McGill team), Kobir Sarkar of Red Pill/Bartenders, and Danielle Rousseau, industry insider, for their support and resource help. H. Samy Alim, Awad Ibrahim, and Alastair Pennycook gave valuable feedback on earlier drafts of this chapter.

Notes

1. See Bourhis (2001), for a political-linguistic summary of the relevant period.
2. A welcome exception is Meghelli's work in Spady, Alim, and Meghelli (2006).
3. The work reported here is being conducted by a team of four researchers based at McGill University in Montreal, with substantial help from research assistants and local Hip Hop community insiders (see Acknowledgments).
4. When Quebec French speakers say "national," they mean Québécois, not Canadian.
5. The title means roughly "People just don't get it."
6. All names are self-styled Hip Hop names and are used, as are some real names, with permission.
7. "514" and "450" are the telephone area codes that cover the Greater Montreal administrative region.
8. The title of this article samples a song by BlackSunz.
9. By law, at provincial level the only official language of Quebec is French.
10. Among them is Loco Locass (e.g., 2000) who have ridden to local fame entirely on the strength of their pro-Quebec independence message. Loco Locass is probably the best-known rap group recording in Quebec today. They typically perform at large-scale events with a general Quebec nationalist appeal, such as the annual June 24th Fête nationale ("National Festival") celebration, rather than at more usual, and generally more underground, Hip Hop venues.
11. As always, these labels ("French," "English," etc.) should be seen as convenient, and certainly not innocent, oversimplifications for present purposes (Janicki, 2006; Pennycook, 2004).
12. See Alim (2004); Cutler (2003); Morgan (2001); and Smitherman (1997), for a discussion of Hip Hop Nation Language words as distinct from other AAVE words.

13. I am indebted to H.S. Alim for pointing out to me that *popo, patnai,* and spliff are also common in Black American Hip Hop. More work is needed to determine just how these and a host of other such words came into American rap, but their route can likely be traced back through the linguistic and musical influence, in the United States, of Creole-speakers from the Caribbean (L. Winer, personal communication, 2006).

14. See also Rampton (1998), on multiethnic youth communities in urban England and "crossing."

15. In this extract we see several examples of codeswitching using Haitian Creole: *bounda* (/bunda/), *sou kote* (/su kote/, "on the side") and *neg pas lave, pafume* (/neg pa lave, pafume/, i.e., "not washed," "perfumed"). J.Kyll frequently raps entire verses in Haitian Creole. A word from European French slang (nana, "chick"), helps the rhyme scheme, as well as incorporating a reference to Black American female rapper Foxy Brown's debut CD *Ill Na Na* (J.Kyll is the "true" ill nana; is Foxy a fake one?). Six of our nine categories are needed to code this short extract.

16. The piece itself is titled in Haitian Creole, a language SP uses without considering himself a fluent speaker (SP, interview, April 9, 2004).

17. Salée (1995) is one of a very few academic commentators to have named these contradictions.

18. The original inhabitants of the territory now known as Quebec were the aboriginal Inuit and First Nations, of which 11 consider themselves to be indigenous to "Quebec" (a label that many First Nations do not recognize as legitimate). The embarrassing situation that Quebec nationalists would find themselves in if they acknowledged the validity of First Nations territorial and other claims has led to the First Nations being even more completely excluded from the Quebec identity debates than other non-White populations of more recent arrival.

19. "That this House recognize that the Québécois form a nation within a united Canada." Controversy about this motion and the reasons it was brought (by the ruling Conservative party) at this time will likely rage in the Canadian press for decades (CBC News, November 27, 2006).

Discography/Webography

All websites for Hip Hop groups accessed and verified April 24, 2006.

Foxy Brown. (1996). *Ill Na Na.* New York: Def Jam. http://www.ill-nana.net/main.htm

IAM. (1997). *L'école du micro d'argent* [School of the silver microphone]. France: EMI–Virgin Music Publishing. http://www.iam.tm.fr/

Loco Locass. (2000). *Manifestif* [Manifestive]. Montréal: Les productions Diphtongue. http://www.locolocass.net/nouvelles/

Muzion. (1999). *Mentalité moune morne* [People just don't get it]. Montréal: BMG Quebec. http://www.vikrecordings.com/muzion/

Sans Pression. (1999). *514-50 dans mon réseau* [514–40 in my network]. Montréal: Les Disques Mont Real. http://www.sanspression.ca/

References

Alim, H.S. (2004). Hip hop nation language. In E. Finegan & J. Rickford (Eds.), *Language in the USA: Themes for the 21st century* (pp. 386–409). New York: Cambridge University Press.

Allen, D. (2006). Who's in and who's out? Language and the integration of new-immigrant youth in Quebec. *The International Journal of Inclusive Education, 10* (2-3), 251–263.

Ancelovi, M., & Dupuis-Déri, F. (1997). *L'Archipel identitaire* [The archipelago of identity]. Montréal: Les Editions du Boréal.

Bazin, H. (1995). *La culture Hip Hop* [Hip hop culture]. Paris: Desclée de Brouwer.

Beaudoin, L. (1999, April 24). Une politique linguistique plus ferme que jamais [A firmer language policy than ever]. *Journal Le Devoir.*(Montréal). Retrieved April 17, 2008, from http://www.spl.gouv.qc.ca/secretariat/t_surviefrancais.html

Bouchard, C. (2002*). La langue et le nombril: Une histoire sociolinguistique du Québec (nouvelle édition mise à jour)* [Language and navel-gazing: A sociolinguistic history of Quebec (rev.ed.)]. Québec: Fides/Les publications du Québec.

Bouchard, G., Jacques, D., & Taylor, C. (1999). *L'avenir de l'état-nation* [The future of the nation-state]. Montreal: McGill University, Programme d'études sur le Québec.

Bourhis, R.Y. (2001) Reversing language shift in Quebec. In J. Fishman (Ed.), *Can threatened languages be saved?* (pp. 101–141). Clevedon, UK: Multilingual Matters.

CBC [Canadian Broadcasting Company] News. (2006, November 27). Retrieved December 21, 2006, from http://www.cbc.ca/canada/story/2006/11/27/nation-vote.html

Chamberland, R. (2001). Rap in Canada: Bilingual and multicultural. In T. Mitchell (Ed.), *Global noise: Rap and hip hop outside the USA* (pp. 306–325). Middletown, CT: Wesleyan University Press.

Chamberland, R. (2006). Le paradoxe culturel du rap québécois. In P. Roy & S. Lacasse (Eds.), *Groove: Enquête sur les phénomènes musicaux contemporains – Mélanges à la mémoire de Roger Chamberland.* (pp. 1–13). Québec, QC: Les presses de l'Université Laval.

Corbett, N. (Ed.). (1990). *Langue et identité: Le Français et les francophones d'Amérique du nord* [Language and identity: French and Francophones in North America]. Québec: Les presses de l'Université Laval.

Cutler, C. (2003) "Keepin' it real": White hip hoppers' discourses of language, race, and authenticity. *Journal of Linguistic Anthropology, 13,* 211–233.

Durand, A-P. (2002). *Black, blanc, beur: Rap music and hip hop culture in the Francophone world.* Lanham, MD & Oxford: Scarecrow Press.

Gagnon, L. (2003, February.) En première? En troisième? [First? Third]. *Journal La Presse* (Montréal), B5.

Harris, R. (1981). *The language myth.* London: Duckworth.

Harris, R. (2002). The role of the language myth in the Western cultural tradition. In R. Harris (Ed.), *The language myth in Western culture* (pp. 1–24). Richmond, UK: Curzon Press.

Ibrahim, A. (2003). "Whassup, homeboy?" Joining the African diaspora: Black English as a symbolic site of identification and language learning. In S. Makoni, G. Smitherman, A. F. Ball, & A.K. Spears, (Eds.), *Black linguistics: Language, society and politics in Africa and the Americas* (pp. 169–185). London: Routledge.

Janicki, K. (2006). *Language misconceived: Arguing for applied cognitive sociolinguistics.* Mahwah, NJ: Erlbaum.

Juteau, D. (1999). *L'ethnicité et ses frontières* [Ethnicity and its borders]. Montréal: Les Presses de l'Université de Montréal.

Kitwana, B. (2005). *Why white kids love hip hop: Wanksters, wiggers, wannabes and the new reality of race in America.* New York: Basic Civitas Books.

Krims, A. (2000). *Rap music and the poetics of identity.* Cambridge, UK: Cambridge University Press.

Laabidi, M. (2006). Culture hip hop québécoise et francophone, culture identitaire [Quebec and Francophone hip hop culture, culture of identity]. In P. Roy & S. Lacasse (Eds.), *Groove: Enquête sur les phénomènes musicaux contemporains–Mélanges à la mémoire de Roger Chamberland* [Groove: Inquiry into contemporary musical phenomena—A mix in memory of Roger Chamberland] (pp. 167–177). Québec: Les presses de l'Université Laval.

Labelle, M. (2005). Le défi de la diversité au Canada et au Québec [The challenge of diversity in Canada and Quebec]. *Options Politiques,* March.

Labelle, M., & Rocher, F. (Eds.). (2004). *Contestation transnationale, diversité et citoyenneté dans l'espace québécois* [Transnational conflict, diversity and citizenship in Quebec space]. Québec: Presses de l'Université du Québec.

Lapassade, G., & Rousselot, P. (1998). *Le rap ou la fureur de dire* (6th ed.) [Rap or the fury of the word]. Paris: Éditions Loris Talmart.

Low, B. (2007). Hip Hop, language, and difference: The N-word as a pedagogical limit-case. *Journal of Language, Identity and Education, 6*(1), 147–160.

Maclure, J. (2003). *Quebec identity: The challenge of pluralism.* [English version of *Récits identitaires,* 2001.] Montreal: McGill/Queen's University Press.

Mitchell, T. (Ed.) (2001). *Global noise: Rap and hip hop outside the USA.* Middletown, CT: Wesleyan University Press.

Mitchell, T. (2004). Doin' damage in my native language: Resistance vernaculars in hip hop in Europe and Aotearoa/New Zealand. In S. Whiteley, A. Bennett, & S. Hawkins (Eds.), *Popular music, space and place* (pp. 108–123). London: Ashgate.

Morgan, M. (2001) Nuthin' but a "G" thang: Grammar and language ideology in hip hop identity. In S. L. Lanehart (Ed.), *Sociocultural and historical contexts of African American English* (pp. 187–210). Athens: University of Georgia Press.

Nadeau, J.-B., & Barlow, J. (2006). *The story of French.* Toronto, Canada: A. A. Knopf.

Newman, M. (2005). Rap as literacy: A genre analysis of rap ciphers. *Text, 25*(3), 399–436.

Newman, M. (2007). "I don't want my ends to just meet; I want my ends overlappin'": Personal aspiration and the rejection of progressive rap. *Journal of Language, Identity and Education, 6*(1), 131–145.

Pennycook, A. (2003). Global Englishes, Rip Slyme, and performativity. *Journal of Sociolinguistics, 7*(4), 513–533.

Pennycook, A. (2004). Performativity and language studies. *Critical Inquiry in Language Studies, 1,* 1–19.

Pennycook, A. (2007). *Global Englishes and transcultural flows.* London: Routledge.

Poirier, C. (Ed.) (1998). *Dictionnaire historique du français québécois* [Historical dictionary of Quebec French]. Ste. Foy, Quebec, Canada: Les Presses de l'Université Laval.

Rampton, B. (1998). Language crossing and the redefinition of reality. In P. Auer (Ed.), *Code-switching in conversation* (pp. 290–317). London: Routledge.

Rose, T. (1994). *Black noise: Rap music and black culture in contemporary America.* Hanover, NH: University Press of New England.

Said, E. (1994). *Representations of the intellectual.* New York: Vintage Books.

Salée, D. (1995), Espace public, identité et nation au Québec: Mythes et méprises du discours souverainiste [Public space, identity and nation in Quebec: Myths and misunderstandings in the discourse of sovereignty].[Special issue]. *Cahiers de recherche sociologique, 25,* 125–153.

Sarkar, M. (2006). "La vraie langue française [n']existe plus": Français parlé et pratiques multilingues comme stratégies identitaires dans le rap montréalais ["The true French language (no longer) exists": Multilingual practices in spoken French as identity strategies in Montreal rap]. *Grenzgänge, 13*(25), 30–51.

Sarkar, M., Low, B., & Winer, L. (2007). "Pour connecter avec le Peeps": Québéquicité and the Quebec hip hop community. In M. Mantero (Ed.), *Identity and second language learning : Culture, inquiry and dialogic activity in educational contexts* (pp. 351–372). Greenwich, CT: Information Age Publishing.

Sarkar, M., & Winer, L. (2006). Multilingual code-switching in Quebec rap: Poetry, pragmatics, and performativity. *International Journal of Multilingualism, 3*(3), 173–192.

Smitherman, G. (1997) The chain remain the same: Communicative practices in the hip hop nation. *Journal of Black Studies, 28,* 3–25.

Spady, J., Alim, H. S., & Meghelli, S. (2006). *Tha global cipha: Hip hop culture and consciousness.* Philadelphia, PA: Black History Museum Press.

Taylor, C. (1989). *Sources of the self: The making of the modern identity.* Cambridge, MA: Harvard University Press.

Termot, M. (1999). *Perspectives démolinguistiques du Québec et de la région de Montréal à l'aube du XXIe siècle: Implications pour le français langue d'usage public.* [Demolinguistic perspectives in the Montreal region of Quebec in the early 21st century: Implications for French language usage]. Québec, QC: Conseil de la langue française.

Walcott, R. (Ed.). (2000). *Rude: Contemporary Black Canadian cultural criticism.* Toronto: Insomniac Press.

Yon, D. (2000). *Elusive culture: Schooling, race and identity in global times.* Albany, NY: State University of New York Press.

"Respect for Da Chopstick Hip Hop"
The Politics, Poetics, and Pedagogy of Cantonese Verbal Art in Hong Kong

ANGEL LIN

My message is to ask people to reflect, to use their brains to think and their hearts to feel—MC Yan.

Introduction: The Arrival of Hip Hop onto the Music Scene in Hong Kong

The music scene in Hong Kong has been dominated by Cantopop (Cantonese pop songs) since the mid-1970s. The early prominent Cantopop lyricists and singers such as Sam Hui were legendary in laying the foundation of the genre and the tradition of the lyrical styles which appeal to the masses through the rise of local Cantonese cinema and television. With easy-listening melody and simple lyrics about ordinary working-class people's plight, Sam Hui's music and lyrical style marked the genesis of a new popular music form in Hong Kong, known as Cantopop (Erni, 2007). Cantopop has arisen as an indigenous music genre that the majority of Hong Kong people identity with. It has served as "a strategic cultural form to delineate a local identity, vis-à-vis the old British colonial and mainland Chinese identities" (McIntyre, Cheng, & Zhang, 2002, p. 217).

However, Cantopop since the 1990s has become increasingly monopolized by a few mega music companies in Hong Kong that focus on idol-making, mainly churning out songs about love affairs, and losing the early versatility that had existed in the themes of Cantopop lyrics (e.g., about working-class life, about friendship and family relationships, about life philosophy, etc.) (Chu, 2007).

It was against this background that Hip Hop as a music genre became visible in the mainstream music scene in Hong Kong in the mid-1990s, when the local underground band LMF (LazyMuthaFuckaz) suddenly emerged above ground and enjoyed a popular reception for some years with their angry lyrics about

159

the everyday reality of working-class youths in their debut song, "Uk-chyun-jai" (Housing Projects Boys) (Chan, 2003). However, LMF's music style was actually a fusion of rock and Hip Hop genres. Researching on the historical development of LMF, I interviewed Davy Chan, a former LMF member who composed and produced most of the music and songs for LMF in his studio—"a.room". According to Davy, who was also a founding member of the local indie rock band, Anodize, in the early 1990s, LMF was originally an ad hoc band loosely formed by members from different rock bands to jam music for fun at the end of major underground music events. It was Prodip, a rock guitarist and graphic designer, who turned the loosely organized LMF into a formally organized band by gathering members from several indie rock bands (e.g., Anodize, NT) and by managing negotiations with major music labels and sponsors. LMF gave the audience the impression of Hip Hop mainly due to the presence of DJ Tommy and MC Yan. Davy invited DJ Tommy to join LMF in the late 1990s for "they wanted to try something new, perhaps Hip Hop." MC Yan was a vocalist and rapper from the rock band, NT, in the early 1990s, and joined LMF with other NT members. Of the final 12 members of LMF in the early 2000s, only two members (MC Yan and DJ Tommy) had a Hip Hop music background.

LMF was disbanded in 2003. According to Davy, it was partly due to the loss of advertising sponsors along with increasingly negative coverage of LMF in the media, and partly because a managing executive of Warner-Brothers, who had signed LMF and had given them great creative autonomy, left the company. The constant touring, performing, and advertising jobs had also robbed them of the time and space for creating new songs. As artists who did not want to repeat themselves, they decided that it was time to disband.

The Hip Hop scene in Hong Kong has never been as animated since the disbanding of LMF. However, Fama, a two-emcee group was formed in 2000. In 2002 the two emcees came under the tutelage of DJ Tommy, and were signed by DJ Tommy's music production company. Fama has strived to keep local Hip Hop music alive in Hong Kong. Although still marginal to Cantopop in the mainstream music scene, it is popular among college and high school students and it is the only local Hip Hop group since LMF to enjoy some degree of commercial success.

Fama, however, has its own style, which they seem to want to distinguish clearly from the LMF style. LMF rocked the local music and media scene by being the first local popular band to put Cantonese *chou-hau* (vulgar speech) into their lyrics in publicly released albums and live performances, and by taking a strongly resistant, defiant, media-critical stance (see studies by Ma, 2001, 2002a, 2002b). LMF's lyrics were largely Cantonese, and when English was used, it was mainly English slang; for instance: "Do you know what the fuck I'm saying?! *Hahm-gaa-ling!*" (a Cantonese *chou-hau* expression literally meaning: "To hell with your whole family!"). LMF's sociolinguistic positioning can be said to be mostly that of the Hong Kong Cantonese working-class youth—the speaking style projects a powerful, defiant, angry, Cantonese, working-class, masculine image, with lots of "rage"—*fo* (fire) in Cantonese (more on this later).

Fama, however, from day one, seemed to want to rectify the popular notion in Hong Kong (largely due to LMF's influence) that Hip Hop music is related to Cantonese vulgar speech or the angry young man image. Li (2006), in her unpublished MPhil study of Hip Hop music in Hong Kong, pointed out that Fama seemed to want to rectify Hong Kong people's misconceptions about Hip Hop music. In a song by Fama called "F.A.M.A. Praise," Fama rapped explicitly in their lyrics about these misconceptions. They seemed to want to draw a line between themselves and the image of MC Yan, in particular, as a politically outspoken figure.

Fama thus seems to aim at dissociating themselves from the politically conscious image projected by MC Yan, who aligns himself with the Muslim cause and writes conscious raps that criticize the Bush government (e.g., in his song, "War Crime"). Fama also never uses Cantonese *chou-hau* in their lyrics. While LMF's lyrics were chiefly Cantonese (except for some vulgar English words), Fama readily uses English and crafts out Cantonese-English bilingual lyrics which sound more like middle-class bilingual college boys than LMF's Cantonese working-class men (Lin, 2007).

To date there has been only one published research project on alternative band culture in Hong Kong. Eric Ma's ethnographic studies on alternative bands in Hong Kong represent the first academic attempt to bring under lenses of cultural studies the emotional energies and cultural practices of alternative bands (Ma, 2002a, 2002b). After months of intensive ethnographic field work (e.g., hanging around with LMF band members in their recording studios, concerts, their everyday/night activities, interviewing band artists and their fans, observing the behavior of the audiences in the concerts, etc.), Ma published a series of research papers and photography books on the alternative band, LMF. Summarizing his analysis in an article, Ma (2002a) wrote:

> As illustrated in this case study, the emotional energies generated by Hong Kong alternative bands are polymorphous. They are partly fuelled by the rebellious spirit of independent music incorporated translocally…; they can be charged by personal frustrations in schools, families and the workplaces…; their production can be a tactic of differentiating a youth identity in contrast with the adult and the established world; they can be exploited by some privileged group members to serve as fashionable identity labels…. Emotional energies can also be political. In the particular juncture of the post-1997 Hong Kong, subcultural energies have [been] articulated and channeled into popular anti-establishment discourses. There are obvious thematic parallels between alternative music and public sentiments on the widespread dissatisfaction with the tabloid media, the education system and the conservative polity. (p. 198)

While Ma seemed to be deeply sympathetic with the sentiments of the alternative band, his ethnographic analysis yielded less than optimistic findings about the progressive potential of the subcultural practices of the band members. Ma wrote critically about the lack of political critique of the band members he studied (Ma, 2002a).

It is at this point that we find Ma's ethnographic analysis, albeit rich and cogent in many aspects, lacking a sociolinguistic perspective. As a cultural studies researcher without any sociolinguistic background, Ma has not conducted any detailed linguistic analysis of the lyrics and might have thus drawn his conclusion a bit too hastily based mainly on the interview comments of some LMF members. The dearth of serious attention paid to the Cantonese *chou-hau* verbal art of Hip Hop lyrics by independent Hong Kong MCs might also explain the lack of understanding of how youthful (defiant) voices and agency are mediated first and foremost in *language* in their raps. I will turn to my attempt at such an analysis in the next section.

Cantonese Youth Verbal Play in Hong Kong: Cantonese *Chou-Hau* as a Transgressive Act Defying Mainstream Middle-Class Norms

Despite Hong Kong's international cosmopolitan appearance, over 90% of its population is ethnic Chinese; Cantonese is the mother tongue of the majority. The British were a minority that until July 1, 1997 had constituted the privileged class of the society. That was the date when Hong Kong's sovereignty was returned to China and Hong Kong became a Special Administrative Region (SAR) of China. The English-conversant bilingual Chinese middle classes have, however, remained the socioeconomically dominant group in Hong Kong, and English is still the most important language of social mobility even in the post-1997, post-British-rule era. English continues to be the medium of instruction in most universities and professional training programs in Hong Kong and English Medium Instruction (EMI) secondary schools are generally perceived by the public as "first class" while Chinese Medium Instruction (CMI) schools are generally perceived as "second rate."

As a local, taken-for-granted language, Cantonese is undervalued and invisible both in education and the "high" domains of society, yet it is a central, valuable medium in popular culture. However, for the majority of working-class children in Hong Kong, English remains something beyond their reach. Unlike their middle-class counterparts, they typically live in a lifeworld where few will (and can) speak or use English for any authentic communicative or sociocultural purposes. The English classroom often becomes a site for their local struggles and oppositional practices involving a great deal of creative work in the form of Cantonese verbal play. And this verbal play often capitalizes on the use of Cantonese *chou-hau* expressions to create a transgressive, subversive effect. For instance, in Lin's (2005) study of the Cantonese verbal play of Hong Kong working-class students in English lessons, a boy was seen to reply to the teacher's reading comprehension question using a euphemistic expression ("fell onto the street") to hint at the Cantonese *chou-hau* expression, *puk-gaai*. Literally, *puk* means "fall (onto)" and *gaai* means "street," but the illocutionary force of *puk-gaai* is similar to: "drop dead!" or "go to hell!". His fellow students' loud laughter upon hearing this seems to have arisen from this student's clever, implicit, transgressive rendering of a taboo Cantonese *chou-hau* expression as an answer to the teacher's formal question.

Cantonese *chou-hau* thus seems to be an unfailing linguistic marker of working classness in Hong Kong. The mere uttering of a Cantonese vulgar word or expression constitutes a highly marked, transgressive act, violating middle-class etiquette and sensibilities, often supposed to arouse unease and contempt from a mainstream middle-class audience. While swearing and cursing have constituted a legitimate research topic overseas and there has long existed a research literature on English slang and cursing (e.g., Hughes, 1991; Jay, 1992; Partridge, 1970), the research literature on Cantonese *chou-hau* is extremely limited. It must be pointed out that Cantonese *chou-hau* is much more socially taboo in Hong Kong than what the English word *slang*, suggests. While the word *slang* in English usually refers to colloquial expressions or jargon of specific social groups, Cantonese *chou-hau* is seen as highly "vulgar," conjuring up explicit sexual images, and is highly taboo in mainstream society in Hong Kong. It is perhaps due to the taboo nature of this topic that only two academic publications by two Western scholars can be found: Bolton and Hutton (1995, 2005). In the 1995 research paper, Bolton and Hutton studied triad language (the "triad society" is a criminal syndicate in Hong Kong) and related it to antilanguages and taboo language. The taboo nature of Cantonese vulgar speech and its connection to bad language, triad society, censored language, and law enforcement is made even clearer in the foreword written by Ip Pau-Fuk (a retired chief inspector of the Hong Kong Police Force) for Bolton and Hutton's *Dictionary of Cantonese Slang* (2005). In the foreword, Ip mentioned that the dictionary "will prove very useful to many people…,including legal personnel, social workers, teachers, and even law enforcement officers" (p. vii). Just as Bolton and Hutton (1995) pointed out, so far, serious official attention that has been paid to the study of Cantonese vulgar speech is mainly for social control and censorship purposes (e.g., legal enforcement, court witnesses). However, it seems that Bolton and Hutton themselves do not want to stereotype Cantonese vulgar speech; in their insightful words:

> All societies have taboos.… What makes a society modern in this context is therefore not the absence of linguistic taboos, but debate about those taboos in the context of debates about free speech and censorship. (Bolton & Hutton, 2005, p. 10)

In a sense, Hong Kong society might be seen as not having reached a modern level if judged by the above criteria: local studies of Cantonese *chou-hau* do not exist at all (i.e., none by local Chinese scholars). The only exception is a recent Chinese book by Pang Chi-Ming (a local cultural critic and newspaper columnist) musing about the origins and meanings of different Cantonese *chou-hau* expressions (Pang, 2007). It, however, has to use a euphemism as the title of the book to escape censorship: *Siu gau laahn chaat haaih* (literally meaning: the puppy is too lazy to shine shoes; tone pattern: 2-2-5-3-4), which is actually a phonological recoding of five common Cantonese *chou-hau* words: *diu, gau, lan, chaht, hai*—all related to sexual organs/acts (tone pattern: 2-1-2-6-1). This recoding is a prime example of clever Cantonese verbal play capitalizing on Cantonese tonal features: by changing one initial consonant (*diu* → *siu*), changing the tones of four of the taboo words, and lengthening two vowel sounds (*chaht→chaat*; *hai→haaih*), the recoded expression keeps almost all the rhymes of the original words intact (i.e., *iu, au, an, at, ai*), while changing the meaning to that of an innocuous, almost "cute" expression. However, phonologically the euphemism is highly suggestive of the original taboo words. The sharp contrast between the cute meaning of the euphemism and the taboo meaning of the original words creates a clever, playful, transgressive effect.

Similar to the observation made by Paul Willis of working-class youths in Britain, there seems to be "work...in their play" (Willis, 1990, p. 2). Cantonese verbal play thus seems to be a kind of folk symbolic creative work and implicit ideological critique through mocking laughter and transgressive play (Bakhtin, 1981) to subvert mainstream linguistic taboos and social norms. While the government and mainstream middle classes in Hong Kong have made the everyday speech of the working classes taboo in the public spheres (e.g., TV, radio, newspapers, books), clever cultural critics and artists will always find a playful, mocking way to transgress these social, linguistic norms.

In MC Yan's words (more on him later), his use of Cantonese vulgar words is both deliberate and natural: "I want to test the boundary of free speech...these are the most lively expressions...this is the language of working-class people; this is the way we speak every day; we don't want to pretend to be those gentlepeople; this is who we are; we just want to be ourselves!" Using Cantonese vulgar words in his playful lyrics, MC Yan seems to be deliberately trying to shout out with a working-class voice about everyday working-class reality.

It is the aim of this paper to bring to the fore samples of the kind of Cantonese creative work that some independent Hip Hop MCs are displaying when they engage in Hip Hop music practices in Hong Kong. These independent (indie) artists seem to have found in this translocal music genre and subculture the powerful symbolisms to express their defiant working-class voices to mainstream society. Through Cantonese-language rap, these artists express their sharp critique of society, of the education system, and of what they see as mainstream hypocritical practices and political injustice. Through using Cantonese vulgar speech in their artful and inventive rap lyrics, they construct alternative discursive spaces where their defiant voices and sharp social critiques can be heard when they perform their both poetic (aesthetic) and political raps.

In the next section, I shall draw on interviews conducted with a well-known first-generation Hip Hop artist in Hong Kong—MC Yan of the former Hong Kong alternative band LMF—and I shall analyze the Cantonese verbal art of his Hip Hop lyrics. In the concluding section, I shall connect the analysis to a discussion of the birth of Conscious Rap in Hong Kong.

Cantonese Slang and Verbal Art in MC Yan's Hip Hop Lyrics

Little attention has been paid to the Cantonese verbal art that is displayed in much of the lyrical work of Hong Kong MCs. A key element of Hip Hop is personal ownership of lyrics—you "rap your own shit"—the choice of language is very much part of an individual MC's lyrical style. MC Yan was the main rap vocalist in LMF, writing the hooks for many of the songs, while other songs were based on the heavy metal and rock styles inherited from the former underground rock bands before they came to form the LMF. In what follows, I want to draw mainly on MC Yan's works as he is by far the most respected and widely recognized first-generation Cantonese MC in indie Hip Hop circles in Hong Kong.

MC Yan has written and rapped many songs, and in his words, they were songs "with a message." His works (lyrics and rapping) appeared in songs such as: "Respect for Da Chopstick Hip Hop," "New Opium War," "Big City Night Life" (collected in the album by DJ Tommy—*Respect for Da Chopstick Hip Hop*, which has the same title as the song), "War," "Beautiful Skin," "Hong Kong Place" (collected in the album by Edison Chan—*Please Steal This Album*). The album, *Respect for Da Chopstick Hip Hop*, is worth noting, as it is a transregional collaboration among Japanese, Korean, and Hong Kong artists. MC Yan told the author that the album was meant to foster an alliance of Hip Hop artists from East Asia, especially from Japan, Korea, and Hong Kong. In all these three places, chopsticks are used, so they called their album *Respect for Da Chopstick Hip Hop*.

The album has only a niche audience (i.e., it's not part of the mainstream pop music scene). That is because independent or nonmainstream Hip Hop is still a marginal practice in Hong Kong and Asia; and although some mainstream commercial Cantopop songs have appropriated some Hip Hop rapping and musical styles, they are generally not regarded as "real" Hip Hop by independent or nonmainstream Hip Hop artists.

The latter album, *Please Steal This Album,* is often seen as part of the pop music scene mainly because Edison Chan is a Hong Kong Cantopop singer. The themes of the songs written by MC Yan usually convey some serious messages of social or political critique. Yan has written many songs on the theme of war. For instance, "War" conveys the theme of a war against the relentless tabloidization of mass media practices in Hong Kong. "Big City Night Life" offers a sharp observation and critique of the money-oriented lifestyles of many Hong Kong people. "New Opium War" offers a historical reminder of the British imperial invasion of China in the 19th century and reasserts a Chinese identity. The song,

"Respect for Da Chopstick Hip Hop," expresses the message of respect for and solidarity of different cultures and music styles of East Asian Hip Hop artists. "Beautiful Skin" is a tribute to women: praising the contribution of wives and mothers to humanity, which is not a pervasive theme in Hip Hop songs whether Western or Eastern.

In this paper I shall focus on MC Yan's indie Hip Hop song, "War Crime" (*Jin-Jan Jeuih-Hahng*), because it is a song regarded by Yan himself as most representative of the recurrent themes in his songs.

MC Yan made the song "War Crime" in his home studio with DJ Frankie. He started circulating songs like "War Crime" on the Internet after launching his own website in 2002 (www.chinamantaggin.org). In the beginning it just consisted of beats, and then demos and the full song were released in 2003 on the Internet. MC Yan also sent it to his Hip Hop artist friends in the United States who were doing a compilation of anti-Gulf War songs at that time. MC Yan's anti-Gulf War song ("War Crime") was the only song from Asia in this compilation. The beats of "War Crime" were made by DJ Frankie, and the lyrics were created by MC Yan. He did the lyrics first and then chose the beats from Frankie's creations.

The idea of "War Crime" came from his anger about the Gulf War, as MC Yan described, "The song's lyrics were inspired by the current affairs." Both MC Yan and DJ Frankie thought that they should do something to voice their protest against the blatant injustice shown in the war. In Table 8.1, I first present my transcription of the Cantonese rap lyrics of "War Crime" using the Yale system (which is a well-established writing system for transcribing Cantonese in the linguistic literature), and then my English translation of the Cantonese rap lyrics.

"I started to bring in this style of writing lyrics since the 1990s," said MC Yan in an interview with the author. The "style" that MC Yan refers to is the style of Zack de la Rocha, a rapper, musician, poet, and activist in the United States. Zack is best known as the former lead vocalist and *lyricist* of the rock band, Rage Against the Machine (RATM), one of the most politically charged bands ever to receive extensive airplay from radio and television. Zack became one of the most visible champions of left-wing causes around the world. MC Yan said from day one both he and members of his former rock band (NT) were influenced by Zack. Yan first came into contact with Zack's music when he was studying visual art in France in the early 1990s. (Yan did not make it in the competitive Hong Kong education system. After high school, he worked for a while and then went to France to study visual art because tuition fees were cheap in France.)In a rock concert in France he witnessed the power of Zack's music and was deeply impressed by his message. Since then, Yan has tried to infuse his lyrics with political messages by using word puns or words that signify political events.

Yan has also been under the influence of Western politically oriented, Conscious Rap artists such as Public Enemy. According to *All Music Guide* (www.allmusic.com, an authoritative source of information on music artists),

Table 8.1 "War Crime" (lyrics written and rapped by MC Yan[1])

Stanza 1

1. 依家 終於知撚道
   yih-gaa jung-yu <u>ji-lan-dou</u>

2. 乜野叫做道理唔通講陰功, 公然當全世界 無到
   mat-yeh *giu-jouh* "douh-leih mh-tung gong yam-gung", gung-yihn dong chyuhn sai-gaai *mouh-dou*

3. 乜撚野叫做渣住雙重標準 黎做
   <u>mat-lan-yeh</u> *giu-jouh* jaa-jyuh seung-chuhng biu-jyun *laih jouh*

4. 乜野大恰細 乜撚野叫做 霸道
   mat-yeh daaih-hap-sai, <u>mat-lan-yeh</u> *giu-jouh baa-douh*

5. 人類 文明究竟去撚到邊撚度
   yahn-leuih mahn-mihng gau-ging heui-lan-dou bin-lan-douh

(There are 16 lines in Stanza 1 and 12 lines in Stanza 2, but due to limited space only the first 5 lines of Stanza 1 and the lines in the Hook are shown here.)

Hook (x 2 times) (::: indicates lengthening of the final syllable):

1. 唔撚::: 知呢乜撚野叫做戰爭罪行
   mh-lan:::-ji ne mat-yeh giu-jouh jin-jan jeui-hahng

2. 唔撚::: 想再相信新聞
   mh-lan:::-seung joi seung-seuin san-mahn

3. 淨係覺得你條撚樣呢 就目中無人
   jihng-haih gok-dak-neih tiuh lan-yeung ne, jauh muhk-jung-mouh-yahn

4. 淨係見撚到你嚮度恰尻人
   jihng-haih gin-lan-dou neih heung-douh <u>hap-gau-yahn</u>

English Translation of Cantonese Rap Lyrics:
Stanza 1:

1. Now, I finally fucking know
2. What it means to say, "When (your action) is unreasonable, just say (you're) miserable". (The U.S is) publicly treating the (others in the) world as non-existent…
3. What it fucking means to have double standards in one's actions.
4. What (it means to say) "Big boys bullying small ones", (and) what "hegemony" means.
5. Human civilization is heading towards which fucking direction?

Hook (rapped 2 times): (::: indicates lengthening of the final syllable)

1. *don't fucking::: know what is called War Crime.*
2. *don't fucking::: want to believe in TV news any more.*
3. *only feel that in your fucking eyes there are no others.*
4. *only fucking see that you are bloodily bullying others.*

---

1. Yale transcription of original Cantonese rap lyrics (line numbers added for easy reference).

Public Enemy was the most influential and controversial rap group of the late 1980s, pioneering a variation of hardcore rap that was musically and politically revolutionary. With his powerful, authoritative baritone, lead rapper Chuck D rhymed about all kinds of social problems, particularly those plaguing Black communities, often condoning revolutionary tactics and social activism. In the process, he directed Hip Hop toward an explicitly self-aware, pro-Black consciousness that became Hip Hop culture's signature throughout the next decade (Spady & Eure, 1991).

Another influence on Yan was the urban Hip Hop poet, Saul Williams, who started the Slam Poetry Movement in the United States. Yan frequently referred to the political messages of Saul in his urban poetry about different issues of racism and social and global injustice. We can see in the lyrics of "War Crime" that the message of anti-U.S.-military invasion is directly expressed. Although no explicit reference to Iraq is made, "George Bush Airport" in Line 11 (Stanza 1) refers to the Baghdad Airport in Iraq, which was renamed "George Bush Airport" after the U.S. military action. In Line 11 (Stanza 1) the rapper asks which national flag is now erected in the George Bush Airport. According to Yan, this line invokes double layers of meanings and images. The first layer signifies the invasion act of the United States by invoking the image of U.S. forces "erecting" the American national flag in the Baghdad Airport and changing the airport name to "George Bush Airport"—a blatant act of invasion and colonization of the territory of another sovereign country. The second layer invokes sexual connotations of "erection" of the male sexual organ in the act of penetration—the "rape" metaphor/image is invoked to refer to the military invasion of Iraq by the U.S. troops. In Cantonese slang usage, the phrase *che-keih* (*erecting a flag*), is often used to refer to the sexual act of penis erection (connoting the male sexual act and male sexual power).

The Cantonese vulgar word *lan*, is used in almost every line of the "War Crime" lyrics to express an angry voice in protest at and condemnation of the U.S. initiation of war on Iraq. In Cantonese vulgar speech, there are five monosyllabic, sex-related words frequently used to express anger or to intensify emotions: *diu* (to fuck), *gau* (penis), *lan* (penis), *chaht* (penis), *hai* (vagina). Although four of these five words are nouns in their literal meaning, their word class status often changes in different contexts. In the context of the "War Crime" lyrics, the noun *lan* (literally meaning "penis") is used not as a noun but as an emotion-intensifier in most instances. For instance, in Line 1 of Stanza 1, *ji-lan-dou* can be translated roughly as "fucking know." *Ji-dou* means "know" and inserting *lan* into the word (*ji-dou* → *ji-lan-dou*) does not change the basic meaning of the word but only adds a layer of strong emotional meaning—anger, frustration, condemnation, and so on (its meaning very much depends on the context). Almost every line of the "War Crime" lyrics is emotionally intensified by the insertion of *lan* into key compound words in each sentence. Table 8.2 shows some more examples of the emotion-intensifying usage of the vulgar word *lan* in the "War Crime" lyrics.

MC Yan said that the use of Cantonese *chou-hau* adds to the *fo* (fire) or "force" of the song. He said the frequent use of English slang in Western Hip Hop had encouraged him and made him bold enough to use Cantonese *chou-hau* in his songs—to be more lively, to speak in the real voice of *siu-shih-mahn* (literally: "little-city-people"; the expression refers to the underprivileged and powerless people in society). The liberal use of Cantonese vulgar words thus adds to the

Table 8.2 Examples of the Use of the Cantonese Vulgar Word, "lan" (撚), as an emotion intensifier

Examples from Stanza 1:

知道 ji-dou (know) → 知撚道ji-lan-dou (fucking know…) (Line 1)

乜野 mat-yeh (what) → 乜撚野 mat-lan-yeh (what fucking…) (Lines 3 & 4)

去到 heui-dou (go to) →去撚到 heui-lan-dou (go fucking to) (Line 5)

邊度 bin-douh (where) → 邊撚度 bin-lan-douh (where fucking) (Line 5)

卑鄙 bei-pei (despicable) → 卑撚鄙 bei-lan-pei (fucking despicable) (Line10)

至大 ji-daaih (the biggest) → 至撚大 ji-lan-daaih (the fucking biggest) (Line 15)

自大 jih-daaih (self-important) → 自撚大 jih-lan-daaih (self-fucking-important) (Line 16)

Examples from the Hook:

唔知 mh-ji (don't know) → 唔撚:::知mh-lan:::-ji (don't fucking know) (Line 1)

唔想 mh-seung (don't want) → 唔撚:::想mh-lan:::-seung (don't fucking want) (Line 2)

見到 gin-dou (can see) → 見撚到 gin-lan-dou (can fucking see) (Line 4)

defiant tone and mood of the song, expressing the voice of the working classes and the marginalized.

Apart from conveying the attitude of the rapper, the insertion of the Cantonese vulgar word, *lan*, into bisyllabic/bimorphemic compound words to form trisyllabic/trimorphemic compound words (e.g., *jih-lan-dou, mat-lan-yeh, heui-lan-dou, bin-lan-douh*) also serves poetic and musical functions. The resulting trisyllabic units synchronize well with the recurrent three-beat drum patterns of the music. This is a conscious poetic strategy employed by MC Yan to tightly integrate the rapping with the music. Yan deliberately makes use of the special features of the Cantonese morpheme: every morpheme is realized phonologically as one syllable with one of the six different tones (i.e., six different pitches, which can form a melody; tones are meaning-differentiating in the Cantonese language). Yan said he consciously makes the different words (with different tones) function like the music beats made by an instrument such as the piano or the drum. For instance, when he spits out the words *ji-lan-douh*, the three-syllable unit fits well with the three-beat drum rhythm of the music.

We can see that in the first five lines of stanza one, there is a high density of such three-syllable units (see underlined in Table 8.1): jih-lan-dou, mat-lan-yeh (twice), heui-lan-dou, bin-lan-douh. The Cantonese vulgar word *lan*, apart from serving as an emotion intensifier, also serves as a central rhyming pillar of the three-beat drum pattern; that is, X-lan-Y. This contributes to the overall assonance of the first five lines. This rhyme tactic is similar to that found in the lyrics of American rapper, Pharoahe Monch, as discussed by Alim (2003, p. 63); for example, "rhymes to spit," "dimes to git." Another example, in Yan's lyrics, of this pattern can be found in the phrase, *Diu-gau-neih, hap-gau-ngo!* (Fuck you! [You're] fucking bullying me!). The pattern is: X-gau-Y. Again, the vulgar word *gau* serves as a rhyming pillar in each of these three-beat units.

Adding "lan" in the hook also serves another musical function. The word *lan* in the first two lines of the hook are phonologically stressed and lengthened. This fits with the rhythmic pattern of the music for the hook. If "lan" is not inserted, the first word *mh* (don't), as a phonologically nonsalient syllabic nasal, cannot be stressed and lengthened. Inserting *lan* after *mh* to form *mh-lan*::: ("don't fucking:::") serves the need for a stressed/lengthened syllable in the second position of the line while also providing a repeated forceful phrase ("don't fucking:::") to start off the first two lines of the hook.

In this connection it is important to analyze the intertextuality between the "War Crime" lyrical text and other working-class media texts. For instance, the final line of the song, "Diu-gau-neih, hap-gau-ngo!" was actually a sampled conversation (Pennycook, 2007) from Anthony Wong, a popular Hong Kong movie star who plays a social underdog in a 1996 movie, *Yi-bo-laai Behng-Duhk* (The Ebola Syndrome, made by famous Hong Kong movie director, Herman Yau, in his early career). The dark movie was about an ex-prisoner and a social outcast, who perceived himself as being constantly bullied by others. In each instance of such perceived bullying, the male character responded by spitting defiantly the line: "Diu-gau-neih! Hap-gau-ngo!" MC Yan said this line is familiar to most working-class males in their 30s now in Hong Kong. In this short line of merely six monosyllabic words, two of the five powerful Cantonese vulgar words: *diu* (fuck) and *gau* (penis) appear three times. The emotional force of this utterance is very strong as its defiant tone is intensified by a high concentration of Cantonese vulgar words within a short utterance. By ending the "War Crime" song with the sampling of this utterance from Anthony Wong in the movie, it pushes the defiant *fo* (fire or force) of the song to the climax.

Apart from the use of Cantonese slang verbal art, lyrical euphony (i.e., harmony of sounds in the lyrics) in the song "War Crime" is achieved linguistically at several levels simultaneously: through phonetic, lexical, and syntactic units which are structurally parallel. In English-language Hip Hop a lot of rappers mobilize the strategies of homophony, metonymy, and both sentence internal and sentence final rhymes (Perry, 2004). For a comprehensive list, Geneva Smitherman's eight features of signification in rap lyrics are often cited in rap lyrics research: indirection, circumlocution, metaphorical-imagistic, humorous-ironic, rhythmic fluence and sound, teachy but not preachy, directed at person or persons usually present in the situational context, punning/play on words, introduction of the semantically or logically unexpected (cited in Perry, 2004, p. 62). Alim's (2003) fascinating analysis of the complex internal rhymes of Pharoahe Monch's *Internal Affairs* lyrics uncovers the highly sophisticated rhyme tactics that U.S. Hip Hop rhymers have mastered (e.g., compound internal rhymes and chain rhymes, back-to-back chain rhymes and mosaic rhymes).

In MC Yan's lyrics, we see another level of sound and word play that capitalizes on the special tonal and syllabic features of the Cantonese language. Cantonese is a monosyllabic, tonal language. Every character is pronounced as one syllable with a tone (i.e., each character has the following syllabic structure: (C) V (C) + pitch). Every character is usually also a morpheme that combines with other characters (morphemes) to form two-, three-, or four-syllable/character words.

These multisyllabic/morphemic words or phrases have their own tonal patterns; for instance, "mh-lan-seung" ("don't fucking want") (tonal pattern: 4-2-2), which is identical in its tone pattern to: "tiuh-lan-yeung" ("that fucking asshole") (tonal pattern: 4-2-2) (both phrases appear closely together in the Hook lines, see Table 8.1). These two three-syllable phrasal units have the same tonal pattern (4-2-2), share the same central pillar ("lan"), and have the same rhymes in the last syllable ("eung"). MC Yan calls this "double rhyme" or "three-dimensional rhyme," meaning that several levels of phonetic parallelism can be drawn upon to create a multilevel rhyming aesthetic; for example, rappers can use words with same vowels (rhyming), same consonants (alliteration), same sounds (homonyms), same number of syllables, and same or similar syllable-pitch (tone) patterns for multisyllabic words. The aesthetic appeal in the song "War Crime" is partly constructed through different ways of creating a large number of two- or three-syllable words or phrasal units that have similar phonetic features (e.g., same or similar verbs, rhymes, and tonal patterns). This kind of multilevel rhyming is similar to what Alim (2003) calls "a multirhyme matrix" in US Hip Hop and the "moraic assonance" patterns (i.e., rhyming of the "moras"—syllable-like units) in Japanese rock (Tsujimura, Okamura, & Davis, 2007, p. 223). For instance, Pharoahe's multirhyming tactic is shown in a string of quadruple rhymes throughout the verse in Alim's analysis (2003, p. 62):

Feel	in	the	flow
Drill	in	the	hole
Kill	in	the	show
Grill	in	the	dough
Will	in	to	blow
Feelin	'em on	the	low

Similar quadruple but partial rhymes can also be found in MC Yan's "War Crime" lyrics, as shown in Table 8.3.

Apart from using different multisyllabic rhyming tactics, MC Yan also employs pairs of multisyllabic words which differ only in the tone value of one syllable and yet with totally different meanings to creative a contrastive effect. For instance, look at lines 15 and 16 in stanza 1:

15. 全世界至撚大 應該係聯合國
cheuhn sai-gaai *ji-lan-daaih*, ying-goi haih lyuhn-hahp-gwok
16. 唔撚係你 自撚大 阿美利堅 合眾帝國
mh-lan-haih neih *jih-lan-daaih* aa-meih-leih-gin hahp-jung-dai-gwok

[15. In the whole world, *the fucking biggest* (organization) should be the United Nations.
16. It's not you who are self-fucking-important—the American Imperialist Empire.]

Table 8.3 Partially Rhyming Four-Character Clausal, Phrasal, and Lexical Units with Similar Tonal Patterns

4-character clausal units	Tone Pattern	English translation
順你者昌 seuihn neih je cheung	6-5-2-1	… those who obey you will live
逆你者死 yihk neih je sei	6-5-2-2	…those who disobey you will die
4-character lexical units		
堂堂大國 tohng tohng daih gwok	4-4-6-3	… a big country…
合眾帝國 hahp jung dai gwok	6-3-3-3	… the imperialist empire
人道主義 yahn douh jyu yih	4-6-2-6	… humanism
帝國主義 dai gwok jyu yih	3-3-2-6	… imperialism
干預主義 gon yyuh jyu yih	1-6-2-6	… interference-ism

The six tones in Cantonese are marked by numerals: 1 = HL (High Level), 2 = HR (High Rising), 3 = ML (Mid Level), 4 = LF (Low Falling), 5 = LR (Low Rising), 6 = LL (Low Level).

By putting two similar trisyllable units that differ only in the tone of the first syllable in parallel syntactic positions in the two sentences, the meaning of the two words are put in sharp contrast: *ji-lan-daaih* (tones: 3-2-6; *the fucking biggest*) vs. *jih-lan-daaih* (tones: 6-2-6; *self-fucking-important*). In fact, this kind of contrastive lexical play is a characteristic of MC Yan's lyrical style; for example, dan *ngoh wah-neih-ji* (tones: 5-6-2-1; let *me tell you*), *ngoh wah-ji-neih!* (tones: 5-6-1-2; *I couldn't care less about you!*).

Apart from the above-mentioned verbal play, MC Yan also mobilizes metaphors, metonyms, and word puns to connote different levels of political meanings. For instance, as discussed earlier, the Cantonese metaphor of rape (*che-keih*—erecting the flag) is used to refer to the U.S. occupation of Iraq's territory. And in line 10 of stanza 2, "Sitting inside the planes and cannons (trucks), you depend on the fucking TV (screen)," the word *screen* has double references. On the literal level, it refers to the control screen of the military gear (e.g., inside the planes or cannon trucks). On another level, as MC Yan pointed out to the author, the "screen" refers to the screens of people's television sets at home. The whole notion of war, in contemporary times, is shaped and constructed by mass media practices through the "screen," and here MC Yan mentioned to the researcher that the screen (the media) has shaped and determined people's consciousness about the Gulf War—people's idea of the war has largely been shaped by mainstream media discourse ("the screen"). These are the double meanings that MC Yan wants to express through the lyrics in line 10 of stanza 2.

Starting a Conscious Rap Group in Hong Kong: The Yellow Peril

While it seems that there is nothing new in saying that MC Yan has politically and socially conscious messages in his songs; this is, however, significant in the Hip Hop scene in Hong Kong for the mere fact that he is the only Hip Hop artist who has steadfastly done this all through his music career without any commercial support. Like the high school students who rejected progressive rap in the school project that Newman (2007) studied, most Hip Hop artists in Hong Kong have aspirations for commercial success and do not particularly care about politically or socially conscious messages. However, from the outset, Yan and members of his band, NT, have been under the influence of political activists such as Che Guevara and the Dalai Lama: Yan and his band members read Che and the Dalai Lama's books and wrote lyrics inspired by them. Later in the mid-1990s, NT was combined with other less politically oriented rock bands in HK to form the LMF. MC Yan told the author that he had been an odd man out in LMF, given his politically and socially conscious style, but he respected the collective works done with LMF members, for as a member of LMF he could not just have his own way. From the beginning, Yan wanted to do Conscious Rap. He defines his work as part of the translocal Conscious Rap movement, having been influenced by politically conscious artists in the U.S. such as Zack de la Rocha, Public Enemy, Tupac Shakur, Saul Williams, and Blackalicious. By "keeping it real" in the Hong Kong context—drawing on Cantonese *chou-hau* as a confrontational, transgressive lyrical style and defiant voice of the underprivileged—MC Yan can be said to have appropriated the spirit of many Conscious Hip Hop artists worldwide (who also do not shy away from using slang to voice the plight and everyday reality of the marginalized), and sown the seeds of Conscious Hip Hop in Hong Kong. While Yan's lyrics in the LMF days mainly centered on voicing the feelings of the underprivileged working-class youth in Hong Kong, in the song "War Crime" Yan has, in his words to the author, "evolved from talking about just social injustice in Hong Kong to talking about social injustice in the world." In a recent interview (conducted on October 10, 2007), MC Yan told the author that his lyrical style has evolved as he has read more books and learned more things about the world. "I want to self-educate and invite other Hong Kong people to self-educate, by learning about what's happening in the world, and we cannot just sit there and do nothing!"

MC Yan's "War Crime" will be included in a mixtape by a French street fashion webzeen called *Black Rainbow* (http://www.bkrw.com/sommaire). It seems that he is much better received in some European Hip Hop circles than in Hong Kong. Yan wants to start a Conscious Rap movement in HK with his disciples, the three young rappers, ADV, Chef, and Double T in Yellow Peril (see Figure 8.1)—a Conscious Rap group which has recently started and performed their three debut songs ("Choice," "Yellow Peril," and "Unbridled") in recent gigs (e.g., on October 6, 2007, in Cizi—a live club; on October 26, 2007, in the Hong Kong Fringe Club). All of their songs are socially and politically conscious. Although MC Yan and Yellow Peril are rapping about global political issues (e.g., Bush's invasion of the Iraq), Yan's sentiments, I want to argue, are transposed from his previous LMF songs about the working-class youths in HK to the underclasses in the world. Yan himself said he is above class and his music should be right for all classes for it is about the moral issues of social and global justice.

The choice of the name "Yellow Peril" symbolized Yan and his group's reflexivity in their ironic defiance of Western colonial discourse. "Yellow Peril," with its colonial image (Pennycook, 1998), was precisely what Yan wants to remind his group not to forget: how yellow people have been positioned in Western colonial discourse. For instance, when asked why they chose the name "Yellow Peril," Yan said that the word *Nigga* is historically a disparaging name that the Whites called the Blacks; however, his African American Hip Hop friends also call Yan *Nigga*, as an intimate term for "Brother." As many sociolinguistic researchers have pointed out (Low, 2007; Alim, 2006), "Nigga" has undergone semantic inversion to become a name for solidarity among those who are discriminated against by an outside group. In a similar way, Yan wants to infuse *Yellow Peril* with positive meanings, as a solidarity term for Asian people who have historically been under the Western colonialist gaze. "Yellow Peril," Yan said, "was a name given to us by Western colonialists, and we want to remind ourselves not to forget this…we want to be socially and politically conscious, to be self-reflective, so that we won't really become a danger and threat to the world…. If the younger generations in China keep on copying the entertainment and consumption styles of the West, then Chinese people will really become a threat to the world…we want ourselves to realize this first…we must self-educate…not to become like the West…." The choice of "Yellow Peril" as the group's name can thus be seen as a deliberate postcolonial, symbolic act to defy the colonial discourse in the West.

In MC Yan and Yellow Peril's songs, we can witness the birth of Conscious Rap in Hong Kong. By doing their songs totally in colloquial Cantonese, without inserting any English (vs. Fama's Cantonese-English bilingual lyrical style), and by boldly using Cantonese *chou-hau*, which is taboo in mainstream Hong Kong society, MC Yan and his followers seem to be "keeping it real," and keeping it true to the translocal spirit of politically oriented Hip Hop artists such as Public Enemy, Tupac Shakur, and Saul Williams. In this connection, one has to remember that Cantonese *chou-hau* plays a symbolic role in asserting the voice of the working classes in Hong Kong. In defying the linguistic taboos of mainstream middle-class society, one can argue that MC Yan's Cantonese *chou-hau* lyrics communicate his political message through transposing the Hong Kong working classes' defiant sentiments to the translocal underclasses' defiant sentiments.

While MC Yan is often seen as a "radical" even by other indie artists in Hong Kong, interestingly Yan told the author that his graffiti design has been invited to be part of a permanent collection in two museums in Britain, as part of their "China Design" collection. In a way, Yan has got some cultural capital (Bourdieu, 1984, p. 3) internationally, but strangely, not in HK. However, his strategy, as he told the author, is: after he has made a name overseas, he can do this in Hong Kong, "as Hong Kong people worship things overseas, especially those from the Western world." It is ironic that Yan's success in some progressive Hip Hop circles overseas relies precisely on his use of local taboo language that is rejected by the Hong Kong middle classes and inaccessible to the rest of the world.

Yan readily defines himself as a public intellectual and he says he will keep doing what he thinks is the right thing to do, although at present he has only a small audience in Hong Kong. It is, perhaps, by winning the recognition and respect of progressive Hip Hop artists and cultural critics in the West that Yan will eventually gain the cultural capital recognized by local Hong Kong middle-class people. Such an indirect route indicates how progressive cultural movements overseas (such as Conscious Hip Hop) can sometimes lend cultural capital to local artists, ironically, and precisely, because of the colonialist mentality of the local people ("who worship things overseas"). Ironically, the author finds herself employing a strategy similar to Yan's: by publishing in overseas progressive academic journals and books, the author's own research on a taboo topic in Hong Kong—vulgar lyrics in indie Hip Hop songs—might stand a chance of winning respect and recognition from local scholars and researchers.

In conclusion, it seems that there is a possibility of drawing on translocal Hip Hop culture and its artistic and linguistic creative practices as resources for a critical public pedagogy (Carrington & Luke, 1997) that reaches out to youth and people beyond the classroom and the school. There remains a lot of work to be done in this area to chart out what exactly such a pedagogy might look like and what effects that might have. A recent breakthrough for MC Yan is his Postcard Project hosted by *Ming Pao*, a well-respected middle-class newspaper in Hong Kong. Every Sunday, Yan gets a whole page to write and draw his message, and to invite the readers to send him a postcard in response to his message. He has received some interesting responses, as he told the author in an interview on October 10, 2007. MC Yan and Hip Hop artists like him in Hong Kong, albeit few as they are, seem to be the first street fighters in Hong Kong to set up good examples for us on how to figure out local tactics (de Certeau, 1984) when drawing on translocal Hip Hop graffiti art and Conscious Rap culture as resources for a possible public education project.

Figure 8.1 MC Yan (in cap) rapping with Yellow Peril and other indie rappers in a gig at the Hong Kong Fringe Club, October 26, 2007.

Acknowledgments

The author is indebted to MC Yan for sharing his lyrics and his time in numerous research interviews over the past two years. Special thanks go to Francis Lee, Jaeyoung Yang, and Eric Ma for exchanging ideas with the author on this research and for their constant colleagial support. The author is also especially grateful to the editors for their critical and very useful comments on earlier drafts of the paper.

References

Alim, H. S. (2003). On some serious next millennium rap ishhh: Pharoahe Monch, hip hop poetics, and the internal rhymes of internal affairs. *Journal of English Linguistics, 31*(1), 60–84.

Alim, H. S. (2006). *Roc the mic right: The language of hip hop culture.* New York: Routledge.

Bakhtin, M. M. (1981). *The dialogic imagination: Four essays.* Austin: University of Texas Press.

Bolton, K., & Hutton, C. (1995). Bad and banned language: Triad secret societies, the censorship of the Cantonese vernacular, and colonial language policy in Hong Kong. *Language in Society, 24,* 159–186.

Bolton, K., & Hutton, C. (2005). *A dictionary of Cantonese slang.* Singapore: National University of Singapore Press.

Bourdieu, P. (1984). *Distinction: A social critique of the judgement of taste* (Trans. Richard Nice). London: Routledge & Kegan Paul.

Carrington, V., & A. Luke (1997). Literacy and Bourdieu's sociological theory: A reframing. *Language and Education, 11*(2), 96–112.

Chan, Ka Yan (2003, May 4–5). *Exploring youth subculture in Hong Kong: A case study on the local band LazyMuthaFucka (LMF),* MPhil Thesis. (Chinese)

Chu, Y. W. (2007). *Before and after the fall: Mapping Hong Kong Cantopop in the global era.* Paper presented at the International Conference on Inter-Asia Culture: Desire, Dialogue and Democracy, City University of Hong Kong.

De Certeau, M. (1984). *The practice of everyday life.* (S. Rendall, Trans.) Berkeley: University of California Press.

Erni, J. N. (2007). Gender and everyday evasions: Moving with Cantopop. *Inter-Asia Cultural Studies, 8*(1), 86–105.

Hughes, G. (1991). *Swearing: A social history of foul language, oaths and profanity in English.* Oxford: Blackwell.

Jay, T. (1992). *Cursing in America: A psycholinguistic study of dirty language in the courts, in the movies, in the schoolyards and on the streets.* Philadelphia: John Benjamins.

Li, W. C. (2006). *The emergence and development of Hong Kong Hip Hop and rap music since the 1980s.* Unpublished MPhil thesis, Department of Music, Chinese University of Hong Kong.

Lin, A. M. Y. (2005). Doing verbal play: Creative work of Cantonese working class schoolboys in Hong Kong. In A. Abbas, & J. Erni (Eds.), *Internationalizing cultural studies: An anthology* (pp. 317–329). Oxford: Blackwell.

Lin, A. M. Y. (2007, May 30–June2). *Crafting out a bilingual identity with bilingual hip hop lyrics in Hong Kong.* Paper presented at the International Symposium of Bilingualism, University of Hamburg, Germany.

Low, B. E. (2007). Hip hop, language, and difference: the N-word as a pedagogical limit-case. *Journal of Language, Identity, and Education, 6*(2), 147–160.

Ma, E. K. W. (2001). *Underground radicals.* Hong Kong: Ming Pao.

Ma, E. K. W. (2002a). Emotional energies and subcultural politics in post-97 Hong Kong. *Inter-Asia Cultural Studies, 3*(2), 187–190

Ma, E. K. W. (2002b). Translocal spatiality. *International Journal of Cultural Studies, 5*(2), 131–151.

McIntyre, B. T., Cheng, C. W. S., & Zhang, W. (2002). Cantopop: The voice of Hong Kong. *Journal of Asian Pacific Communication, 12*(2), 217–243.

Newman, M. (2007). "I don't want my ends to just meet; I want my ends overlappin": Personal aspiration and the rejection of progressive rap. *Journal of Language, Identity, and Education, 6*(2), 131–145.

Pang, C. M. (2007). *The puppy is too lazy to shine shoes*. Hong Kong: Subculture Hall. (in Chinese)

Partridge, E. (1970). *Slang: Today and yesterday*. London: Routledge.

Pennycook, A. (1998). *English and the discourses of colonialism*. London: Routledge.

Pennycook, A. (2007). Language, localization and the real: Hip hop and the global spread of authenticity. *Journal of Language, Identity, and Education, 6*(2), 101–115.

Perry, I. (2004). *Prophets of the hood: Politics and poetics in hip hop*. Durham, NC & London: Duke University Press.

Spady, J., & Eure, J. (Eds.). (1991). *Nation conscious rap: The hip hop vision*. Philadelphia: Black History Museum Press.

Tsujimura, N., Okamura, K., & Davis, S. (2007). Rock rhymes in Japanese hip hop rhymes. *Japanese/Korean Linguistics, 15*, 222–233.

Willis, P. (1990). *Common culture: Symbolic work at play in the everyday cultures of the young*. Buckingham: Open University Press.

Dragon Ash and the Reinterpretation of Hip Hop

On the Notion of Rhyme in Japanese Hip Hop

NATSUKO TSUJIMURA AND STUART DAVIS

Introduction

Japan has an active and diverse Hip Hop scene with widespread popularity among the younger generation. This is reflected in recent figures cited by Manabe (2006, pp. 3–4) who notes that 15% of all singles classified as gold or above in the first half of 2005 were rap-oriented and that rap is an integral part of the Japanese music scene. The history of Hip Hop in Japan has been delineated in a series of articles by Condry (2000, 2001a, 2001b) and in his 2006 book, *Hip-Hop Japan*. Condry (2001a, p. 228) traces the beginnings of Hip Hop in Japan to the mid-1980s with the release of the film *Wild Style*, a low-budget film featuring the first generation of U.S. rappers, DJs, and breakdancers, and the subsequent release of the film *Breakdance* in 1985 which launched the first of several breakdance booms in Japan. A club called Hip Hop opened in 1986 in the Shibuya district of Tokyo, the district that is the center for fashion, entertainment, and youth culture in Japan. Condry notes that in the period from 1988 to 1992 there was a growing number of clubs sponsoring rappers, DJs, and breakdancers. Specialty magazines began covering the Hip Hop scene in detail from the mid- to late 1980s. The first produced million-selling rap hits in Japan appeared in 1994 and 1995 and the term *J-rap* was coined to represent this new genre (Condry, 2001a, p. 233). In the mid- to late 1990s, Condry divides the J-rap scene into two camps: party rap and underground Hip Hop. According to Condry (2000, p. 177), "Party rap tends to have light, funny lyrics that speak to themes from everyday life (e.g., video games, dating, teenage love songs).... In contrast, underground hip-hop tends to be more abstract, darker, and at times in opposition to mainstream

Japanese society." The two camps had very different followings and were critical of one another. The current Hip Hop scene in Japan, since 2000, according to Condry (2006) is more diverse:

> We find a broad spectrum including rock rap to hard core to gangsta, spoken word/poetry, to conscious, old school, techno rap, anti-government, pro-marijuana, heavy metal-sampled rap, and so on. Alongside the widening diversity with the hip-hop scene, we also see the disappearance of any orientation toward a center.... The era in which underground hip-hoppers debated with party rappers has given way to more personal conflicts between rappers. These conflicts gesture toward ideas of what hip-hop should be about. (p. 82)

Recent trends that Condry notes include the regionalization of Hip Hop within Japan and the incorporation of samurai imagery. What these trends suggest to some is that the global spread of Hip Hop reflects a "cultural homogenization" in the "borrowing" of a particular type of musical genre. However, through a structural poetic analysis of Japanese Hip Hop rhyming, we aim to demonstrate in this chapter the complicated linguistic aspects of cultural appropriation that occur when Japanese Hip Hop is given a local interpretation. Specifically, we illustrate how Japanese Hip Hop artists fuse local, historically Japanese poetic traditions with global, historically Western rhyming practices.

With this as background, this chapter focuses on the adaptation of the notion of rhyme in Japanese Hip Hop. Rhyme, rhythm, and word play are defining aspects of Hip Hop and as Alim (2003) demonstrates, U.S. Hip Hop artists such as Pharoahe Monch use complex and creative multiple rhyme strategies in their lyrics. Traditional Japanese poetry has no notion of rhyme. Yet, over the past two decades, since the arrival of rap music in Japan, a "borrowed" notion of rhyme has become incorporated in many of the lyrics of Japanese Hip Hop. This chapter offers an analysis of the adaptation of rhyme in the lyrics of one Japanese Hip Hop group, Dragon Ash. While much of the work on the language of Hip Hop culture focuses on the politics of language, this chapter focuses more specifically on the poetics of Japanese Hip Hop rhyming and thus contributes to a more technical, linguistic understanding of the language of Hip Hop. But, it also illustrates at a microlevel how a foreign notion of rhyme is given a "local" interpretation within the mechanism of the Japanese language. Before detailing the analysis, we first give background in Section 2 on traditional Japanese poetry. This entails discussion of the notion of mora, a key linguistic unit of both Japanese poetry and the Japanese language more generally. In Section 3 we discuss the rhyming domain found in Japanese Hip Hop. In Section 4, we will offer an analysis of the rhyming lyrics of Dragon Ash contending that it can be best described in terms of *moraic assonance*. In Section 5 we discuss various issues that arise from the analysis. Section 6 concludes the chapter and ties these specific linguistic findings to broader ideas about cultural globalization.

The Mora and Traditional Japanese Poetry

Traditional Japanese poetry, such as Haiku and Tanka, is largely conditioned by mora count. For example, Haiku consists of three lines with 5, 7, and 5 moras in each line, while Tanka is formed by five lines with 5, 7, 5, 7, and 7 moras. Traditional Haiku and Tanka poetry is sampled in (1–2), where mora breaks are indicated by hyphens.

(1) a. Hu-ru-i-ke-ya   b Sa-mi-da-re-o
         Ka-wa-zu-to-bi-ko-mu   A-tsu-me-te-ha-ya-shi
         Mi-zu-no-o-to   Mo-ga-mi-ga-wa

(2) A-ra-za-ra-mu
     Ko-no-yo-no-ho-ka-no
     O-mo-i-de-ni
     I-ma-hi-to-ta-bi-no
     A-u-ko-to-mo-ga-na

While superficially moras resemble syllables, as discussed by Kubozono (1999) and Tsujimura (2007) they are crucially different. A mora is instantiated by (i) a vowel with an immediately preceding consonant if there is one; (ii) a nasal consonant that is not accompanied by a following vowel; or (iii) the first part of a long consonant (i.e., a geminate consonant). Native Japanese speakers naturally divide words into moras rather than syllables. Consider the four Japanese words shown in (3) with their moraic division.

(3) a. ka-mi-ka-ze   b. Lo-n-do-n   c. ni-p-po-n   d. ha-i

The Japanese word *kamikaze* in (3a) is shown with its division into four moras. Here, mora seems to correspond to syllable, but the difference between mora and syllable is made clear by (3b) and (3c). Japanese speakers hear the place name *London* as consisting of four moras while English speakers hear it as comprising two syllables (i.e., Lon-don). Similarly, the Japanese word *nippon* is heard by Japanese speakers as comprising four moras though it consists of two syllables (i.e., nip-pon). The word *nippon* illustrates the three different instantiations of a mora. The first mora, *ni*, contains a vowel with an immediately preceding consonant; the second mora, *p*, is the first part of a geminate consonant; and the final mora, *n*, is a nasal consonant with no following vowel. The final example in (3d), the Japanese word for "yes," *hai*, is pronounced almost identically to the English word *high*. But while the English word is heard as one syllable, the Japanese word is perceived as comprising two moras. This reflects that vowel sequences or diphthongs do not comprise single moras. It also reflects that the prevocalic consonant (i.e., the consonant immediately before the vowel) is not an essential part of the mora.

Given this understanding of mora, what is essential in the examples of traditional Japanese poetry in (1) and (2) is the number of moras per line. Crucially, individual moras in the different lines are not required to be composed of identical or similar sounds. Thus, there does not seem to be anything like the notion of rhyme in Haiku, Tanka, and other types of traditional Japanese poetry (cf. Kawamoto, 2000).

Despite the lack of a poetic tradition in Japanese that incorporates rhyme, it is interesting to note that Japanese Hip Hop lyrics, as investigated by Kawahara (2002, 2005, 2007) and Manabe (2006) incorporate a notion of rhyme. While the rhyming pattern demonstrated in Japanese Hip Hop is somewhat different in nature from its English counterpart as will be discussed in the following sections, the resemblance to English rhyme is readily observed in the parts of two sample songs from Dragon Ash in (4) and (5) where the rhyming parts are underlined. (Note that all the lyrics from Dragon Ash cited in this article are taken from their 2001 album *Lily of da Valley*. We leave all verses untranslated.)

(4) machija nayameru <u>juudaiga</u>
     naihu nigiri aitewa <u>juutaida</u>…
     sonnauchini yumeou <u>monodooshi</u>
     tekundara zettee <u>morochooshi</u> ii

     temeeno ketsuwa temeede <u>motsubekida</u>
     soitsuga wakaru yatsuwa <u>totsugekida</u> (from *21st Century Riot*)

(5) owari aru jinnseidemo <u>yookosoo</u>
     tukamitorerusa <u>kyookoso</u>.…
     tinbaarando humishimeru <u>daichio</u>
     in da round moyasu <u>akaichio</u>

     konomachide <u>tashikani saiteru</u>
     yuri <u>ashitani maiteru</u> (from *Yurino Hanasaku Bashode*)

Both Condry (2001a) and Manabe (2006) observe that rhymes like those illustrated in (4) and (5) are not characteristic of the early Japanese Hip Hop of the 1980s. As mentioned by these authors, Hip Hop of the early period either used word repetition or had very little or no rhyming. However, especially since the early 1990s, Japanese Hip Hop rhyming has evolved and has become more sophisticated over time. It has come to adopt a notion of rhyme even though there is no basis for it in traditional Japanese poetry. In the remainder of this chapter we will consider the nature of rhyming found in contemporary Japanese Hip Hop as exemplified in Dragon Ash's 2001 album *Lily of da Valley*. We will place the nature of Japanese Hip Hop rhymes in the context of Zwicky's (1976) discussion on imperfect rhymes in rock music and in Alim's (2003) analysis of rhymes in U.S. Hip Hop. We will contend that Japanese Hip Hop exemplifies a system of imperfect rhyme that is best described as *moraic assonance*. We will further examine cases where moraic assonance does not seem to hold, and suggest that moraic assonance most frequently occurs with moras whose core is a vowel. First, though, we will consider the domain of rhymes in Japanese.

The Rhyme Domain in Japanese Hip Hop

When we think of the rhyme domain in English, we often think of the domain as being the word. Examples would include one syllable words like *line-sign*, two syllable words like *table-cable*, and three syllable words like *sinister-minister*. Technically, though, the rhyme domain in English is not an entire word but a subpart of the word that extends from the stressed vowel to the end of the word. This is the part of the rhyming words that need to be identical. In the rhyming word pairs cited above, and in examples like *promotion-lotion* and *audition-politician*, it is the stressed vowel and all the following sounds that are identical in the rhyming pairs. This is what constitutes a perfect rhyme in English poetry. Kawahara (2002) observes that in Japanese Hip Hop lyrics, a rhyme domain constitutes at least two moraic elements. He states this principle as the Minimality Principle in (6), and gives examples in (7) and (8) where the underlined moraic elements are pronounced identically.

(6)   Minimality: Rhymes should consist of the agreement of at least two moraic elements. Moraic elements are vowels and consonants at the end of a syllable.

(7)   soshite te ni ireyooze satsut<u>aba</u>
      mitero ore no sokojik<u>ara</u>

(8)   kyoomo T-shatsu ni shibumeno g<u>ooru</u>d<u>o</u> ch<u>een</u>
      shanpan banban akete s<u>ooru</u> t<u>oreen</u>

The example in (7) illustrates that the minimal domain for a rhyme in Japanese Hip Hop is a two mora or bimoraic sequence. Specifically, in (7) the last two moras of the words satsutaba and sokojikara constitute the rhyming domain. Note that the consonants at the beginning of the last two moras of each of these words do not have to be identical for the words to rhyme. In (8) we see a more complicated rhyme where the domain comprises the final word pair of each line with seven moras in each word pair. We note that in the rhyming domain in (8) all vowels are identical as well as the word-final nasal consonant which would constitute a mora on its own. Again, crucially, the consonants immediately before the vowel in the rhyme domain do not need to be identical. Kawahara (2005) further observes that a rhyme domain has its own intonation (or pitch pattern) that is independent of what the pitch of the words would be if pronounced independently. Specifically, the first mora in the rhyming domain is articulated with a high pitch while the other moras are pronounced with a lower pitch. Thus, a rhyming domain is not only marked by the identical nature of the core moraic elements but also by a particular intonation pattern.

One other issue discussed by Kawahara (2002) concerning the domain of rhyme in Japanese Hip Hop stems from the observation that the rhyming domain may contain an "extra" moraic element at a line's end, as in the example from Kawahara in (9). This can be termed *extrametricality* and we use angle brackets to indicate this.

(9) a. Ittuno doori no aarii mo͟oni<n>
      yume kara samereba uso no yo͟oni
   b. hadani karamu nurui ka͟ze
      toroketeru karada wo hurui ta͟te<ru>

This phenomenon seems fairly common in Japanese Hip Hop rhymes and does occur in Dragon Ash.

Japanese Hip Hop Rhymes as Moraic Assonance

Assuming that the rhyme domain in Japanese Hip Hop is minimally bimoraic along with the notion of extrametricality we now turn to an examination of the nature of Japanese Hip Hop rhymes as found in the lyrics of the group Dragon Ash. From one perspective, Japanese Hip Hop rhymes can be considered an instantiation of what are called imperfect rhymes in the poetry literature. In his discussion of imperfect rhymes from a linguistic perspective, Zwicky (1976) gives a classification of imperfect rhymes in terms of how they deviate from perfect rhymes.

(10) Zwicky's (1976) classification of imperfect rhymes in English
    a. One or more of the matched vowels is unstressed:
       kiss—tenderness, scenery—tapestry
    b. Vowels following the stressed one do not match
       face—places
    c. Consonance-stressed vowels do not match but the consonants do
       off—enough, stop—up
    d. Assonance-stressed vowels match but the following consonants do not
       wine—times, sleepin'—dreamin'

    Technically speaking, none of these terms applies to the notion of rhyme that emerges from the Japanese Hip Hop lyrics because Japanese is not a stress-accent language, and, as mentioned, the rhyme domain has its own pitch pattern. In order to see the nature of Japanese imperfect rhyme in Hip Hop, consider the rhyming pairs from the Dragon Ash lyrics in (11) where mora division is indicated by a space between letters.

(11) Hip Hop rhymes in Dragon Ash
    a. mo tsu be ki da—to tsu ge ki da   (*21st Century Riot*)
    b. ko o do o—bo o do o   (*21st Century Riot*)

c. wa i ro ni—ta i ho ni   (*21st Century Riot*)
d. ju u da i ga—ju u ta i da   (*21st Century Riot*)
e. se ma i to ko—de ka i ko to   (*Bring It*)
f. shi n ji ta i—ka n ji ta i   (*Yurino Hana Saku Bashode*)
g. ba su ja k ku—ka su ja p pu   (*21st Century Riot*)

These Japanese imperfect rhymes seem to illustrate Assonance mentioned in (10d) but it should be applied in the context of mora. We shall call it a principle of "moraic assonance". In examining the rhyming data in (11), we see that the moraic elements are identical in each rhyming pair, where core moraic elements are understood to be a vowel, moraic nasal, or the first member of a geminate. The nonmoraic consonant, namely the consonant immediately before the vowel which we will refer to as the onset consonant, may or may not be identical. In (11b), for example, the first rhyming mora pair *ko* and *bo* have an identical vowel but differ in the quality of the onset consonants. This is most telling in (11e) where all core moraic elements in the rhyming pair, namely, the vowels in these cases, are completely identical, but all the onset consonants in the rhyming pair differ. The term moraic assonance thus seems most appropriate to capture the rhyming pattern of Japanese Hip Hop. Notice that in the examples in (11) the moraic elements in the rhyming pairs are identical whether the moraic element is a vowel, as in (11a-e), or a moraic nasal as in (11f). An exception to this seems to be the different geminate consonants in (11g) where a moraic core element [k] is paired off with another moraic core element [p], where each of [k] and [p] is the first consonant of a geminate. However, one can view this as not being exceptional under a traditional view of geminate consonants in Japanese linguistics as being represented by an abstract empty consonant called the Q-element in traditional Japanese phonology (cf. Vance 1987). Thus, we find the generalization that the Japanese Hip Hop songs are subject to moraic assonance which requires that moraic core elements in a rhyming pair be identical, where a moraic core element is either a vowel, moraic nasal, or the first member of a geminate.

A further observation that argues for the notion of moraic assonance in Japanese Hip Hop rhyme, at least as performed by Dragon Ash, is that the rhyming pairs virtually always have the same number of moras (ignoring the possibility of a final extrametrical mora). This is shown in the examples in (11) above as well as the further examples in (12).

(12)   Identical number of moras for each rhyming pair
    a. wa ga—wa da   (*Glory*)
    b. so ma ri—to ba ri   (*Glory*)
    c. ki ka n no ta i yo—ki ga n to a i o   (*Yurino Hana Saku Bashode*)
    d. ta shi ka ni sa i te ru—a shi ta ni ma i te ru   (*Yurino Hana Saku Bashode*)
    e. mo tsu be ki da—to tsu ge ki da   (*21st Century Riot*)

The requirement that rhyming pairs have the same number of moras distinguishes Hip Hop rhyme (at least as manifested by Dragon Ash) from rhymes in English, where identical word length is not required for two words to rhyme. In English, words having different number of syllables can constitute rhymes as long as the stressed vowel and every sound after it is identical. Thus, pairs like *end-offend* and *tore-adore* are good rhymes even though the rhyming words do not have the same number of syllables. It is also clear from the data in Zwicky (1976) that even imperfect rhymes in English do not have to be of the same length. Examples include *kiss-tenderness* and *underfed-kid*. Thus, the notion of moraic assonance in Japanese Hip Hop seems to impose a requirement on the forms in a rhyming relation that they have the same mora length.

As much as this state of affairs in Japanese Hip Hop rhymes may seem unique, our findings together with Kawahara's (2002) observations discussed above are reminiscent of (though not identical to) what Zwicky (1976) calls "rock rhymes" in his investigations of rhyming in English rock music. Zwicky notes that there is a great deal of deviance from traditional classifications of rhyming patterns in rock lyrics, and describes such deviant behavior in terms of the principles that he calls "subsequence rhyme" and "feature rhyme." Crucially, characterizations of Japanese Hip Hop rhymes that we have discussed thus far can also be captured on the basis of these two principles. First, subsequence rhymes are defined in (13).

(13) **Subsequence rhyme**: X counts as rhyming with XC, where C is a consonant

(X may end with a consonant itself, as in pass-fast, or with a vowel, as in go-load). In a relatively infrequent variant on this principle, internal subsequence rhyme, X counts as rhyming with CX (as in proud-ground and plays-waves). (Zwicky, 1976, p. 677)

Given this definition, extrametricality as discussed previously and characterized in (9) can be viewed as an instance of subsequence rhyme: that is, subsequence rhymes generally add extra sounds after the rhyming part of one of the words, and this is precisely what extrametricality is intended to capture. The nature of added elements, however, perhaps should be interpreted somewhat differently in the case of Japanese so that any addition is based on mora, rather than on sounds. Some examples of extrametrical elements from Dragon Ash lyrics are given in (14).

(14) Extrametricality in Dragon Ash lyrics
    a. dooshita—dooshita\<chi\>   (*Glory*)
    b. kanjitai—panchirai\<n\>   (*Yurino Hana Saku Bashode*)

Second, Japanese Hip Hop rhymes do not normally pay attention to the nonmoraic consonant at the onset of each mora. As shown by examples like that in (11), the nonmoraic consonants in the rhyme do not have to be identical, though they can be. Nonetheless, as noted by Kawahara (2005, 2007) there seems to be a certain similarity between two nonmoraic consonants in a rhyme that are not identical. The role of similarity is well captured by Zwicky's second principle, feature rhymes, which is defined in (15).

(15) **Feature rhyme**: segments differing minimally in phonological features count as rhyming. The segments may be vowels (as in end-wind) or consonants (as in stop-rock); the feature in question can even be syllabicity (as in mine-tryin'). (Zwicky 1976, p. 677)

To illustrate this type of rhyme in actual songs, Zwicky (1976, pp. 678, 692) gives the examples in (16–19).

(16) My experience was limited and <u>underfed</u>,
You were talking while I <u>hid</u>,
To the one who was the father of your <u>kid</u>.   (*Dylan, Love is Just a Four Letter Word*)

(17) Well, the technical manual's <u>busy</u>
She's not going to fix it up too <u>easy</u>   (*Joni Mitchell, Electricity*)

(18) Blackbird singing in the dead of <u>night</u>
Take these broken wings and learn to <u>fly</u>
All your <u>life</u>
You were only waiting for this moment to <u>arise</u>   (*The Beetles, Blackbird*)

(19) Me and my gal, my gal, <u>son</u>,
We got met with a tear gas <u>bomb</u>   (*Dylan, Oxford Town*)

In (16) and (17) the vowels that are involved in the rhyming pairs are not identical but can sometimes be perceived to be at least similar in that they only differ by one feature. The examples in (18) and (19) involve similarity of consonants rather than identity. Such "perceptual similarity" may lead to "identity" in actual performance as the musician may modify the pronunciation of the nonmatching sounds so that they are perceived as identical.

Kawahara's (2005, 2007) work on Japanese Hip Hop rhymes has largely focused on the issue of the similarity relation between the nonmoraic (onset) consonants of two units in a rhyming relation. As mentioned, Kawahara notes a strong tendency for perceptually similar consonants to be matched with one another. While the data from Dragon Ash lyrics show similar tendencies in the matching of nonmoraic consonants in rhyming pairs, we note, as Zwicky (1976) does, that there is a real issue as to what counts as perceptually similar given that results of sound similarity studies vary with task, experimental conditions, and subject population. On the other hand, one fairly common phenomena found in

Japanese Hip Hop lyrics is the observation that a nonmoraic (or onset) consonant corresponds with the absence of a consonant in many of rhyming pairs. Examples from Dragon Ash are given in (20).

(20) Examples of rhyming pairs where nonmoraic consonants have a null correspondence (the relevant rhyming part is underlined)
    a. i ta mi ga—hi ka ri ga   (*Yurino Hana Saku Bashode*)
    b. ji ka n to ta i o n—ki ka n no ta i yo o (*Yurino Hana Saku Bashode*)
    c. da ke ma shi te—ka ke a shi de   (*Yurino Hana Saku Bashode*)
    d. yo o sha na ku—yo ko ja na ku   (*My friends' Anthem*)
    e. de ka i o to—se ka i go to   (*Bring It*)

This type of relation is not reported to be found in English imperfect rhymes, but is quite common in Japanese Hip Hop. While such forms may be problematic for a similarity account, they do provide additional evidence for the principle of moraic assonance in Japanese Hip Hop rhymes where the notion of mora plays a crucial role.

Some Linguistic Issues

While we have shown that bimoraic minimality, extrametricality, and moraic assonance constitute major characteristics of Japanese Hip Hop rhymes, we find possible counterexamples to these in our data. In our discussion earlier on extrametricality, it was observed that Hip Hop rhymes may contain an extra mora that is not matched with anything at the end of a word. Two examples from Dragon Ash were provided in (14) to illustrate it. According to Kawahara (2002), since extrametricality is restricted to the "periphery of the form", instances should not be found where a nonfinal mora is considered extrametrical, as Kawahara schematizes in (21). (C stands for a consonant and V for a vowel.)

(21) CV <CV> CV
       | |
      CV   CV

Precisely the type illustrated in (21) has been observed in our sample. This is shown in (22) and (23).

(22) rensashite hiraku mi ra i   ga
                   | | | |
      sonosakiga   mi ta i <n> da   (*Yurino Hana Saku Bashode*)
(23) menomaeni   ka su ka   na
                    | | | |
      demo tashikana ka chi ka <n> ga   (*Yurino Hana Saku Bashode*)

In each of (22) and (23), the extrametricality surfaces in the penultimate mora. In fact, violations of extrametricality seem to always involve a moraic nasal. Thus, while the data in (22) and (23) are exceptional to extrametricality in that there is a nonperipheral mora that appears inside the rhyming domain, it seems to be a regular pattern that such nonperipheral extrametricality tends to involve a moraic nasal.

A second related problem concerns the principle of moraic assonance. Under moraic assonance, the expectation is that the core moraic elements of two rhyming units be identical. This is illustrated by the Dragon Ash data in (11), (12), and (20). Occasionally, however, there are examples where moraic assonance does not hold, as is shown by the examples in (24) and (25) from the lyrics of *Yurino Hana Saku Bashode*, where the moras at issue are capitalized.

(24) hidoku yaseta <u>koOyao</u>
      hosiga aseta <u>koNyamo</u>
(25) ikinukunowa <u>koNnande</u>
      daremoga mina <u>soOnande</u>

In each example, the capitalized moras, one being a vowel and the other a moraic nasal, are intended to rhyme, but they do not; and hence, assonance is not observed. Such examples, however, seem to be more common involving the pairing of a vowel and a moraic nasal. In fact, we find several examples of the same sort in our sample, as is illustrated in (26).

(26) a. ju <u>n</u> ba n ni—ju <u>u</u> ma n shi   (*Glory*)
      b. to <u>o</u> a ke ro—do <u>n</u> da ke no   (*Glory*)
      c. ku <u>u</u> ka n ni—ju <u>n</u> ba n ni   (*Glory*)
      d. ji ka n to ta i o <u>n</u>—ki ka n no ta i yo <u>o</u> (*Yurino Hana Saku Bashode*)
      e. ko <u>n</u> na n de—so <u>o</u> na n de   (*Yurino Hana Saku Bashode*)

This may suggest that while the principle of moraic assonance is stronger for moras whose core element is a vowel, its deviant pattern may also form a certain regularity.

These apparent counterexamples bring up the issue of modification of pronunciation in the actual performance of the lyrics. In our investigations of some of Dragon Ash songs we note that they modify their pronunciation of lyrics during performance in such a way that rhyming is achieved. A rather drastic example of this is given in (27).

(27) saa kakenukeyooze <u>dooshita</u>
      yuri no moto tudotta <u>dooshita</u>chi
      yo ima dakara koso <u>tooshi da</u>shi
      <u>don't stop</u> tomo ni mezasu eekooe e ikoo   (*Glory*)

In (27) the vowel sequences of the underlined rhyming domain in the first three lines are identical, with the second and third lines containing extrametricality, but the English phrase in the last line, "don't stop," is modified in pronunciation so that it rhymes with the first three lines: in fact, "don't stop" sounds exactly like "dooshita" in performance. Other examples of English words that involve altering pronunciation are given in (28) and (29).

(28) hai ni intoro bai ni <u>sindoo o</u>
      makiokosu Lilyda <u>sindoroo</u><mu>
(29) mune hukuramasite <u>kanjitai</u>
      kono omoio <u>panchi rai</u><n>

The last words of the second line in (28) and (29) are the English words syndrome and punch line, respectively. While the final mora of these words seems to be extrametrical in the rhyming scheme, upon listening to the actual songs, they are virtually inaudible. The phenomenon described in (27–29) is indeed reminiscent of Alim's (2003) illustration of deliberate change in pronunciation observed in Pharoahe Monch's lyrics. Alim (2003, p. 64) cites the instance from the album *Internal Affairs* where the sequence "vertebraes," "heard of me," "third degree," and "surgery" may not seem to rhyme but are modified in performance so that they do so more closely.

To be clear for Japanese, modification in pronunciation is not restricted to loan words, as the examples in (30) and (31) illustrate.

(30) suusennen himitsuno <u>beeru</u>
      tsutsumareta michinaru su<u>keeru</u>
      toodaikara naniga <u>mieru</u> doodai
      kyoodaieno <u>eeru</u>   (*Yurino Hana Saku Bashode*)
(31) sonna nakani yume ou <u>monodooshi</u>
      tekundara zettee <u>morochooshi ii</u>   (*21st Century Riot*)

The four underlined words in (30) are intended to be targets of rhyming. Notice that the third word mieru, the Japanese verb meaning "see," does not appear to rhyme with the rest of the words perfectly. In order to keep the rhyming pattern, however, the musician pronounces it as *mieeru*, lengthening the second mora of the verb. In (31) the last two moras, *ii*, in the second line, which is a Japanese word, is obviously an extra element while what precedes it perfectly rhymes with *monodooshi*. In this case, since these extra vowels are identical with the final vowel of the rhyming element in the second line, *morochooshi*, it is not detectible in performance, nor is it perhaps even relevant, whether the vowel gets strictly lengthened.

As a final issue, it is interesting to place Dragon Ash's use of moraic assonance in the context of Alim's (2003) discussion of the use of assonance and complex rhymes in the Hip Hop lyrics of the U.S. artist Pharoahe Monch. Alim (2003,

p. 73) notes Pharoahe Monch's use of assonance in examples like those in (32); the relevant vowels are given in bold.

(32) a. "N**e**v**e**r you d**e**vils, my l**e**vel's that of a high **e**volutionary r**e**bel"
      b. "the d**e**sk of **a**ny r**e**dneck r**e**cord **e**x**e**c"

While assonance is used by Pharoahe Monch, it is only one of various possibilities that he uses along with alliteration and various different types of rhymes. We have contended that assonance, specifically moraic assonance, is the primary means that Dragon Ash uses to create rhymes in Japanese Hip Hop.

Alim (2003, p. 70) also shows how Pharoahe Monch incorporates internal rhymes in lyrics such as those in (33).

(33) a. "Every <u>line</u> to word of <u>mine</u>…"
      b. "<u>Unobtainable</u> to the <u>brain</u> it's <u>unexplainable</u> what the verse'll do"

While we have not discussed the use of internal rhymes by Dragon Ash, they do occur in their lyrics as in the couplet in (34) where the internal rhymes are indicated in bold.

(34) kake**dashite** imawa ke**gashite**
      age**dashite** kizudake **mashite**   (*Yurino Hanasaku Bashode*)

Relatedly, it is not uncommon to find in Dragon Ash instances where the first word of a line rhymes with the last word of the previous line. While one example of this was shown in (27) above, we give a fairly complicated example in (35), taken from *Glory*, where all the rhyming domains are in bold.

(35) a. munenonaka nanika kizuitara kanjiru **taka**
          narini makase kanaderu u**taga**
          nakamatachito wakachiau **waga**
          hokorashiki yurino nano **wada**
          mada mikaitakuno kuu**kanni**
          junbanni konoshirabe juu**manshi**
      b. konomachija neonde **somari**
          owarinaki yono **tobari**
          towani tuzukuyoodemo **ichigo**
          ichienanda jinnseiwa moo**ichido**

We note that the first word of the fifth line in (35a) and the first word of the third line in (35b) each rhyme with the last word of their preceding lines. This type of rhyming pattern is fairly common in Dragon Ash and we suspect that it is not uncommon with other Hip Hop artists. What is interesting about the two rhyming schemes in (35) is that they exhibit examples of what Alim (2003) terms *bridge rhyming*. This is a complex technique where a rhyming sequence ends in the first part of a line and a new rhyming sequence begins at the end of that line. Thus, in (35a), the word *mada* at the beginning of the fifth line ends a rhyming sequence and a new sequence starts at the end of that line. Similarly in (35b), *towani* at the beginning of the third line serves as a bridge marking the end of one rhyming sequence, and a new sequence starts at the end of that line. Thus, examples like (34) and (35) testify to the complexity of rhyming schemes that are utilized by Japanese rappers.

Conclusion

In this chapter we have proposed that Japanese Hip Hop musicians use the principle of moraic assonance in their rhyming scheme. This principle can be seen as combining the traditional notion of mora count in Japanese poetry with the notion of assonance (vowel identity) in Western poetry. Thus, rhyming units in Japanese Hip Hop lyrics ideally should have an identical number of moras and the corresponding moraic elements should agree in quality. We have noted slight deviations from this scheme, but they are often compensated for by modified pronunciation in performance. We have also noted the use of internal rhymes and bridge rhyming that hint at the complexity of rhyming schemes used by the Japanese Hip Hop artists.

The way in which rhyme has been incorporated into Japanese Hip Hop is enlightening to the discussion of how Hip Hop can simultaneously be realized as both global and local forms of expression. Rhyme, a defining aspect of Hip Hop, is foreign to traditional Japanese verse, and yet it is assimilated into Japanese Hip Hop. One can view its adoption as reflecting a global form of expression characteristic of Hip Hop worldwide. On the other hand, the way in which rhyme is adapted into Japanese Hip Hop is localized to the context and resources of the Japanese language by having it faithfully conform to the notion of mora, a crucial linguistic concept of the language, but not necessarily relevant in many others. Once the notion of rhyme is incorporated into Japanese Hip Hop, we then witness the complexities of rhyming schemes, such as internal rhymes and bridge rhyming shown for Dragon Ash that are found with U.S. Hip Hop artists and undoubtedly with others. In conclusion, we would contend that moraic assonance is a means internal to the Japanese language that allows for the adaptation of the foreign notion of rhyme and reflects with respect to language what Condry (2001b, p. 372) calls "a dynamic process by which the meaning of Hip Hop is reinterpreted to fit into the Japanese context."

Acknowledgments

We thank Shigeto Kawahara for sharing his work with us and to Kyoko Okamura for her input on a preliminary version. Thanks also go to the editors for their valuable suggestions. We are particularly grateful to H. Samy Alim for his encouragement and inspiring comments that have been extremely helpful in shaping this chapter. Some of the material in this chapter was presented at the 15th Conference on Japanese/Korean Linguistics held in Madison Wisconsin in October 2005 and we acknowledge the audience there for their comments. Any errors are our responsibility.

References

Alim, H. S. (2003). On some serious next millennium rap ishh: Pharoahe Monch, Hip Hop poetics and the internal rhymes of *Internal Affairs*. *Journal of English Linguistics, 31*, 60–84.

Condry, I. (2000). The social production of difference: Imitation and authenticity in Japanese rap music. In, H. Fehrenbach & U. Poiger (Eds.), *Transactions, transgressions, and transformations* (pp. 166–184). New York: Berghan Books,

Condry, I. (2001a). A history of Japanese hip-hop street dance, club scene, pop market. In, T. Mitchell (Ed.), *Global noise: Rap and hip-hop outside the USA* (pp. 222–247). Middletown, CT: Wesleyan University Press,

Condry, I. (2001b). Japanese Hip-Hop and the globalization of popular culture. In G. Gmelch & W. Zenner (Eds.), *Urban life: Readings in the anthropology of the city* (pp. 357–387). Prospect Heights, IL: Waveland Press.

Condry, I. (2006). *Hip-Hop Japan: Rap and the paths of cultural globalization*. Durham, NC: Duke University Press.

Kawahara, S. (2002). Aspects of Japanese hip-hop rhymes: What they reveal about the structure of Japanese. Paper presented at the 5th ICU Language Study Workshop, International Christian University, Tokyo, Japan, June 21–23.

Kawahara, S. (2005). *Linguist's delight: Similarity, half-rhyme, and hip hop*. Paper presented at the University of Massachusetts, Amherst, June 17.

Kawahara, S. (2007). Half rhymes in Japanese rap lyrics and knowledge of similarity. *Journal of East Asian Linguistics, 16*, 113–144.

Kawamoto, K. (2000). *The poetics of Japanese verse: Imagery, structure, meter*. Tokyo: University of Tokyo Press.

Kubozono, H. (1999). Mora and syllable. In N. Tsujimura (Ed.), *The handbook of Japanese linguistics* (pp. 31–61). Oxford: Blackwell.

Manabe, N. (2006). Globalization and Japanese creativity: Adaptations of Japanese language to rap. *Ethnomusicology, 50*(1), 1–36.

Tsujimura, N. (2007). *An introduction to Japanese linguistics* (2nd ed.). Oxford: Blackwell.

Vance, T. (1987). *An Introduction to Japanese phonology*. New York: SUNY Press.

Zwicky, A. (1976). Well, this rock and roll has go to stop. Junior's head is hard as a rock. *Chicago Linguistic Society, 12*, 676–697.

"That's All Concept; It's Nothing Real"

Reality and Lyrical Meaning in Rap

MICHAEL NEWMAN

Introduction: "Hip-Hop's Most Notorious Problems"

In an early discussion of sexism and violence in rap, Lott (1992, p. 79) claims, "As a dominant influence on black youth, rap music articulates the perspective of a black *lumpenproletariat*." However, he almost immediately adds the following: "This underclass status of rap, however, tends to conceal the fact that it has certain social and political dimensions that suggest that something other than pathology is occurring."

With this claim, Lott articulates a position repeated in a number of subsequent academic textual critiques of rap music (Garofalo, 1994; Grant, 1996; Lawson, 2003; Rose, 1994; Shusterman, 2003); that is, the use of a Marxist sociological lens to frame a dichotomy between positive and negative influences of rap. The harmful influences relate, of course, to the violent and sexist themes that Thompson (2005, p. 123) calls "hip-hop's most notorious problems." By contrast, what Shusterman (2003, p. 422) refers to as rap's "better aspects" express heightened social consciousness and progressive politics.

Thompson, however, problematizes this critical lens by pointing out that it crucially depends on a specific referential assumption, what he calls "the message view." The term refers to a famous metaphor of Chuck D's that, "rap is the Black CNN." The idea is that rap, like a news program, provides reports or messages about Black life. In essence, the "message view" assumes that rap lyrics have *transparent* interpretations; that is, they mean what they say superficially. Importantly, Chuck D is as an early practitioner of a type of art that Shusterman favors.

Thompson identifies an opposing assumption, the "as-if view," which he associates with Young Buck's idea that rap "is just putting words together, so that you gotta be your own judge of how real it is" (Satten, 2004 cited in Thompson,

2005, p. 120). In other words, Buck believes rap lyrics should be seen as *opaque*; that is, expressing deeper meanings in addition to or even in place of the superficial events described. Buck, it should be noted, has made use of violent and sexist motifs in his work.

In this chapter I depart from the position that the interpretation involves interpreters, and therefore it is an empirical question how creators and listeners construe a text. Critique can identify interpretations, but it cannot determine what meanings people actually take from texts. In the case of rap, this point is supported by ethnographic studies (e.g., Alim, 2004, 2007; Dimitriadis, 2001; Ibrahim, 1999, 2003; Keyes, 1996; Norfleet, 1997; Sarkar & Allen, 2007; and various chapters in this volume), which find complex interpretations of lyrics by creators and audience. Dimitriadis (2001, p. 46), for instance, makes the following observation regarding the teenage rap listeners in his study:

> Many have argued…that [the traditional African American] community has been lost to an out-of-control generation of black youth—most often symbolized by and through rap music…. Yet…these teens attempted to create a kind of cultural continuity through these same popular resources—an insight that simply could not be prefigured by textual analysis of rap lyrics alone. (Dimitriadis, 2001, p. 63)

The present study explores meaning making in relation to the "notorious problems" in a group of young MCs all of whom used violent, sexist motifs. Specifically, it examines how these MCs:

- interpreted the violent and sexist lyrics in their own and others' work,
- understood violence and sexism in real life, and
- related the two.

The goal is to understand why the MCs were attracted to these motifs, and suggest whether, for them at least, they really deserve their notoriety.

Class Conflict: "They Have Good Ideals, but They Wouldn't Work"

The MCs in the study attended a class called Hip-Hop Poetry and Production from 1999 to 2002 at the Urban Arts Academy (UAA) a small alternative secondary school in New York City. The class formed part of UAA's arts program and met once a week for half a day. Membership varied during the study period, but macrosocial characteristics broke down roughly as follows:

- **Ethnicity:** mostly Jamaican Americans and Latinos.
- **Social Class:** working class or low income.
- **Origin:** born in New York or arrived before age 10.
- **Age:** 15 to 18.
- **Gender:** heterosexually identified males.

I entered UAA as a researcher in part because I had worked there as a teacher three years previously, and three of the MCs were former students: Hilarrius, TopDawg, and Kareem.[1] Upon Kareem's graduation and matriculation in college, I hired him to transcribe interviews and songs, interview his friends, and provide his own analyses.

The controversy surrounding "the notorious problems" was not merely theoretical to the participants. The rap class teachers cultivated a socially conscious style in the tradition of Chuck D. They once used an in-class cipha, for example (see Alim's introduction, this volume) to analyze violence as arising from economic exploitation (Newman, 2001, 2005). They also used rap to model appropriate responses to conflict. One teacher, for instance, recounted in rap how he peacefully but firmly responded to a challenge from someone who tried to take the mic from him in a show. The teachers also discouraged students from "spittin'" sexist, homophobic, or violent lyrics while encouraging solidarity and greater political awareness and activism.

As I argued elsewhere (Newman, 2001, 2005, 2007), the students said they learned a lot about rhyming and production but rebuffed the political messages. Even "Hilarrius," the student MC closest to the teachers, showed little attraction to progressive ideology inside or outside rap. For instance, he identified the politically conscious crew Dead Prez as "socialist," which he said involved "good ideals" but "wouldn't work." The other MCs' responses to many artists who rapped about progressive political themes were even more dismissive. By contrast, the students listened to and emulated successful commercial artists such as Eminem, Jay-Z, Ludacris, and the then-emerging 50 Cent whose work was known for violent and sexist themes.

Verbal Violence: "Like No Rapper Says Something Real"

The teachers' lyrical exploration of violence and modeling of a response to conflict were representative of how they often relied on transparent interpretations for their raps. The students, however, presented a more complex panorama referentially. In the following comment, a defense of Eminem, Tropics, a UAA MC, appears to assume that rap is generally opaque, and that transparent readings are misinterpretations:

Tropics: What politics did they just made him seem like this bad guy who hates fags, hates all this other stuff, wants to kill them, can't stand them. He kills his wife. He hates his wife, but if you think about it logically, that's all concept; it's nothing real. Like no rapper says something real. They just talkin' about what they think, and what they wanna write like, "Oh, that's a good idea; I should write that."

The term *concept* refers to opacity because it indicates an idea behind the motif, whatever that might be.

Nevertheless, it was apparent that opacity and transparency were both available for the MCs. A clear example of normatively transparent interpretations involved *thug rap*, a term the MCs used for rhymed autobiographical recountings of violent or criminal life. This definition is implicit in another MC, Kaliph's, effort to correct my misclassification of Wu-Tang Clan as thug rappers. Although, Wu-Tang spit images of violent criminality, and members are known for having participated in such activities, Kaliph believes their violent images were really opaque:

Kaliph: Wu-Tang has like their own style. I mean it is thug but like not really. I don't know how to explain it.
MN: Cuz there's more there? Is that what you're trying to say?
Kaliph: It's like sorta like survival, and getting out of certain places.
MN: What do you like about that? What does it tell you?
Kaliph: That anyone can do it. It sorta like motivates me.

Interestingly, Kaliph transferred from a vocational high school to UAA because, "I thought I could do more with myself than be like an electrician." He thus got out of a certain place himself, using his own skills. Wu Tang's lyrics metaphorically reflected his own struggles.

It would be a mistake to construe a dismissal of transparent "thug rap" from Kaliph's words. Instead, the MCs repeatedly articulated a doctrine of authenticity whereby anyone they labeled a thug rapper should be an authentic thug in life (Jones 2006; Keyes, 1996; Norfleet, 1997). This idea was expressed by Tropics, when interviewed by Kareem, although in doing so he contradicted his earlier claim that "no rapper says something real":

Tropics: Like if you say, "I'm gangsta I'll shoot you," but if you don't shoot him, you're not gangsta.... If you say something, you do it. If you say something, you live it. If you talk it, you are it.

This doctrine was so widely accepted that only one MC, Sega, expressed any dissent from it, and in doing so he also contradicted himself. In an interview with me, he went along with the legitimacy of thug rap when performed by real thugs, but when he was interviewed by Kareem a few months later, the doctrine was given only a cursory nod, despite Kareem's framing that view for him:

Kareem: What's your view on like thug rappers?
Sega: I'm not really, really behind that because I don't live that life. If you live that life, go ahead, you can portray it, but don't say you do this, and you do that if you don't. You know I don't endorse it because I don't tell anybody that's the best rap there is because I don't think it is. That's not my particular type of rap to listen to.

Kareem: So you don't think most thug MCs are real or what?

Sega: Nah, I think a lot of them are, but that's not what rap is about. That's not what rap was made about.

It is curious that the White adult interviewer was told an opinion that violated mainstream norms, which he might reasonably be expected to subscribe to, while the close Black friend heard the more conventionally acceptable one, which violated an in-group dogma.

The legitimating of thug rap created a dilemma for the MCs because it implied a high valuation of a thug life that they, in fact, did not live since none were involved in drug dealing, violence, or gang membership. When interviewed by Kareem, Tropics and Cherub's solution was to turn the dilemma on its head by framing their lack of thug status as a kind of disadvantage that they overcame through their authenticity:

Cherub: I'm gangsta. I'll tell you right now I'm gangsta. I'm gangsta because, know what I'm sayin', I'm not a thug, and I'll tell you I'm not a thug. I won't be goin' in my raps tellin' you how I shoot people in the face.

Tropics: That's a studio gangsta.

Cherub: That's a studio thug, studio thug, but I don't do none of that. I'll tell you who I am, and I'm bein' true. I'ma spit it at you 'namean? You can take it, or you can leave it. That's the way I am.

Cherub's final statement implies that the MCs actually rapped about their real lives, and, when asked about appropriate themes, a number responded that rap artists should do just that. Hilarrius, for instance, said, "If you are an airplane pilot MC down with hip-hop, you rap about flyin.'" However, I found not a single case of transparent raps about school, family or social life, teenage angst, or real interpersonal conflicts, the stuff their lives were actually made of. Sega, in fact, considered such material, particularly the angst and family problems, to be more typical of rock genres. The idea that rappers should rap about what is real was fulfilled in the breach; their raps were always laden with what Tropics called "concept"; that is, nothing real.

An interesting twist was that the concepts were almost always violence, sex, and verbal one-upmanship, but the MCs were careful to mark these references as opaque, using various signals to mark their words as not reflecting their real lives. For instance, violence was frequently explicitly labeled as verbal, as in these lines:

- I'm gonna teach you all a lesson/how to use nouns and adjectives and verbs as weapons. (Cherub)
- Niggas get shot up/Not by bullets but by these lyrics. (Tropics)

- It's like I inflict verbal fatality. (Hilarrius)
- Verbal ammunition was unloaded/and it was only one round. (Sega)

In other cases, the MCs made violent or sexual adventures highly irrealist by making fantastic claims, inserting pop-cultural references into the middle of the narration, or staging action in mock-religious/mythological settings.

Conflict in Rap and Life: "There's No Reason for You to Take It to the Heart"

The-violence-as-verbal metaphor is particularly significant because it replaces the thug, who battles in reality, with a lyrical equivalent: the *MC Warrior* (Keyes, 1996), who battles in lyrics, so articulating a substitutional relationship between real and verbal violence. Specifically, verbal violence in the form of MC battles—rhymed verbal dueling—could replace the real equivalent, a function with a long history in rap (Norfleet, 1997). However, again principles and reality diverged. Battles were common between the UAA MCs, but Sega described them as friendly sport:

MN: When you're battlin' someone can it ever be serious?
Sega: Sometimes if you take things to the heart, which you shouldn't, cuz it's all lyrical, and it's all fun; you know we're just tryin' to have fun. There's no reason for you to take it to the heart cuz it's just playin' around.

Only one battle fit the substitute-for-violence model. The "beef" or conflict motivating it was described by Tropics as arising when he observed I-mation violating the taboo against "biting"; that is, plagiarism.

Tropics: He came out, and [his rhyme] was just like similar to mines, and I'm like, "wow…cuz I had said this verse last year."

This biting required an assertive response because I-mation's motives were normatively interpreted as a challenge, rather than the more likely desperate casting around for something to rhyme:

Tropics: To bite rhymes is to slap an MC in the face. Cuz if you take someone else's rhyme, you're basically sayin', "I could say what you say better" to an MC. An MC takes that real harsh, "You can say my word better than me?" So you know that's why a rapper really takes that to the heart. No rapper could avoid [responding to] rhyme biting! Cuz, you know, you gotta point the issue out.

MN: And that would lead to a battle or something?

Tropics: …most people, they're like, "Oh, oh, I'ma duff him out; I'ma fight him." I'm like, "It's hip-hop. Like if he woulda stole like my shirt, that's my personal business, but this is hip-hop. I gotta handle it the way a MC should"; so I battled him instead of tryin' to take it to somethin' personal.

Compared to this one case of substitution of word for "somethin' personal," there were two in which a "duffin' out" took place, although they never actually achieved the level of a full-scale fistfight. In the first case Kareem was challenged by a younger MC, Damien, who was resentful because Kareem had removed him from the studio when he was supposed to be in class. As it was recounted later by a number of MCs, Damien ambushed Kareem on the way to the subway, and Kareem tried to avoid fighting. Although Damien made that impossible by refusing to get out of his way, one of Kareem's friends ended it before it began by punching Damien.

Interestingly, Kareem did not lose respect by trying to decline to fight or having it ended for him. On the contrary, Damien received considerable ridicule afterwards. Later, Kareem came up with the most important observation for our purposes. He said that even if Damien had won the fight, he would have lost anyway because by resorting "to fists" he would be admitting that he was too incompetent to fight lyrically. Skills at lyrical conflict were more highly valued than physical ones.

The other incident arose from nonrap verbal play, "taken to the heart." The verbal putdowns that characterized rap battles were also frequent in conversational interactions. They were not necessarily meant to be taken transparently, but instead created conditions for display of verbal agility and toughness in the face of verbal attack. Group hierarchy was also involved according to Kareem who said that, "any sign of weakness" would lead to a group member's being taken advantage of, "just like in prison." As I observed it, the target of an insult was expected to return the abuse in kind and proportion. If no resistance was offered, he was considered soft and an appropriate target for public humiliation; but if he lost his temper, he was considered to be thin skinned and unstable. One MC was described as having "an anger management problem" in part because of his overreactions in these situations.

Nevertheless, it was not always clear that the insults were not really meant. Everyone knew that some classmates did not like each other, and actual feelings were sometimes unclear. Also, even insults not meant to injure could cause a strong response if the target was on edge or if the words struck a sore point. What is surprising then is that insults degenerated into a physical attack only once. In this case, Delphee responded to some teasing remarks by Hilarrius in the hallway by punching him. Interestingly, Delphee was not necessarily blamed for overreacting in part because his "happy-go-lucky" reputation contrasted with Hilarrius's rep for a sharp tongue. The aftermath was described to Kareem by Tropics and Cherub:

Tropics: You know what was funny was that nobody felt mad that that happened to Hilarrius.

Cherub: Hell no! It was like, everybody like, they real feelings came out. "You know, Hilarrius do play too much."

This interpretation coincided with that of the assistant principal, who lamented Hilarrius's inability to realize that not everyone took his constant jibes lightly.

In sum, we find the MCs navigating, mostly but not always successfully, a complex system relating verbal and real violence and conflict generally. Potential violence could be shifted to the virtual form of battles, but verbal insults, in or out of battles, could be subject to transparent or opaque interpretations, although the choice between them was not always clear.

Violence in the Lifeworld: "It Comes From the Street"

To round out the understanding of the MCs' construction of lyrical conflict, it is necessary to examine the roles of conflict, violence, and criminality in their lifeworlds, Husserl's (1970) term for the "world of every day lived experience" (Cope & Kalantzis, 2000, p. 206). The lifeworld is a phenomenological construct representing how elements of reality are individuated and assigned significance by a living agent (Schutz & Luckmann, 1973). A key concept in the MCs' lifeworlds was "the street" a construction of the urban environment, in particular norms and expectations concerning respect, assertiveness, aggression, and self-defense (Spady & Alim, 1999).

The teachers, in the in-class cipha mentioned briefly above, attempted to elicit from the students a progressive understanding of violence. As part of this effort, TopDawg was directly asked where he thought violence came from. His answer invoked the street:

1. It comes from the street,
2. But I still will defeat.
3. I don't have to use a gun.
4. I can use my lyrical tongue.

The question assumes that violence could be eliminated by attacking the root cause. TopDawg's invocation of the street as the source (line 1) entails that violence is inevitable, an assertion that implies that the teachers' understanding is unrealistic, and not in accord with "street consciousness" (Spady & Alim, 1999). Lines 2 to 3 emphasize the response to violence (lines 2–4) as a kind of harm-reduction strategy explicitly associated with rap. A later contribution, by LocoMan, elaborates these views, although more pessimistically:

1. I was in Spanish Harlem the other day.
2. I was walkin' the street.
3. Yo three little kids was about five
4. or seven. They was robbin' these Chinese guys
5. for their chicken wings and french fries.
6. There were three. I'm dead serious that ain't no joke.
7. they had a bat.
8. they slapped
9. him with it.
10. They slapped in the head almost broke his scull up.
11. They almost leave him toe up.
12. You can even see his brain inside his skull.
13. You can even see the nigga crawlin' on the floor.
14. Nobody helped him out 'n' nobody said nothing.
15. 'cause in the streets nobody else be frontin',
16. or else nobody else be snitchin'.
17. 'cause there's no rat niggaz.
18. 'cause if there's a rat you're gonna get killed.
19. just like burst of the steel.
20. yo, that's what I saw. I'm telling you the truth, yo.

This rhyme is quite remarkable in its horrific imagery, which combines and then exaggerates a number of clichés regarding the street:

- extreme youthfulness of perpetrators (lines 4–5)
- excessive violence (line 8–13),
- miniscule rewards achieved (line 6),
- victimization of hard-working immigrants (line 5),
- fearful passivity of the urban community (lines 15–16).

The rap closes with what amounts to a dark moral about the inescapability of the agonistic world of the street (lines 15–20).

The villain and hero of the street is the thug, and there is evidence that the MCs developed a kind of cult of this figure. First, there is the negative response to falsely claiming thug credentials in raps, which were thus seen as something an MC had to earn rather than be ashamed of. Additionally, some MCs, including Kareem, read magazines like F.E.D.S. (*Finally Every Dimension of the Street*) that are essentially celebrity magazines of criminal life, with federal penitentiaries replacing Hollywood as the prime venue. Finally, no one ever criticized the drug dealers and gang members at UAA—the real thugs—for their actions or lifestyle.

However, whereas Kareem could claim that the rough verbal interactions in his group led to a jailhouse atmosphere, the UAA thugs exhibited no such illusions. When I naively asked a gang member I had not seen for a week about where he had been, he told me with a bitterness I will never forget, "the place no one should ever go." Another gang member (and former student of mine) gave this memorable depiction of the pathology, anger, and hurt of real thug life even outside prison:

Rashid: I believe…what goes around, doesn't necessarily come around. Cuz, I did a lot of bad things in my life, and I am not ashamed to say it; and a lot of bad things happened to me in my life, but on the scale, a numerous, many, many, many, many, way more bad things has happened to me than good things. So, by everything goes around, by that belief, I must wake up in the morning and find a lottery check on the floor or somethin' for a couple a million dollars because I been through a lot in my life. Somebody owes me, if that's the way, if everythin' goes around comes around, somebody owes me somethin'. Somebody, somewhere owes me somethin'; they owe me somethin' that I deserve.

The MCs maintained good relations with their thug classmates, but they were not intimate friends with any. It appears almost as if they were caught between their decision to avoid thug life, their respectful relations with real thugs, and their romanticization of those classmates' quite painful lives. An academically successful rap fan in the school captured how he dealt with this dilemma:

Claudio: I'm cool with [the thugs]—you know what I mean? You know, we hang out, whatever. They respect the fact that I want kids, house, wife, car, everything, you know what I mean? This is the only way I know to do it. You have another way? Go ahead. Hey, I respect that; you're still my boyz [=friends].… You got your way; I got my way. We respect each other.

Similarly, Delphee, who had a particularly hard childhood, described having mugged someone when he was 13. His reason for deciding not to continue down a thug path was, like Claudio's, expressed in terms of practicality. The profits had been minimal, he said, and so, "I didn't do it again because it was stupid."

"I'm Strugglin' Through My Whole Life While Everybody Else Is Just Livin'": Divergent Interpretations, Divergent Lives

It has to be admitted that the textual critics' assumption of transparency of hardcore rap is compatible with the association of that style with the idealization of thug life. The assumption also receives support from the reasons Rashid, the gang member, gave for his attraction to this style:

Rashid: I mostly listen to music like rappers that they live the same life as me in my neighborhood, but they from different neighborhoods. So it's good to hear somebody rhyming about something you actually live through, that way you can say to yourself, "A'ight good, I'm not the only one." I am glad that I am not the only one. Make me feel like I'm strugglin' through my whole life while everybody else is just livin'.

MN: And you're not alone.

Rashid: No, I'm not alone, when I listen to rap, I hear like the life that I live out on the avenue.

Nevertheless, there was simply no evidence that rap influenced the MCs in this study to adopt the thug lifestyle they idealized (see Dimitriadis, 2001; Dyson, 1996). It did not even seem to be a temptation that they succeeded in avoiding, any more than it would be for well-off European American rap fans untouched by racism and poverty. The MCs' goal was inevitably to make it in rap, or, failing that, become economically successful by some other *conventional* means. As Cherub put it, "either I'm makin' some cheese, or I'm just getting a straight job." If someone who sees a straight job in their future is idealizing thug life, the most likely analysis is that they are invoking the general archetype of the outlaw, which is by definition an opaque reference. Dimitriadis (2001) puts it as follows:

Part of the gangsta's wide cultural currency comes from the universally extractable nature of his narrative. The violent outlaw, living his life outside of dominant cultural constraints, solving his problems through brute power and domination, is a character type with roots deep in popular American lore.... He embodies such capitalist values as rugged individualism, rampant materialism, strength through physical force, and male domination, while he rejects the very legal structures defining that culture. He is both deeply inside and outside of mainstream American culture,... The gangsta is a romantic figure, a ready-made tool for teen rebellion. (p. 29)

In other words, the cult of the thug was not, for the MCs, about being a thug but holding up the thug as symbolically compelling. To drive this point home, note that Delphee's move away from thug life coincided with his development as an MC. The thug world shifted from a way of life he tasted one evening in a park with his boyz, into a narrative motif that was explicitly removed from reality through various rhetorical conventions. Instead of being a thug, he conjured up a warrior MC, who used, to cite TopDawg, "his lyrical tongue," instead of a gun.

Sexism and Homophobia: "Did You Know He Was Really a Bitch?"

The quote from Dimitriadis above connects violence with sexism, the other "notorious problem," through the figure of the thug. Examination of the MCs' rhymes shows a related but somewhat different pattern in which sexist and homophobic motifs were employed as verbal weapons in battle rhymes. A popular conceit involved using sexual penetration as expression of dominance. This image is probably the most fundamental archetype of "hegemonic masculinity," an association of supremacy with masculine attributes (Connell, 1987), and it thus rests upon a profoundly sexist worldview.

Nevertheless, this image was often employed in bizarre and improbable ways. Tropics, for instance, boasted that he had raped the devil because, "Did you know he was really a bitch?" This nominally homosexual image was rare, but there was no shortage of depictions of highly stylized heterosexual conquests, such as this excerpt of a song by Sega:

1. You on top nigga?
2. Nah! Maybe when you fuckin'
3. You know who to watch nigga
4. Nah! You could stay hiding and
5. Ducking
6. Rhyming or something
7. While I'm wining and dining
8. you wife/inside of her while she
9. still lies to her husband
10. decide or keep frontin'

Grant (1996) argues that similar exaggerations in the lyrics of commercial artists are a kind of last-ditch defense of male privilege in the face of feminist demands for fairness. However, this excerpt is about a conflict with another male; the act of cuckolding is how he achieves his victory. Furthermore, as with lyrical violence the patently irrealist nature of these depictions supports an opaque interpretation. After all, it seems more plausible that a 16-year-old boy's rhymed depiction of himself as the rapist of a mythological personification of evil is more a poetic grotesque than a bunker for his male self-regard.

Another reason to prefer an opaque interpretation of these motifs is the wide-ranging use of images of nonsexual penetration, ranging from the bizarre to the realistic, as symbols of supremacy:

- The devil sent me to kidnap baby Jesus/and pump the Virgin Mary full of 500 diseases. (Tropics)
- Let my thoughts come out of my mind into yours/Cherub kick open all doors. (Cherub)
- Cherub is guaranteed to spit a dart right through your heart. (Cherub)
- I'd rather send shots through your stomach/Leave your bladder soaked in gauze. (Sega)

Gender in the Lifeworld: "All the Ill Ones Don't Be Walkin' Around Showin' They Tits"

The absurdity of most of the MCs' sexist images does not necessarily absolve them of holding sexist attitudes; equating a woman with a trophy is evidently a form of objectification. Still, it does indicate that these motifs were not simply about male dominance over women. To understand how these motifs related to real constructions of gender requires comparing them to how their creators related to gender in their lifeworlds generally.

UAA provided an excellent venue for determining one aspect of this relation because, on the one hand, the MCs made frequent use of homophobic slurs such as *faggot, cocksucker,* and *homo,* while on the other, male homosexuality was a part of the fabric of life at the school. During the study, there were five openly gay boys, one of whom was elected senior class president, and one of the most popular and respected teachers was also openly gay. In addition, some MCs were aware that I am gay from my time as a teacher. It was therefore not surprising that the MCs denied that they had anything against gays despite their constant use of homophobic slurs.

Kareem claimed that the words were not about homosexuality at all, but referred to softness. This explanation may appear to be clumsy adolescent dissembling, but it is supported by the fact that none of the gay students considered the MCs particularly homophobic. Also, I observed no attempts on their part to police canonical gender roles. Finally, though, counterintuitively, some MCs readily admitted to verbally harassing one presumably gay student. This student was the exception that proves the rule because he was widely considered closeted. When I asked Kareem why this boy was harassed but not his openly gay classmates, he reported that there was no point in accusing someone of being gay if they would just admit it. In other words, the boy's perceived fakeness and fear opened him to attack, not his sexual orientation, which in the context of UAA was not much of an issue.

The case of girls and women, by contrast, appeared more problematic. Kareem told me that the MCs did not accept the condemnation of the double standard that prizes male promiscuity but censures the female equivalent. Lil' Kim, for instance, was widely dismissed as "a ho" because of her overt sexuality whereas Ludacris, who famously boasts of his promiscuity, was admired. In school, Sega sampled a sexist hook of his in one of his own songs, which, he let it be known, was aimed at a girl he felt had betrayed him. Nevertheless, whatever their desires, the MCs were not the macho playaz they boasted about being in their rhymes. Sega, for instance, became contrite to a (different) girlfriend when he felt he had acted badly toward her.

Some UAA students gendered urban music systematically, with rap associated with boys' and R&B considered the girls' domain. The MCs were dismissive of this position, arguing that there were female rap fans and artists. Still, girls were rarely found in the studio, although a few did join the boys on trips to open mics and clubs. While there were no female MCs at UAA, the MCs nevertheless were open to them joining at least in theory, and they admired some commercial and underground female artists. In fact, they respected one who taught briefly in the program because she won a televised rap battle. When Kareem asked Tropics and Cherub about women rap artists, the answers reflected this ambivalence:

Cherub: I think they're ill, especially when they got a bang up body, yo. [K laughs].... Well yo I think female rappers is ill, cuz [pause]. Yo, niggaz (= males) is ill too.... But you don't want a group of niggaz. You want some females. When you start touring....

Tropics: Yo, I think there aren't enough female rappers. Either the ones that are out are wack, just tryin' too hard. I think they just feel too damn intimidated to come into the game.

Cherub: I think all the ill ones are not given as much respect as they deserve.

Kareem: I think the ill ones is ugly.

Cherub: All the ill ones, they don't be walkin' around showin' they tits.

Kareem: They be too butch.

Cherub: They be too gangsta for that, so they don't shine as much as like the Li'l Kims, know what I'm sayin, or the Fox Boogies, 'n' junk. They don't be showin' the tits and the ass.

These conflicting data suggest that the sexist motifs were distorted reflections of a real sexist worldview. If this is the case, the MCs' contradictions may respond to a conflict between the traditional sex roles still present in their families and communities and those promoted in school and the media they listened to. Whatever the cultural stigma against gay males, ultimately it was relatively easy to accommodate them because their disruptions of the traditional gender roles had little effect on the MCs, and they were not going back in the closet in any case. However, this accepting approach was more difficult in the case of women and girls, with whom the MCs needed to negotiate or struggle over their roles in relationships, and so it was not as fully realized. Still, the images of male superiority they expressed, as playaz, bore little resemblance to the way they conducted themselves in life; the lyrics remained primarily opaque.

"Hip Hop's Like Mad Diverse": Discussion

Comparing the music listened to and produced by the MCs with how they lived their lives leads to the conclusion that their lyrical sexism and violence were related to the cult of the thug. Nevertheless, however distasteful many may find such images, it seems hard to support the conclusion that they were pernicious behaviorally. In fact, five years after the fieldwork ended, it appears that no UAA MC has had any encounters with the criminal justice system. Given Delphee's evolution, perhaps the notorious problems really did serve as verbal substitutes for the destructive features in the street. Like a rap battle that transfers a beef from the physical to the virtual realm, hardcore rap affords a verbal expression of "street conscious identity" instead of a behavioral one that is risky for oneself and harmful to others.

There is some theoretical support for this view. Eckert (1989, 1999) reveals how peer cultures like Hip Hop serve as vehicles for youths to try out and cultivate values and practices associated with adult social identities. Her study in a racially homogeneous European American high school examined the opposition between two class-based groups. One included *jocks,* who cultivated corporate values and practices such as competitiveness and working through established structures. The other involved *burnouts,* who valued the unionlike values of solidarity, group self-sufficiency, and resistance to authority. The jock–burnout dichotomy allowed for social mobility because a working-class youth could become a jock and a middle-class youth a burnout, but both peer cultures were more about continuity than change. They preserved the status, practices, and values of both classes into the next generation.

The working-class UAA MCs combined burnouts' resistance to authority with the jocks' competitive individualism. Differences are not surprising. Eckert studied European Americans toward the end of the relatively stable economy of the post-World War II United States whereas the MCs' were minorities living in a postindustrial age characterized by flux. As Boyd (2002) and Bynoe (2004) argue, rap reflects elements of its time and place, particularly the clash between the hard limits of the urban street and the hope unleashed from the uneven decay of the structures of U.S. racism. As Boyd (2002, p. 18) says, Hip Hop "transcends the boundaries of culture, race, and history, while being uniquely informed by all three."

On this point, it must be noted that only two MCs had African American roots, and these involved only one parent in each case. Nevertheless, all the MCs considered themselves "minorities," being either Black Jamaican Americans or Latinos. Importantly, minority identity is traditionally multiracial in New York City due to the post-World War II Puerto Rican immigration. Sega, a Nuyorican (New Yorker of Puerto Rican heritage) saw Hip Hop as reflecting this multiracialism:

Sega: Hip Hop is like mad diverse. I mean like the industry now is like there's more like African American rappers out there, but if you go toward the underground, there's so many like Chinese rappers, White rappers, Spanish rappers; all over there's everything, Hindu rappers.

By participating in Hip Hop, the MCs constructed identities for themselves as inner city community members. The argument I wish to make is that the problematic motifs served to help locate that identity through the figure of the thug.

To understand how this worked, it is useful to see thuggish elements as backgrounds; that is, as the environment in which a narrative takes place rather than the point of the narrative. Thug actions and the thug ethos mark the agonistic nature of that environment. The warrior MC moves in that harsh environment but always defeats opponents through some form of penetration and collects trophies: hos, money, and other symbols of dominance. Almost like an avatar in a role-playing computer game, the MC acts out sequences of events involving survival and success in a stylized universe.

These goals were fictitious reflections of the MCs own actual imagined futures. Recall that Cherub, for instance, saw himself as making money through conventional means, which involves the assumption that he, a Black male, will be able to get a well-paying "straight job." In fact, he was careful in making sure he took that path, which led to admission to a respected four-year state university, and recently graduate school. His friend Tropics was salutatorian (second highest grade point average) of his graduating class, and also completed college. The remaining MCs were not as successful academically. Some went to college but then dropped out; others never finished high school. Some went to technical schools. Yet all appeared to believe, realistically or not, that they would have options for a prosperous future on the basis of their intelligence, knowledge of the music industry, if not their rap skills.

The combination of aspirations held and challenges faced clarifies why strength, skills, realism, and determination were highly prized, and weakness, fakeness, and particularly softness—a readiness to give in—deprecated. Their lives involved little violence, but the street provided an icon for the difficulties and disadvantages they certainly did face as young minority working-class or low-income males. It also provided them with grounding in a community and culture they were proud of. Its toughness made their survival testimony to their skills and strength as it provided them with a sense of belonging and identity.

Conclusion

In this study, the UAA MCs show how the "notorious problems" of rap were semiotic representations of street reality, closely associated with a cult of the thug. The opaque use of sexist and violent themes rooted the MCs' lyrics in the agonistic world of the street. The lyrics connected their creators to this potentially hostile environment, while allowing them to remain at a relatively safe distance from its physical and moral dangers. The motifs were resources in identity construction as well as tools for creative self-expression. By contrast to the MCs' largely opaque use of these themes, thugs, such as Rashid, could view them transparently as reflections of their lives. Rashid's transparent interpretation does not make the themes responsible for his actions; how they influenced or did not influence Rashid is probably not possible to determine. Certainly, outlaws and outlaw icons predate rap by millennia, as do controversies over the relations between the two.

Clearly, how people define themselves in relation to their larger society involves a multifaceted and complex set of historical, social, and psychological processes. Michael Eric Dyson in an interview with Jones (2006, p. 789), for instance, describes individuals such as Rashid, as having "been thrown by social circumstance and personal choice" into a thug profile. After all, anyone in his circumstances runs into the limits Dyson refers to as "the sad existential truths of young black male life" (Jones 2006, p. 788). Rashid, who described himself as "a prisoner of the ghetto" because his whole life had been circumscribed by his low-income neighborhood before he went to UAA, felt those sad truths particularly acutely. When I interviewed him, the knife scar running across his handsome face spoke louder than his words the price he was still paying for his response to those sad truths. As he saw it, "this was the game that was left for me to play," and he decided that therefore, "so I'm gonna play it."

Most, though not all, of the MCs had happier personal histories, and all perceived more opportunities open to them. They certainly took different paths from Rashid. What the violent and sexist motifs of the UAA MCs raps did, however, was to align them with the thug figure. They portrayed, highlighted, and romanticized the thug's response to those cruel and unjust limitations they all felt to some extent. Their words, then, positioned them as taking the thug's perspective toward the social circumstances of turn of millennium America. They portrayed ideas about the world and their place in it.

In the end, authenticity, a constant hip-hop preoccupation, lies beyond the specifically referential questions of opacity and transparency. As Dyson says:

> Should the authenticity of a model of reality inform the art, or vice versa? Can life be informed by the protocols and machinations of art? Can it be suitably a source of moral and ethical energy that should be transmitted to others who inherit a certain vocabulary of self-regard and self-reflection? Why can't that be the case? I think that seeing things this way is part of the ingenuity of hip-hop. (Jones, 2006, pp. 794–795)

It seems hard to deny that the UAA MCs are doing their best to authentically reflect their lifeworlds, and little more can be asked from a verbal artist than to do that well.

Note

1. Participants are identified by pseudo rap names.

References

Alim, H. S. (2004). *You know my steez: An ethnographic and sociolinguistic study of styleshifting in a Black American speech community* (pp. ix–xxiii.). Durham, NC: Duke University Press/ American Dialect Society

Alim, H. S. (2007). Critical hip-hop language pedagogies: Combat, consciousness, and the cultural politics of communication. *Journal of Language, Identity, and Education, 6*(2), 167–176.

Boyd, T. (2002). The new NHIC: The death of civil rights and the reign of the reign of hip hop. New York: New York University Press.

Bynoe, Y. (2004). *Stand and deliver: Political activism, leadership, and hip hop culture*. Brooklyn, NY: Soft Skull Press.

Connell, R. W. (1987). *Gender and power*. Oxford: Polity Press.

Cope, B., & Kalantzis, M. 2000. Designs for social futures. In B. Cope & M. Kalantzis (Eds.), *Multiliteracies: Literacy learning and the design of social futures* (pp. 203–234). London: Routledge.

Diamatridis, G. (2001). *Performing identity/Performing culture: Hip-hop as text, pedagogy, and lived practice.* New York: Peter Lang.

Dyson, M. E. (1996).*Between God and gangsta rap.* Oxford: Oxford University Press.

Eckert, P. (1989). *Jocks and burnouts: Social categories and identity in the high school.* New York: Teachers College Press.

Eckert, P. (1999). *Language variation as social practice: The linguistic construction of identity in Belten High.* New York: Blackwell.

Garofalo, R. (1994). Culture versus commerce: The marketing of black popular music. *Public Culture, 7,* 275–287.

Grant, J. (1996). Bring the noise: Hypermasculinity and the power to pose in heavy metal and crossover rap. *Journal of Social Philosophy, 27*(2). 5–30.

Husserl, E. (1970). *The crisis of European sciences and transcendental phenomenology.* Evanston, IL: Northwestern University Press.

Ibrahim, A. (1999). Becoming Black: Rap and hip-hop, race, gender, identity, and the politics of ESL learning." *TESOL Quarterly, 33*(3), 349–369.

Ibrahim, A. (2003). "Whassup homeboy?": Joining the African diaspora: Black English as a symbolic site of identification and language learning. In S. Makoni, G. Smitherman, A. Ball, & A. Spears (Eds.), *Black linguistics: Language, society, and politics in Africa and the Americas* (pp. 169–185). London: Routledge.

Jones, M. D. W. (2006). An interview with Michael Eric Dyson. *Callaloo, 29*(3), 786–802.

Keyes, C. (1996). At the cross-roads: Rap music and its African nexus. *Ethnomusicology, 40*(2), 223–248.

Lawson, B. E. (2003). Microphone commandos: Rap music and political ideology. In T. L. Lott & J. P. Pittman (Eds.), *A companion to African-American philosophy* (pp. 419–428). Malden MA: Blackwell.

Lott, T. (1992). Marooned in America: Black urban youth culture and social pathology. In B. Lawson (Ed.), *The underclass question* (111–126). Philadelphia: Temple University Press.

Newman, M. (2001). "Not dogmatically/It's about me": Contested values in a high school rap crew. *Taboo: A Journal of Culture and Education, 5*(2), 51–68.

Newman, M. (2005). Rap as literacy: A genre analysis of Hip-Hop ciphers. *Text, 25*(3), 399–436.

Newman, M. (2007). I don't want my ends to just meet. I want my ends overlappin. *Journal of Language, Identity, and Education, 6*(2), 131–145.

Norfleet, D. M. (1997). *Hip-hop culture in New York City: The role of verbal musical performance in defining a community.* Unpublished Doctoral Dissertation, Columbia University, New York.

Rose, T. (1994). *Black noise, rap music and Black culture in contemporary America.* Hanover, NH and London: Wesleyan University Press.

Sarkar, M., & Allen, D. (2007). Hybrid identities in Quebec hip-hop: Language, territory, and ethnicity in the mix. *Journal of Language, Identity, and Education, 6*(2), 117–130.

Schutz, A., & Luckmann, T. (1973). *The structures of the life-world.* Evanston, IL: Northwestern University Press,

Shusterman, R. (2003). Rap as art and philosophy. In T. L. Lott & J. P. Pittman (Eds.), *A Companion to African-American philosophy* (pp. 419–428). Malden MA: Blackwell.

Spady, J., & Alim, H. S. (1999). Introduction. In J. Spady, C. Lee, & H. S. Alim (Eds.), *Street conscious rap* (pp. 71–89). Philadelphia: Black History Museum Press.

Thompson, S. L. (2005). "Knowwhatumsayin'?" How hip-hop lyrics mean. In D. Darby & T. Shelby (Eds.), *Hip-hop and philosophy* (pp. 119–132). Chicago: Open Court.

Creating "An Empire Within an Empire"

Critical Hip Hop Language Pedagogies and the Role of Sociolinguistics

H. SAMY ALIM

Let's imagine, for example, a populist teacher who refuses this right of correction [correcting students' language] and says "Anyone who wants to speak should just speak; the most beautiful French is street French...." When it comes to defining the laws of the specific market of his classroom, the teacher's freedom is limited, because he will never manage to create "an empire within an empire", a sub-space in which the laws of the dominant market are suspended. (Bourdieu, 1977/1993, p. 63)

I have suggested that teachers should be about the serious business of educating young black minds to deal with (and if necessary, on) a society of power politics and incredible complexity.... As agents of change, teachers can work to help mold American society into a humane and pluralistic social universe. Effectuating changes in language attitudes and policies, in the classroom and beyond, is a major step in this direction. What teachers would be doing, then, amounts to a social and political act, which, like charity, begins at home. Can I get a witness? (Smitherman, 1977/1986, p. 241)

This chapter has two related goals. The first is to address the daily cultural tension, or cultural combat, that linguistically profiled and marginalized students engage in as they form their linguistic identities in creative and often unexpected (by teachers) ways through their participation in Hip Hop Culture. And the second goal is to present a critical language pedagogy while speaking broadly to the field of sociolinguistics about its involvement in language pedagogy, policy-making, and politics. By providing a case of sociolinguistic involvement in language pedagogies, I will be simultaneously addressing ways in which we can interrogate and reverse (rather than merely "suspend" as Bourdieu wrote above) the laws of the dominant linguistic market through the development of critical pedagogies rooted in students' diverse cultural-linguistic realities, in this case, critical Hip Hop language pedagogies (CHHLPs). This particular sociolinguistic approach to education, being overtly political, is as concerned about speech as it is about speakers, and thus functions on multiple levels (pedagogy, policy, politics) and in multiple contexts (wherever learning occurs). The rise of Hip Hop Culture at the same time that Smitherman and Bourdieu were addressing sociolinguists and educators is an interesting coincidence, since all three represent movements addressing social crises of and through language. This chapter speaks to all of those audiences (the Hip Hop Nation, sociolinguists, and educators) in hopes of improving the educational and social welfare of all students.

I present CHHLPs as a holistic approach aimed at both students *and* teachers, incorporating theory *and* practice, so that innovative approaches might begin to be implemented in classrooms. I begin by locating the school as a primary site of language ideological combat, and situating CHHLPs within the frame of critical language awareness. I argue (as Smitherman does in the opening quotation) that linguists and educators are obligated to present the current social and linguistic reality to students who are economically, politically, and culturally subjugated in mainstream institutions. To this end, several pedagogical approaches will be presented and discussed, including the "Real Talk" project, "Language in My Life" project, "Hiphopography: The Ethnography of Hip Hop Culture and Communication," and "Linguistic Profiling in the Classroom," in an effort to develop CHHLPs. I conclude with a vision for critical, reflexive language pedagogies and a call to mobilize the full body of language, social, and cultural theory to produce consciousness-raising pedagogies. As sociolinguists, we must reconsider both our roles and our goals in studying educational institutions.

"I Ain't Tryna Get Caught Up in That No More": Hip Hop Language Ideologies and Droppin that Catch-22

As speakers of nondominant languages can testify, the politics of language often leave linguistically profiled and marginalized groups in a "cultural catch-22." Smitherman (1977/1986, pp. 206–207), shocking the American sociolinguistic establishment by soundly obliterating the false distinction between "difference" and "deficit" theorists, explained that difference theorists merely "pay lip service" to the "systematic" and "highly verbal" linguistic practices of Blacks. At the same time, these theorists indirectly maintain the position of the "dominant culture," *not* by believing in its superiority, but rather by tacitly accepting that "the white middle class either cannot or will not accept" Black Language (hereafter "BL") and continuing to tell the "gross lie" that "speaking White English guarantees economic advancement." We see the continued telling of this lie 30 years later in 2007. In much the same way as economic and political institutions are gentrifying Black communities around the nation and offering unfulfilled promises of economic independence, one can also say that educational institutions have been attempting to gentrify and remove BL from its speakers with similarly unfulfilled promises of economic mobility. In both cases, the message is: "Economic opportunities will be opened up to you if you just let us clean up your neighborhoods and your language."

Most Blacks in the United States since integration can testify that they have experienced teachers' attempts to eradicate their language and linguistic practices (Baugh, 2000) in favor of the adoption of White cultural and linguistic norms. Many U.S. Blacks can also testify that their desire for group solidarity and identification—as well as linguistic creativity (as with much of the Hip Hop generation)—has rendered this coercive process of cultural and linguistic norming all but irrelevant. Morgan (2001, p. 188) describes the language ideology of the Hip Hop Nation as "consciously and often defiantly based on urban African American language norms, values, and popular culture constructed against dominant cultural and linguistic norms." The Hip Hop Nation's language ideology, she writes, "relies on the study, knowledge, and use of African American English (AAE) and General American English (GAE) linguistic features and principles of grammaticalization." This ideology, which claims urban, working-class BL as its prestige variety, has led to a dramatic increase of localized lexicon and, as Latasha points out below (as did Morgan), a greater emphasis on phonology as a cultural, class-based, regional identifier within Black America:

Latasha: Yeah, like the way I talk to my teacher ain't the same way I talk with the 3L Click.

Alim: 3L Click? What's that?

L: All of our names begin with "L," so we named our click after that, the 3L Click. It's me, LaToya, and Lamar....

A: And how is the way y'all talk different from the way you talk to the teacher?

L: Well, it's like, you know that rapper, Nelly?

A: Yeah, yeah.

L: How he say everything like "urrrr," like for "here" he'll be like "hur-rrr"?

A: Yeah! [Laughing] "I ain't from round hurrrr!"

L: [Laughing] That's how we try to talk!

A: Why, though?!

L: Cuz we like it!

When Latasha's favorite rappers, Nelly and the St. Lunatics, bust onto the Hip Hop scene, they were among the first rappers to represent St. Louis, Missouri on an (inter)national scale. Language was an essential part of establishing their identity in the fiercely competitive world of Hip Hop. In a popular single, they emphasized every word that rhymed with "urrrr" to highlight a well-known (and sometimes stigmatized) aspect of Southern/Midwestern pronunciation (also popularized by St. Louis' Chingy and New Orleans' Mystikal, among others). By intentionally highlighting linguistic features associated with their home turf, they established their tenacity through language as if to say, "We here now!" As we see from the dialogue above, northern California-based Latasha and the 3L Click borrow this phonological feature of BL and fashion themselves as multiregional and multilectal Hip Hop Heads.

This phenomenon of Hip Hop Heads borrowing regionally marked phonology is occurring around the nation and has been noted by Perry (2004) in her literary criticism of Hip Hop. She describes an "uncanny experience" of visiting a movie theater in Boston only to encounter employees speaking as if they were from the "Deep South." She writes:

> It wasn't until after I left the theatre that it occurred to me that this phenomenon of southern language entering Boston might have something to do with the massive success of hip hop artists from the South such as the Cash Money Millionaires, Master P, and the 504 Boys. That region had taken center stage nationally. (pp. 22–23)

What these instances demonstrate is that Hip Hop language ideologies are often more concerned about playing with and exploiting interregional differences in BL than they are with remaining trapped in the "catch-22" that pits the "standard" against their own varieties. Or as one of my students put it, they "ain't tryna get caught up in that no more."

"Everything Is Just 'Was'": The School as a Primary Site of Language Ideological Combat

CHHLPs build upon the research in the field of language ideologies, brought into focus by Schieffllin, Woolard, and Kroskrity (1998) and Kroskrity (2000). Those who have conducted long-term research in schools are well aware that teachers' language ideologies are remarkably consistent in their elevation of the "standard" language variety and their devaluation of all other varieties (Alim, 2004a, 2004b). In fact, one could argue that most members of any society (even linguists are not immune) have purchased and are deeply, if unconsciously, invested in the hegemony of the "standard" language (DeBose, 2007). Teachers are the shared focus of CHHLPs because they are the ones charged with the awesome responsibility of educating culturally and linguistically diverse students. They hold the same deeply entrenched set of folk linguistic mythologies and ideologies of language as most citizens, yet they are required to enforce "rules" which reproduce the current sociolinguistic order in a very direct way through language teaching, thus placing them in a tremendous position of power.

The teacher, by virtue of the education system's dialectical relationship to the labor market, is a primary conduit of the cultural reproduction of prescriptive and sometimes prejudicial language ideologies (Bourdieu, 1991, pp. 48–49, in particular). Writing about the construction, legitimation and imposition of an official language, Bourdieu ascribes a decisive role to the educational system:

> Georges Davy goes on to state the function of the schoolmaster, a *maitre à parler* (teacher of speaking) who is thereby also a *maitre à penser* (teacher of thinking): "He [the primary schoolteacher], by virtue of his function, works daily on the faculty of expression of every idea and every emotion: on language. In teaching the same clear, fixed language to children who know it only vaguely or who even speak various dialects or *patois*, he is already inclining them quite naturally to see and feel things in the same way; and he works to build the common consciousness of the nation."

Bourdieu articulates language education in much broader terms than the mere acquisition of a "standard variety"—in fact, he places language education as central to the construction of a common national consciousness. Many teachers still view their role to be one in which they "work daily on the faculty of expression" in order to "build the common consciousness of the nation." The establishment of that "same clear, fixed language" to speakers of diverse linguistic varieties is, as one teacher put it, "the thing that teachers...*combat* the most" (see dialogue below).

In this context, CHHLPs view the school as a primary site of language ideological combat, and begin with efforts to uncover and understand the complex and conflicting language ideologies within particular educational institutions. The school is a key site for the construction, legitimation, and imposition of an "official language." One of the goals of CHHLPs is to uncover both the official, articulated language ideologies of the school, as well as the unofficial, unarticulated language ideologies of teachers and students. In this particular case below, teachers consistently engage in behaviors that aim to produce a homogenous "academic language," while many students are busy celebrating, highlighting, and consciously manipulating "diverse language varieties."

This dialogue with a teacher from Haven High in Sunnyside, a diverse, working-class suburb in the United States, serves as the entry point to our discussion of how BL, and its speakers, are viewed in American educational institutions. We enter the dialogue as the teacher describes the "communication" goals of the school, and the language and communication behavior of her Black students:

Teacher: They [Haven High] have a lot of presentation standards, so like this list of, you know, what you *should* be doing when you're having like an oral presentation—like you should speak slowly, speak loudly, speak clearly, make eye contact, use body language, those kinds of things, and it's all written out into a rubric, so when the kids have a presentation, you grade on each element. And so, I mean, in that sense, they've worked with developing communication. I mean, I think the thing that teachers work with, or *combat* the most at Haven High, is

	definitely like issues with standard English versus vernacular English. Um, like, if there was like one of the *few* goals I had this year was to get kids to stop sayin, um, "he was, she was…"
Alim:	They was?
T:	"They was. We be." Like, those kinds of things and so we spent a lot of time working with that and like recognizing, "Okay, when you're with your friends you can say *whatever you want* but…this is the way it is. I'm sorry, but that's just the way." And they're like, "Well, you know, it doesn't make sense to me. This sounds right." "She was." Like, and that's just what they've been used to and it's just…
A:	Well, "she was" is right, right? You mean, like, "They was"?
T:	"They was."
A:	And "we was" and that kinda thing…
T:	Yeah, "we was." Everything is just "was."
A:	[Laughter]…

The teacher goes on to note that her students' language is "unacceptable," "disrespectful," and "abrasive"; that they "can't codeswitch," at least not to the point where it's "natural"; and, although she desires better training, that she is "not equipped" to tell them "why they have to play the game" and speak the dominant variety. This teacher presents an interesting case in that she is genuine about her commitment in seeing as many of her students attend four-year colleges as possible. And later in the interview when she states, "I have to say it's kind of disheartening because like despite *all* that time that's been spent focusing on grammar, like, I don't really see it having helped enormously," one gets the sense that she is actually disheartened and saddened by her lack of results.

What teachers like this one are probably not aware of is how they are enacting Whiteness and subscribing to an ideology of linguistic supremacy within a system of daily cultural combat. It is very revealing that the teacher describes the language of her Black students as the thing that teachers at Haven High "*combat the most.*" In fact, her attempt to eradicate the language pattern of her Black students has been "one of the *few* goals" she has had throughout that academic year. The teacher not only works to eradicate the language pattern of her Black students, but also responds negatively to what she calls "unspoken language," or the students' "tone." Further, the attribution of negative characteristics (such as "abrasive" or "disrespectful") due to cultural differences has been noted frequently in studies of intercultural communication (Gumperz, 1982a, 1982b).

Interestingly, the teacher notes her students' failure to speak "standard English"—particularly in the case of what's known as the generalization of *was* to use with plural and second person subjects (Wolfram, 1993)—while she fails to make several linguistic distinctions herself. Not only does the teacher erroneously point out "he was" and "she was" as cases of BL and imply that BL has a random system of negation, but she is also clearly not aware of the stylistic sensitivity in the use of *was* and *were*. When the teacher says, rather exasperatedly, "Everything is just 'was,'" she is not recognizing the subtle stylistic alternation of *was* and *were* that is employed by BL speakers, where speakers alternate their use of *was* and *were* based upon various contextual and situation factors. In fact, the teacher goes as far as to say that her Black students do not have the ability to "codeswitch," a point which is soundly disproven in Alim (2004a).

Much ethnographic research on language in schools has shown how educational institutions deem particular linguistic and communicative competencies "acceptable," "rewardable," and even "truthful" and other competencies (and they are usually not seen as "competencies" by the institution) as "unacceptable," "punishable," and yes, "untruthful" (Alim, 2004a; Heath, 1983; Hornberger, 1988). While the notion of language ideologies may be absent from most traditional approaches to language pedagogies, and the development of language pedagogies may be absent from many language ideological studies, ideologies and pedagogies are linked in that language pedagogies are inherently ideological, enforcing certain norms at the expense of others (Blommaert, 1999; Collins & Blot, 2003; Jaffe, 1999).

As Kroskrity (2000) writes, emphasizing the need for a critical linguistic anthropology:

> Never before have the relations of language, politics, and identity seemed so relevant to so many. We live in a time when English-only legislation is zealously proposed in many of the United States; when many speakers of minority indigenous languages around the world struggle to retain their mother-tongues in the face of all manner of state-supported linguistic discrimination; and when the mere mention of nonstandard varieties of languages such as "Ebonics" inspires animated debate on the subject of language and its educational virtues. (p. 1)

Further, as other researchers have shown, we live in a time when the mere mention of "nonstandard varieties of languages" inspires more than animated debate; it incites profoundly racist and discriminatory discourses about the speakers of those varieties (Baugh 2000; Collins 1999; Rickford & Rickford, 2000,). It is within this highly charged political field—in the sense of "*state* politics" as well as "*cultural* politics"—that CHHLPs emerge with the aim of not just teaching language, but to inspire pedagogies that make explicit the link between language, power and social process.

In this important respect, CHHLPs draw heavily from the perspectives of Critical Language Awareness (CLA) (Fairclough, 1995; Wodak, 1995) and Critical Applied Linguistics (CAP) (Pennycook, 2001). Though CLA and CAP differ in some important ways, both view educational institutions as designed to teach citizens about the current sociolinguistic order of things, without challenging that order. This view of education interrogates the dominating discourse on language and literacy and foregrounds the examination and interconnectedness of identities, ideologies, histories/herstories, and the hierarchical nature of power relations between groups. Importantly, CLA and CAP are not concerned with the study of decontextualized language but rather with the analysis of "opaque and transparent structural relationships of dominance, discrimination, power and control as manifested in language" (Wodak, 1995) and how these relationships are performed and contested (Pennycook, 2004).

CHHLPs create a Freireian critical pedagogy (Freire, 1970) of language that educates linguistically profiled and marginalized students about how language is used and, importantly, how language can be used against them. Questions central to the overall project are: "How can language be used to maintain, reinforce, and perpetuate existing power relations?" And, conversely, "How can language be used to resist, redefine, and possibly reverse these relations?" CHHLPs engage in the process of consciousness raising; that is, the process of actively becoming aware of one's own position in the world and what to do about it (as in the Black, Chicana/o, Women's, and LGBT Liberation movements). By learning about the full scope of their language use (see below) and how language can actually be used against them (Baugh, 2003; see also Bertrand & Mullainathan, 2003), students become more conscious of their communicative behavior and the ways by which they can transform the conditions under which they live.

Bearing critiques of critical language awareness in mind (Reagan, 2006), the remainder of this article will focus specifically on pedagogical approaches that empower diverse students. Although each project is really a unit, and can be described at much greater length, the following sections introduce the main pedagogical initiatives and provide sample exercises. This pedagogical framework furthers what Gutierrez (2005) refers to as "sociocritical literacy" by providing a progression of language learning experiences that illustrate a developmental approach, one that brings a theoretically grounded and socioculturally rich pedagogy alive. Moreover, as Morrell (2004) has shown, engaging students in critical research relating to popular culture can be particularly effective, especially when deep and meaningful learning is too often preserved for more privileged others.

"That's Real Talk": Developing an Awareness of Sociolinguistic Variation

"Real talk" is an idiomatic expression in the language of the Hip Hop Nation that builds upon what generations of Black Americans have referred to as "straight talk." Real Talk is the Hip Hop generation's version of an evolving discourse on language and authenticity in the Black community. CHHLPs borrow the phrase "Real Talk" to create an alternative metalinguistic discourse on language in educational contexts. The project utilizes "real talk" (naturally occurring conversations) to socialize students into an awareness of sociolinguistic variation. This project builds upon the "dialect awareness" programs spear-headed by Walt Wolfram and his colleagues at North Carolina State University and supported by Carolyn Adger and Donna Christian of the Center for Applied Linguistics

(Wolfram, Adger, & Christian, 1999). In short, these programs seek to infuse the fundamental principles of sociolinguistic variation into school curricula. The programs get students excited about the inherent variability of language and meet standards proposed by the International Reading Association and the National Council of Teachers of English that students should "develop an understanding of and respect for diversity in language use, patterns, and dialects across cultures, ethnic groups, geographic regions, and social roles" (NCTE/ IRA, 1996, p. 3). One of the most exciting aspects of the programs is that they encourage students to become ethnographers and collect their own speech data from their local communities.

The "Real Talk" project begins with the sociolinguistic analysis of a conversation with one of the Bay Area's most well-known street Hip Hop artists, JT the Bigga Figga. The class exercise begins by listening to an audiotaped interview, and copies of the tape are then distributed to the students, each of whom has a tape recorder. Each student is instructed to transcribe the first small portion of the tape *exactly as they hear it*. What we then find out as a class is that we have each produced a unique transcript of the same speech sample. Invariably, some students will "standardize" the speech samples, and others will "vernacularize" them. As we search for differences between our transcriptions, students begin to notice sociolinguistic patterns in the rapper's speech (e.g., "In the first sentence he said, "He run everything," and then later he said, "He runs everything.""). We take this one feature of the rapper's spoken speech (third person singular –s variability) and conduct a sociolinguistic analysis of his speech, which leads to a larger understanding of the structure and systematicity of spoken speech. Students are not only learning about the sociolinguistic variation of spoken language, they are also being introduced to a curriculum that introduces it as a viable modality for learning.

"Mostly in Slang, or Ebonics, but Sometimes in Standard English": Language Learning Through Reflexive, Ethnographic Analyses

After learning about the systematicity of spoken speech, and that sociolinguistic variation refers to the variable frequencies of certain features within a linguistic system, we introduce the concept of variation in terms of language use, or "ways of speaking." The "Language in My Life" project begins by introducing students to Dell Hymes' (1964, 1972) theory of the "Ethnography of Speaking" and ends with student-conducted, reflexive, ethnographic analyses of their own speech behavior. The goal is for students to answer the question: How do I use language in my life? They are given an "Ethnography of Speaking" reference sheet that they keep in their binders throughout the unit. The sheet reviews basic concepts in this area, such as *speech situation*, *speech event*, and *speech act*, as levels of analysis in a communicative encounter. (In this case, the speech situation is a Hip Hop concert in Oakland, CA; the speech event is an interview with Juvenile; and speech acts include greetings, jokes, etc.).

Table 11.1 Interview with Juvenile

A:	Wassup, Juve?
J:	Wassup, woadie?
A:	What's goin on?
J:	Chillin, you know me. I'm chillin.
A:	How would you describe the last year/year and half for you?
J:	Spectacular, man! I've been blessed, you know.
A:	It's a blessing, ha?
J:	Workin real hard, you know. Just a lot of things. A lot of things have been goin on and so far everything's been goin right. I've been makin the right moves…

J = Juvenile
A = Alim

Students are presented with another sample of "Real Talk"—this time with New Orleans rapper Juvenile (in order to use a speaker that is *not* from their local community)—and are guided through an "ethnography of speaking" analysis of an interview, which they learn is a "speech event." A small sample from the interview (see Table 11.1) is used to create a worksheet (full interview appears in Spady, Alim, & Meghelli, 2006).

Students are encouraged to notate the transcript in detail. They are usually adept at identifying a certain level of informality (through the use of "slang" like "wassup," "chillin," "you know what I'm saying?") as well as regionalisms in the New Orleans-based rapper's speech (such as "woadie," which can mean, "man, homie"; "It's all gravy!" for the commonly used "It's all good."), and my use of "ha?" as an attempt to build rapport with (or "be cool with") the rapper by using one of his most famous expressions.

But, of course, the students are told, you can only gather so much information by reading a transcript—you have to "go out into the field." After introducing the theory and doing a hands-on ethnography of speaking analysis, I wanted the students to be able to analyze their own communication behavior in their everyday environments, from their actual lived experiences. After challenging students and asking them if they thought that *they* could do an ethnography of speaking with their own language data, I introduced the "Language In My Life" project. The students were instructed to analyze their own communication behavior as it shifted across contexts and situations. As ethnographers, they were charged with carrying an ethnography notebook and documenting their communicative encounters. The notebook consisted of grids that were to be filled in throughout the day. See Table 11.2 for an example from an 8th grader.

Immediately, this project validates the language practices that students engage in outside of the classroom—e.g., *rappin* or *battlin*—by allowing the students to see their speech behavior taken as a subject of analysis. Further, after collecting data on their own speech, students gain a much higher level of metalinguistic

Table 11.2 Language in My Life

Date:
November 22nd

Time:
Early in the morning, like, 7am

Mode of Language (reading, speaking, writing, listening, etc.):
Speaking, listening, rappin

Name of Language:
Mostly in slang, or Ebonics, but sometimes in standard English because my aunt was there and she talks like that.

Context (who's involved, where is it happening, what's happening):
I was sitting in the kitchen with my dad, eating cereal before I had to go to school. Before that, I was reading this rap I had wrote over and over again in my room, so I wanted to rap it for my dad. I did, and he was feelin it! He said the he could do a better one, so he tried, but it wasn't better. He called my mom and aunt over from the other room and told me to rap for them and I did. My mom was like, "Wow, Lamar! You bad!" I said, "I know." (Being cocky, as I am!) And my aunt said, "What a talented young man." My dad said he was gonna battle me after school.

Comments on the style(s) of language used:
The language with me and my dad was mostly in slang, or Ebonics, as I like to call it. Nah, I mostly say slang. And my mom, too. But my aunt, she talks standard English. I don't know, maybe because she's older.

---

awareness (speaking of themselves as styleshifters possessing multiple languages and a range of speech styles) that allows them to not only better understand the abstract theory of "speaking," but also to better understand the linguistic landscape of their social worlds. These worlds are not marginalized in the classroom, or "checked-in at the door," as some teachers would have it. They are made central to the students' language learning experience.

"Aight, Rogue": Hiphopography—The Ethnography of Culture and Communication

After the students have learned about and conducted sociolinguistic and ethnographic analyses of their own speech behavior, we expand the scope of the pedagogy and encourage students to "go back into the field" to study their social worlds through an analysis of their peer group and peer culture. As seen in this example below, one of the primary ways to accomplish this is through the study of localized lexical usage. We begin by raising students' awareness to the variety of lexical innovations within Hip Hop Culture (of course, most students are already aware of this, since they actively participate in these innovations). To peak their interest, as well as to localize the dialogue by focusing on the Bay Area, we provide a specific example of a research interview about the language of Hip Hop Culture with JT the Bigga Figga. In the short excerpt below, JT provides an "emic" view of Hip Hop's evolving lexicon (full interview appears in Spady et al., 2006).

[J = JT the Bigga Figga; A = Alim]

A: What does it mean to be CERTIFIED WITH GAME?

J: CERTIFIED mean you official…. How it got incorporated into our language in the streets, from my first experience with the word in the streets, was from MOBB CARS. And the mobb cars is Caprice Classics or Chevy Impalas '87 to '90. Them three years right there. And if you get a mobb car and it don't have a certain seal on it, it's not certified. So when dudes buy the car, it have to have that seal. You want yo car to be certified, you know what I'm saying? And that's just like if you into the collector's cars and if it don't have the same steering wheel or if you change something it's not certified no more. So it's original, you know what I'm saying? And another meaning for certified meaning that you OFFICIAL…. If I say, "Man, Alim's gon handle it. If he said he gon handle it, he certified, man. He gon handle it." So somebody who word is good.

Upon reading the transcript aloud as a class, students immediately respond by critiquing phrases, calling some out-of-date, providing new or similar phrases, comparing with other regional phrases, etc. This excitement is channeled into further training in ethnographic methods. For this particular case, we borrow from the introduction to linguist Geneva Smitherman's *Black Talk: Words and Phrases from the Hood to the Amen Corner* (1994/2000). The following worksheet translates academic language into a familiar Hip Hop-stylized way of writing (again, validating both academic language and the language of Hip Hop Culture).

Ethnographic Methods Used by Geneva Smitherman to Write *Black Talk: Words and Phrases from the Hood to the Amen Corner.* We should use all of these methods in writing our own book (by the way, we need a title—what's up?)

(1) *Written language surveys and word lists* completed by Black people. She made up surveys and gave them to some folks that she knew, and many that she didn't, and asked them to fill out the surveys. What would a survey look like?

(2) *Songs and hit recordings.* Basically, she blocked out 30 minutes or so in her daily schedule to play some of her CD's and tapes. As the songs played, she listened really closely for any unique words and phrases. Most of us listen to music way more than 30 minutes a day, right? I know I do.

(3) *Radio shows.* My radio stay *locked* on KMEL, so this one should be easy. Whether you listen to Chuy in the morning or Big Von in the evening for the 7 O'clock Drop, you'll hear tons of slang words and phrases.

(4) *Movies and television.* You can block out 30 minutes to watch your

favorite TV show (*106th and Park, Rap City*, BET, whatever) and catch all the slang that's being used. If you happen to be watching a movie that day, or that week, pay extra attention to the slang. You can probably get *hecka* words from one movie.

(5) *Collecting words from* community bulletins, leaflets, magazines, announcements or other written material. Can you think of any that you might use?

(6) *Face-to-face interviews.* You can literally ask people if they know any slang words or phrases that you can include for your slang dictionary. Sometimes we can't think of all of these terms by ourselves, right, so we need some help from our people. How would you ask somebody to help you? Who would you ask?

(7) *Eavesdropping.* I ain't gotta tell y'all about that one. Mmm-hmm-mm...

(8) *Participant observation.* Participant observation means that you are not only *observing* the event or the scene, but you are also *actively participating* in it. In what events or scenes do you hear lots of slang talk? I bet you the talk at lunchtime is full of slang words and phrases, huh? This is your first official ethnographic assignment. You are to be a participant observer at lunch tomorrow (Thursday) and at least one other day before we meet again next Wednesday. Keep your lil notebooks handy so you can jot words down as you hear them. I know some of you are dying to ask, so yeah, you can combine this with *eavesdropping*, but if you get popped in the eye, I'ma be like Silkk the Shokker and say, "OOOOOH, it ain't my fault!"

Students are given further training in these methods as we move through the unit. This type of assignment generates intense interest in ethnographic fieldwork and some students go above and beyond expectations by interviewing peers, family members, neighbors, and others until they completely run out of tape! One thing that needs to be emphasized is that this is not just a way to "get students excited" about language, but rather, students are told that they are contributing to the body of scholarly literature on BL. They are charged with the historical responsibility of archiving Black culture—in this case, Hip Hop Culture—through words. In my experience, students have contributed much to the literature. One example is the term *rogue*, a localized example of semantic inversion that highlights a very specific regionality, as it is used *only* within the 2.5 square miles of Sunnyside (Alim, 2004a).

"My Problem with English": From Language Use to Language Discrimination

Thus far, I have outlined projects that develop students' metalinguistic awareness, particularly in the area of language use. As I stated earlier, our goal is to develop CHHLPs that do more than provide students with the tools to analyze language and to theorize its use in their local, social worlds (which is a substantial development in its own right). But beyond this, we are also obligated to expose the nature of power relations vis-à-vis language that exist within and beyond our students' social worlds. Many of our students, particularly those who speak marginalized language varieties, are already acutely aware of the fact that people can use language to discriminate against "others"—they and their families are often those "others." Other students, those for whom a more "standard" variety of English is native, may not have had similar experiences— yet, as Baugh (1998) has already argued, those students also need an education that makes explicit linguistic discrimination, one that recognizes the privileged status of native "standard" English speakers in relation to linguistically profiled and marginalized groups.

In an effort to incorporate the full range of what linguists know about language and its use in society, we begin this lesson by drawing from sociolinguistic research conducted on *linguistic profiling*. Baugh (2003) describes linguistic profiling as the auditory equivalent of racial profiling. This type of profiling (usually occurring over the phone), for example, can prevent potential homeowners from moving into certain neighborhoods. Linguistic profiling covers the full range of discriminatory practices based on racial, geographic, gender, class, sexuality inferences made from speech alone.

Students are introduced to this compelling research by watching a video of recent cable news coverage of the Linguistic Profiling Project (LPP in Alim, 2005). The LPP research findings (Purnell, Idsardi, & Baugh, 1999), which show that the overwhelming majority of us can make correct racial inferences based on the pronunciation of the single word *Hello*, inspire a whole unit of activities designed to investigate this phenomenon. After introducing *linguistic profiling* research as "applied linguistics," the students collect data from the community about similar experiences.

It is at this point in the developmental progression of CHHLPs that students begin to explore the relationships between language and discrimination, as well as the connective marginalities across linguistically profiled and marginalized populations. One brief example illustrates this point. While one Black American student interviewed his aunt and discovered that she had a very painful experience of discrimination in the housing market (that is, she would often be told that units were "still open" only to be turned away upon arrival), a Latina student shared a narrative from her father in which he was fired from his truck-driving job because of "phony" charges of tardiness. In the first case, the Black American aunt spoke "proper" on the phone, but she was still often denied access to housing based on the visual representation of her race ("When they saw I was a Black person"). And in the second case, the Latino father spoke English as a second language and believed that he was fired *not* because of his job performance (or his race) but his "problem with English," as he put it. These narratives are sites of exploration and critical interrogation of the links between language, discrimination, and power.

Conclusion: The Role of the Sociolinguist

Before designing pedagogies, we need to seriously consider the language ideological combat that is being waged inside and outside of our classroom walls. Otherwise, we will continue to produce language pedagogies that fail our students. As Richardson's (2006) work on the global circulation of Hip Hop language ideologies suggests, as well as several chapters in this volume (especially Ibrahim, Lin, and Sarkar), the language ideological struggles within educational institutions in relation to Hip Hop youth is a global issue that impacts youth around the world. In the United States, explanations of academic failure as the result of students' ideological opposition to formal schooling and "acting White" often miss the complexity and multidirectionality of ideological combat. More directly, ethnographic studies (Alim, 2004a; Carter 2005) reveal that teachers can spend as much time devaluing students' language and culture as students spend rejecting that devaluation (which is not the same as rejecting "acting White"). Further, while Bourdieu (1977/1993, pp. 63–64) insists that students will continue to maintain the laws of the dominant linguistic market despite the intentions of "radical" and "populist" teachers, actual teaching experience suggests otherwise. The irony is that even as some teachers spend an inordinate amount of time "focusing on English grammar," and as some social theorists spend an equally inordinate amount of time on macrophenomena, our students are busy takin English to a *whole nother level*; that is, "grammaticalizing" it (Alim, 2006).

In order to keep it real with our students, we need to recognize that the full body of available research on language, its structure, its use, and its role in constructing identities and mediating intergroup relations, is not produced solely for the consumption of scholars. Rather, this knowledge can be used to develop pedagogies that create high levels of metalinguistic awareness through reflexive ethnographic and sociolinguistic analyses of speech. In this way, CHHLPs operationalize the vast body of research on language for the purposes of raising the linguistic and social consciousness of all students.

And as we read above, students ain't the only ones that's strugglin. Teachers of linguistically profiled and marginalized youth often struggle with the contradictions emerging from their own ideological positions, training, lived experiences, and sometimes overwhelmingly antidemocratic school cultures and practices. To this end, more research on teachers' language ideologies and experiences is needed. CHHLPs aim to use this research to engage teachers in the same type of critical language pedagogies outlined for students in this chapter. Teachers, too, can benefit greatly from reflexive analyses of their own language behaviors and ideologies. In fact, it is only once teachers develop a meta-ideological awareness that they can begin to work to change them—and be more fully prepared to teach all students more effectively.

Arriving at this awareness is seen as the first step in challenging a given social order (including the structure of the dominant linguistic market), a "wake-up call" that encourages students and teachers to interrogate received discourses on language, which are always connected to issues of race, class, gender, sexuality, and power. As Fairclough (1989, cited in Reagan, 2006, p. 14) has pointed out, critical language pedagogies have a "substantial 'shock' potential" and "can help people overcome their sense of impotence by showing them that existing orders of discourse are not immutable." Training in critical language issues can help teachers be not only well-meaning but also well-informed enough to address student questions about the imposition of dominant language norms. With such an approach, teachers can stop apologizing for "the way things are," and begin helping their students envision the way things can *be*. As sociolinguists and scholars of language, we can help teachers become those "agents of change" whom Smitherman wrote so passionately and eloquently about in the opening quotation. Armed with this knowledge, and these approaches, teachers can work to push the limits of a Bordieuian analysis; that is, they *can* create "an empire within an empire" by creating a subspace in which the laws of the dominant market are more than suspended—they are interrogated and, over time, dismantled with the goal of providing equal language rights for all.

For too long, scholars of language have studied educational settings for the purposes of addressing "the most fundamental questions in the sociology of language (or sociolinguistics)" (Bourdieu 1977/1993, p. 61) while choosing not to get their hands dirty with the practical processes of teaching and learning. Following Pennycook (2001, p. 176), we must recognize that language teaching and learning, as well as the study of these practices, is "always already political and, moreover, an instrument and a resource for *change*, for challenging and changing the wor(l)d." Change begins with one teacher, one classroom, one school, one district, and this cannot be overemphasized. How many countless social changes have been initiated and bolstered through the active work of educational institutions? Understandings of gender, racial and sexual identification and orientation, for example, have benefited greatly through changes in the official discourses of schools. As Rampton (1995) cautioned, it would be a "major mistake to rule out any possibility of schools engaging constructively" with these difficult issues. Change from the school outwards carries the potential of creating a deeper understanding of linguistic diversity. As sociolinguists, we must do more than study the relationships between language, society and power—we must do what we can to alter those relationships. That's real talk.

Acknowledgments

I would like to acknowledge the support of the Spencer Foundation, without which I would not have been able to complete this research. I'd also like to thank my coeditors, Awad Ibrahim and Alastair Pennycook, for their critical feedback.

This chapter has also benefited from comments by Kris Gutierrez, Austin Jackson, David Kirkand, Ernest Morrell, Marjorie Orellana, Geneva Smitherman, and the two anonymous reviewers of this volume, all of whom made excellent suggestions. Conversations with Alessandro Duranti (especially on Bourdieu), Candy Goodwin, and Paul Kroskrity have also greatly enhanced this chapter. Last but not least, much love to all the Sunnysidaz out there *DO*in it real BIG and gettin they grown self on! (Yeah, yee yee!)

References

Alim, H. S. (2004a). *You know my steez: An ethnographic and sociolinguistic study of styleshifting in a Black American speech community.* Publications of the American Dialect Society, No. 89. Durham, NC: Duke University Press.

Alim, H. S. (2004b). Hearing what's not said and missing what is: Black language in White public space. In C. B. Paulston & S. Keisling (Eds.), *Discourse and intercultural communication: The essential readings* (pp. 180–197). Malden, MA: Blackwell.

Alim, H. S. (2005, October). Critical language awareness in the United States: Revisiting issues and revising pedagogies in a resegregated society. *Educational Researcher, 34*(7), 24–31.

Alim, H. S. (2006). *Roc the mic right: The language of hip hop culture.* London: Routledge.

Alim, H. S., & Baugh, J. (Eds.). (2007). *Talkin Black talk: Language, education, and social change.* New York: Teachers College Press.

Baugh, J. (1998). Linguistics, education, and the law: Educational reform for African American language minority students. In S. Mufwene, J. Rickford, G. Bailey, & J. Baugh (Eds.), *African-American English: Structure, history and use* (pp. 282–301). London: Routledge.

Baugh, J. (2000). *Beyond Ebonics: Linguistic pride and racial prejudice.* New York: Oxford University Press.

Baugh, J. (2003). Linguistic profiling. In S. Makoni, G. Smitherman, A. F. Ball, & A. K. Spears (Eds.), *Black linguistics: Language, politics and society in Africa and the Americas* (pp. 114–126). London: Routledge.

Bertrand, M., & Mullainathan, S. (2003). *Are Emily and Greg more employable than Lakisha and Jamal? A field experiment on labor market discrimination.* NBER Working Paper No. 9873.

Blommaert, J. (Ed.). (1999). *Language ideological debates.* Berlin: Mouton de Gruyter.

Bourdieu, P. (1991). *Language and symbolic power.* (J. B. Thompson Ed. & Introduction; G. Raymond & M. Adamson, Trans.). Cambridge, MA: Harvard University Press.

Bourdieu, P. (1993). *What talking means. In Sociology in question.* London: Sage. (Original work published 1977)

Carter, P. (2005). *Keepin' it real: School success beyond black and white* (pp. 60–71). New York: Oxford University Press.

Collins, J. (1999). The Ebonics controversy in context: Literacies, subjectivities, and language ideologies in the United States. In J. Blommaert (Ed.), *Language ideological debates* (pp. 201–234). Berlin: Mouton de Gruyter.

Collins, J., & Blot, R. (2003). *Literacy and literacies: Texts, power, and identity.* Cambridge, UK: Cambridge University Press.

DeBose, C. (2007). The Ebonics phenomenon, language planning, and the hegemony of standard English. In H. S. Alim & J. Baugh (Eds.), *Talkin Black talk: Language, education, and social change* (pp. 31–42). New York: Teachers College Press.

Fairclough, N. (1989). *Language and power.* London: Longman.

Fairclough, N. (1995). *Critical discourse analysis: The critical study of language.* London: Longman.

Freire, P. (1970). *Pedagogy of the oppressed.* New York: Seabury Press.

Gumperz, J. (1982a). *Discourse strategies.* Cambridge, UK: Cambridge University Press.

Gumperz, J. (1982b). *Language and social identity.* Cambridge, UK: Cambridge University Press.

Gutierrez, K. (2005). *Building sociocritical literacies: A decolonizing tool for contemporary demographics of inequality.* Paper presented at the American Educational Research Association.

Heath, S. B. (1983). *Ways with words: Language, life, and work in communities and classrooms.* Cambridge, UK: Cambridge University Press.

Hornberger, N. H. (1988). *Bilingual education and language maintenance: A southern Peruvian Quechua case*. Berlin: Mouton.

Hymes, D. (1964). Introduction: Towards ethnographies of communication [Special issue]. *American Anthropologist, 66*(6), 1–34.

Hymes, D. (1972). Models of interaction of language and social life. In J. Gumperz & D. Hymes (Eds.), *Directions in sociolinguistics* (pp. 35–71). New York: Holt, Rinehart & Winston,.

Jaffe, A. (1999). *Ideologies in action: Language politics in Corsica*. Berlin: Mouton de Gruyter.

Kroskrity, P. (Ed.). (2000). *Language ideologies: The cultures of language in theory and practice*. Santa Fe, NM: School of American Research.

Morgan, M. (2001). "Nuthin' but a G thang": Grammar and language ideology in hiphop identity. In S. Lanehart (Ed.), *Sociocultural and historical contexts of African American vernacular English* (pp. 185–207). Athens: University of Georgia Press.

Morrell, E. (2004). *Becoming critical researchers: Literacy and empowerment for urban youth*. New York: Peter Lang.

NCTE/IRA [National Council of Teachers of English/International Reading Association]. (1996). *Standards for the English language arts*. Newark, DE: IRA/NCTE.

Pennycook, A. (2001). *Critical applied linguistics: A critical introduction*. Mahwah, NJ: Erlbaum.

Pennycook, A. (2004). Performativity and language studies. *Critical Inquiry in Language Studies, 1*(1), 1–19.

Perry, I. (2004). *Prophets of the hood: Politics and poetics in hip hop*. Durham, NC: Duke University Press.

Purnell, T., Idsardi, W., & J. Baugh. (1999). Perceptual and phonetic experiments on American English dialect identification. *Journal of Language and Social Psychology, 18*, 10–30.

Rampton, B. (1995). *Crossing: Language and ethnicity among adolescents*. London and New York: Longman.

Reagan, T. (2006). The explanatory power of critical language studies: Linguistics with an attitude. *Critical Inquiry in Language Studies, 3*(1), 1–22.

Richardson, E. (2006). *Hiphop literacies*. New York & London: Routledge.

Schieffelin, B., Woolard, K., & Kroskrity, P. (Eds.). (1998). *Language ideologies: Practice and theory*. New York: Oxford University Press.

Smitherman, G. (1986). *Talkin and testifyin: The language of Black* America (rev. ed.). Detroit: Wayne State University Press. (Original work published 1977)

Smitherman, G. (2000). *Black talk: Words and phrases from the hood to the amen corner*. Boston: Houghton Mifflin. (Original work published 1994)

Spady, J. G., Alim, H. S., & Meghelli, S. (2006). *Tha global cipha: Hip hop culture and consciousness*. Philadelphia: Black History Museum Press.

Wodak, R. (1995). Critical linguistics and critical discourse. In J. Verschueren, J. Ostman, & J. Blommaert (Eds.), *Handbook of pragmatics* (pp. 204–210). Philadelphia: John Benjamins.

Wolfram, W. (1993). A proactive role for speech-language pathologists in sociolinguistic education. *Language, Speech and Hearing Service in Schools, 24*, 181–185.

Wolfram, W., Adger, C. T., & Christian, D. (1999). *Dialects in schools and communities*. Mahwah, NJ: Erlbaum.

Takin Hip Hop to a Whole Nother Level

Métissage, *Affect, and Pedagogy*
in a Global Hip Hop Nation

AWAD IBRAHIM

[I]t seems that [Tanzanian youth] are redefining their local environments in transcultural terms associated with the cultural capital of global Hip Hop, and at least some of the time, they are using mostly local linguistic resources to fashion themselves for this imagined yet locally salient context. (Higgins, this volume)

J'check Rob: '*What up dog?*'
—'*What up yo!* ' Shit, les rues sont <u>fucked up</u>!'
<u>Enough talk</u>. Check le reste du *squad*.
On *set* un *get* ce soir. <u>Peace</u>. <u>Hang up the phone.</u>
J'<u>step</u> dehors. Dès que j'sors, des nègs <u>blast</u> des *teck*, percent mon corps.
J'saigne, <u>fucked up</u>, à l'hôpital, presque mort.
    <u>Help me</u> *y'all!* (Sarkar, this volume, quoting MC Impossible of Muzion)

The irony is that even as some teachers spend an inordinate amount of time "focusing on English grammar," and as some social theorists spend an equally inordinate amount of time on macrophenomena, our students are busy takin English to a whole nother level; that is, "grammaticalizing" it (Alim, this volume)

This book has attempted to navigate between these three quotes, expressing three different yet interrelated areas: desire, *métissage*, and pedagogy. Our hope was to put together some good tracks (i.e., chapters) that are intertextually talking to and building upon each other. Brother Alim began this CD (i.e., book) with,

I think, a really strong, clear, and comprehensive prologue. I will attempt now to write an epilogue. To do so, I will frame the book around three questions: (1) What does it mean to localize Hip Hop culturally, linguistically, agentively, and representationally? That is, what meanings do we make from the Aboriginal Australian Wire MC's contention that, "Hip Hop is a part of Aboriginal culture, I think it has always been"? (cited in Pennycook and Mitchell, this volume); (2) What does it mean to affectively desire, engage, translate, appropriate, and claim Hip Hop as one's own? That is, similar to Bakari Kitwana's question, "Why do White, Brown, African, Asian, Aboriginal, South American and European kids love Hip-Hop?"; (3) From an educational and pedagogical perspective, *so what* that kids globally love Hip Hop? Socrates once said, the most banal is the most difficult. The last question, for me, is the most difficult and hence I will spend more time in answering it. I will give each question equal attention, but most of the moral panic against Hip Hop in the United States (cf. Peterson, Esbensen, Taylor, & Freng, 2007) and globally (Mitchell, 2001), for me, stems from seeing Hip Hop as useless verbal violence that has nothing to do with pedagogy and education. I will discuss a pedagogical framework in response to this moral panic to show, much like Newman and Alim in this volume, that Hip Hop is a "null curriculum" (Eisner, 1979). This is an inventive, boundary breaking, boundary pushing, which may best be referred to as *Creative Margin Curriculum* that is deeply related to students' lives, and which students use as a site of learning and identity formation, but is not considered a necessary site for pedagogical engagement.

Métissage: Localizing the Global and The Politics of "Coevalness of Origins"

> The echoes around the world of new Hip Hop cultures may be understood not so much as subvarieties of global Hip Hop, but rather as local traditions being pulled toward global cultural forms while those traditions are simultaneously reinvented (Pennycook & Mitchell, this volume)

This book has been about, on the one hand, what this new landscape of Global Hip Hop Nation might (ethnographically?) look like and, on the other, how the process of creolization or *métissage* is taking place in such innovative ways that it calls for new theorizations, making the division between the local and the global problematic. *"Pratique de métissage"* or cultural, linguistic, and musical creolization, Édouard Glissant argues, "is not part of some vague humanism, which makes it permissible for us to become one with the other" (cited in Françoise Lionnet, 1989, p. 4). On the contrary, *métissage* is a radical concept which means "the constant interaction, the transmutation between two or more cultural components with the unconscious goal of creating a third cultural entity—in other words, a culture [and I would add musical genre, language and identity]—that is new and independent even though rooted in the preceding elements." Here,

Lionnet (1989) explains, "each one changes into the other so that both can be transformed" (p. 15). *Métissage* assumes two or more cultural entities that are equally valorized; hence it is an egalitarian hybridity, where ambiguity, multiplicity, fragmentation and plurality become the new landscape. These cultural entities, however, are not found in complete isolation as Homi Bhabha (1990) argues because there is no cultural form that is "plainly plenitudinous, not only because there are other cultures which contradict its authority, but also because its own symbol-forming activity…always underscores the claim to an originary, holistic, organic identity.… [Therefore,] the "original" is never finished or complete [and the] "originary" is always open to translation" (p. 210).[1]

Pennycook and Mitchell's chapter addresses these processes head-on. They frame their chapter around this question: "At what point does the local take over the global, or at what point do we need to focus on the local host culture appropriating Hip Hop rather than Hip Hop becoming localized?" To answer their question, Pennycook and Mitchell talked to Wire MC (Aboriginal Australian) and K'Naan (African Canadian of Somali origin). They describe both artists as a product of *métissage*, as "abodigital" (to use Wire MC's term): "They are 21st century artists who draw on and change traditional, cultural forms." That is, "they are part of the global Hip Hop movement, identifying with and also rejecting different aspects of its global formation; they benefit from and participate in the rapid flows of music and ideas made possible in the digital age and yet they remain highly critical of Western ways of viewing the world and of the bias in particular forms of historical reasoning" (Pennycook & Mitchell, this volume). They refer to the tension between the global and the local as "coevalness of origins," where K'Naan and Wire MC can claim Hip Hop as theirs, identifying "with aspects of Black American Hip Hop while resisting and changing parts of its message and style that they find inappropriate to their local circumstances." In an effort to appreciate the complexity of localization, Hip Hop is turned into Hip Hops and has, in the words of Wire MC, always been "a part of Aboriginal culture." Wire MC is not suggesting, Pennycook and Mitchell explain, "that Hip Hop as a global cultural formation was invented by Indigenous Australians"; rather he is arguing "that what now counts as Aboriginal Hip Hop is the product of a dynamic set of identifications—with African-American music, style, and struggle—and a dynamic set of reidentifications—with Indigenous music, style, and struggle."

Pennycook and Mitchell then make two central conclusions vis-à-vis the notion of *métissage* that are directly related to the chapters by Androutsopoulos, Higgins, Omoniyi, and Sarkar. (1) "[I]t is not fruitful to pursue the true origins of Hip Hop, as if these could be found either in the village of Africa or the ghettoes of North America, but rather to appreciate that once Hip Hop is taken up in a local context, the direction of appropriation starts to be reversed: No longer is this a cultural form that has been localized; now it is a local form that connects to several worlds: Australian Aboriginal Hip Hop [for example] does connect to African oral tradition but not as much as it connects to Australian Aboriginal practices." (2) "Ultimately,…whether we are dealing with the global spread of English or the global spread of Hip Hop, we need to move beyond an image only of spread and adaptation, beyond only a pluralization by localization (global englishes and global Hip Hops) in order to incorporate as well the self-fashioning of the already local."

Vertical and Horizontal *Métissage*

In his chapter, Jannis Androutsopoulos first builds on Pennycook and Mitchell's conclusions and, second and very significantly, invokes John Fiske's distinction between *vertical* and *horizontal intertextuality*. The latter, for Androutsopoulos, "captures explicit relations between individual texts with regard to their genre or content" while the former "refers to relations of a…text to texts that assume a different function in the circuit of popular culture." Put otherwise, horizontality expresses diversity and frequency while verticality expresses intensity and depth. I want to use the same metaphor in relation to *métissage,* hence making a distinction between *vertical* vs. *horizontal métissage.* We see both forms in Androutsopoulos' chapter. Situating his discussion within Germany and Greece, in the former's case, Androutsopoulos explains, we witness technical mastery and intense similarities between German, Greek, and U.S. Hip Hop—so much so that, Androutsopoulos concludes, "Talking about 'Greek rap' or 'German rap' might be a useful shortcut for comparative purposes, but turns out to be a crude simplification as we focus on a particular local scene in more detail."

These similarities are stark especially in topics, speech act patterns, rhetorical resources, and linguistic variation. He offered these lyrics from Wu-Tang Clan, Spax (translated from German), and Ζωντανοί Νεκροί (translated from Greek), respectively: "I crystallize the rhyme so you can sniff it"; "my stuff 100% pure dope uncut"; "a hit of my rap is more than enough to send you to Strofi for detox." Even though the last two examples are in German and Greek, the similarities in terms of topic and language suggest at least three things. First, for the Global Hip Hop Nation (GHHN), *langue* (that is, speaking English, Cantonese, French, or Zulu) matters less than *langage* (that is, what they speak about and their ways of speaking about it). Second, that German and Greek MCs are not only familiar with, but full-fledged "citizens" of the Global Hip Hop Nation. Spax is not linguistically "crossing" (Rampton, 1995) anywhere here, he is using the German phrase, "*Wort drauf!*" while evoking both phonetically and metaphorically *word* or *word up*, the globally spread African American Hip Hop idiom. Androutsopoulos thus concludes, when it comes to crossing and *métissage,* "at least in the German case,…the point is less *stepping into* an alien ethnic territory ('Blackness') [sic] than *stepping out* of one's own national boundaries (in this case: 'Germanness') and into a [G]lobal Hip Hop [N]ation that is not necessarily imagined of in primarily racial or ethnic terms."

But, third, Spax is also ritualizing Hip Hop through his use of what Androutsopoulos calls "the default code" of Hip Hop: African American Vernacular English (AAVE). This is the second, *horizontal* form of *métissage*. The intent here is not to display a full mastery of the GHHN and its language, but to invoke the GHHN and its commonly ritualized expressions (such as "*Word*" or "*Whadap homeboy?*") as sites of identification and as a performative gesture of desire and identity formation (see especially Higgins, this volume). We see a similar process in Sarkar's chapter. In the opening quote in this chapter, MC Impossible of Muzion actually used different languages. Through her meticulous sociolinguistic analysis, a particular kind of *métissage* is revealed, one where "descendants of the early 17th-century colonists from France are rubbing shoulders—and rhyming—with other urban youth whose roots go back to very different corners and colors of the globe" (Sarkar, this volume). The only reason why this rubbing of shoulders is possible because both groups (the colonized and the historical colonizer) are not only familiar with, but again full-fledged "citizens" of the GHHN and its Language (i.e., GHHNL, see Alim's Introduction, this volume).

Christina Higgins and Tope "Sky" Omoniyi take this idea of *métissage* and situate it squarely within postcolonial contexts, Tanzania and Nigeria, respectively. They both ask the same questions: "Are [Tanzanian and Nigerian] youth *crossing* (Rampton, 1995) from Tanzanian [and Nigerian Pidgin] varieties of English into AAE [African American English], borrowing the linguistic and semiotic styles of another culture? Or, are they *appropriating* what may be better described as Global Hip Hop Nation Language to fit their local East [and West] African context, their language use resulting in a simultaneously localized, yet global, form of expression, such as *raplish*?" (Higgins, this volume). Higgins and Omoniyi joined Pennycook and Mitchell's (this volume) conclusion that we need to appreciate the complexity of localization and that "It is not so much the case that Hip Hop merely takes on local characteristics, but that it has always been local."

In her analysis, Higgins demonstrates a horizontal *métissage* where Tanzanian youth expressed an identification with GHHNL through linguistic gestures. Both linguistically and in terms of their clothes, Higgins concludes, their intent is not to show a full mastery of the GHHNL but to invoke it as a symbolic gesture to their familiarity with it. Higgins also illustrates the complex ways in which Tanzanians manage global and local aspects of Hip Hop linguistically. Like Omoniyi's analysis, she moved beyond a unidirectional analysis of global Hip Hop's influence on local contexts, and illustrated aspects of Tanzanian indigeneity that have produced localized Hip Hop language and culture. On his part, Omoniyi brings us closer to what Halifu Osumare (2007) calls "the Africanist aesthetic" of Hip Hop. Here, we see "how African and Nigerian Hip Hop artists discursively carve out a recognizable creative patch and a legitimate nonsubordinate local identity whilst retaining membership of the global community." We see the discursive strategies deployed by Nigerian artists, for example, in an attempt to articulate Nigerian yet global identities. Here, the mantra of "keepin it real" is taken to a *whole nother level*: locating oneself exactly at the local, where Hip Hop "has always been local."

At this point in the chapter, it is worth thinking about what Omoniyi (this volume) calls "alternative narratives of origin and identity." While we need to keep alive the contentions proposed by these chapters and organically integrate them in our work, a word of caution is necessary, especially for "the linguist" who is not as familiar with GHHN. When Bill Yousman (2003) and Bakari Kitwana (2005) question the conventionally accepted notion that, "White suburban kids are Hip Hop's primary audience" (Kitwana, 2005, p. 81), they are not questioning statistics. Instead, they are asking the question, "Why is this discussion about hip-hop's primary listening and/or audience buying audience important in the first place?" (p. 101). What matters for Yousman and Kitwana is not *who* is buying the music, but *why* this detail has been emphasized. I think a similar line of questions is needed in relation to these alternative narratives of Hip Hop origin and identity.

Yes, there are multiple points of entrance and origin to Hip Hop and yes, the "original" has never been finished or completed and the "originary" has always been open to translation. Furthermore, Hip Hop belongs as much to the South as it does to the North; and Wire MC and K'Naan can claim it as much as King Crazy GK of Tanzania (Higgins), Manzo or SolValdez of BlackSunz of Québec (Sarkar), Dragon Ash of Japan (Tsujimura & Davis), Mano Brown of Brazil (Roth-Gordon), MC Yan of Hon Kong (Lin), and Kaliph of New York City (Newman). These chapters are both acknowledging and pushing beyond the South Bronx narrative of origin. At least for me, they are calling attention to an ongoing, globalcentric Hip Hop production. The collective point is that we need to explore the "global cipha" (Spady, Alim, & Meghelli, 2006) and appreciate the complexity of localization, both in content and form. We further need to think about the process of *métissage* discussed above as a dialectic relation between the global and the local (a point that some U.S.-based Hip Hop is yet to fully understand). We also need, however, not to reverse the old mantra of "Black creation, White imitation" into "Black creation, global imitation." Clearly, as all the chapters in this volume show, the processes of cultural globalization are far more complicated than these clichés suggest.

Hip Hop Desire(d)

Taking Hip Hop to a *whole nother level* calls forth questions of desire. In his chapter, Michael Newman (this volume) illustrates why Hip Hop, especially "hardcore rap," appeals to Rashid, one of the MCs in his study: "I mostly listen to music like rappers that they live the same life as me in my neighborhood, but they from different neighborhoods. So it's good to hear somebody rhyming about something you actually live through, that way you can say to yourself, 'A'ight good, I'm not the only one.' I am glad that I am not the only one. Make me feel I'm strugglin' through my whole life while everybody else is just livin'."

Rashid is raising at least three very significant points as to why global(ly) young people love Hip Hop. First, rappers live in the same neighborhood,[2] and thereby demonstrate the globally circulating Hip Hop ideology of the primacy of locality (a running theme throughout this volume). Second, Rashid gets to know what others are thinking and talking about, allowing him to expand his network and ways of thinking about the world. And third, in so doing, he is glad he is not the only one who is experiencing or talking about "the issues" that are important to him.

This is the appeal of Hip Hop. It speaks to people, speaks about their "issues," and hence creates a *space of identification* (Ibrahim, 2003). As Grossberg (1992) and Masny (2005) argue, the processes of affective investment eventually make this space of identification "home," we thus authorize it to speak on our behalf. We see this *global space of identification* in the chapters by Tsujimura and Davis, Roth-Gordon, Cutler, Androutsopoulos, and Lin (and to a lesser extent in Higgins and Sarkar). As I showed elsewhere (Ibrahim, 2004a), identification is the initial stage of identity formation and for identification to function as such, it requires two things: desire and time. Angel Lin's chapter is exemplary in how this space of identification is both formed and performed. In her conversation with MC Yan, a member of the Hong Kong Hip Hop group LMF (LazyMuthaFuckaz), Lin delineates the complex, poetic, and political ways in which the desire and identification with Hip Hop has changed the value of the Cantonese language in Hong Kong.

While Tsujimura and Davis show how Hip Hop has changed the nature of poetics in Japanese language by introducing "rhyme" for the first time in/to the Japanese language, the desire and identification with Hip Hop take on a stylistic turn in Hong Kong. It is the idea of Hip Hop being a "street language" that seems to capture the imagination of the Hip Hop scene in Hong Kong, especially LMF. Still using Hip Hop's default code (AAVE), the Hip Hop language in Hong Kong both in content and style turned to Cantonese slang for poetic and political inspiration. Cantonese slang, Lin explains, is taboo; devalued and considered as an "inappropriate" language by the middle class in Hong Kong. Significantly, this is a moment of *vertical métissage* where Hip Hop has single-handedly moved the periphery—the "inappropriate" Cantonese slang—to the center and made it a *locus of enunciation* (Mignolo, 2000): a site of knowledge production and of engaging linguistic, class, ethnic, social, and local reality. *Word up*, MC Yan might have said, *just keepin it real!* These are the "Hip Hop Realists, who are telling it like it was, how it is and how it should be…[it is] about real issue and real passion" (Blaktrax, 2005, cited in Pennycook, 2007, p. 141).

These real issues and real passion along with their default code were taken again to a *whole nother level* in Cecelia Cutler's chapter. Besides being a space of identification and desire, AAVE is turned into a "marker" of Whiteness. Cutler is dealing with how ethnic boundaries get negotiated between a White contestant (Eyedea) and his African American opponents (R.K., E-Dub, and Shells) in an MC Battle. By marking his Whiteness, Cutler explains, Eyedea is taking up and *identifying* with African American linguistic marking of Whiteness on the one hand, but on the other he is *desiring* to be seen in his own terms as a White MC; not as another Eminem or Vanilla Ice, but as a capable MC who can stand his own ground.

Both in Roth-Gordon and Androutsopoulos we see Hip Hop as a political site of identification and desire. It is mostly the so-called conscious rap (Spady et al., 1999; Newman, this volume) that seems to appeal to local, grassroots groups. Hip Hop is a political statement in Brazil while in Germany, especially within immigrant groups, it is used to make sense of their migrant experiences. Here, Roth-Gordon and Androutsopoulos explain, people "dissociate themselves from gangsta rap and orient to Public Enemy, whose work they read as a political message against racism and social justice" (Androutsopoulos, this volume). Fans are seldom just fans, as Androutsopoulos argued. Like Omoniyi, Sarkar, Roth-Gordon, Lin, and Higgins show, young people identify with particular images, representations or musical genres because they "speak to" and interpellate them as sites where they may invest their identities and desires. There is a particularly difficult psychic work of desire that needs further research. Yet, this psychic investment, this moment of *jouissance* was so pronounced in Roth-Gordon's research that another moment of *vertical métissage* was produced: one where Rap radically changed the racial politics in Brazil by calling for a "racialized revolution"—in a country "where overt racial conflict, legal separatism, and identity politics are readily viewed as 'un-Brazilian'"—and where the poor Black and Brown *marginais* (marginals) of the *favela* can affirm: "We are marginalized. We are not marginals" (Roth-Gordon, this volume).

The "Main Text" and the Grammaticalization of What We Don't Teach

We are left then with a number of research and pedagogical questions that I think are worthy of further research. First, where (and how) do our youth form their identities if not within and in relation to the realm of popular culture, which is negated most often within formal education settings (Alim, 2007; Dimitriadis & McCarthy, 2001; Giroux & Simon, 1989a, 1989b) and, second, what are the implications of this negation in reframing and reconceptualizing critical curriculum studies? Put otherwise, do social identities, especially race and gender, and their formation processes have any significant role in the process of learning; how do we engage these identities; and how can critical educators bring student-based and student-produced knowledge into the classroom, not to be consumed but rather to be critically engaged, deconstructed? This, furthermore, raises questions of voice and experience. How do we acknowledge previous experience as legitimate content and challenge it at the same time? How do we affirm student voices while simultaneously encouraging conscientization (Freire, 1993): the interrogation of such voices? And how do we avoid the conservatism inherent in simply celebrating personal experience and confirming what people already know? (cf. Alim, 2004, 2007; Eisner & Powell, 2002; Giroux & Simon, 1989a; Newman, in this volume; Quinn & Kahne, 2001).

These questions cannot be understood separately from a diagnosis of the modern condition of what Dimitriadis and McCarthy (2001) call "the age of difference," of multiplicity and *métissage*. Unfortunately, however, the age of difference is also the age of what Nietzsche calls "ressentiment" (resentment): the "practice by which one defines one's identity through the negation of the other" (Dimitriadis & McCarthy, 2001, p. 4). The Other is here capitalized, absolutized, and rancorously put either in the "inner-city" or "overthere" in the Third World. Our aim in this book, especially at a pedagogical level, is to disrupt this dichotomy between Self/Other, Urban/Suburban, Third World/First World, and Local/Global.

When it comes to Hip Hop Pedagogy, Pennycook (2007) contends, "The point is not just to relocate our pedagogical gaze to the street, but to understand the fluidity, fixity and flow of cultural movement" (p. 157). So, as authors, researchers, and organic intellectuals we wanted to *enter the image*, to go through and experience the *School of Reality* (Bankie Santana, cited in Alim, 2007) not as others have described them for us but as an on-going, organic, shifting, and fluid Reality that is of interest to us personally. If one reads between the lines, each of the authors in this volume is deeply involved and committed to the community she or he researches. In fact, one may argue, most if not all of us are unapologetic in blurring the boundaries between "the researcher" and "the research subjects" and find these terms unsatisfactory.

This is because we bore witness to the outcome of *ressentiment*. In education, the politics of *ressentiment*, particularly as expressed by mainstream (conservative?) educational theorists, tends to "draw a bright line of distinction between the established school curriculum and the teeming world of multiplicity that flourishes in the everyday lives of youth beyond the school" (Dimitriadis & McCarthy, 2001, p. 2). Nowhere in the United States is this narcissistic line (and its moral panic) more drawn than against Black popular culture in general and Hip Hop in particular. Clearly, race as much as political agenda determine who gets to be represented and how and, in education, they regulate and govern who gets to be included in the curriculum—what Maxine Greene (1992) refers to as the "main text." "In truth," she writes, "I do not see how we can educate young persons if we do not enable them on some level to open spaces for themselves—spaces for communicating across the boundaries, for choosing, for *becoming different* [my emphasis]…so that…[they] will be less likely to confine themselves to the main text" (p. 2).

For Elliot Eisner (1979) the "main text" can be divided into three typologies: implicit, explicit, and null curriculum. In the explicit curriculum, students enter a discourse and culture whose common signifier is "schooling," with publicly sanctioned goals. These goals are usually presented as ideologically neutral and pedagogically necessary if one is to become a "functional citizen." In the implicit curriculum, also known as the "hidden curriculum" (Apple, 2004), students are expected to conform and follow certain patterns of cultural practices of schooling that are not stated explicitly and the ultimate "hidden" goal or secret education, for Eisner (1979), is that students are expected to follow and comply to purposes and agenda set by another (see also Eisner, 2005). The "null curriculum" (which I am referring to as *Creative Margin Curriculum* [CMC]) is defined as "what schools do *not teach*" (Eisner, 1979, p. 83; original emphasis). CMC is a configuration of knowledge and a mattering map that are linked to students' identities and ways of knowing and learning—representing their *School of Reality*—but not directly addressed in their schooling processes. Eisner argues that most subject matters that are now taught in school systems are taught out of habit. Eisner is not arguing that geography, math, chemistry, and so on, are not important; he is, however, reminding us of this question, which is rarely asked in educational settings: Why are we teaching what we are teaching? Hence, Eisner concludes, "we ought to examine school programs to locate those areas of thought and those perspectives that are now absent in order to reassure ourselves that these omissions were not a result of ignorance but a product of choice" (1979, p. 83).

It is here, I am contending, that we should locate Hip Hop as a creative margin, a cultural space of affective and identity investment that accommodates both internal tensions and dynamic cultural ciphers. That is, Hip Hop is complex, fluid, and a curriculum site full of possibilities that are not readily apparent to the uninitiated. Both here and in his book, *Roc the Mic Right* (2006), Alim offers theoretical and practical approaches to studying Hip Hop. For him, Hip Hop will "mediate the corrosive discourse of the dominating society while at the same time function as a subterranean subversion" (Spady, 1993, p. 93).[3] Hip Hop is a *Creative Margin Curriculum* that is so subtle and subterranean that Ice-T likened it to a home invasion. He is worth quoting at length:

> Homes are being invaded by Hip-Hop theories and Hip-Hop flavors. White kids are being injected with black rage and anger. People like KRS-One, Public Enemy, Cube are stimulating kids to question authority. And moms says, "My home has been invaded by these new ideas. How did it get here?" It comes through the walkman. These homes are being invaded by us [rappers]. And they know it. They know we are in their homes. (cited in Spady, 1993, p. 95; for full interview, see Spady et al., 1999)

The Brother is SICK, as Alim has commented on Ice-T's quote; that is, unbelievably perceptive. His quote appoints him not only as a Social Theorist but as a Critical Curriculum Educator. Moms are freaking out because their homes are being "invaded by these new ideas," which come "through the walkman." Ice-T basically summed up what we have seen in Sarkar, Higgins, Omoniyi, and Pennycook and Mitchell's chapters: the processes of production and distribution of Hip Hop and the impact and influence of Hip Hop in the many lives to which Hip Hop matter.

But, Maxine Greene (1997) warns us, this home as well as school invasion and bombardment of popular culture images frequently has the (negative) effect of freezing the imaginative thinking of youth, thus potentially whirling them into "human resources" as opposed to "centers of choice and evaluation" (p. 57). For critical educators, the latter will happen only when we as critical pedagogues recognize the temporal and nonstatic nature of youth identities, and when the youth themselves are able to gaze back at these images and consciously "read" (through) them. This gaze will be developed only when youth are conscious participants in Hip Hop artwork, in its "going out of energy," and have the "ability to notice what there is to be noticed" (Greene, 1997, p. 58).

David Star and Limitless in Newman's chapter show us what it means to be a critical Hip Hop educator, and in his chapter, Alim offers concrete ways on how to enable students to gaze back and become their own subject. Following Greene, our interest in CMC is a recall to emphasizing the intersectionality between identity, politics, experience, pedagogical dis/engagement and the process of learning. Building on this, I showed elsewhere that students do appropriate and develop aspects of CMC as part of their identity formation; and in the case of Hip Hop, such a curriculum can be utilized in and as a form of critical pedagogy and praxis (Ibrahim, 1999, 2000a; Newman, this volume). This way, I concluded, we may contribute to bringing in students' previously unwarranted and non-validated forms of knowledge, address the feeling of alienation that (Black and Brown) students have in relation to Eurocentric curricula, and contribute to an integrative antiracist curriculum (Dei, 1996).

Affect and the Pedagogy of Hip Hop: A Conclusion

> Hiphopness—the dynamic and constant sense of being alive in a hip hop, rap conscious, reality based world—is actually where many young…people are today. As we enter [the 21st Century], it becomes even more important to realize that significant changes are taking place in the rapidly growing hip hop world. To stand back, wack crack style is to succumb to the inertia of the past. And yet, to become a participant in this highly fluid, ritual-ized space is to exercise an act of freedom that may very well change your constitutive being. (Spady, 1993, p. 96)

This is another SICK quote that basically sums up what it means to be a member of the Global Hip Hop Nation: it is "to exercise an act of freedom that may very well change your constitutive being." This exercise of the *Hip Hop Act of Freedom* involves as much "the researcher" as it does "the research subjects" and has deep pedagogical implications. In what follows, I want to explore further what I am calling (along with Alim, this volume, 2007; Pennycook, 2007) "Hip Hop Pedagogy." Before doing so, however, I raise the question: What does it mean for Hip Hop to become a *locus of enunciation*—a pedagogical site of identity forma-tion, identification, affect, desire, teaching, and learning? Focusing primarily on

Michael Newman's chapter (this volume), I will attempt to link pedagogy and affect through the "mattering map" metaphor. Hip Hop, I am suggesting, is a site of *multiplicity* that is replete with as much dangers as possibilities and the essence of Hip Hop Pedagogy is to live in this dialogic space between dangers and possibilities. It is here that resides what I called elsewhere "pedagogy of *jouissance*" (Ibrahim, 2004b), which is introduced as a "third ear" (Lacoue-Labarthe, 1989), as a mattering map and a pedagogical framework that links Hip Hop, identity investment, and the process of critical teaching and learning.[4]

This site of multiplicity is explored best in Newman's study, where students at the Urban Arts Academy (UAA) become MCs, thus transforming the teacher-students relationship, the notion of knowledge production and eventually creating a new pedagogical praxis where affect is an integral part of what it means to teach and learn. As MCs, students not only become knowledge producers but also, and probably more significant, curriculum architects. At UAA, students live unapologetically between "knowledge rap" (a.k.a. *conscious rap*) and "hardcore rap" (a.k.a. *thug/gangsta rap*). They are conscious of what it means to travel both verbally and emotionally between the two (see Spady et al., 1999 for the problematic distinction between "conscious rap" and "commercial rap").

Yet, as pedagogues we are sometimes unable and in most cases unwilling to deal with this multiplicity, this move. Our unease stems from three different areas: (1) lack of knowledge about Hip Hop generation, culture, and language; (2) fear of blurring the boundaries between students' lives outside school and in-school activities; and finally (3) we are dealing with affect. William Ayers (2004), Peter McLaren (2007), William Pinar (2004), and bell hooks (1994) all call attention to the latter point. They contend that only through affect can we really make students love the material we teach. That is, when students love what we teach, teaching and learning move from the traditional paradigm of "work" to a paradigm of pleasure, identity investment (where, consciously and unconsciously, what is taught directly impacts, engages, and reconfigures students' sense of self), and hence learning becomes a cornerstone in the process of personal transformation.

For students to love what we teach they have to invest into what Lawrence Grossberg (1992) calls "mattering map." For Grossberg (1992), *mattering map* is a broad linguistic, cultural and sociosemiotic space where people's identities and everyday lives are formed, performed, and make sense, and where no investment is haphazard. Much like "investment portfolios," mattering maps determine where, how, and the intensities and degrees of investment. They "tell" people how to use and how to generate energy, and thus regulate not only the passion, investment, and texture of their affect, but eventually their identities, identification, and the possibilities of what they could become. Clearly, as we saw in this volume, Hip Hop has become a global mattering map for identity investment and pedagogical engagement, where critical Hip Hop language pedagogies become possible.

As explored in this book, the issues at stake in Hip Hop Pedagogy are as follow. First, there seem to be two contradictory "texts"—tendencies, if you like—in education today. They are best described by Maxine Greene (1997), "one has to do with shaping malleable young people to serve the needs of technology in a postindusturial society[5]; the other has to do with educating young people to grow and to become different, to find their individual voices, and to participate in a community in the making" (p. 64). Oscillating toward the latter, the Hip Hop Pedagogy proposed here is a pedagogy of affect and *jouissance*, of voice and ear. The lives of our research participants in this volume would be the starting point, if not *the* base, for a critical inclusive curriculum. A curriculum that, (1) sees Hip Hop as a pedagogical site of teaching and learning; (2) deconstructs Hip Hop as a site of multiplicity, celebration, and critique; (3) sees students' lives as providing the basis for reconceptualizing culture and identity as dynamic social productions; (4) notes that what might constitute reality for students may not be the teacher's reality; (5) draws on students' creativity, subjectivity, and experience; (6) sees Hip Hop as a space of *métissage* of the global and the local, where students are defining their local environments in transcultural terms by using mostly local linguistic resources to fashion themselves within a Global Hip Hop Nation (as Higgins put earlier); and, finally (7) sees social differences of identity enactments or a global understanding of them as part of a critical inclusive curriculum—hence, they need serious engagement and deconstruction.

These seven elements are theorized from three literacy, literary, and educational programs: the Urban Arts Academy in New York (Newman, 2001, this volume), Da Bomb Squad Comprehensive Literacy Development Program in Haven High in the Bay Area, California (Alim, 2007), and the African Diaspora Participatory Literacy Communities (ADPLCs) in northern California (Fisher, 2004). In the first program, Newman looks at how students at UAA have moved from the category "student" to "MCs" and in so doing, they radically changed the idea and the pedagogical approach to teaching and learning. Teaching became a courageous act of reciprocal engagement while learning became an affective yet highly intellectual semiotic space for knowledge production. Hip Hop was no longer a trigger to something else within the "main text," but a "main text" in its own terms.

Departing from exactly the same point, Alim implemented his course, "Hiphopgraphy: The Ethnography of Hip Hop Culture and Communication," at Haven High in the Bay Area, California. The course began with three premises. (1) Students *are* the sources, investigators, and archivists of varied and rich bodies of knowledge rooted in their cultural-linguistic reality—what Bankie Santana calls the *School of Reality* (cited in Alim, 2007); (2) Hip Hop Culture *is* a serious subject of scholarly investigation that necessitates a distinction between "cultural-linguistic reality curriculum" and "culturally relevant curriculum"; finally (3) "There's no room for ignorance no more." Alim showed how his sixth graders became ethnographers, linguists, researchers, social critics, and a voice to a silenced community. They joined the Brazilian *favela's* poor in affirming that: "We are marginalized. We are not marginals."

Maisha Fisher's (2004) project explored how the "marginals" were able to create their own poetic, literary, and literacy centers that enabled them to speak. The margin was turned here into a *creative space* for poetic and knowledge production. "Cafés have been transformed into literary salons and bookstores into educational centers" (p. 292). Fisher described two open mic poetry venues in Black-owned-and-operated bookstores that recall the feeling and communal centrality of jazz clubs and literary circles of the Harlem Renaissance. Fisher showed that these ADPLCs have become a Mecca, sites for multiple literacies for many men and women of African descent to access both spoken and written words, and "speaking [became] a natural outgrowth of reading and writing" (p. 292). As such, these ADPLCs placed "orality" beside "literacy" in the vernacular tradition of African American writing and similar to Newman and Alim's programs, the prevailing theme in this open mic project is that everyone has a message worth conveying – eventually, creating a "new era of Black words" (p. 292).

Second, in chapter 8 of his book, *Global Englishes and Transcultural Flows*, Pennycook (2007) discusses close to 10 studies that are dealing with what Walter Ong and Tricia Rose call "postliterate orality," which they define as the "orally influenced traditions that are created and embedded in a postliterate, technologically sophisticated context" where rap music "blurs the distinction between literate and oral modes of communication" (Rose, 1994; cited in Pennycook, 2007, p. 147). The lyrical skills of MC-ing, Pennycook contends, "suggest a more complex form of postliterate orality produced amid complex literacy skills and in a culture of sampling" (p. 147). Invoking this idea of *sampling* as "a new way of doing something that's been with us for a long time," as a place where "you recontextualize the previous expression of others," and where "there is no such thing as an 'immaculate perception,'" Pennycook (p. 149) draws our attention to how rap is redefining the idea of literacy, authorship, ownership, knowledge, originality and creativity.

Because of its highly sophisticated linguistic use and communicative patterns, rap for Pennycook represents a significant tool for language awareness and the experience of beauty and pleasure are displayed through language, thus "making language available to scrutiny" (p. 146). Because of "biting," reenactment, and the mobilization of a Confucian-style form of imitation and respect, Pennycook concludes, Hip Hop Pedagogy has entered a "post-authorial era" (p. 149). What Pennycook, Fisher, Alim, and Newman point to is a New Literacy, new approaches to Hip Hop Pedagogy where rhyme, rhythm, dialect, performance, and difference are all salient elements in Hip Hop Culture and Rap. These approaches are built around the "phonocentric" tradition—being concerned with fostering diversity and "allowing non-powerful knowledges, cultures and voices of the disadvantaged to be heard" (p. 144)—and the spoken word becomes an organic extension and a powerful expression of deep intellectual rigor, thus requiring and at the same time performing "a natural outgrowth of reading and writing," as Fisher has put it.

Third, Higgins offers a wonderful way to think about Hip Hop as a global space of/for *intercultural communication*. Pennycook and Mitchell also make the case for the dialogic nature between the local and the global and Alim's notion of Hip Hop Nation Language gives it a cartography and structure. In Sarkar's chapter, we see the colonizer and the colonized "rubbing shoulders." For me, this argument is summed up best by Higgins in the opening quote of this chapter. As Bloomaert put it (cited in Higgins), the *Kihuni* (a form of Global Hip Hop Nation Language mixed with Swahili) offers the *wahuni* (i.e., gangsta) in Tanzania a linguistic repertoire "that allows them to 'get out' of Dar es Salaam culturally, to culturally relocate their local environment in a global semiotics of class, status, blackness, marginalization." This is also the case with Omoniyi, Lin, Tsujmura and Davis, and Roth-Gordon, where Hip Hop moves youth from "moja" (Swahili for "one") to "pamoja" ("togetherness").

Fourth, we know that students do not come to our classrooms as generic disembodied individuals. On the contrary, the racial and gender identities formed outside the classroom are crucial in the learning process. Specifically, I showed elsewhere that Hip Hop is and can be on-and-off-school site where learning can and indeed does take place (Ibrahim, 2003; see also Alim, 2007). If this is so, then we are confronted with a pedagogy where learning may mean *investing into* hybrid cultural and linguistic practices that are not valued by the dominant culture or outside the "main text." The Fisher, Alim, and Newman programs are hopeful notes in how this New Literacy can be introduced as a subject of investigation.

Fifth and finally, Hip Hop is an invented semiotic language, an aesthetic form that is historically specific. As such, it is neither immune to social ills such as homophobia and sexism nor is it above critique. When Brother Nas declared, *Hip Hop Is Dead*, for me, he is not dissin Hip Hop, he is asking us to lovingly kill that which is undesirable within Hip Hop. We kill it by critiquing it and in its stead we lovingly create that which is desirable. That way we speak about a Hip Hop "pamoja" that engages seriously Daara J of Senegal, Dragon Ash of Japan, Wire MC of Australia, MC Yan of Hong Kong with KRS-One of New York, and the list is long to be exhausted. In the Fisher, Alim, and Newman programs, we saw a language of concrete possibilities that saw Hip Hop as a site of multiplicity and hope: (1) A hope that those who do not see themselves represented in the curriculum, those who cannot relate to the "main text," those who are wittingly or unwittingly kept silent, may find a subject matter they can relate to and identify with; a subject matter that brings their experience to the forefront so it can be valued and critically engaged. The Urban Arts Academy has to be cited as an exemplary site of how students desilence themselves when they find a "mattering map" that engages them. Here, students became an organic part of the curriculum design process. That is, they became knowledge producers;

and where they invested their desire and self was turned into a curriculum site worthy of study. (2) A hope that educators will not be stuck in the notion that they do not know much about Hip Hop, and hence it is better kept dormant. (3) A hope that we as adults, academics, teachers, and pedagogues are able to use our "third ear"; because the consequence of not envisioning Hip Hop as a subject of investigation, Weaver, Dimitriadis, and Daspit (2001) have argued, has "been deafening" in that "[a]s youth have become attuned to the world of Hip Hop, most adults [particularly academics] have lost the ability to understand the artistic power of Hip Hop, thereby losing a major route to understanding the concerns, fears, hopes, and dreams of youth" (p. 10). (4) A hope that teachers will engage the different mattering maps where students invest their identities, learning, and desires. In my research, as well as Newman and Alim, one must ask, whose identity are we assuming if we do not engage Hip Hop and rap in our classroom activities?

"By ignoring the cultural and social forms that are authorized by youth and simultaneously empower or disempower them educators risk complicitly silencing and negating their students," Giroux and Simon (1989a) contend. "This is unwittingly accomplished by refusing to recognize the importance of those sites and social practices outside of school that actively shape student experiences and through which students often define and construct their sense of identity, politics, and culture" (p. 3). Ultimately, the issue at stake is for students to become their own subject and locate themselves in time and history and at the same time critically interrogate the adequacy of that location. If "all is rhythm; the entire destiny of man [sic] is one celestial rhythm," as the German poet Hölderlin has put it, it is time to unleash youth creativity, set them free to form their own voice and knowledge, to use their "lyrical tongue" (Newman, this volume), to ask their own questions and become their own person. It is time to begin the improvised script, set the stage and take the pedagogy of pleasure and *jouissance* very seriously. Only then can life be off da hook: taken as *is* not as some think it *should be*. Word up—straight outta Compton, straight outta Global Zulu Nation—Hip Hop's in da house!

Notes

1. Bhabha uses "hybridity" instead of *métissage*. In fact, one may argue, *métissage* does the work in French that hybridization does in English.
2. In the African American experience, neighborhood or simply "hood" is as much a geographic space where people actually live as it is a metaphor, a state of mind, and a way of being. This is why folks say you can take the nigga out the hood but you can't take the hood out the nigga. If you take the hood out the nigga, then you left him or her with nothing (Smitherman, 2000). I am using it here in a metaphoric sense to represent a nation, with its culture and language.
3. Hip Hop, Russell Simmons has recently explored in an interview with the *City Paper* of Toledo, is inherently political, from its inception. He argued, "Hip Hop has always been about politics. It was and is a means to an end. I wouldn't be here [at the University of Toledo] today if it wasn't. But, now it is time for Hip Hop to assert itself. Politics has changed. It used to that the Democrats were there for the underdog, they supported civil rights and the poor. Now, that shit's out the window." Hip Hop, he continues, is also an economic force, a way into the

corporate capitals and decision making towers. He wonders, "So, why shouldn't we who are in Hip Hop start making a difference with the influence we have? Again, Hip Hop's purpose was to develop a way out. We now have the ability to give youth a way out of poverty" (*City Paper*, March 6–12, 2003, p. 14; can also be accessed through www.toledocitypaper.com).

4. The metaphor of the ear invokes one of Hip Hop's most significant elements: orality, especially its spoken word, voice, and rhythm. As we shall see, Hip Hop pedagogy is in fact a pedagogy of the ear, of listening.

5. Dewey (1916) calls this "the traditional scheme, "which for him "is, in essence, one of imposition from above and from outside. It imposes adult standards, subject matters, and methods upon those who are only growing slowly toward maturity." He goes on to explain, "The gap is so great that the required subject matter, the methods of learning and of behaving are foreign to the existing capacities of the young. They are beyond the reach of the experience the young learners already possess" (p. 120).

References

Alim, H. S. (2004). Hip hop nation language. In E. Finegan & J. Rickford (Eds.), *Language in the USA: Themes for the 21st century* (pp. 386–409). New York: Cambridge University Press.

Alim, S. (2007). "The wig party don't exist in my hood": Knowledge, reality, and education in hip hop nation. In S. Alim & J. Baugh (Eds.), *Talkin black talk: Language, education, and social change* (pp. 12–23). New York: Teachers College Press.

Apple, M. (2004). *Ideology and curriculum* (3rd ed.). New York: Routledge.

Ayers, W. (2004). *To teach: The journey of a teacher*. New York: Teachers College Press.

Bhabha, H. (1990). The third space: Interview with Homi Bhabha. In Rutherford, J. (Ed.), *Identity, community, culture, difference* (pp. 26–33). London: Lawrence & Wishart.

Dei, G. (1996). *Anti-racism: Theory and practice*. Halifax, Nova Scotia: Fernwood.

Dewey, J. (1916). *Democracy and education*. New York: Free Press

Dimitriadis, G., & McCarthy, C. (2001). *Reading the postcolonial: From Baldwin to Basquiat and beyond*. New York: Teachers College Press.

Eisner, E., & Powell, P. (2002). Art in science? *Curriculum Inquiry, 32*(2), 131–159.

Eisner, E. (1979). *The educational imagination on the design and evaluation of school programs*. New York: Macmillan.

Eisner, E. (2005). *Reimagining schools: The selected works of Elliot W. Eisner*. London: Routledge.

Fisher, M. (2004). "The song is unfinished": The new literate and literacy and their institutions. *Written Communication, 21*(3), 290–312.

Freire, P. (1993). *Pedagogy of the oppressed*. New York: Continuum.

Giroux, H., & Simon, R. (1989a). Schooling, popular culture, and a pedagogy of possibility. In H. Giroux & R. Simon, (Eds.), *Popular culture, schooling, and everyday life* (pp. 219–235). Boston: Bergin & Garvey.

Giroux, H., & Simon, R. (1989b). Popular culture as a pedagogy of pleasure and meaning. In H. Giroux & R. Simon (Eds.), *Popular culture, schooling, and everyday life* (pp. 1–29). Boston: Bergin & Garvey.

Greene, M. (1992). Texts and margins. In M. Goldberg & A. Phillips (Eds.), *Arts as education* (pp. 1–17). Boston: Harvard Educational Review.

Greene, M. (1997). Art and imagination: Reclaiming a sense of the possible. In E. Clinchy, (Ed.), *Transforming public education: A new course for America's future* (pp. 56–65). New York: Teachers College Press.

Grossberg, L. (1992). *We gotta get out of this place: Popular conservatism and postmodern culture*. New York and London: Routledge.

hooks, b. (1994). *Teaching to transgress: Education as the practice of freedom*. London: Routledge.

Ibrahim, A. (1999). Becoming Black: Rap and hip hop, race, gender, identity and the politics of ESL learning. *TESOL Quarterly, 33*(3), 349–369.

Ibrahim, A. (2000a). "Whassup Homeboy?" Black/popular culture and the politics of "curriculum studies": Devising an anti-racism perspective. In G. J. S. Dei & A. Calliste (Eds.), *Power, knowledge and anti-racism education: A critical reader* (pp. 57–72). Halifax, Nova Scotia: Fernwood.

Ibrahim, A. (2000b). Trans-re-framing identity: Race, language, culture, and the politics of translation. *trans/forms: Insurgent Voices in Education, 5*(2), 120–135.

Ibrahim, A. (2003). "Whassup homeboy?" Joining the African diaspora: Black English as a symbolic site of identification and language learning. In S. Makoni, G. Smitherman, A. Ball, & A. Spears (Eds.), *Black linguistics: Language, society and politics in Africa and the Americas* (pp. 169–185). London: Routledge.

Ibrahim, A. (2004a). Performing desire: Race, identity, identification, and the politics of becoming Black. In C. Nelson & C. Nelson (Eds.), *Racism eh? A critical interdisciplinary anthology on race in the Canadian context* (pp. 120–135). Toronto: Captus University Press.

Ibrahim, A. (2004b). Operating under erasure: Hip Hop and the pedagogy of affect(ive). *Journal of Curriculum Theorizing, 20*(1), 113–133.

Ibrahim, A. (2006). Rethinking displacement, language, and culture shock: Towards a pedagogy of cultural translation and negotiation. In N. Amin & G. Dei (Eds.), *The poetics of anti-racism* (pp. 33–45). Halifax, Nova Scotia: Fernwood Books.

Kitwana, B. (2005). *Why White kids love hip hop: Wankstas, wiggers, wannabes, and the new reality of race in America.* New York: Basic Books.

Lacoue-Barthe, P. (1989). *Typography: Mimesis, philosophy, politics.* Palo Alto, CA: Stanford University Press.

Lionnet, F. (1989). *Autobiographical voices: Race, gender, self-portraiture.* Ithaca, NY: Cornell University Press.

Masny, D. (2005). Learning and creative processes: A poststructural perspective on language and multiple literacies. *The International Journal of Learning, 12*(5), 149–156.

McLaren, P. (2007). *Life in schools: An introduction to critical pedagogy in the foundations of education.* New York: Longman.

Mignolo, W. (2000). *Local histories/Global designs: Coloniality, subaltern knowledges and border thinking.* Princeton, NJ: Princeton University Press.

Mitchell, T. (Ed.). (2001). *Global noise: Rap and hip-hop outside the USA.* Middletown, CT: Wesleyan University Press.

Newman, M. (2001). "Not dogmatically/It's all about me": Ideological conflict in a high school rap crew. *Taboo, 5*(2), 51–68.

Osumare, H. (2007). *The Africanist aesthetic in global hip-hop: Power moves.* New York: Palgrave.

Pennycook, A. (2007). *Global englishes and transcultural flows.* London: Routledge.

Perry, I. (2004). *Prophets of the hood: Politics and poetics of hip-hop.* Durham, NC: Duke University Press.

Peterson, D., Esbensen, F., Taylor, T., & Freng, A. (2007). Youth violence in context: The roles of sex, race, and community in offending. *Youth Violence and Juvenile Justice, 5*(4), 385–410.

Pinar, W. (2004). *What is curriculum theory?* Mahwah, NJ: Erlbaum.

Quinn, T., & Kahne, J. (2001). Wide awake to the world: The arts and urban schools—Conflicts and contributions of an after-school program. *Curriculum Inquiry, 31*(1), 11–32.

Rampton, B. (1995). *Crossing: Language and ethnicity among adolescents.* London: Longman.

Simmons, R. (2001). *Life and def: Sex, drugs, money and God.* New York: Crown.

Smitherman, G. (2000). *Black talk: Words and phrases from the hood to the amen corner.* New York: Houghton Mifflin.

Spady, J. (1993). "I ma put my thing down": Afro-American expressive culture and the hip-hop community. *TYANABA Revue de la Société d'Anthropologie. 20*(2), 93–98.

Spady, J., Lee, C., & Alim, S. (1999). *Street conscious rap.* Philadelphia: Black History Museum.

Spady, J., Alim, S., & Maghelli, S. (2006). *The global cipha: Hip-Hop culture and consciousness.* Philadelphia: Black History Museum Press.

Weaver, J., Dimitriadis, G., & Daspit, T. (2001). Hip-hop pedagogies and youth cultures: Rhythmic blends of globalization and the lost third ear of the academy. *Taboo: Journal of Culture and Education, 5*(2), 7–13.

Yousman, B. (2003). Blackophilia and Blackophobia: White youth, the consumption of rap music and White supremacy. *Communication Theory, 20*(2), 360–371.

Hip-Hop Headz aka List of Contributors

Jannis Androutsopoulos started his research on the language and discourse of Hip Hop in 1998, when he embarked, with Arno Scholz, on European rap research, a comparative study of rap lyrics in five European languages. Hip Hop research accompanied him since then through various academic positions to his current post as Reader in Sociolinguistics & Media Discourse at King's College London. In the process, he organized Hip Hop related conferences and academy-meets-community events in Germany and Greece, and published a number of papers as well as the volume *HipHop: Globale Kultur — Lokale Praktiken* (2003, transcript). His current research interests are located at the interface of sociolinguistics and media discourse with particular emphasis on computer-mediated communication, multilingualism and style. His recent publications include an edited theme issue of *Journal of Sociolinguistics* on "Sociolinguistics and Computer Mediated Communication" (September, 2006).

H. Samy Alim is an Assistant Professor of Anthropology at the University of California, Los Angeles. Recent works include *Roc the Mic Right: The Language of Hip Hop Culture* (Routledge, 2006), *Tha Global Cipha: Hip Hop Culture and Consciousness* (with James G. Spady and Samir Meghelli, Black History Museum, 2006) and *You Know My Steez* (Duke, 2004). His research interests include style theory and methodology, language and race(ism), and Global Hip Hop Culture(s).

Stuart Davis is Professor and Chair of the Department of Linguistics at Indiana University. His primary area of research is in phonology and phonological theory with a secondary area of research in African American English. His work in phonology has focused on languages such as English, Arabic, Japanese, and Korean. He has taught courses on the Ebonics controversy and on the grammar and history of African American English. His work has appeared in a wide variety of journals including *Linguistic Inquiry*, *Phonology*, *Studies in Language*, *Linguistics*, and *American Speech*.

Christina Higgins is an Assistant Professor in the Department of Second Language Studies at the University of Hawai'i at Manoa. She teaches graduate courses in sociolinguistics, qualitative research methodology, discourse analysis, and English as an international language. She has researched sociolinguistic aspects of multilingualism in East Africa for 10 years, focusing on codeswitching, language variation, stylized speech, and gendered language. Aspects of this research will be compiled in a forthcoming book on linguistic hybridity with multilingual matters. Her current research project investigates discourse and cultural models among non-governmental organizations that sponsor HIV/AIDS education in Tanzania.

Awad Ibrahim is an Associate Professor at the Faculty of Education of the University of Ottawa, Canada. He used to teach in Education and American Culture Studies Program at Bowling Green State University, Ohio. He is a doctoral graduate of the University of Toronto (Canada) and teaches and publishes in the areas of Hip-Hop studies/Black pop culture, minority adolescents, racially and linguistically mediated identities, critical curriculum studies, applied sociolinguistics, and cultural studies. His book, *"Hey, whassup homeboy" Becoming Black: Hip-Hip Culture and Language, Race Performativity and the Politics of Identity in High School* (University of Toronto Press) is forthcoming.

Angel Lin received her PhD from the Ontario Institute for Studies in Education, University of Toronto. She is an Associate Professor in the Department of English, City University of Hong Kong. She teaches and researches in the areas of sociolinguistics, critical discourse analysis, urban ethnography, critical pedagogy, feminist media studies, youth literacies, and cultural studies.

Tony Mitchell is a senior lecturer at the University of Technology, Sydney. He is the author of *Popular Music and Local Identity: Rock, Pop and Rap in Europe and Oceania* (University of Leicester Press, 1996), editor of *Global Noise: Rap and Hip Hop outside the USA* (Wesleyan University Press, 2001), co-editor of *Sounds of Then, Sounds of Now: Popular Music in Australia* (Australian Clearning House for Youth Studies) and numerous articles and book chapters on global Hip Hop, film, and popular music in Australia, New Zealand, Italy, Singapore, China and Hong Kong. From 1997 to 1999 he was chairperson of IASPM (the International Association for the Study of Popular Music) and he is currently working on Local Noise (localnoise.net.au) a project on Australian Hip Hop funded by the Australian Research Council grant. He also writes reviews and articles about Australian Hip Hop, rock and jazz for *Music Forum* magazine.

Alastair Pennycook is concerned with how we understand language in relation to globalization, colonial history, identity, popular culture, and pedagogy. Most recently this has included collaborative projects with Tony Mitchell on Hip Hop in Australasia as well as coediting with Samy Alim a special issue of the *Journal of Language, Identity and Education*. Publications include *The Cultural Oolitics of English as an International Language* (Longman, 1994), *English and the Discourses of Colonialism* (Routledge, 1998), *Critical Applied Linguistics: A Critical Introduction* (Erlbaum, 2001) and *Global Englishes and Transcultural Flows* (Routledge, 2007). Alastair is Professor of Language in Education at the University of Technology, Sydney.

Jennifer Roth-Gordon is Assistant Professor of Linguistic Anthropology at the University of Arizona. Her research joins critical race studies, linguistic anthropology, and the study of youth in Rio de Janeiro, Brazil, to explore the racialization of language and the marginalization of poor, Black, shantytown youth. Her study of Brazilian Portuguese *gíria* ('slang') has resulted in recent publications in *Journal of Sociolinguistics* and *Journal of Linguistic Anthropology*.

Natsuko Tsujimura is Professor of East Asian Languages and Cultures at Indiana University. Her research areas include lexical semantics and various topics in Japanese linguistics. She is the author of *An Introduction to Japanese Linguistics* (2nd ed., 2007, Blackwell) and the editor of *The Handbook of Japanese Linguistics* (1999, Blackwell), and *Japanese Linguistics: Critical Concepts* (Vols. I–III, 2005, Routledge). She has also been published in journals such as *Linguistic Inquiry*, *Natural Language and Linguistic Theory*, and *Studies in Language*. She has served as the editor-in-chief of the *Journal of Japanese Linguistics* and as an associate editor of *Language*.

Index